ML
3477
M88
1997

MUSICS OF

Multicultural
America

MUSICS OF

Multicultural America

■

A STUDY OF
TWELVE MUSICAL COMMUNITIES

edited by
Kip Lornell and Anne K. Rasmussen

Schirmer Books
An Imprint of Simon & Schuster Macmillan

Prentice Hall International
London   Mexico City   New Delhi   Singapore   Sydney   Toronto

Schirmer Books
An Imprint of Simon & Schuster Macmillan
1633 Broadway
New York, NY 10019

Library of Congress Number: 97-19860

Printed in the United States of America

Printing number

1   2   3   4   5   6   7   8   9   10

Library of Congress Cataloging-in-Publication Data

Musics of Multicultural America : a study of twelve musical
    communities / edited by Kip Lornell and Anne K. Rasmussen.
              p.   cm.
        Includes index.
        ISBN 0-02-864585-5 (alk. paper)
        1. Popular music—United States—history and criticism. 2. Music
    and society—United States. I. Lornell, Kip. II. Rasmussen, Anne K.
    ML3477.M88 1997
    780'.973—dc21
                                                    97-19860
                                                        CIP
                                                        MN

This paper meets the requirements of ANSI/NISO Z39.48-1992 (Permanence of Paper).

table of contents

preface

Musics of Multicultural America is about the role of music in the social and cultural life of the United States. Comprising twelve discrete case studies and a companion compact-disc recording of musical performances, the book provides historical and contemporary accounts of the American musical landscape. Collectively, the authors augment the more abundant, more readily available, and better-known literature about African American, European American, and Native American traditions to include a consideration of the music making of a small number of vibrant American subcultures. As such, Musics of Multicultural America responds to the growing need on college campuses to teach a "new American canon," one characterized by diversity as well as the continuing creation, interaction, and regeneration of multiple multicultural voices.

Because the case studies in this collection do not presuppose any particular expertise in music on the part of student or instructor, we confidently recommend Musics of Multicultural America for both music and humanities courses. The book may be used as a primary text for an undergraduate course or as a point of departure or supplementary text in an upper-level undergraduate or graduate seminar. You will notice that this book is not a standard textbook, nor is it collection of scholarly essays. Moreover, we decided not to present students with a cumbersome and incomplete survey of "ethnic" music, an impossible task given the gaps in scholarship. Rather, Musics of Multicultural America is a reader that presents students with an intellectual and historical framework for exploring a diversity of music making and music through a series of specific ethnographic case studies. It is our hope that these highly focused studies of music and community life provide a variegated sample of musical activity from across the United States and that the collection both represents and meets the needs of our admittedly postmodern yet still highly regionalized culture.

The introduction outlines a number of themes and theoretical issues that are found throughout this collection of essays, which are written by authors from several different fields. Any of the unifying themes and issues of the collection or any of the specific communities presented in the book may be explored in greater depth. Suggested literature, audio, and visual materials listed at the end of each chapter are intended to facilitate further exploration.

Our investigation of musical diversity in United States complements existing course materials in the areas of ethnomusicology, American music, and ethnic studies. Our focus on music in American life complements existing literature for multicultural curricula in both American Studies and the Humanities; thus, it is our belief that this reader, with its interrelated essays, will benefit not only students of music but also students of American history and culture.

Making music is a more complex undertaking than the mere process of playing an instrument or singing. Musical activity often facilitates community interaction. A music and dance event, a concert, an evening in a nightclub or community clubhouse, a wedding, or a festival may actually set in motion the social processes and rituals that bind people together, giving them a shared identity. Each chapter in this collection illustrates the ways in which the musical practices of a particular community are intertwined with other facets of culture, such as language, religion, social and political ideology, constructs of gender, folklore, and history. The authors share the conviction that understanding musical activity in America is key to understanding multicultural America.

This project arose because of the co-editors' mutual experience teaching multicultural American music and their consistent frustration in finding easily available materials that could be used in the classroom. We wish to thank our team of authors for their willingness to contribute to the collection and for so cogently distilling their longer works, which were aimed at a more specialized or scholarly audience. We are indebted to the College of William and Mary and the Smithsonian Institution for their support, as well as to our editors at Schirmer Books, particularly Jonathan Wiener, and the manuscript's anonymous reviewers who offered much insightful critique. On a more personal level we thank, in order of their ages, our families for their encouragement and understanding: Katherine, Cady, Hansen, Dan, and Kim.

Kip Lornell
Anne K. Rasmussen

Recorded Selections

1. Svestkova Alej (The Prune Song). Romy Gosz. 3:15.

2. Wedding Polka. Yuba Bohemian Band. Courtesy of the Library of Congress, Archive of Folk Culture. 1:48.

3. Unzer Toirele. Abe Schwartz and His Orchestra. From Shanachie/Yazoo 7001, *Dave Tarras: Yiddish-American Klezmer Music—1925–1956.* Courtesy of Shanachie Entertainment, 37 East Clinton, Newton, NJ 07860. 3:05.

4. Berdichever/Mazel Tov. Kapelye. From Shanachie 67005, *Kapelye on the Air: Jewish-American Radio.* Courtesy of Shanachie Entertainment, 37 East Clinton, Newton, NJ 07860. 4:11.

5. Ma Hadi Zayeh (No One Was Ever Distressed; excerpt). Moses Cohen, vocalist; Naim Karakand, violinist; unknown qanun player. From field recordings courtesy of Anne Rasmussen. 0:53.

6. 'Atuba, Mijana, and 'Ala Daluna. Rana and Naim Homaidan and Anne Rasmussen. From field recordings courtesy of Anne Rasmussen. 3:26.

7. Wedding music (excerpt). Afra al-Yemen. 0:59.

8. Wedding music (excerpt). The Bells Band. From field recordings courtesy of Anne Rasmussen. 1:27.

9. Fire Coming Down. Pan Rebels. Courtesy of Basement Recordings & Trevor John. 6:07.

10. Las Mananitas. Mariachi Los Camperos. Courtesy the artist. 2:48.

11. El Jabali. Mariachi Los Camperos. Courtesy the artist. 2:31.

12. La Delgadina. Brenda Romero. Courtesy of the artist. 1:34.

13. Matachine no. 1. Features Adelaido Martinez and Daniel Culacke. Recorded by John Donald Robb, Dec. 29, 1974. 0:55.

14. Matachine no. 2. Features Gabriel Casiquito and Daniel Culacke. Recorded by Brenda Romero, Jan. 1, 1993. 0:59.

15. Son del Toro. Features Adelaido Martinez and Daniel Culacke. Recorded by John David Robb, Dec. 29, 1974. 1:37.

16. The Fast Monarcha or Jemez Man Song. Features Brenda Romero and Daniel Culacke. Recorded by Brenda Romero, Jan. 1, 1993. 0:59.

17. First Stop Waila. Southern Scratch. From *Em-we: hejed—For All of You* (CR-8097) by Southern Scratch. Courtesy of Canyon Records Productions, 4143 N. 16th St., Suite 6, Phoenix, AZ 85016 (800-268-1141). 2:22.

18. Libby Bird Mazurka. Gu Achi Fiddlers. From *The Gu-Achi Fiddlers* (CR-8082). Courtesy of Canyon Records Productions, 4143 N. 16th St., Suite 6, Phoenix, AZ 85016 (800-268-1141). 3:15.

19. Holy Manna. The Southern Harmony, led by Ray Mofier. Field recording courtesy of Ron Pen and the Univ. of Kentucky. 3:15.

20. Promised Land. The Southern Harmony, led by Ron Pen. Field recording courtesy of Ron Pen and the Univ. of Kentucky. 3:14.

21. Roll, Jordan, Roll. The Harmonizers. Courtesy of High Water Records, CCFA, the University of Memphis, Memphis, TN 38152. 3:25.

22. I John Saw. Spirit of Memphis. Courtesy of High Water Records, CCFA, the University of Memphis, Memphis, TN 38152. 3:12.

23. Tampopo. Nobuko Miyamoto. Courtesy of the artist. 3:01.

24. Hibakusha. Mark Izu. Courtesy of the artist. 3:05.

25. Sprite Commercial. The Mountain Brothers. Generously provided by the Mountain Brothers. 0:59.

26. Gas, Food, Satan. Double Zero. Courtesy of the artist. 2:22.

27. Killing for Pleasure. Selena Wahng. Courtesy of the artist. 4:23.

Contributors

Susan M. Asai is a professor in the Music Department at Northeastern University. Her publications include articles on *nomai,* a folk dance drama of northern Japan and issues of music and identity in Japanese American music. Her other research interests include Asian popular music and music education.

Gage Averill is an associate professor in the Music Department at New York University. He received is Ph.D. in ethnomusicology from the University of Washington in 1989 and taught previously at Wesleyan University and Columbia University. He is the author of *A Day for the Hunter, a Day for the Prey: Popular Music and Power in Haiti* (Chicago, 1997) and co-editor of *Making and Selling Culture* (Wesleyan, 1996). He has directed steelbands for eight years.

Theo Cateforis and **Elena Humphreys** are both products of the State University of New York at Stony Brook. Ms. Humphreys, in addition to her popular music career, completed graduate training in the arts. Mr. Cateforis has been associated with the Department of Music and his strongest scholarly interests are in contemporary American popular music.

Jim Griffith is known locally as one of the driving forces behind the "Tucson Meet Yourself" festival and as the head of the Southwestern Folklife Center at the University of Arizona. In addition, he has published extensively on regional vernacular music traditions found along the border of the United States and Mexico.

Kip Lornell has been researching American vernacular music since the late 1960s. He is the author or co-author of five previous books, including *The Life and Legend of Leadbelly* (with Charles K. Wolfe, 1993) and *Happy in the Service of the Lord: African-American Sacred Vocal Harmony Quartets in Memphis* (University of Tennessee Press, 1995). Since receiving his Ph.D. from the University of Memphis in 1983, Mr. Lornell has worked at the Blue Ridge Institute of Ferrum College and taught at the University of Virginia, the Johns Hopkins University, and George Washington University. At present he is a research associate at the Smithsonian Institution.

James P. Leary is a faculty associate in the Folklore Program at the University of Wisconsin. Since the mid-1970s he has authored and collaborated on numerous publications, media productions, and exhibitions on the folklore of America's culturally diverse Upper Midwest.

Ron Pen has been associated with the University of Kentucky, where he is currently an associate professor and director of the John Jacob Niles Center for American Music, since the mid-1980s. He has been singing from shape note books for many years, and is most often found addressing his students on the subject of American music.

Anne K. Rasmussen received her Ph.D. in ethnomusicology from the University of California at Los Angeles in 1991 and has taught ethnomusicology and directed Middle Eastern Music Ensembles at Oberlin College, the University of Texas at Austin, and the College of William and Mary, where she is now on the faculty. She has done extensive fieldwork in Arab American communities and recently spent a year in Indonesia studying Islamic performance.

Brenda M. Romero is an assistant professor of ethnomusicology in the College of Music at the University of Colorado in Boulder. Her current research focuses on traditional music and ritual of Latino and American Indian cultures of New Mexico and Colorado, with an emphasis on genres that reflect cultural interaction. She is regionally known for her performances of the old songs that are the subject of her research, and a compact disc of her recordings is forthcoming.

Henry Sapoznik is a musician/writer, record producer, and the executive director of Living Traditions, which sponsors KlezKamp: The Yiddish Folk Arts Program. He is currently working on a book on the history of klezmer music and a series on the story of Yiddish-American broadcasting for National Public Radio.

Daniel Sheehy is an arts administrator with the federal government, an active musician, and a scholar of Latin American mestizo music. He is co-editor (with Dale Olsen) of the forthcoming volume of the Garland Encyclopedia of World Music covering Mexico, Central and South America, and the Carribean. He has performed Mexican mariachi music professionally since 1968.

Deborah Wong has taught at Pomona College and the University of Pennsylvania. She is currently assistant professor of music at the University of California at Riverside. Ms. Wong was trained in ethnomusicology and incorporates her work on the music of Asian Americans, currently emerging traditions, and the theory and method of the discipline into her teaching and publishing.

MUSICS OF
Multicultural America

CHAPTER 1

Music and Community in Multicultural America

Kip Lornell and Anne K. Rasmussen

*M*usics of Multicultural America is a collection of twelve essays on music in the United States. Through a series of case studies, we present a sampler of American music and a glimpse of music making in a handful of American communities at the end of the twentieth century. All of the authors contributing to this volume are interested in the diversity of musical styles, genres, and repertoires that make up the American soundscape. Our focus throughout this reader, however, is on the varied and complex roles of music making in community life. Through the process of research, oral history, and ethnographic fieldwork with musicians and their audiences, all of the contributors to this volume investigate how people make and experience music on a local level.

WHAT IS AMERICAN MUSIC?

What is American music? Most Americans are aware of the commonly accepted definitions and delineations of American music. For example, we know that the United States is heavily indebted to the African and European roots that were originally imported and implanted in American soil between the period from the early 1500s to the mid-1800s. African and European musical roots have become entangled at various points in history to produce such extraordinarily popular and influential hybrids as jazz or rock 'n' roll. Both jazz and rock 'n' roll are American musics that have not only become monumental features of our own cultural landscape but that are also played and enjoyed worldwide.

As artists, audiences, consumers, and students of American music, we may recognize distinctions between so-called fine art music, vernacular music, folk music, popular music, religious music, music for the stage, and so forth. Moreover, we are often aware (either tacitly or overtly) of the general differentiations that are made between "high" and "low" culture, distinctions eloquently articulated in the writings of Lawrence W. Levine (1988), and that are frequently and liberally applied to music, literature, dance, and other cultural manifestations in the United States.

Universities, conservatories, and ensembles like symphonies and opera companies are among the elite institutions that teach students, employ faculty, and contract artists in the "fine arts." This strata of musical activity is the one most directly and openly sanctioned by institutions of higher education, corporations, and arts agencies as part of their agenda to support high culture. Occupying the other end of the cultural spectrum are folk, vernacular, traditional, and popular musics. Families, local taverns, neighborhood festivals, and places of worship are among the institutions that generally patronize and promote these musics of the people. Since the late 1930s, for example, small neighborhood clubs on the Southside and Westside of Chicago (such as the Checkerboard Club or Smitty's) have attracted patrons with live blues performances by such local black performers as Memphis Minnie, Muddy Waters, and Hound Dog Taylor. Grassroots, community musics may often be less bound to specific venues and thus are experienced in a number of contexts. Religious performance, for example, occurs in communities throughout the country; however, so-called sacred music can also transcend the context of the regularly scheduled religious service in a church, temple, or mosque and be heard at a festival or a fair.

Mass media is probably the most powerful force in music promotion and patronage in the twentieth century. The radio, since the 1920s, and major record companies, beginning at the turn of the century, are two of the media that have promoted popular music in the United States. Since the 1950s, late-night television shows, most notably *The Tonight Show,* have featured popular musicians for an adult clientele. The middle 1960s featured such programs as *Shindig* and *Hullabaloo,* shows that brought contemporary popular music to a "teen audience" for one-half hour each week. Today MTV and VH1 bring popular music to cable-connected consumers twenty-four hours a day. These media tell us—and help to reinforce—what songs are the most popular across the country during any particular day or week. While music that is grounded in community is likely to be somewhat more resistant to change, popular music fueled by mass media is, by definition, ephemeral, ever changing, and the most likely to shift according to fads. Sweeping trends may be sparked by an individual (like Frank Sinatra or Elvis Presley) or by a single popular music group, such as the Beatles. As is the case with an influential genre of music, for example rock or hip hop, music can serve as a symbol of, and impetus for, change across an entire culture.

Located in ethnic communities or among groups with a common social bond or agenda, musical activity that falls outside of the generally recognized categories of mainstream American music is embedded in our cultural fabric and plays on, largely unnoticed by the general public. Perhaps the most important aspect of this book is our effort to broaden our audience's notion of American music and to recognize and appreciate the myriad musical sub-cultures that constitute an integral part of our cultural landscape. Throughout the United States, regional grassroots musical cultures not only exist, they thrive!

UNIFYING THEMES AND ISSUES IN THE COLLECTION

Musics of Multicultural America celebrates the multiplicity and diversity of musical communities within the United States. While the ethnographic studies in this collection focus on a wide variety of communities from across the United States, they only represent a sampling of our musical landscape. There are literally scores of groups, for example, Hawaiians, Korean-Americans, South and Southeast Asian Americans or Cajuns, that might have been included in this book. The number of groups is simply too great to be discussed in a volume that is meant to be adapted to a one-semester course. Two other limitations need to be mentioned. The first is that many of these musical communities have not been adequately investigated and documented, which precludes their inclusion here. Second, such an all-encompassing survey would be embarrassingly superficial. We believe that the essays presented here represent a combination of depth and diversity that is more important than the facile breadth offered by a sweeping survey.

The collection underscores and celebrates the wonderful variety of music in the United States. Our authors, too, write from varied perspectives: some emphasize the historical, others the contemporary; some focus on the theoretical and the political, others the music and the ritual. Nonetheless, a number of themes exist that unify our collection of vignettes of American musical life. Most of the themes, questions, and other issues that are examined in these case studies are almost certainly relevant for other studies of music and community. Any of these topics might be used as a point of departure for independent research and fieldwork projects by students. Nine themes run through the essays and are touched upon as well in the rest of the Introduction:

1. The intersection between music, community, and identity.
2. The role of core cultural institutions, such as churches, festivals, families, that support musical activity within a community.
3. The actions of individual musicians (both professional and amateur) who lead music-making activities.
4. The trends related to musical preservation, innovation, renewal, or atrophy that occur at different times or simultaneously with a musical subculture.

5. The ways in which music is transmitted among generations, sometimes skipping a generation or more.

6. The ways in which musical performance articulates, challenges, and teaches gender roles and other social constructs.

7. The evaluation of a group's access to and use of mass and electronic media in the construction of community within and across often tenacious geographical boundaries.

8. The phenomenon of music as a commodity in the commercial marketplace, on a local, regional, national, or even international level.

9. The importance and effect of the fieldwork experience in shaping our view of the music.

Several of the case studies included in this book explore the ways in which musical traditions are brought to the United States from outside our geopolitical boundaries and adapted to fit a new environment. In his chapter on polka music in Wisconsin, Jim Leary traces the history and development of the music of Czech Americans, who immigrated, along with millions of Europeans, to the United States during two great waves of immigration from the middle of the 1800s to about 1920. Polka music and dance, in addition to surviving the test of time among Czech Americans, has also become an official emblem of the State of Wisconsin.

Henry Sapoznik, in his contribution on klezmer music, describes a musical genre brought to America by Ashkenazi Jews of Eastern Europe, many of whom migrated to the United States beginning in the late nineteenth century. Although klezmer music was a well-established cultural phenomenon among Jews in Eastern Europe, it took on a life and sound of its own in the United States. As the Jewish community in America embraced mainstream values and practices of the 1950s and '60s, klezmer music went into "hibernation." Since the 1970s, however, klezmer has experienced a revolution of renewal and has come to represent and express Jewish identity, not only in the United States but in Europe as well.

Anne Rasmussen describes a vibrant Arab American musical scene in Detroit that was established decades ago but has been greatly enriched by the wave of immigration since 1965 and the social and political events in the Middle East that have fueled an urgent and populous migration of thousands. With the current Lebanese, Iraqi, Yemeni, Palestinian, Syrian, Egyptian, Saudi, and North African musical mix, Arab music in the Detroit area of Michigan reflects an American musical microcosm of the contemporary Arab world. A transnational exchange of musicians and music media from cassette tapes to cable television keeps musical trends circulating throughout the Arab diaspora and the insistence of Arab families to keep their expressive culture alive facilitates a bustling Middle Eastern musical subculture in midwestern America.

In his chapter on Americans from the Caribbean, Gage Averill identifies the circulation of Caribbean cultural expressions throughout the diaspora as essential to the creation of a pan-Caribbean ethnicity in the United States. The New York Carnival is a well-established late summer event for Americans of Caribbean heritage who have come to use the event and the music of the panyards in the process of celebration but also to the end of inculcating the values of ethnic pride, education, and responsibility among the youth of the community.

Dan Sheehy's essay about mariachi music and musicians reveals just one aspect of a cultural exchange across the shifting Mexican American border that has been ongoing since the eighteenth century. By tracing the history of the genre of mariachi music in Mexico, Sheehy reveals a cultural phenomenon that was constructed by and through mass media—particularly film and radio—and used to represent a new urbanized Mexican identity. When adopted by Mexican American musicians in the United States, mariachi became a flexible category of performance that works in almost every context from the ritual to the festive and across the spectrum of social and economic class. Perhaps like polka in Wisconsin, mariachi has become emblematic of the southern and the western regions of the United States, even for mainstream America.

Two of the ensuing chapters discuss musical traditions among Native American and Mejicano people in the Southwest that have evolved from the processes of borrowing and shaping of forms of expressive culture. In her chapter on matachines, Brenda Romero discusses a ritual music and dance drama that is maintained through performance by both native Pueblo communities and Mejicano populations of Hispanic heritage. The matachines music and dance complex that developed from the confluence of Hispanic and Native American culture in southern Colorado and northern New Mexico also reveals roots from medieval Moorish Spain, a detail that adds to the history and, as Romero writes, the contemporary authenticity of this cultural performance.

In describing another aspect of Native American performance, Jim Griffith portrays the evolution and current practices of wailia musicians who reside in southern Arizona. Like matachines, waila draws from the ceremonial and entertainment musics of numerous local groups including the Tohano and O'odham peoples (also known as Pima Indians), the Yaqi, Mexican Americans, and country and western musicians and audiences. These chapters by Griffith and Romero, as well as the chapter on mariachi music by Sheehy, give us a sampling of the rich southern border culture of our country—a culture that knows numerous manifestiations in the performing arts.

Although relatively recent immigration trends that have occurred since the post–Civil War Reconstruction era have influenced much of our contemporary indigenous music, the core African American and Anglo American cultures have also significantly contributed to the foundation of our musical landscape. African and Anglo American musical practice have set the foundation for nearly all of what we think of as American music, such as blues, jazz, rock 'n' roll, and gospel. Two distinctive forms of sacred music, both of which are rooted in four-part harmony singing, constitute two essays in this book.

Ron Pen explores the Anglo American tradition of singing from shape-note hymn books in central Kentucky. Through a historical narrative that begins before American independence and brings us up to the present day, Pen explores not only the history of this strong American musical tradition, but the evolution of the unique social context and performance practice of the communities he calls "the fasola folk." Pen's chapter examines not only the longevity of the tradition maintained through the continuous oral transmission of one relatively homogenous Christian Anglo American community, but also the emergence of a more recently self-identified community of shape-note singers of ecumenical heritage, ethnicity, and religion.

The community of gospel quartet singers that thrived in Memphis, Tennessee, from the 1920s through the 1950s, is the focus of Kip Lornell's essay. Through his description of the social organization, the training, and the performance practices of quartets in Memphis, Lornell reveals a musical tradition that developed its own unique musical community. This community has interacted not only with other gospel groups but with singers performing in the realm of popular music as well.

An affiliation with contemporary American popular or "new" music characterizes three of the chapters in this collection. Susan Asai looks at the music making of Americans of Japanese heritage across three generations. She focuses on third-generation Japanese Americans, called *nisei,* and the ways in which they learn about, choose, perform, and experience music of their cultural heritage. Because of the eradication of much Japanese American cultural practice in the internment camps on the West Coast during World War II, young musicians of Japanese heritage do not always have the simple option of drawing from the traditions of their parents. Rather as innovative individuals, every Japanese American musician must search for and define Japanese musical memory and expression for themselves.

In her chapter on Asian American musicians, Deborah Wong interprets the cultural politics of the recording industry and the African American and now pan-national cultural movement, hip hop. Placing a group of three Chinese American rappers at the center of her chapter, Wong discusses how rap and hip hop culture have been appropriated and then tailored to become one of the many expressions of Asian American identities. Analyzing the interface of Asian American artists and mass media, Wong ascertains that by merely making a space for themselves in the production and dissemination of mediated musical forms, Asian Americans are creating and affirming unique identities.

A musical culture of and for young women called Riot Grrrls is presented by Theo Cateforis and Elena Humphreys. Much like contemporary punk and clean edge, both recent rock phenomena, Riot Grrrl is also a movement that promotes independence, self-reliance, and takes a decidedly anti-corporate stance. While the essay in this volume narrates the origin and development of the New York scene, Riot Grrrl is a national musical and cultural movement with hubs across the country. Communication between members is greatly fostered by modern technology—not only by way of phonograph records or cassettes (usually self-produced), but also by ephemeral magazines created by and for the community, called "fanzines."

ON THE CONTRIBUTORS

The contributors to this reader are scattered across the United States and work in universities and in the so-called public sector. Trained in the academic fields of ethnomusicology, folklore, American studies, anthropology, history, ethnic studies, and international studies and languages, we share a common interest in and commitment to music in the United States as it is most broadly defined. We are all engaged in fieldwork among the communities we introduce in *Musics of Multicultural America*. Some are players, singers, or dancers in the traditions about which we write. Although many do not share the same social and cultural background as the people we studied and wrote about, a few of us qualify as "insiders" in these communities. Asai, herself a third-generation Japanese American; Romero, who grew up as a Mejicana in the Southwest; and Sapoznik, who accidentally tripped over his own Jewish musical roots while playing American "old time" music, all bring a valuable perspective to the cultures they have chosen to explore.

Whatever our status as researchers, we are all aware of the potential power of our positions as patrons and publicists of our community consultants and their cultural practices. We inevitably became involved in the maintenance and development of their communities' cultural performances through playing, singing, dancing, and teaching. We have also stimulated and extended exposure to these traditions through the production of such documentary endeavors as conference papers, books, articles, recordings, and films, and through the presentation of live performance.

Through our involvement in festivals and concerts, sponsorship of educational and public projects, and the documentation of musicians and their communities, we have assumed active roles as advocates. Since the 1970s, multicultural festivals have become important forums for groups to show-case their unique contributions to American society. Virtually every city in America presents celebrations of culture that are orchestrated and executed by local groups, often with some assistance by local arts agencies. For example, Urban Gateways has for many years conducted educational and cultural programs that highlight the contributions of various Hispanic, African American, Eastern European, and other communities in the Chicago metropolitan area. In addition to the dizzying array of neighborhood and holiday festivals in New York, such arts agencies as City Lore and the Ethnic Folk Arts Center devote their energies full time to the documentation and promotion of the culturally diverse communities of New York's five boroughs.

On the national level is the Festival of American Folklife, held annually on the Mall in Washington, D.C., and sponsored by the Smithsonian Institution's Center for Cultural and Folklife Studies. This multicultural festival, which is mounted for ten days at the end of June and early July, is supported by a triad of the Smithsonian Institution, corporate sponsorship, and money contributed by the states and countries that are featured each summer. The Los Angeles Festival, an enormous multicultural festival that has been held twice in the 1990s, is also notable for its global and local focus. Held in venues throughout the city, the L.A. Festival attempts to gather the arts and artists of the city's multifaceted population with their counterparts in Asia, the Pacific, Africa, and the Middle East.

Festivals that showcase music and musicians can also be completely self-supporting by way of grassroots organization and planning, and community and corporate sponsorship. Milwaukee (which boasts one of the highest percentage of German Americans in the United States) hosts an Octoberfest complete with high-fat sausage and dark beer. This annual event draws tens of thousands of people to the city. Similarly, the German American community in New Ulm, Minnesota (home of the Bohemian American polka legend, Whoopie John Whilfart), hosts an annual fair in October with local and regional polka bands that perform daily. The annual Arab World Festival, in the heart of Detroit, is planned and presented every summer through a complex process of negotiation among the community leaders and artists in Michigan's multifaceted Arab American community. And in Brooklyn, New York, during the late summer, people from throughout the Caribbean participate in a unique American version of Carnival (usually associated with the end of Lent in early spring) when many blocks are taken up with food and soca, steel band, reggae, calypso, and dance!

Many of the authors for this volume have done research, contacted artists, acted as interpreters, built stages, written grant proposals, advised festival planners, produced, and even performed in festivals. And as advocates of the public presentation of community arts, we have taken increasingly central roles in their manifestation, simply as an extension of our fieldwork.

All of the authors are attentive to the potential reverberations of our research in the communities in which we have worked. Many have had the opportunities to see and begin to understand the ways in which our work may elicit a range of emotions among community members. The festivals, concerts, exhibits, or other performances in which we assisted or participated may have lasted only a few hours or even for several weeks, but their impact reverberates long afterwards. Such public performances may help to revitalize or rejuvenate a musical genre. Only one example of this process is the overwhelming enthusiasm for klezmer music, a tradition that has enjoyed a nationwide renaissance since about 1980.

Meanwhile, we wrestle with the search for objectivity in our studies of these communities. We are challenged by the mission of representing the opinions and explanations of people whose stories about the same events may be inconsistent or in conflict because of differing political agendas or personal histories. We feel compelled to be nonjudgmental in scholarly presentations and publications because these products provide what may eventually be the most permanent documentation and interpretation of the communities and their cultural expressions. As players in a continuously evolving intellectual tradition, we have a self-imposed mandate to assume a reflexive stance in the crafting of our respective chapters and to evaluate the importance of the fieldwork experience in shaping our own view of the people and the music whose stories fill the following pages. It is ironic that these scholarly works may be irrelevant, even invisible, to the people who helped to generate them. It is hoped that *Musics of Multicultural America* will reach a readership that includes students with connections to the communities represented herein and will be accessible to those who helped us write it.

MULTICULTURAL AMERICAN MUSICS AND CONTEMPORARY DISCOURSE

Musics of Multicultural America speaks to an audience that is interested in both the sound of American music and in American music as a social and cultural phenomenon. We write with reference to a family of allied academic fields that includes American studies, ethnomusicology, folklore, and multicultural studies. We build on a literature from American music, cultural geography, the study of world music, and scholarship on ethnicity and identity; a selection of important works from these fields are cited and suggested for further reading at the end of this chapter. Because of the interdisciplinary nature of our work, these case studies do not fall neatly into conventional academic categories; however, we believe that an interdisciplinary framework is essential to the understanding and appreciation of music in multicultural America.

EARLY STUDIES OF AMERICAN MUSIC

Until the 1950s research by academic scholars about American music was primarily focused upon European-derived musical forms that were attributed to schooled (usually male) composers and represented in staff notation. This is particularly true for historical musicologists, those academically trained music historians who followed a Germanic model of scholarship that evolved in the late nineteenth century. They often overlooked or deliberately ignored American vernacular and popular music and limited their research to the analysis of musical works and the writing of biography. Although the paradigms of musicology are now under scrutiny by the scholars themselves (see, for example, Bergeron and Bohlman 1992), many twentieth-century musicologists continue to define the study and teaching of music history in terms of "Great (Western European) Men" and their "Great (Western European) Works."

There were, of course, a handful of pioneering scholars—almost none were trained in historical musicology—who worked outside these established academic boundaries. Beginning in the middle 1920s, Sigmund Spaeth wrote elegantly and at length about popular music (1927); Frederic Ramsey and Charles Edward Smith coauthored the first book devoted to jazz (1939); George Pullen Jackson published studies of white gospel music in the southeastern states (1933); John and Alan Lomax wrote a study of the life and lyrics of the Texas songster Lead Belly (1936). Ruth Crawford Seeger and her husband, Charles Seeger, were among the handful of exceptions; during the 1930s they studied and taught courses that included American vernacular music. They were especially interested in American folk music and worked with traditions as varied as old-time fiddle tunes, children's play songs, and Appalachian folk music (Crawford Seeger 1953).

The first edition of Gilbert Chase's masterly survey, *America's Music,* helped to challenge the Eurocentric hegemony in the mid-1950s (Chase 1987). Chase (who initially trained in historical musicology and also worked as a music critic and teacher) broadened the scope of scholarly discourse by including information about jazz and Tin Pan Alley composers. Subsequent editions of Chase's book embraced even more styles of vernacular music as the author added facts and insights about black American and popular music. This trend has gradually escalated and today we not only have fairly well-balanced surveys of American music history but specialized textbooks that are devoted to such vernacular forms of American music as jazz, rock, and folk.

Since the 1970s the number of scholarly books about American vernacular music (written by both academic and nonacademic authors), has increased dramatically. Most of these books discuss a single topic, for example Bill Malone's panoramic *Country Music U.S.A.* or the even more geographically focused *Big Road Blues,* a study of Mississippi blues by David Evans. In

1972 the University of Illinois launched the first scholarly series, "Music in American Life," devoted exclusively to this subject. The first book in the series, *Only a Miner: Studies in Recorded Coal-Mining Songs,* is Archie Green's classic study of mining lore, songs, and music (1972). Since its inception this series has published books on topics as diverse as Chicago soul music, cowboy songs, the music of Jewish immigrants, bluegrass, music at the White House, Kansas City jazz, and the definitive biography of country music legend, Jimmie Rodgers. More recently, in 1995, the University Press of Mississippi launched its own series in American music, but with a focus on the South and a mission to reach a wider audience that includes nonacademics.

AMERICAN MUSICAL GEOGRAPHY

Musics of Multicultural America puts a spotlight on topics that have been underserved by the sweeping surveys written by Charles Hamm (1979, 1983), Gilbert Chase (1987), H. Wiley Hitchcock (1988), and Daniel Kingman (1990)—the American music texts that are most frequently used today. *Yesterdays: Popular Song in America* is Hamm's look at this aspect of American music since the country's inception. Chase's most recent edition of *America's Music* covers American musical history in roughly chronological order, including sections about blues, ethnic traditions, and rock music. *American Music: A Panorama,* by Kingman, looks at this massive topic through seven strains, including sacred and secular music, jazz, classical music, folk and ethnic music, and diverse regional musics. The trend, quite clearly, is toward the inclusion of previously marginalized musical cultures.

Kingman's nod to regionalism—which works in tandem with race and ethnicity as an important way to define difference in our musical culture—suggests the significance of cultural geography. Since the time of the seventeenth-century New England Psalmodists, American music has been classified according to its "hearth" area of origin. Such geographical classifications may be indicative of an entire genre, consider for example "Appalachian folk music," which refers to the mostly white folk music found from northern Georgia through upstate New York. In the late 1940s, the classic Chicago blues was developed primarily by black migrants from the Mississippi Delta, who basically updated their music by adding a rhythm section and amplifying their instruments to create a distinctive sound. Other types of folk music, for example cowboys songs, Cajun music, and the African American fife and drum band tradition, also recognize distinctive regional boundaries.

Cultural geography also provides an important way to understand popular music and American jazz. A tour of jazz styles, for example, begins in early twentieth-century New Orleans and then moves upward and outward to Chicago, New York City, Kansas City, and other locations during the 1920s and 1930s; later West Coast cool jazz emerges distinct from East Coast be-bop. While jazz was originating in the South, the popular music industry was established in the Tin Pan Alley area of New York City. Over the intervening decades, popular music diffused across the country. Popular music in the post–World-War-II period exploded with geographical attributions: the Motown sound, California surf bands, Gamble and Huff's sound of Philadelphia, Seattle grunge, the psychedelic sound from San Francisco, swamp-pop from Louisiana, Brooklyn's doo-wop groups, or the Southern rock of such groups as Lynard Skynard and the Allman Brothers.

The geographical implications of music, as George Carney (1994) has amply demonstrated, are more complicated and significant than the mere origin of a particular music in a city, state, or region of origin. Musical genres and styles have the power to actually evoke American places in the same way that individual artists and their repertoires can become emblematic of towns, cities, states, or entire regions. Country musicians are well known for regional identification; consider, for example, Bill Monroe and the Blue Grass Boys (bluegrass), Bob Wills and the Texas Playboys (western swing), or Charlie Poole and the North Carolina Ramblers (old-time stringbands). Perhaps at first, a geographical reference in a song's title or lyrics ignites a memory of place; but over time musical sounds themselves can evoke a sense of place in a way that is matched, perhaps on a personal level, only by the particular aromas in the kitchen or the sight of grandmother's home.

A consideration of American cultural geography must also include the diffusion or movement of musical styles from one section of the United States to another. The physical movement of such pivotal blues musicians as Muddy Waters, Sonny Boy Williamson, Elmore James, and Howlin' Wolf from the deep mid-South to Chicago in the late 1940s and 1950s helped to establish the previously mentioned sounds of the Delta to the north. Thus the term Chicago Blues in fact not only refers to musical innovations but implies the migration of a music from south to north, and from rural to urban. Similarly, immigrants from the dust bowls of Oklahoma and Texas brought their music with them to California. This expanded audience caused Bob Wills to relocate (albeit for only a few years) to Southern California in the late 1940s. Similarly, the interest in blues in California was heightened by the black Americans who left the same region in search of economic prosperity in California. This same migration pattern, though it was primarily stimulated by the availability of shipyard and other related jobs in the San Franciso Bay area, holds true also for the Cajuns who left southwestern Louisiana and brought their musical culture with them.

CULTURAL GEOGRAPHY AND THE MULTICULTURAL MIX

The blend of cultures in the United States at the end of the twentieth century makes the American cultural landscape especially rich. The United States is presently the home to people from across the entire world. On the West Coast, for instance, Asian immigrants have had a profound impact. The southernmost states form a "border culture" where the music, fashion, and food from Mexico, Central America, and the Caribbean permeate every strata of society. In the so-called heartland of our country (the American Midwest), African Americans, as well as people of Northern European and Scandinavian heritage share the map with Middle Easterners and people from Eastern Europe. Every large city in the United States, from Boston to San Francisco, is a virtual cauldron of ethnicity, race, nationalism, class, and social groups. *Musics of Multicultural America* challenges its readers to develop a sense of American musical life that matches the diversity and complexity of the American population.

Just as is the case with American vernacular and popular music, American multicultural music may often serve as a window into the history of migration and transplantation. The movement of Mexican American peoples from the Southwest throughout the United States has established a number of important Mexican-American styles, including for example, *conjunto*, mariachi, and *tejano*, in the north and east. As people of Norwegian, Swedish, Czech, and Bohemian background permanently leave their northern homes and become wintertime "snowbirds," they bring with them the polka bands and dances that find new audiences in places like Arizona and Florida. The very popularity of Cajun culture and music illustrates that certain types of regional or ethnic music become trendy and undergo waves of popularity that extend beyond their place of origin. Beginning slowly in the 1960s and rapidly gathering momentum over the past ten years, gumbo, button accordions, and two-stepping have become chic. Hundreds of miles from the bayou, throughout much of the United States, not only have the sheer number of Creole, Cajun, and New Orleans style restaurants increased radically, the interest in Cajun music and dance has mushroomed. In the late 1980s there were usually one or two Cajun or zydeco dances per month in the Washington, D.C., area alone, and at this writing there are dances nearly each week at several venues as well as a regular Wednesday night gathering of people who like Cajun music and culture. There are even escape weekends at seaside resorts and mountain retreats that plunge their participants into Louisiana food and music and dance. Nevertheless, even with today's nationwide and even international fascination with things Cajun, we rightly associate Cajun music and culture with southwestern Louisiana and southeastern Texas. Looking into the history of Cajun music and culture reminds us of this community's original migration from France to eastern Canada and then from the maritime Provinces to present-day Louisiana.

When a music that has a significant set of stylistic features—for example, melodies, ryhthms, instruments, or lyrics—that originate outside of our borders, that music brings a rich sense of place with it. For some, who iden-

SQUEEZE BAYOU
Cajun Dance Music

Sunday-May 21 - Tornado Alley
11319 Elkin St. Wheaton Md.   (301) 929-0795
Workshop - 5:00 - 6:00   Dancing - 6:00- 8:30
Admission - Adults $7.00 , Kids free

Wed.-June 7 - Columbia, Md.
Sunset Serenade Concert
Centennial Park South,   Columbia, Md.
If weather is questionable call (410) 313-4451 for recorded announcement
Music - 7:00-8:30   Admission - Free

Tuesday- June 20 - Crescent City
1120 King St., Old Town, Alexandria Va,   (703) 684-9505
Great Cajun food !   Wooden floor for dancing.
Music - 8:30-11:30   Admission - Adults $3.00

Sunday-June 11 - Silver Spring
Montgomery Co. Ethnic Heritage Festival
City Place Stage   Silver Spring, Md.
Music : 12:00-12:45   Admission - Free

Saturday-July 29 - Borders Books
White Flint Mall,   Rockville, Md.
Music : 1:00-3:00   Admission - Free

Sunday-July 30 - Tornado Alley
11319 Elkin St. Wheaton , Md.   (301) 929-0795
Workshop - 5:00 - 6:00   Dancing - 6:00- 8:30
Admission - Adults $7.00 , Kids free

For more info : (301) 270-2586

Figure 1.1. Flyer from Lornell collection.

tify their heritage as originating outside of the nation, and others who are learning about their heritage through community performance, music *invents* homeland. Collections edited by Falassi (1987) and Stokes (1994) offer numerous examples of the power of music, dance, festival and ritual, to actualize community through referencing its sights, sounds, smells, customs, and world views. George Lipsitz in his *Dangerous Crossroads* (1994) extends the discussion to embrace mediated popular music in a global postmodern context and its power to communicate a "poetics of place." Whether remembered from "over there" or learned here, music has the power through lyrics, instruments, ornaments, scales, intonation and a host of other features to reference time and place in special ways. When we have in the United States the sounds of Puerto Rico and Cuba in salsa, of the Caribbean in reggae, soca, and calypso, of Northern and Eastern Europe in polka and klezmer, of Japan in new age, of the Middle East in kef-time, of Spain and Mexico in Native American matachines—what we have is quite a lot of world music within our own national boundaries.

THE STUDY OF WORLD MUSIC

Although the study of "world music"—often the work of ethnomusicologists—has been part of college curricula for nearly three decades, it still remains largely on the fringe. The major art and folk music traditions of Asia, the Middle East, Eastern Europe and the Balkans, Latin America, Africa, and Native America are well represented in survey courses of world music and academic forums, such as scholarly conferences, journals, and books. Serious consideration of world music tradition in the United States (for example Chinese music in America, or Chinese-American music) has lagged far behind due to the privileged position of the authentic in academia (see, for example, Handler and Linnekin 1984). Over the past two decades, however, ethnomusicologists have expanded the purview of their discipline to include not only musical practices characterized by age, place, and purity, but also those rich with the complexities of the contemporary, the mediated, the transnational, and the postmodern, phenomena that have been identified and theorized by contemporary thinkers, perhaps most notable among them Arjun Appadurai (see, for example, Appadurai 1990).

Ethnomusicologists then, among others, have reinforced the fact that the "New World" is as rich a field of study for contemporary scholars as the "Old World" has been for historical and comparative musicologists and their colleagues. Thanks to the time and energy ethnomusicologists have invested toward the understanding of multiple musical languages, they have much to offer contemporary study of American music. At this writing, the discipline of ethnomusicology itself is characterized as much by approach as by geographical orientation. Taking a nod from anthropology, ethnomusicologists look at music in and as culture, as a fundamental activity of humankind. Unlike musicology, which traditionally has taught the important moments, the major figures, and the essential works of Western music history, ethnomusicologists are often less interested in charting and ranking musical repertoires than they are in understanding the ways people use, practice, and ascribe meaning to music. Ethnomusicologists aim to gain some understanding of native systems of musical practice and aesthetics and to adopt a relativistic view of musical sounds and systems.

College students often have an interest in world music because they have taken related courses in anthropology or the histories, religions, and literatures of non-Western cultures. Furthermore, many students now come to world music classes because their interest has been piqued by "world beat" artists and international pop stars, such as Algerian rai-singer Cheb Khaled or Nigerian juju musician King Sunny Ade, whose recordings fill the eclectic international sections of music retail stores and mail-order catalogues. Others are there because they have heard some so-called world music in their own backyard—a conjunto band on a Texas radio station, a salsa group performing at a New York City nightclub, klezmer music at a friend's wedding, or the religious and holiday songs that accompany their own family celebrations.

Those of us who teach world music courses are challenged and excited by our assignment to teach "the world" in one or two semesters. Yet, while our colleagues teach a comparatively compact geographical and temporal slice of Western fine art music, we can be frustrated by the marginalization of world music by some who consider any kind of global studies as extra, exotic, faraway, foreign, or mostly for fun. A residual dichotomy between "the West and the rest" remains an influential paradigm in many academic institutions despite moves within our educational system to address the need for a more global perspective in the areas of art, history, literature, philosophy, religion, and related fields in the humanities. An inclusive investigation of musical activity in our own nation testifies that the sacred dichotomy between things Western and non-Western is one that is perhaps falsely perpetuated and subsidized by our educational and political institutions (see also Bloom 1987, Levine 1996, and Palumbo-Liu, ed. 1995). The sounds of much of the world ring out across the United States. American music is simply a by-product of the diversity of the American population (see Takaki 1993).

MUSIC, ETHNICITY, AND IDENTITY

Studies of ethnicity as a profound and enduring social construct of humankind have gained unmatched momentum since the mid-1960s. Building upon the interests of such sociologists and anthropologists as Herskovitz (1945) and Gordon (1964), who monitored processes of assimilation, adaptation, and acculturation among both African Americans as well as the teeming masses of the first and second wave of immigrants to the United States, scholars from music to political science developed a keen interest in ethnicity and race as a key to American identity and in the "practice of tradition" as evidence of such identities (see Cohen [1985] and Barth [1969]). For early scholars, explains Anya Peterson Royce (1982), tradition meant the old customs and modes of behavior that were passed down and inherited from generation to generation. The natural processes of assimilation and acculturation in the New World were catalysts for the erosion of "authentic" Old World traditions that resulted in the gradual meltdown of ethnic distinctions into the American pot. As the civil rights movement in the 1960s legitimized difference, new academic paradigms emerged that focused not on the meltdown of tradition but on the constant reworking and rearticulation of tradition through idea and action. Cohen, Barth, and Peterson Royce are among the scholars of ethnicity who have studied the ways in which communities are constructed, the ways in which boundaries are defined, and how symbols are manipulated. In the 1980s and 1990s, studies of race and ethnicity and the construction of identity have been extended by numerous scholars from within ethnic groups, who, writing as insiders, have given prominence to the complexity and richness of identity formation.

The conclusions of researchers and their consultants from the myriad communities they study is that ethnicity and identity are far from static. In spite of the fact that we are born into families, into socioeconomic classes, and into religious groups, our identities are largely constructed through the daily processes of personal interaction, choosing associates, and through participating in social activities—from singing a song to making a deal. The sense of who we are is not predetermined at birth; rather it is invented throughout the life cycle and reinterpreted from generation to generation. Ethnic and community identity—confirms such studies as those by Waters (1990) and Alba (1990)—are fluid, vigorous, and to certain extent, voluntary.

In such disciplines as anthropology, sociology, American history, and cultural studies, the investigation of ethnicity as the wellspring of individual and group identity has become a major focus, and this is clearly reflected in the literature and curricula generated by scholars in these fields (for example, Erikson 1993, McCready ed. 1983, and Sollors 1989). Notions of ethnic identity and the ways in which identities in general are constructed, however, have been particularly fascinating to ethnomusicologists and folklorists. "The construction of identity and community through and around performance" has inspired a wealth of papers, conference sessions, entire conferences, dissertations, books, book series, and college courses. As many of our colleagues—Kirshenblatt-Gimblett (1983), Slobin (1993), Stern and Cicala (eds. 1991), to name only a few—have illustrated, scholars of performance are especially well situated to comment on the construction of identity because ethnicity or community is practiced through a wide variety of cultural acts including music, dance, language, food, dress, religion, humor, story, ritual, and almost always through a composite web of several of these acts at once.

Every essay in *Musics of Multicultural America* exemplifies the way in which music making contributes to the creation, maintenance, and transfer of individual and group identity. The preparation for a musical performance and the experience shared by artists and audience alike helps to spark the construction of community. For example, reliving Carnival every year in the streets of New York brings Caribbean Americans together in an almost obligatory celebration that reaffirms their heritage and their solidarity as a people, however dispersed are their residences in America. For communities such as these, the musical event may be in fact the only time during which group members—of disparate ages, income levels, and educational backgrounds—gather together. For other communities, such as the gospel quartet community in Memphis or Yemeni Americans in Detroit, interaction often occurs in a number of domains (at home, at school, or in the workplace), but the musical event may be the time during which bonds are especially strong. Rather than merely reflecting and repeating a community's pre-established ideology and practice, however, the creation and performance of music can generate—to borrow from immigration scholar Rodolph Vecoli—"a sense of peoplehood."

With this volume, we extend and revisit the theoretical attention to "the construction of community" and view this extraordinary but very natural human process through the lens of performance. Furthermore, we believe that the agents that are at work for an ethnic group in their construction of community through music and dance are at work for any community, however self-identified. Certainly a community-generated festival at the Los Angeles Thai Temple stands in sharp relief to an African American go-go dance held at a skating rink in the Anacostia section of Washington, D.C. But are the fundamental processes of choosing ways to dance, which clothes to wear, how to worship, what to eat, or when to sing really that different for Thai Americans of Los Angeles and the thousands of Americans who gather each weekend at go-goes? We suggest that the answer is no. Participation in music, whether as a player or a listener, implies making choices, choices that are sometimes made in the light of ethnicity and heritage but at other times may be made according to a political, social, professional, or artistic agenda.

Switching codes between American popular music at a school dance at the gym and, for example, Mexican American mariachi at a family graduation party are part and parcel of multicultural America. The process of code switching may also occur over a longer span of time—during the life cycle (as has been the case with Linda Rondstadt, profiled in Dan Sheehy's chapter) or from generation to generation (as is discussed by Susan Asai in her chapter on Japanese American music making). In the context of a wedding, young Americans of Arab heritage, for example, may move easily between Casey Kasem's "top forty" and the most recent Arab hits from Lebanon. That Kasem—the host of the nationally syndicated "Casey Kasem's Coast to Coast" and thus the long-reigning "King of top-forty"—is himself a Lebanese American who is a willing and highly visible supporter of Arab American social causes and cultural events, is indicative of the complex web of multiple identities that Americans may negotiate within the course of a day or their life span. In their own way, each of the communities profiled in *Musics of Multicultural America* defiantly and proudly proclaim—in the words of *Polka Happiness* authors, Keil, Keil, and Blau—a resounding "'No!' to monoculture."

Why experience music? Why play, listen, dance, sing, and feel music? Cateforis and Humphreys assert that music was the most visible and audible emblem around which Riot Grrrls could coalesce. Romero writes that the Pueblo themselves invest the performance of matachines with such a sense of authenticity that it is absurd for the scholar to even evaluate continuity and change in what is obviously a very old but also quite flexible performance complex. Pen suggests that religious and cultural impulses, many of which are steeped in decades of tradition, underpin the singing from the shape-note books used by people in central Kentucky. Wong, on the other hand, asserts that the contemporary hip-hop culture is so pervasive that even the most recent East Asian immigrants come under its sway.

The ability of music to consistently generate powerful symbols of social alliance, tradition, heritage, place, love, hate, nationalism, and a host of other emotions is often overlooked in the existing studies of American music. A profound sense of spirituality may permeate certain audience members at a gospel quartet performance who normally may not articulate their religious orientation. At the annual Arab World Festival in Detroit, spirited nationalism may rise unexpectedly among individuals who are normally ecumenical in their view of the Arab world. Thus, what may not be even hinted at in spoken and written discourse, for example, may be vividly obvious or subtly encoded in a music event. This team of authors looks to musical activity as a rich repository of information about cultural and social issues.

CLOSING THOUGHTS

Musics of Multicultural America is meant to broaden the horizons of those interested in music found in the United States. We hope that this small sample of case studies will stimulate students to more carefully access and explore the multitudinous musical communities untouched by this collection. We further hope that students using this book will become aware of the diversity of music making in the United States and understand that our musical heritage extends far beyond the familiar folk, rock, pop, jazz, and country to encompass an enormous range of music that is built upon the bedrock of immigration and innovation.

In closing, we find it important to stress that musical taste and cultural identity in the United States is a matter of choice. People of Jewish heritage may cringe at the sound of klezmer, African Americans may never have experienced a Sunday afternoon gospel program, Americans of Caribbean heritage living in Kansas may just simply be too far from the New York Carnival loop to have ever gotten involved. Furthermore, it is important to be cognizant of the intellectual history of the United States of America and the many emotional and ideological shifts in perspective that our nation has undergone and continues to experience regarding cultural diversity (see U.S. Commission . . . 1994). The popularity of the familiar *melting-pot* metaphor has waxed and waned with movements toward nationalism and xenophobia on the one hand or toward proud promotion of cultural diversity on the other. Consider for example the immigration quotas of 1924, which reflected the concern to limit the racial and ethnic contamination of America by immigrants from Asia and Eastern Europe. Recall, for example, Alex Haley's *Roots* and the numerous, publications, television programs, and trips to Ellis Island to check the passenger records for an ancestor that his powerful book inspired in its wake. Contrast the inclusionist messages of multiculturalism in popular culture and corporate advertising with the defensive rhetoric, in the mid-1990s, surrounding California's Proposition 187.

Whichever way the winds of ideology, politics, and policy may blow in America, it is clear that people are becoming hooked on musical diversity. When commercial jingles are tinged with world percussion and harmonies and when people are dancing Cajun in the north and polka in the south, it seems that individuals are searching for ways in which they can listen to and participate in an increasingly diverse set of musical options. The musics profiled in *Musics of Multicultural America,* in addition to thousands of others, have provided these options. There is little doubt that these American musics will play on and continue to provide powerful catalysts for artistically creative and socially positive experiences.

FOR FURTHER READING

Alba, Richard D. 1990. *Ethnic Identity: The Transformation of White America.* New Haven, Conn.: Yale University Press.

Anderson, Benedict. 1983. *Imagined Communities: Reflections on the Origin and Spread of Nationalism.* London: Verso.

Appadurai, Arjun. 1990. Disjuncture and Difference in the Global Cultural Economy. *Public Culture.* 2, no. 2: 1–24.

Barron, Robert, and Nick Spitzer. 1992. *Public Folklore.* Washington, D.C.: Smithsonian Institution Press.

Barth, Frederik. 1969. *Ethnic Groups and Boundaries: The Social Organization of Cultural Difference.* Boston: Little, Brown.

Bergeron, Katherine, and Philip V. Bohlman. 1992. *Disciplining Music: Musicology and Its Canons.* Chicago: University of Chicago Press.

Berlin, Edward. 1980. *Ragtime: A Musical and Cultural History.* Berkeley and Los Angeles: University of California Press.

Bloom, Alan. 1987. *The Closing of the American Mind: How Higher Education Has Failed Democracy and Impoverished the Souls of Today's Students.* New York: Simon & Schuster.

Briggs, Vernon M., Jr. 1992. *Mass Migration and the National Interest.* Armonk, N.Y.: M. E. Sharpe.

Caraveli, Anna. 1985. The Symbolic Village: Community Born in Performance. *Journal of American Folklore* 99 (289): 260–86.

Carney, George O. 1994. *The Sound of People and Places.* 3rd ed. Lanham, Md.: Rowman and Littlefield.

Chase, Gilbert. 1987. *America's Music: From the Pilgrims to the Present.* 3rd ed. Urbana: University of Illinois Press.

Charters, Samuel. 1975. *The Country Blues.* Reprint, New York: Da Capo Press. Original edition, 1959.

Ch'maj, Betty E. M., ed. 1993. *Multicultural America: A Resource Book for Teachers of Humanities and American Studies.* Lanham, Md.: University Press of America.

Cohen, A. P. 1985. *The Symbolic Construction of Community.* London: Tavistock Publishers.

Crawford, Ruth Seeger. 1953. *Animal Songs for Children.* Garden City, N.Y.: Doubleday and Co.

Epstein, Dena. 1977. *Sinful Tunes and Spirituals: Black Folk Music to the Civil War.* Urbana: University of Illinois Press.

Erikson, Thomas Hylland. 1993. *Ethnicity and Nationalism: Anthropological Perspectives.* London: Pluto Press.

Jeff Todd Titon, ed. Special Issue: Music in the Public Interest. *Ethnomusicology: Journal for the Society of Ethnomusicology* 36:3.

Evans, David. 1982. *Big Road Blues: Tradition and Creativity in the Folk Blues.* Berkeley and Los Angeles: University of California Press.

Falassi, Alessandro. 1987. *Time Out of Time: Essays on the Festival.* Albuquerque: University of New Mexico Press.

Georges, Robert A., and Stephen Stern. 1982. *American and Canadian Immigrant and Ethnic Folklore: An Annotated Bibliography.* New York: Garland Publishing.

Glazer, Nathan, and Daniel P. Moynihan, eds. 1975. *Ethnicity, Theory, and Experience.* Cambridge, Mass.: Harvard University Press.

Gordon, Milton. 1964. *Assimilation in American Life: The Role of Race, Religion, and National Origins.* New York: Oxford University Press.

Gronow, Pekka. 1982. Ethnic Recordings: An Introduction. *Ethnic Recordings in America: A Neglected Heritage.* Edited by Richard Spottswood. 1–31. Washington, D.C.: Library of Congress.

Hamm, Charles. 1979. *Yesterdays: Popular Song in America.* New York: W. W. Norton.

———. 1983. *Music in the New World.* New York: W. W. Norton.

Handler, Richard, and J. Linnekin. 1984. Tradition, Genuine or Spurious. *Journal of American Folklore* 97(385):273–90.

Harvard Encyclopedia of American Ethnic Groups. 1980. Edited by Stephan Thurston. 128–36. Cambridge, Mass.: London: The Belknap Press of Harvard University Press.

Heilbut, Tony. 1985. *The Gospel Sound: Good News and Bad Times.* 2nd ed. New York: Simon & Schuster.

Herskovits, Melville J. 1945. *Acculturation and the Study of Culture Contact.* New York: J. J. Augustin.

Hitchcock, H. Wiley. 1988. *Music in the United States: A Historical Introduction.* 3rd ed. Englewood Cliffs, N.J.: Prentice Hall.

Humphrey, Theodore C., and Lin T. Humphrey. 1988. *"We Gather Together": Food and Festival in American Life.* Ann Arbor: U.M.I. Research Press.

Jackson, George Pullen. 1964. *White Spirituals in the Southern Uplands: The Story of the Fasola Folk, their Songs, Singings, and "Buckwheat Notes."* Reprint, Hatboro, Pa.: Folklore Associates. Original edition, 1933.

Kiel, Charles, Dick Blau, and Angeliki Keil. 1992. *Polka Happiness.* Philadelphia: Temple University Press.

Kingman, Daniel. 1990. *American Music: A Panorama.* 2nd ed. New York: Schirmer Books.

Kirshenblatt-Gimblett, Barbara. 1983. Studying Immigrant and Ethnic Folklore. In *Handbook of American Folklore.* Edited by Richard M. Dorson. Bloomington, Ind.: Indiana University Press.

Klymasz, Robert B. 1983. Folklore of the Canadian-American Border. In *Handbook of American Folklore.* Edited by Richard M. Dorson. Bloomington, Ind.: Indiana University Press.

Levine, Lawrence W. 1988. *Highbrow/Lowbrow: The Emergence of Cultural Hierarchy in America.* Cambridge, Mass.: Harvard University Press.

Levine, Lawrence W. 1996. *The Opening of the American Mind: Canons, Culture, and History.* Boston: Beacon Press.

Lipsitz, George. 1994. *Dangerous Crossroads: Popular Music, Postmodernism and the Poetics of Place.* London: Verso.

Lomax, Alan. 1960. *The Folk Songs of North America in the English Language.* Garden City, N.Y.: Doubleday and Co.

Lomax, John. 1938. *Cowboy Songs and Other Frontier Ballads.* Rev. ed. New York: Macmillan.

Lornell, Kip. 1995. *"Happy in the Service of the Lord": African-American Sacred Vocal Harmony Quartets in Memphis.* 2nd ed. Knoxville: University of Tennessee Press.

Loza, Steven. 1993. *Barrio Rhythm: Mexican American Music in Los Angeles.* Urbana and Chicago: University of Illinois Press.

Malone, Bill. 1985. *Country Music, U.S.A.* Rev. ed. Austin: University of Texas Press.

McCready, William C., ed. 1983. *Culture, Ethnicity, and Identity: Current Issues in Research.* New York: Academic Press, Inc.

Naficy, Hamid, and Gabriel Teshome. 1993. *The Making of Exile Cultures: Iranian Television in Los Angeles.* Minneapolis: University of Minnesota Press.

Oliver, Paul. 1974. *The Story of the Blues.* Reprint, New York: Chilton Books. Original edition, 1969.

Omni, Michael, and Howard Winant. 1994. *Racial Formation in the United States: From the 1960s to the 1990s.* 2nd ed. New York: Routledge.

Palumbo-Liu, David, ed. 1995. *The Ethnic Canon: Histories, Institutions, and Interventions.* Minneapolis: University of Minnesota Press.

Pena, Manuel. 1985. *The Texas Mexican Conjunto: History of a Working-Class Music.* Austin: University of Texas Press.

Peterson Royce, Anya. 1982. *Ethnic Identity: Strategies of Diversity.* Bloomington, Ind.: Indiana University Press.

Porterfield, Nolan. 1979. *Jimmie Rodgers: The Life and Times of America's Blue Yodler.* Urbana: University of Illinois Press.

Ramsey, Frederic Jr., and Charles Edward Smith. (1939) 1977. *The Jazzmen.* DaCapo.

Spaeth, Sigmund. 1977. *Read 'em and Weep: The Songs You Forgot to Remember.* New York: Da Capo Press. Original edition, 1926.

Schuller, Gunther. 1989. *The Swing Era: The Development of Jazz, 1930 through 1945.* New York: Oxford University Press.

Simonson, Rick, and Scott Walker, eds. 1988. *Multicultural Literacy: Opening the American Mind.* St. Paul, Minn.: Greywolf Press.

Slobin, Mark. 1993. *Subcultural Sounds: Micromusics of the West.* Hanover, N.H.: Wesleyan University Press.

Slobin, Mark. 1982. *Tennement Songs: The Popular Music of the Jewish Immigrant.* Urbana, Ill.: University of Illinois Press.

Spottswood, Richard K., ed. 1990. *Ethnic Music on Records: A Discography of Ethnic Recordings Produced in the United States, 1893–1942.* Champaign-Urbana: University of Illinois Press.

Sollors, Werner, ed. 1989. *The Invention of Ethnicity.* New York: Oxford University Press.

Stern, Stephen, and John Allan Cicala, eds. 1991. *Creative Ethnicity: Symbols and Strategies of Contemporary Ethnic Life.* Logan, Utah: Utah State University Press.

Stokes, Martin, ed. 1994. *Ethnicity, Identity, and Music: The Musical Construction of Place.* Oxford: Berg Publishers.

Takaki, Ronald. 1993. *A Different Mirror: A History of Multicultural America.* Boston: Little, Brown and Company.

Tawa, Nicholas E. 1982. *A Sound of Strangers: Musical Culture, Acculturation, and the Post–Civil War Ethnic American.* Metuchen, N.J.: Scarecrow Press.

Toll, Robert. 1974. *Blacking Up: The Minstrel Show in Nineteenth-Century America.* New York: Oxford University Press.

U.S. Commission on Immigration Reform. 1994. *U.S. Immigration Policy: Restoring Credibility.* Report to Congress by the U.S. Commission on Immigration Reform, chaired by Barbara Jordan. Washington, D.C.: U.S. Government Printing Office.

Waters, Mary C. 1990. *Ethnic Options: Choosing Identities in America.* Berkeley, Los Angeles, Oxford: University of California Press.

CHAPTER 2

Czech American Polka Music in Wisconsin

James P. Leary

*I*n this essay, Jim Leary, a folklorist who teaches at the University of Wisconsin at Madison, examines the evolution of one strand of polka music in the Dairy State. Although he briefly mentions the German, Polish, and Slovenian communities of the region and the love for polka music that they share, the author specifically focuses on the Czech enclaves, especially those in eastern Wisconsin. Leary traces the history of Czech American polka music from its origins in the 1850s, with a special emphasis on the changing contexts in which the music has been performed: from the Bohemian halls built by Czech fraternal organizations during the late nineteenth and early twentieth centuries, to Depression-era ballrooms, to contemporary polka festivals. These settings and the close-knit Czech American communities of Wisconsin have helped to bridge the gulf between the old world and the new while contributing to the Slavic, German, and Scandinavian cultural pluralism that distinguishes Wisconsin and the Upper Midwest. Leary addresses one strand of the multiethnic polka community that until the 1980s, barely received serious attention from scholars in American vernacular music—despite its mainstream status among so many citizens of the United States from Texas to Minnesota. Today, because of the work undertaken by Leary, Richard March, Victor Greene, Charlie Keil, Manuel Peña, Robert Walser, and a handful of others, polka music is finally being treated with respect.

■   ■   ■   ■

POLKA MUSIC, AMERICAN MUSIC

Polka is the vernacular music of rural and working-class ethnic Americans whose ancestors immigrated from Europe in the nineteenth and early twentieth centuries to labor in factories, in lumber and mining camps, and on farms. Incorporating not only the polka, but also such other nineteenth-century couple dances as the waltz, the schottische, the ländler, the mazurka, and assorted "mixers," polka music is typically played by small ensembles consisting of some combination of brass, reed, percussion, and stringed instruments. Most at home in community halls and amidst weddings and local festivals, polka music has, throughout the twentieth century, entered into every form of mass media. Not surprisingly, it has been influenced by and has occasionally contributed to American popular music. And it has affected and intermingled with such other American folk traditions as the Cajun and zydeco music of southwest Louisiana, the Mexican-American *conjunto* music of south Texas, and the *waile* or "chicken scratch" music of Arizona's Tohono O'odham peoples.

Prominent in the industrial cities of southern New England and the Middle Atlantic states, the farming communities of the eastern Great Plains, the mining towns and alpine resorts of the Rocky Mountains, the ports and valleys of the Pacific Northwest, and the retirement havens of the Sun Belt, polka music is practiced most vigorously in the Midwest. In 1994, for example, the Wisconsin legislature designated the polka as the official state dance.[1] The genre's recognition was particularly appropriate since, because of Wisconsin's long history of cultural pluralism, the state's borders encompass a greater variety of polka substyles than anywhere else in the world.

For self-described "polka people," ethnicity has been the primary feature in distinguishing among the Dairy State's profusion of polka sounds. Austrians, Belgians, Croatians, Finns, Irish, Italians, Jews, Mexicans, Norwegians, Swedes, and Swiss have all made contributions within their respective enclaves. Czechs (Bohemians), Germans, Poles, and Slovenians, however, have done the most to shape Wisconsin's polka music. Indeed this quartet of ethnic-American polka styles, each with its innovative practitioners and evolving substyles, dominates the nation's polka scene (Leary 1991).

Despite its diversity, ubiquity, longevity, and clear contribution to the peculiarities of American musical life, polka music has received scant attention from folklorists, ethnomusicologists, and other students of American folk and vernacular music, especially in comparison to the considerable research devoted to America's Anglo-Celtic and African-derived musical traditions. There are several obvious reasons for this neglect, most of them descendent from the conservative, Anglophile, implicitly xenophobic, upper-class, academic origins of scholarship concerning American life and culture, including American folk music.

First, as the music of Germans, Italians, Jews, Slavs, Scandinavians, and other non-English-speaking immigrants, polka has been regarded as "foreign," a survival from the old country, and therefore less worthy of full musical citizenship than folk performances by those of "old stock" Anglo-Celtic heritage. Second, as a European-American genre, polka has, for the European

Americans who dominate folk-music scholarship, lacked the exoticism of African- and Native-American musical traditions. Third, as a multifaceted, pluralist, and widely dispersed genre, polka music—in terms of style, community, and place—has been far less geographically circumscribed, and consequently far less easy to study definitively, than the music of such otherwise comparable ethnic-regional Americans as Cajuns and Chicanos. Fourth, as a musical movement whose brief flirtation with American popular music was swept away in the early 1950s by the emergence of rock 'n' roll, polka music and, by association, the accordion have been regarded by the nation's tastemakers as hopelessly square.[2]

Happily, however, scholars have begun to discover polka music in increasing numbers since the 1980s (see especially Greene 1992; Keil, Keil, and Blau 1992; and Spottswood 1990). Part of this turnabout stems from the reassessment and broadening of canons in many fields, including folk music, since the late 1960s (Bohlman 1988; Slobin 1993). Part is attributable to a parallel expansion of the number and backgrounds of scholars researching American folk music: as more people do more work, they draw from a greater range of experience, and invariably some have grown up amidst the polka scene. Finally, the robust emergence of public folklore in the late 1970s, with its emphasis on culturally diverse folklore practitioners in every state (Feintuch 1988; Baron and Spitzer 1992), has provided both mandate and opportunity for the study of such previously neglected genres as polka music.

My own experience is instructive. I was born in 1950 in Rice Lake, an ethnically diverse farming and logging community in northwestern Wisconsin. While growing up in the 1950s and 1960s, I heard or heard about local Bohemian, German, Norwegian, Polish, Slovenian, Swedish, and Swiss polka bands performing live on WJMC radio, and at the Moose Club, Sokup's Tavern, the Pines Ballroom, Virgil's Bunny Bar, the Bohemian Hall, the Barron County Fair, Mount Hardscrabble's ski chalet, and an occasional wedding or barn dance. The music was everywhere.

In the early 1970s, however, when I began studying folk music as a graduate student, I could discover almost nothing about my hometown's polka scene and its broader American context. Neither course syllabi nor academic publications so much as acknowledged the genre's existence. Determined to learn more, in the late 1970s I began to buy polka recordings by Wisconsin bands, hang out at dances, and photograph and interview musicians (see, for example, Fig. 2.1). About the same time, Richard March—a fellow folklorist with polka roots and Wisconsin connections—and I began to get research contracts from various public folklore agencies for the purpose of documenting regional folk music traditions. For nearly twenty years, in collaboration or working on our own, we have been responsible for the inclusion of polka music in numerous festivals, documentary sound recordings, videos, radio programs, exhibits, and folk artist award ceremonies.[3] Along the way,

Figure 2.1. Joe Tomesh plays Czech music while Albert Tomesh and his sister, Dorothy Schwab, dance. John, Rose, Regina, and Tony Tomesh look on. House party, Haugen, Wisconsin, 1990. Photo: Jim Leary.

we have learned a great deal about polka music, especially through the musicians themselves, and we have published steadily on the subject (for example, Leary and March 1996). Our commitment to the polka music of America is likewise a commitment to a pluralist vision of American folk music. This essay draws upon my work, Richard March's, and that of other polka scholars in an effort to illuminate one more rich territory on America's polka map—that occupied by Wisconsin's Czechs.

CO CECH, TO MUZIKANT

> There were so many great bands in a small area . . . It's the Bohemians. They all love music and they love to show off. They either played or wanted to.
>
> — "Tuba Dan" Jerabek[4]

On a summer's night in 1988, Dan Jerabek took a break from playing at Americano's, an old wooden ballroom slated for razing in the modernizing paper-mill city of Appleton. An all-star lineup of polka bands and a floor full of dancers were sending the place off. We stepped outside into the parking lot, I propped a tape recorder on my car's hood, and—with brass and reeds blending in the background—Dan offered an old-world proverb that recalled a past and plotted a future guaranteed to withstand urban renewal: "Co Cech, to muzikant" (every Czech is a musician).

These words and sentiments have long echoed throughout Wisconsin's Czech communities: Hillsboro and Yuba in the lower Wisconsin River watershed; Ashland on the shores of Lake Superior; Haugen and Phillips in the northern cutover; and the Manitowoc and Kewaunee area along Lake Michigan. Here, music has been as vital as bread. Here, playing a tune has been no less important than ploughing a field. Here, the hard play of dances and weddings has been regarded as the natural complement of the hard work on farms and in factories.

One of nine children, Dan Jerabek was raised on a forty-acre farm near Kewaunee. "My dad wanted to keep us on the farm and out of mischief, so he gave us instruments." Jerry played piano, concertina, and bass clarinet; Bill was on drums and the button accordion; John favored the cornet; Joe and Ann switched off on clarinet and saxophone; while Dan blew the tuba. In the early 1950s the Jerabeks played variety shows in Manitowoc and Kewaunee Counties. "We didn't make any money, but we could start and end together. And the old people liked us," recalled Dan.

When Dan Jerabek was fifteen, a local musician needed a tuba player and offered eight dollars for a wedding job. Over the next two decades Dan played with over forty bands, either as a full-time or a fill-in player. By the late 1970s he had formed the Polkalanders, now known as the Tuba Dan Band, which comprised himself as the energetic bass horn player, his wife, Corky, on the drum, and their son, Dan Junior, on the clarinet, saxophone, and button accordion. Versatile enough to perform country music, rock, and some jazzy pop, the Jerabeks of the 1990s remain a polka band at heart, with a distinctive repertoire of Czech dance tunes and songs that is likely to persist well beyond the year 2000.

FROM OLD WORLD TO NEW

The roots of the Tuba Dan Band extend across nations and centuries. While some Czech immigrants found work in America as factory hands, tradesmen, and domestics in such urban centers as New York, Cleveland, and especially Chicago, more than half, like Dan Jerabek's ancestors, sought land. Most came from the German-dominated province of Bohemia (hence their designation as "Bohemians"), while others were from Moravia. Whether Bohemians or Moravians, Czechs constitute America's largest population of rural Slavs. Accordingly their old world village traditions have evolved more slowly than has been the case for their urban counterparts. Immigrant farmers arrived in Wisconsin first in the 1860s, but they were soon coming to agrarian east-central Texas in large numbers, sailing from the German ports of Bremen and Hamburg to Galveston. Today Texas outranks all other states in the total number of Czech Americans, with Wisconsin, Nebraska, Iowa, and Minnesota next in line. Settling in sufficient numbers to form their own cultural institutions, and often coexisting with immigrant Germans and Poles (their old-world neighbors), rural Czechs tempered the assimilative forces of Anglo-America to establish distinctive regional and ethnic identities (Leary 1995).

The fact that seven-eighths of America's four hundred thousand Czech immigrants arrived between the liberal revolutions of 1848 and the onset of World War I had an enormous impact on their music. That period coincided with the emergence and pan-European popularity of the polka, the flowering of brass-band music, the career of Frantisek Kmoch, the invention and mass production of the accordion, an interest in folksongs among intellectuals, and the association of folksongs and new songs in a folk style with nationalism: all of which profoundly influenced what has become Czech American polka music (Leary 1987a).

Performed by a couple executing a hop-step close-step pattern in $\frac{2}{4}$ time, the polka emerged around 1830 in northern Bohemia near the German and Polish borders. Although the dance draws upon earlier ethnically diverse forms, its oft-printed legend of origin, suffused with the era's romantic nationalism, suggests that Anna Slezak, a Bohemian peasant girl in the village of Elbeteinetz, improvised a tune and steps one summer afternoon. The local schoolmaster noticed Slezak's invention, taught it to his students, and sparked an international dance craze (Shaw 1948, 67–69). Certainly the polka had entered the genteel ballrooms of Prague by the mid-1830s; by the mid-nineteenth century, dancing masters had pupils dancing the polka in Vienna, Paris, London, and New York City. Like its couple-dance contemporary, the waltz, the polka was the perfect dance for an immigrant people to carry to new surroundings: rooted in the soil of peasant life, yet valued by the upper classes; an extension of old-world village customs, yet the fashionable rage in modern ballrooms; distinctly Czech, yet internationally adapted (Keil, Keil, and Blau 1992, 10–14).

Although perhaps first played on some combination of fiddles, clarinets, *cymbaly* (hammer dulcimers), or bagpipes, Czech folk instruments of the early 1800s, polka melodies were popularized through military brass bands. A Bohemian regimental brass band was playing polkas in Vienna, the Hapsburg seat of imperial power, as early as 1840. The military influence, technological innovations enabling the mass production of relatively inexpensive standardized instruments, and musical literacy prompted the formation of many late nineteenth-century village bands, whose members donned military garb and scanned musical staffs while blowing their horns for Sunday afternoon concerts and dances.

Frantisek Kmoch, the "Czechoslovak March King," wrote roughly four hundred marches and polkas for brass ensembles during a lifetime extending from 1848 to 1912. A trumpeter who combined traditional melodies with peasant themes and nationalist sentiments, Kmoch popularized his compositions, beginning in the 1870s, through European tours with his own brass band. Sheet music versions of such Kmoch compositions as "Koline, Koline," "Andulka Safarova," and "Muziky, Muziky" were carried to America by immigrants or purchased here from midwestern ethnic entrepreneurs. In an era when the martial winds of John Phillip Sousa swayed all Americans, Czech Americans could draw similar inspiration from one of their own (Greene 1992, 50–51).

More humble than the booming brass band, the diatonic button accordion and its instrumental relatives, the concertina and the piano accordion, likewise prospered in the late nineteenth and early twentieth centuries when German and, later, Italian companies produced inexpensive models in quantity. Most of the musicians who strapped on so-called squeezeboxes learned by ear rather than through formal training. With a voice that simultaneously replaced and sustained the reedy bite of bagpipes, the accordion could either accompany a clarinet, a violin, a cymbalum, or it could stand alone, a veritable one-man band, as its player punched out melodies with the right hand while articulating bass patterns with the left. Absent on the nineteenth-century village bandshell, the accordion became the central instrument for taverns, house parties, and weddings where revelers sang folksongs in polka and waltz tempos.

The period of Czech immigration to America was, finally, an era when intellectuals throughout Europe documented and celebrated the folksongs of peasants as exemplary of their people's essential spirit. Valued for their indigenous "natural" poetry, these folksongs were also elevated for their protonationalist sentiments—sentiments that Slavic foes of the Germanic Hapsburg empire expressed overtly in folk-inspired anthems like "Kde Domov Muj" (Where Is My Home), with its declaration that the old province of Bohemia is "God's country" and the rightful home of Czechs. The patriotic veneration of Czech folksongs was furthered in old world and new by the emergence of liberal-thinking Sokol organizations that, like the German Turners, established halls for the promotion of artistic, athletic, and political activities (Kolar 1979).

As a consequence of their common cultural history, the first generation of Czech Americans shared a fondness for polkas, waltzes, and related couple dances; they formed brass bands that often relied on arrangements written down by composers like Kmoch; they numbered many accordionists among them; and they sang traditional songs in homes and ethnic halls that merged peasant memory with ethnic allegiance.

BRASS BANDS AND BOHEMIAN HALLS

The early experiences of many Wisconsin Czechs exemplify the foregoing musical pattern. Consider Martin and Ludmila Stangle, both born in

Bohemia, who emigrated to Ashland, Wisconsin, in 1905 (Leary 1988). Ludmila played harmonica and button accordion by ear. Martin, a clarinetist, could read music. Martin's immigrant baggage, in the recollection of his son, Stanley, included

> green books, red books, blue books. And they all had categories of music in each one . . . little notebooks with printed staffs on them . . . schottisches, and waltzes, and polkas.

During a three-hour interview in the music room of his Ashland home, Stan Stangle enthusiastically recalled his first instrument, a baritone horn imported from Czechoslovakia, and his dad's improvised instructions.

> I'll never forget that first lesson my dad gave me. He just had a piece of paper, I think it was the back end of a calendar. He made the staff out and he wrote the scale for me. I was as tall as the doorknob and that's where he made a slit in the paper and hung it on the door-knob. And he said, "Get this note." And he'd sing it: "Da." Then the next note, first and third valves . . . from there on it was nothing to it. . . . And I loved to practice. There were times when he'd work nights and he'd have to sleep during the day. I'd go out to the wood-shed and sit on a coal pile or a stump, or close the barn door, and go to it.

The family soon had a band with Ludmila on button accordion, Martin on clarinet, Stan on trumpet, and a brother and sister on baritone horns.

Besides encouraging the talents of his children, Martin Stangle was a driving force behind his community's Bohemian Brass Band. Ashland in the early twentieth century was a patchwork of ethnic working-class neighbor-hoods—Norwegian, Swedish, Finnish, Polish, and Czech—stitched east to west near the sawmills and iron-ore docks that hugged the shores of Lake Superior (Leary 1984). Each enclave had one or several organizations. These collective entities, created to sustain ethnic and ideological solidarity, not only offered life insurance, athletic training, cultural programs, and social events, but also erected halls. Ashland's Bohemian Hall, "the jewel of the east side," was erected in 1910 by the ZCBJ or Západni Česko-Bratrská Jednota (Western Fraternal Life Association). It had an ample basement kitchen, a stage with painted backdrops of old-world scenes, and an open space that doubled as gymnasium and the best dance floor in town. Stangle's Bohemian Brass Band, garbed in militaristic, black uniforms and visored caps, held forth in the hall from 1910 through the late 1920s.

In the Band's final years, Stan, his brother, and other youngsters filled in for the old timers. Stan Stangle recalled about seven members. There was usually two cornets, two clarinets, baritone, tuba—there were no drums, no piano—and peckhorn, maybe two peckhorns. Peckhorn is an upright alto that gives that "oooh aaah" for rhythm.

With tuba and twin alto horns oompahing a powerful rhythm, and clarinets, baritone horns, and cornets weaving melody and harmony, the band set dancers swirling until the floor shook.

> We usually started out with a polka. That gets 'em out on the floor. Oh boy, they can hardly wait. Then a nice waltz. And then there was another type of waltz called the ländler. It was similar to a waltz, almost in the time of a waltz, but it had a different feeling to it. Then we'd go into another polka. We'd even play marches and they'd dance around to that.

The band also played the galop, a cousin of the march that is distinguished by its rollicking promenade. Similarly, many polkas and waltzes featured residual elements of marches in introductions and bridges framing the dance melodies.

Dances at the Bohemian Hall welcomed entire families. Before Stan Stangle was old enough to perform, he squirmed with other kids on chairs surrounding the dancers. Parents and grandparents frequently pulled their offspring onto the floor for impromptu lessons. And whenever musicians took a break, Stan and his peers capered and slid across the waxed wood floor, an experience he still relished half a century later.

> WHOOSH! We'd skid on our bellies, our new clothes. Our parents didn't think anything of it, because we were having a good time. As long as we behaved, they were having a good time dancing, so we could have a good time too.

Good food and cold beer were always plentiful at Bohemian Hall dances. Band members slaked their thirst by pulling bottles from an iced tub at the back of the stage. Sometimes drink brought mischief, as Stan recalled filling a baritone-horn player's instrument with brew. Beer also inspired songs from the dancers. Braced by several draughts in the hall's basement, old gentlemen, especially, would ascend and crowd in front of the stage singing:

> "Ma roztomila Baruska" [my beloved Barbara] . . . Oh it was fun. And the old guys would sweat. They'd be all dressed up in the suit they're going to die in and get buried in. And their ties would be over here [askew], you know. And the women would be sitting

there staring because the men wouldn't be dancing with them . . .
They'd get their [Stan sings] "Pivo, pivo, pivo cerveny" [beer, beer,
red beer] and they'd down it.

Besides "Baruska" and "Pivo Cerveny," favorite songs included "Louka
Zelena" (Green Meadow), "Cerveny Satacek" (Red Handkerchief), "Modre
Oce" (Blue Eyes), and "Svestkova Alej" (The Prune Song).

The latter, with its typical peasant setting, universal theme, reliance on
natural metaphors, and subtle shifts from familiar (Anca/Annie) to formal
(Andula/Ann) terms, is perhaps the best-known Czech American song. [Listen
to the classic version by Romy Gosz on the accompanying compact disc.]

> Za naši vesnici, na hlavní silnici,
> Bosenský rostou švestky. Bajo!
> Ančou jsme hlidali švestky jsme jidali bejvalo, to moc hezký.
> Vždycky jsme seděli vedle sebe, na hvěz dy čuceli a na nebe,
> A teďko sám a sám, na všecko vzpomíńam, chtěl bych být blizko tebe.
>
> CHORUS: V tej naši aleji, švestky se váleji
> Já dneska nehlidám, oči mně páleji.
>
> Za naši vesnici, na hlavní silnici, švestky jsou jako pěsti. Bajo!
> Anča nic neřekla ode mně utekla, ted nemám žad ne štěstí.
> Andula sjiný m teď švestky hlídá, už naše providla neuhlid á.
> Dřív tady hvězdičky vidali věcičky, o tom se nepovídá.
>
> CHORUS:
> Za naši vesnici, na hlavní silnici, švestky jsou očesaný. Bajo!
> Šaty mám v almaře a sjinou na faře, máme to podepsaný.
> Snad až se oženim zapomenu, pak ti to Andulo připomenu.
> Co jsi to provedla žejsi mně provedla švestky teď nemanj cenu.
>
> CHORUS:
> Behind our town on the main road, Bosenky, grow plums. Bajo!
> We looked for plums, Annie, we ate plums; it was real nice.
> We sat together, we looked at the stars in the sky.
> And now, all alone, I remember. I'd like to be close to you.
>
> CHORUS:
> In our alley, plums are lying around.
> Today I'm not looking, my eyes are burning.

Behind our town on the main road, plums grow as big as fists. Bajo!
Annie said nothing and ran away, now I have no luck at all.
Ann is looking for plums with someone else, she'll not look on our
familiar places anymore.
And little stars of former times saw what happened, nothing more
can be said.

Behind our town on the main road, the plums are picked. Bajo!
I have clothes in the closet and have signed the banns at the par-
sonage with another girl.
Perhaps when I marry I'll forget, perhaps I'll tell you Ann:
What did you mean when you said that plums have no price?[5]

Just as "Svestkova Alej" has been sung repeatedly, the Stangle family's experiences have been replicated, with slight variation, again and again throughout Wisconsin's Czech enclaves. In the 1940s Helene Stratman-Thomas of the University of Wisconsin's Music Department journeyed for the Library of Congress into the Czech communities of southwestern Wisconsin.[6] In family kitchens and community halls she recorded such standards as "Svestkova Alej," "Baruska," and Frantisek Kmoch's "Koline, Koline" from a capella singers and squeezebox players, as well as polkas and marches from the brassy Yuba Band. [Stratman-Thomas's recording of the wedding polka by the Yuba Band is included on the accompanying compact disc.]

Founded in 1868 by Martin Rott, Sr., who had emigrated from Bohemia to the Richland County hamlet of Yuba, the Yuba Band persisted through the mid-1950s (Levy 1987). The band's performances for life cycle and seasonal events—characteristically complementing religious ceremonies in this over-whelmingly Catholic community—included funerals as well as weddings (see Fig. 2.2 for a similar band's participation in a wedding), and winter frolics as well as summer picnics. Regarding funerals, Helene Stratman-Thomas offered the following in her 1946 journal:

I was told that the band would precede the hearse and march from the church to the cemetery, a distance of a mile and a half. When I asked the band if they would record one of their funeral marches, they selected "Bohemul," which was the march played for the funeral of . . . Martin Rott [Sr.] in 1932. Although this custom is passing, one elderly lady who was standing near me remarked, "When my husband died, the children didn't think we should have the band, but I insisted. I knew their father wouldn't think it right to be buried without playing the funeral procession" (Peters 1977, 33).

Figure 2.2. Adolph Blahnik's Orchestra leads the Pauline and Philip Plansky wedding party to St. John's Church, Krok, Wisconsin, June 20, 1911. Courtesy Kewaunee County Historical Society.

Beyond musical funeral processions, Czech and Catholic performance traditions merge during Masopust, the Czech Mardi Gras: a two-day celebration that precedes the prolonged abstinence of Lent (Barden 1982, Kallio 1987).

Literally translated as "without meat," Masopust occurred on the Monday and Tuesday prior to Ash Wednesday. During a 1991 interview in his Yuba home, Raymond Liska, born in 1913, told me that the festivity's Monday night dance was always a masquerade. "Before midnight everybody paraded around, then three judges would pick out the best." In keeping with old-world village traditions of animal and cross-gender disguise amidst moments of seasonal transition, Ray once deceived even close neighbors by masquerading as a young woman. "I won first prize that year," he told me with mischievous chuckle.

The party continued all day and into the night on Tuesday, especially if there were "no cows to milk." But as the clock struck twelve, music and dancing ceased. Then the revelers blackened each other's faces with burnt corks in rowdy parody of the ashes to be marked on foreheads by the priest the following morning.

POLKA BANDS AND BALLROOMS

Masquerades and ashen faces have vanished from Yuba winters. The custom of musical funeral processions, "passing" in the 1940s, ceased a decade later with the Yuba Band's demise. The gradual decline of Czech speakers and family farms, together with the outmigration and Americanization of younger generations, loosened the venerable hold of seasonal custom and community hall. Yet Yuba's Masopust continues, albeit with a shift to weekend nights in recognition of the participants' clockbound schedules. Similarly, descendants of Yuba Band members still play Czech music for a new, self-consciously ethnic festival, *Cesky Den* (Czech Day), that emerged in the 1970s. Wisconsin's Czechs generally, and its musicians in particular, have found ways to accomodate the changes in American life through the creative transformation of their cultural heritage.

As early as 1870, southwestern Wisconsin Czechs, perhaps some of them members of Martin Rott's Yuba Band, participated in their region's musical ferment with an eclectic fervor that combined the dance repertoires of continental Europeans, Anglo-Celts, and African Americans. As Franco-American Charles Mon Pleasure, a fiddler and sometime house painter, observed in his autobiography:

> When winter [1870] set in, I did not do any painting, but organized a quadrille band of six pieces. At that time we used the old-fashioned post horns [i.e. small European horns that were coiled in a circle and used to announce the arrival of mail coaches] and bugles, so we had the first violin, second violin, double bass, post horn, clarinet, and bugle. They were all Bohemians but myself. I guess we would look like monkeys nowadays [1910] with such a band, but it was all right in those days. The first ball that we played for was for old George F. Switzer, a big old fat Dutchman, a darned good fellow too . . . I had the only quadrille band in Prairie du Chien. Jim Williams, a negro, had a band across the [Mississippi] river at South McGregor [Iowa]. He sometimes played in Prairie du Chien and I would play in McGregor (Mon Pleasure 1910).

By the early twentieth century, the northeastern Wisconsin Czechs of Manitowoc and Kewaunee Counties had embarked upon musical innovations that rivaled the interest paid to French quadrilles and black performers by Mon Pleasure's Bohemian cohorts.

As was the case in the hinterlands of Ashland and Yuba, these Czechs included squeezebox and brass players, they established ethnic halls, they held Masopust dances, and they observed weddings and funerals with musical processions. In contrast, however, they also drew considerable musical inspiration from their Lake Michigan neighbors in Chicago, where Czechs occupied a niche within that cosmopolitan metropolis.

Exporting such treasured rural commodities as goose down for feather pillows and dried mushrooms for cookery to their ethnic kin in Chicago, northeastern Wisconsin Czechs were recompensed with instruments, sheet music, and sound recordings. Situated on West Eighteenth Street in Chicago's

"Little Bohemia," Joseph Jiran's store, established in 1898, was the first of a succession of Czech music businesses operated by such immigrant entrepreneurs as Anton Grill, Louis Vitak, and Joseph Elsnic (Greene 1992, 51–55). Czech musicians from Chicago traveled to New York City in 1911 to make recordings for Columbia. Four years later that label made its first Czech recordings in Chicago, and by the 1920s Chicago bands lead by Vaclav Albrecht, Anton Brousek, Vaclav Fiser, Anton Grill, and others had cut scores of 78 rpm discs (Spottswood 1990, vol. 2, 602–8, 612–17, 625–27, 632–33).

Grounded in old-world village traditions, the sheet music and sound recordings of Chicago Czechs were simultaneously urbane, often incorporating elements of American popular music and of Chicago's emergent jazz scene. The influence of these innovations on northeastern Wisconsin communities accelerated in the mid-1920s, when radio stations like Chicago's WLS bombarded the region with a broad musical spectrum. The Manitowoc-Kewaunee area's numerous brass bands began an instrumental transformation: reed players supplemented clarinets with saxophones, the afterbeat of dual alto horns was replaced by a piano or piano accordion, while the new addition of trap drums emphasized dance rhythms. Seven-piece bands became the standard: a front line of two trumpets and two reeds, with reed players switching from clarinet to saxophone, and a rhythm section of piano, drums, and bass horn. The remnants of military band music were diminished by the abandonment of marches and promenading galops. Some bands rejected their old-world repertoire entirely to embrace the popular music of the day. Others performed an occasional "modern" fox trot while grafting a jazzy feel onto older Czech polkas, waltzes, and ländlers (Janda 1976). Like their traditional yet modern southern Anglo-Celtic counterparts, these northern Czech Americans self-consciously promoted their hybrid sound as "old-time music" and, eventually, as "polka music."

From the 1930s through the 1950s in particular, many of them made recordings, performed for live radio broadcasts, and traveled a widening dance hall circuit. With the end of prohibition in 1933, dance halls proliferated throughout ethnic Wisconsin. Typically "mom and pop" operations, they largely superceded the old ethnic halls by combining the functions of a tavern, weekend eatery, and community hall. Despite fierce competition, there were enough musicians and dancers to keep the floors filled. When interviewing the area's Czech musicians in 1988 for a Wisconsin Public Radio documentary on their musical scene, I heard many poetic testimonies of the sort offered by Jerome Wojta, a polka disc jockey on Kewaunee's WAUN and the leader of a Czech polka band, the Two Creeks Farmhands:

> We'd go to country dances. And a typical country dance would consist of people of all ages. This was everyone from the grandchild to the grandmother. You could go to a dance each night of the week.

It's really hard to tell someone who hasn't experienced it what it was really like. When you get a group of people going, and happy, and dancing, it would be just like watching big waves on the sea.

Wojta's home Manitowoc County, likewise the territory of Tuba Dan Jerabek, boasted twenty such dancehalls, with evocative and personal names like Terrace Gardens, Peterson's Modernistic Ballroom, Forst's New Hall, the Maribel Ballroom, and Romy's Ballroom.

JUMP AND TOSS WITH ROMY GOSZ

Romy's Ballroom, situated at a crossroads called Polivka's Corners, was run by Romy Gosz, the leading exponent of northeastern Wisconsin's updated Czech American polka sound (Fig. 2.3). Roman Louis Gosz was born in 1911 in Rockwood, north of Manitowoc. His father, Paul, ran a family band that sometimes doubled as a basketball team, playing for both local sporting events and dances in the early 1920s. By 1928, Romy had taken over the band, and he made his first recordings in 1931 for Port Washington, Wisconsin's Broadway label. Gosz was recording in Chicago two years later. From his first session to his death in 1966, Romy Gosz recorded roughly 170 tunes on the

Figure 2.3. "Polka King" Romy Gosz makes prominent reference to his media stature on the poster for a 1965 dance on the border of Wisconsin's Manitowoc and Kewaunee Counties. Courtesy Jim Eisenmann.

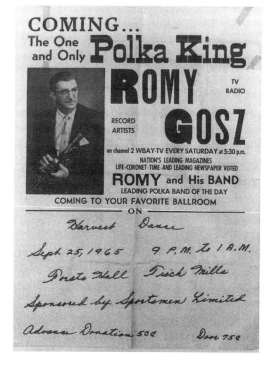

Broadway, Brunswick, Columbia, Decca, King, Mercury, Mono, Okeh, Polka King, Polkaland, and Vocalion labels. Playing for countless dances in the Manitowoc area, Gosz also barnstormed throughout Wisconsin: south to Milwaukee and Watertown, north to Green Bay and Wausau, and west to Stevens Point. He performed on radio and television and was pronounced the "polka king" by both his followers and such national magazines as *Coronet* and *Time* (Greene 1992, 164–67; Janda 1976, 6–7; March 1991, 391–93).

Originally a piano player, Gosz won admirers with his trumpet. Czech bandleader Jerome Wojta, himself a trumpet player, expressed awe:

> Romy Gosz had a style all his own. His tone was clear and pene-trating. He had a very good lip, a lip of steel. His music was smooth, it was humorous. A fellow like Romy comes along once in every five hundred years.

The overall Gosz style was distinguished by a slow tempo, a dignified pace, and a heavy feel anchored by a stolid tuba. A piano, or increasingly the more portable piano accordion, contributed rhythm and fills but seldom took a lead voice. Gosz's trumpet, often in chorus with a second trumpet and saxo-phones, introduced the melody, with clarinets frequently answering a phrase or chiming in with a countermelody. Ethnomusicologist Charles Keil has written of "Romy's buttery tone, vibrato, [and] loose surging phrases," aspects of instrumental articulation that folklorist Richard March suggests draw upon a prior Czech folk aesthetic that emphasizes rather than mini-mizes the natural slurring "whaaa" of the trumpet and the tendency of clar-inets toward reedy quavering, not clear bell-like tones (Keil 1982, 55; March 1991, 392; March in Leary and March 1996, 76–78). [Listen to "Svestkova Alej" on the accompanying compact disc.] In this way the rough passionate old-country edges of Gosz's instrumental attack merged with the hot, bluesy intonations of African American jazz. In keeping with jazz-age conventions the Gosz band played chiefly instrumentals or sang truncated versions of tra-ditional songs in the latter half of a given performance. The singers' har-monies, like those of jazz brethren, were at once well conceived and imbued with a loose feeling echoing the horns' controlled abandon.

Much to the chagrin of the region's high school band teachers—who have favored round notes and square rhythms, while valuing external rather than local traditions—Romy Gosz inspired young musicians throughout northeastern Wisconsin, and his influence remains powerful thirty years after his death. Like Kentucky's Bill Monroe, whose pioneering Blue Grass Boys provided both a standard and a training ground for subsequent bluegrass generations; like Muddy Waters, who inspired legions of urban performers with his amplified update of Delta blues, Romy Gosz and his band spawned fervent disciples. Since the 1930s a succession of bandleaders, some of them former sidemen, have built upon the Gosz sound.

Many of them—Larry Hlinak, Dan Jerabek, Mark Jirikovic, Jimmy Nejedlo, Rudy Plocar, Jerome Wojta, Louie Zdrazil—have been of Czech heritage, but perhaps more have been German Americans: Elroy Berkholtz, the Greiner Brothers, Gene Heier, Joe Karman, Ludger Karman, Quirin Kohlbeck, Bob Kuether, Gordy Reckelberg, Don Schliess, Harold Schultz, Tom Siebold, Jerry Voelker. Such cross-ethnic affinity for Czech music may be partially attributed to old-country roots in the mixed Czech and German villages of southwestern Bohemia (Rippley 1992, 5–8). When nineteenth-century German immigrants settled northeastern Wisconsin in tandem with their old world Czech neighbors, their already established musical synergy persisted. The wind-driven Pilsen Brass Band, for example, was northeastern Wisconsin's most prominent old style Bohemian band in the decades prior to the modern transformations wrought by Romy Gosz (Janda 1976:2). Its members' surnames balance the Czech (Janda, Nejedlo, Sladky) with the German (Altman, Schliess, Suess).

More than anything else, however, Gosz's sound and his memorable public performances inspired allegiance irrespective of ethnicity. As Russ Zimmerman, a Swiss-American, explained in liner notes for the album *Old Bohemian Memories* (K-2039), recorded in the 1960s for Sauk City, Wisconsin's Cuca Records:

> This album is truly a collection of good-time Bohemian melodies that were originally recorded many years ago by the famous "Polka King" and were accepted by the public, nationwide, as the most popular songs of the era.

With its insular assumption that all readers will understand the royal reference to Romy Gosz, its equation of an ethnic sound with American popular music, and its hopeful expansion of a regional fan base to include the entire nation, Zimmerman's comments amply demonstrate the power of Gosz, at least in his home territory, to command loyalty and transcend boundaries. The Gosz legacy came to be the collective heritage of all the people of northeastern Wisconsin.

Consider the experience in the 1960s of a youthful Cletus Bellin, a Belgian American, who, like fellow ethnics Marvin Brouchoud and Gene LeBotte, was charmed by Gosz-inspired music. Growing up in that northeastern Wisconsin "border country" where Czechs and Germans intermingle with members of America's largest settlement of Walloon Belgians, Clete Bellin learned to speak his ethnic elders' Walloon French dialect as well as English. His region's musical language and lineage, however, was decidedly Czech.

I first started playing polka music with a local band, and we used to play in the Czech villages and Czech settlements in my neighborhood. Especially if we played one of the popular Czech songs . . . people would come to the bandstand and say, "Why don't you sing it? You have a beautiful voice." I used to tell them, "I don't know the Czech language." Well, they told me, "You should learn." So from that point on, I made it a kind of a life endeavor.

Bellin sought out a Kewaunee County tavernkeeper, Ella Warczyk, who came "from a family of exceptionally good Czech musicians and singers" in the hamlet of Slovan. He asked her to teach him the correct pronunciation of Czech songs, she was delighted to comply, and Bellin proved a dedicated student. In the 1990s the Clete Bellin Band, featuring its leader's vocals, has become northeastern Wisconsin's premier Czech polka band.

A REAL CZECH ORCHESTRA

While Clete Bellin and his contemporaries sustain the Gosz legacy, they have also departed from it in ways that match the changing context of Czech polka music in Wisconsin—and beyond. Romy Gosz's modernization of Czech music beginning in the 1930s was paralleled by other performers throughout Czech America. In eastern Nebraska, for example, a greater number of Czechs worked the button accordion into their bands, and they were far more likely than the jazz-smitten Gosz to sing full, not incidental, versions of Czech songs. In Texas Czech communities, polka bands likewise favored singing, and they often fused their sound fascinatingly with the western swing and honky-tonk music of Anglo-Celtic neighbors (Machann 1983). Like Wisconsin's Romy Gosz, many Nebraska and Texas Czechs made recordings and, branching out on radio and the ballroom circuit, expanded their local followings to the surrounding territory.

Not surprisingly, Czech bands from distant American regions began to cross paths. Contact was, at first, largely through recordings and radio airplay. But since the 1970s, the growing phenomenon of polka festivals has regularly lured fellow polka travelers from around the country. Attributable both to an ongoing ethnic revival movement that gained momentum during America's 1976 bicentennial and to the new mobility of retirement-aged ethnic Americans raised on polka music, the polka festival also filled the void created by the gradual decline of ballrooms from their zenith in the early 1950s. Transregional musical exchanges accelerated between Czech polka bands. Vocalist Clete Bellin, for example, was attracted by the singing Nebraska bands, incorporating elements from their repertoires to treat his Wisconsin audiences to something new.

During the 1980s and early 1990s, the gradual dissolution of the "Iron Curtain," Czechoslovakia's "velvet revolution," and the eventual creation of the Czech Republic resulted in an increase of trans-Atlantic cultural exchanges. Czech Americans traveled to the old country, Czechs visited America. Some American polka bands organized tours to their ancestral homes, while state-sponsored Czech musical aggregations launched extensive tours to the mostly rural communities of Czech America. Recruited from the most virtuosic of village performers, garbed in generalized folk costumes, and expertly playing an "authentic" repertoire sanctioned by ethnologists, such all-star groups as Moravanka made a powerful impression on their new-world kin through highly structured concert performances intended to conjure the essence of Czech folkness.

The impact of such culturally imbued showmanship on Czech American audiences and musicians, including those in Wisconsin, was immediate. Clete Bellin concurred when I interviewed him just after a festival gig in October, 1995: "Moravanka, when they toured the country, were a big popular hit, so people asked me, 'Clete, will you do some of those songs?'"

It was not enough to do them, they had to be done right. Soon Bellin was not only buying the group's recordings but incorporating critical elements of its style into the musical attack of his own band.

> I wanted a real Czech orchestra like the Czech country bands in Europe. I wanted to play the Czech music as close to the original style as you possibly can, with the Czech tempos and the Czech vocals.

Unlike many Czech American bands who favor shortened renditions of old country originals, or whose performances fuse several styles, the Bellin Band is committed to the characteristic Czech emphasis on full versions that frame familiar melodies with distinct introductions and choruses.

Clete Bellin's emulation of such polished contemporary old-world troupes as Moravanka has won him followers beyond the normal sphere of Czech American polka enthusiasts. Like any other ethnic group, Czech Americans include upper-class or upwardly mobile members with rigid notions of authenticity and quality. For them, Czech American compositions are akin to the bastard offspring of noble stock: of questionable lineage since they did not originate fully in the Czech homeland. For them, folk music, whether Czech or Czech American, is likewise crude stuff, rendered worthy only through the refined transformations of classical composers like Anton Dvořák and Bedřich Smetana, or through the more populist, but no less carefully arranged, works of "march kings" like Frantisek Kmoch.

From this strongly held, albeit not widely shared, perspective, the Clete Bellin Band stands at the tip of the Wisconsin Czech polka pyramid—a point brought forcefully to my attention in the spring of 1995. The Smithsonian Institution was preparing for the summer Festival of American Folklife, which would include participants from the Czech Republic for two weeks on the national mall in Washington, D.C. Aware of my work in Wisconsin, and wishing to include a Czech American band, the Smithsonian's senior ethnomusicologist, Tom Vennum, asked for my advice. I recommended the Clete Bellin Band *and* the Tuba Dan Band as the leading candidates. Vennum wondered if one was playing soon, so that he might hear for himself. As it happened, the Tuba Dan Band was playing near my home that weekend. Tom flew out, was delighted, and booked the group. He was also very impressed with the tape I played of the Clete Bellin Band. Yet, given the logistical complications of organizing a festival, the serendipitous face-to-face encounter with Tuba Dan carried more weight. Within a few weeks, however, after word of the invitation had circulated, Vennum received a letter from the head of a small Wisconsin Czech cultural organization. Citing classical music credentials, the writer offered his services regarding who ought or not be included in the Festival of American Folklife. He went on to laud the authenticity and quality of Clete Bellin's Band, while deriding Tuba Dan's music as a crude hodgepodge.

Tom Vennum called for my advice before declining the writer's help with polite firmness. From my own point of view—I told Vennum as I would tell anyone—the Tuba Dan and Clete Bellin bands are both equally remarkable, equally legitimate. Both move in musical directions that are simultaneously fresh and familiar. Like polka bands throughout America, and certainly in Wisconsin, both approach the twenty-first century with their sonic coordinates fixed on the old-world past and the new-world present.

Indeed, Czech American polka music, like any other vibrant musical tradition, flows in more than one direction. Drawing upon the exuberant brass bands and village songs of immigrants, the jazz-tempered innovations of Romy Gosz, and the classicized memorialization of folk music by those who stayed in Europe, Wisconsin Czech polka bands, each in their own way, not only persist but continue to evolve.

NOTES

1. Legislation was sponsored by State Senator Gary Drewiecki, a Polish American from Pulaski in northeastern Wisconsin and a polka musician proficient on the German or Cheminitzer concertina.

2. Lawrence Welk, whose television program persists through reruns four decades after its origin in the 1950s, has come to represent in the popular media all that is cornball and saccharine about polka music. It is worth pointing out, however, that, although Welk's roots were in the German-Russian polka traditions of North Dakota, he was not really a polka musician, but essentially a practitioner of "sweet" jazz and pop music.

3. Some of the research for this essay was conducted from 1978 through 1996 in connection with public folklore projects undertaken or funded by the Cedarburg Cultural Center, the

Minnesota Historical Society, the Folk Arts Program of the National Endowment for the Arts, the Smithsonian Institution's Office of Folklife and Cultural Studies, the Wisconsin Arts Board, the Wisconsin Folk Museum, and the Wisconsin Humanities Council. I thank these organizations for their support.

4. Unless otherwise indicated, all quotations from musicians are drawn from tape-recorded interviews conducted by the author. Full citations appear in the list of interviews that follows.

5. Czech lyrics and translations are by Clara Belsky Sveda, of Ashland, Wisconsin; originally published in Leary 1986.

6. On August 19, 1941, Stratman-Thomas recorded Czech musicians in Prairie du Chien; Archives of Folksong (AFS) discs 5020–5022, 5025. She also recorded musicians in Yuba on September 25, 1946; AFS 8436–8439 (see also Leary 1987b and Peters, 28, 33).

INTERVIEWS
(All interviews were recorded on tape by James P. Leary.)

Bellin, Cletus. 1995. Cedarburg, Wisconsin, 7 October.

Jerabek, Dan ("Tuba Dan"). 1988. Appleton, Wisconsin, 4 May.

Liska, Raymond. 1991. Hillsboro, Wisconsin, 9 March.

Stangle, Stanley. 1980. Ashland, Wisconsin, 6 November.

Wojta, Jerome. 1988. Two Creeks, Wisconsin, 3 May.

REFERENCES CITED

Barden, Thomas. 1982. The Yuba Masopust Festival. *Midwestern Journal of Language and Folklore* 8:1:48–51.

Baron, Robert and Nicholas Spitzer. 1992. *Public Folklore.* Washington, D.C.: Smithsonian Institution Press.

Bohlman, Philip V. 1988. *The Study of Folk Music in the Modern World.* Bloomington: Indiana University Press.

Feintuch, Burt. 1988. *The Conservation of Culture: Folklorists in the Public Sector.* Lexington: University Press of Kentucky.

Greene, Victor. 1992. *A Passion of Polka: Old-Time Ethnic Music in America.* Berkeley: University of California Press.

Janda, Robert. 1976. Entertainment Tonight: An Account of Bands in Manitowoc County Since 1900. *Occupational Monograph* 28. Manitowoc, Wisc.: Manitowoc County Historical Society.

Kallio, Sandra. 1987. In Yuba, It's Masopust. *Wisconsin State Journal,* 18 February, section 3:1.

Keil, Charles. 1982. Slovenian Style in Milwaukee. In *Folk Music and Modern Sound,* edited by William Ferris and Mary L. Hart, 32–59. Jackson: University Press of Mississippi.

Keil, Charles, Angeliki V. Keil, and Dick Blau. 1992. *Polka Happiness.* Philadelphia: Temple University Press.

Kolar, Roger. 1979. Early Czech Dance Halls in Texas. In *The Czechs in Texas: A Symposium,* edited by Clinton Machann, 122–27. College Station: Texas A & M University College of Liberal Arts.

Leary, James P. 1984. Old Time Music in Northern Wisconsin. *American Music* 2, no. 1:71–88.

———. 1986. *Accordions in the Cutover*, booklet to accompany the double LP listed below. Ashland, Wisc.: Northland College.

———. 1987a. Czech Polka Styles in the U.S.: From America's Dairyland to the Lone Star State. In *Czech Music in Texas*, edited by Clinton Machann, 79–95. College Station, Texas: Komensky Press.

———. 1987b. *The Wisconsin Patchwork: A Companion to the Radio Programs Based on the Field Recordings of Helene Stratman-Thomas*. Madison: University of Wisconsin, Department of Continuing Education in the Arts.

———. 1988. Brass Bands and the Bohemian Hall. *The Folklife of the Upper Midwest* 4, no. 3:4–5.

———. 1991. Polka Music, Ethnic Music: A Report on Wisconsin's Polka Traditions. *Wisconsin Folk Museum Bulletin* 1. Mount Horeb, Wisc.: Wisconsin Folk Museum.

———. 1995. Poppies, Pillows, and Polkas: Czech-American Folk Culture. In *1995 Festival of American Folklife*, edited by Carla M. Borden, 58–59. Smithsonian Institution: Center for Folklife Programs and Cultural Studies.

Leary, James P. and Richard March. 1996. *Down Home Dairyland: A Listener's Guide*. Madison: University of Wisconsin-Extension.

Levy, Marcella. 1987. Richland Ramblings. *The Richland Observer*, three-week series: 12, 19, 26 February.

March, Richard. 1991. Polkas in Wisconsin Music. In *The Illustrated History of Wisconsin Music, 1840–1990*, edited by Michael Corenthal, 385–97. Milwaukee: Yesterday's Memories.

Machann, Clinton. 1983. Country Western Music and the "Now" Sound in Texas-Czech Polka Music. *JEMF Quarterly* 19, no. 69 (Spring): 3–7.

Mon Pleasure, Charles W. 1910. *Adventures of a Violinist: The Autobiography of Charles W. Mon Pleasure*. Originally serialized in the *Platteville Witness and Mining Times*, typescript copy courtesy of Alan D. Goff, Fort Wayne, Ind.

Peters, Harry. 1977. *Folksongs Out of Wisconsin*. Madison: State Historical Society of Wisconsin.

Rippley, LaVern J. 1992. *The Whoopie John Wilfahrt Dance Band: His Bohemian-German Roots*. Northfield, Minn.: St. Olaf College German Department.

Shaw, Lloyd. 1948. *The Round Dance Book*. Caldwell, Idaho: The Caxton Printers, Ltd.

Slobin, Mark. 1993. *Subcultural Sounds: Micromusics of the West*. Hanover, N. H.: The University Press of New England.

Spottswood, Richard K. 1990. *Ethnic Music on Records: A Discography of Ethnic Recordings Produced in the United States 1893–1942*. Vol. 2. Urbana: University of Illinois Press.

COMPANION CD SELECTIONS

CD Track 1. Romy Gosz, "The Prune Song."

CD Track 2. Yuba Bohemian Band, "Wedding Polka."

ADDITIONAL SOURCES

Recommended Recordings

Accordions in the Cutover: Field Recordings of Ethnic Music from Lake Superior's South Shore. Double LP with booklet. Distributed by the Folklore Program, 305 Ingraham Hall, University of Wisconsin, Madison, Wisconsin 53706.

Down Home Dairyland. Half-hour radio programs on "The Manitowoc Bohemian Sound" and "Czech and Slovak Music in Wisconsin." Distributed by the Folklore Program, University of Wisconsin.

Hofner, Adolph. *South Texas Swing.* CD reissue of western swing and Czech recordings from the late 1930s through the early 1950s. Arhoolie, 10341 San Pablo Avenue, El Cerrito, California 94530.

———. *Texas Czech: Historic Recordings 1929–1959.* CD reissue by Arhoolie, ibid.

J&P Czech Record Sales maintains the largest catalogue of Czech and Czech American polka bands, including recordings by the Clete Bellin and Tuba Dan Bands: 931 Saunders Avenue, Lincoln, Nebraska 68521-2325.

Polkaland Records has reissued the bulk of the recordings made by Romy Gosz and many other northeastern Wisconsin polka bands from the 1930s through the 1970s: Greg Leider, Polkaland Records, 109 North Milwaukee Street, Fredonia, Wisconsin 53021.

CHAPTER 3

Klezmer Music: The First One Thousand Years

Henry Sapoznik

*W*hen it comes to studying and performing klezmer music, Henry Sapoznik *is a musical insider. The son of a cantor, Sapoznik, a music practitioner, was initially attracted to "old-time" country music, mostly as a researcher and banjo player. In the middle 1970s, however, he became increasingly interested in klezmer, the music of his Jewish heritage. Using the life story of the master clarinetist Dave Tarras, Sapoznik looks at the development of klezmer music in the twentieth century. Although Tarras was not the sole proponent of klezmer music in America, he has clearly emerged as a key figure in the transmission of klezmer to the New World in the early part of the century as well as a major contributor to its dynamic renewal beginning in the 1970s. This chapter underscores the importance and impact that one individual can have within a specific musical genre. In looking at the longer evolution of klezmer music, Sapoznik also makes the connection between itinerant Jewish musicians in the Middle Ages and their counterparts in contemporary urban settings in the United States. It is a story that explores the marginalization of Jewish culture in the old world followed by its near extinction under the Nazi regime. Ironically, although klezmer gains a foothold in the American context, it subsequently dissipates, a phenomenon fueled in part by the Jewish American experience of post–World War II prosperity and the rise of suburban American lifestyles. Sapoznik's musical choices and experience prior to his (re)disovery of klezmer are in some ways conditioned by that era of post–World War II, pre–civil rights "Americana." The transformation of his musical identity from American folk musician to klezmer musician reflects a characteristic of American identity politics, whereby "ethnic" identities may be "born into," rejected, discovered, created, and embraced at various stages of a person's life. Sapoznik's story narrates his own arrival on the scene as one of a select* *group of musicians who inspired a renewal in the klezmer tradition that has not only taken America by storm, but that has also reached back to the roots of Jewish culture in Europe.*

■   ■   ■   ■

INTRODUCTION

It would seem nearly impossible. A music born during the dark years of the Middle Ages by a people deprived of a homeland, buffeted by persecution, dispersion, wars, revolutions, assimilation, and the Holocaust, makes a dramatic worldwide comeback in post-Woodstock America. In a nutshell, that is the story of klezmer music, the traditional instrumental music of the Jews of Eastern Europe. And no life story better exemplifies this near millenium of musical and cultural history than that of clarinetist Dave Tarras.

Tarras, trained in Europe, arrived in New York to enter the tumult of the Yiddish music world. By sheer dint of technique, intuition, and presence, he managed to shape the way people heard the distinctive sound of the klezmer clarinet from that moment on. Tarras's playing transformed the second generation of Jewish clarinetists with its new sense of style, interpretation, and orchestration and completely overwhelmed the previous European approach to the music.

The revival of klezmer music, which I helped to stimulate, had as its inspiration veteran players like Dave Tarras. When I formed Kapelye in 1979, there were only two other bands in the United States. Since then more than 150 groups have sprung up across North America and half that number again in Europe, most amazingly in Germany, the place where the Jewish presence was nearly extinguished a half century ago. The function of new bands like the Klezmatics in New York, Nisht Gerferlakh in Montpelier, Vermont, the Mazeltones in Seattle, among others, is to act as the cultural conscience for communities that have lost touch with their folk identities. The 1970s so-called roots movement that began in the African American community had great resonance with other minority cultures who were struggling to reconnect with their own identities. The expression "the children try to remember what the parents tried to forget" aptly describes the process of those of us who reunited our community with a vibrant part of its history.

This is a history that most music historians have ignored. It is a history that until recently existed only in the anecdotes and memories of elderly musicians who had run out of people with whom to share them. Someone like myself. The quotes featured here by Dave Tarras were collected by me over a period of years in a variety of venues: at his little kitchen table while we munched on cookies and sipped endless glasses of tea; in the hospital,

Figure 3.1. Dave Tarras (ca. 1940s).
Courtesy Henry Sapoznik.

where I visited Dave after his heart attack; on the boardwalk on Coney Island; at my parent's house when Tarras came for a Sabbath dinner. Most times my tape recorder was there, quietly humming as Dave's vision turned inward and he became misty and wistful or harbored anger over a wrong done him long ago. At times, a tape recorder was not available and I had to concentrate on memorizing his fleeting recollections. I need not have worried: his voice, his words, his whole demeanor are as fresh and present to me now as they were when we first began our chats in 1977.

"IN THE BEGINNING . . .": MUSIC IN THE OLD WORLD

Yiddish music may be described as the informally accumulated history of the Jews of Eastern Europe and America. In numerous forms, from folk songs to fiddle tunes, a clear picture emerges of the people through their music.

The Yiddish language and its culture sprang from the Western European Jewish communities that had settled and grown during the Middle Ages along the river Rhine in Germany (*Ashkenaz*). It was the success of Moses Mendelssohn's *Haskalah* (Enlightenment) movement in the late eighteenth century that gradually ended the use of the Yiddish language and its attendant culture in Germany while it continued to grow and thrive in Eastern Europe.

The most influential form of musical expression within the Jewish community was the singing of the *khazn* (cantor). No aspect of Jewish music remained unaffected by the performance and content of this principal form. The centrality of this vocal style is due to a formative and historic chapter in Jewish musical life. After the destruction of the Second Temple in Jerusalem (70 C.E.), the rabbinate (the association of religious authorities), then in mourning, banned instrumental music. Following this profound event, the only officially sanctioned music was unaccompanied liturgy. Even with the cantors' commitment to the content of the prayers, there are examples of rabbinical reprimands against them because of their beautiful voices, which—it was claimed—distracted the worshippers from the piety of the prayers. In addition to his role as a leader in the dynamic performance of community prayer, the *khazn* was also responsible for training the future generations of *khazonim*. The apprentices (*meshoyr'rim*) would learn the rudiments of the special prayer modes to accompany the cantor; some of them might later become cantors themselves. In smaller towns that had no *khazn,* prayers were led in the synagogue by such talented "amateurs" as the *ba'al tfile* (master of prayer) and the *ba'al koyre* (master of reading) or community services were led by one of many traveling *khazonim.* Religious music also thrived in the *kheyder* and *yeshiva* (primary and secondary schools), where the whole of Jewish law and traditions were taught to students with the help of specific mnemonic melodies. (In the study of religious texts, the writings are set to simple modal melodies to help students remember them.)

Also influential were the myriad forms of unaccompanied folksongs that reflected the broad diversity of East European Jewish life. These included songs of love and marriage, lullabies and children's songs, work songs, and ballads detailing natural and national disasters. Sung in a plain manner—as opposed to the more florid and virtuosic *khazonic* style of singing—they would, by the beginning of the twentieth century, form a rich source for music of the Yiddish theater. Most of these songs were learned through an "oral tradition," that is, from family and friends and, later, from theater performances, recordings, or the radio.

The Hasidim, a charismatic religious sect, developed a spiritual interpretation of piety encouraging song and dance, as opposed to religious texts, as a valid approach to prayer. Their fervor accorded a great value to compositions called *nigunim* (wordless songs), whose melodies bypassed the "burden" of words in the quest of a oneness with God. These tunes, sung on holidays and celebrations, would build in intensity as they progressed, accompanied by clapping, stamping, and enthusiastic dancing. Because of the religious mandate of separation of men and women, there was no mixed dancing; thus, specific men's and women's dance traditions were created.

All of these forms were to have a profound influence on the instrumental music of the klezmer. The term *klezmer* (plural, *klezmorim*) is a Yiddishized contraction of two Hebrew words, *kley-zemer*, meaning vessel of melody. Although the original Hebrew meaning connotes the musical genre, *klezmer*, the Yiddish meaning refers to the musician himself, a *klezmer*, or a group of them, *klezmorim*. Though looked down upon by the rabbinate for promoting "frivolity," instrumental music was an important part of both sacred and secular events in Jewish life.

The influence of the *khazn* could be heard in the music of the klezmer. Not only did the klezmer emulate the vocal stylings and inflections of the *khazn* but also the specific modes and scales used by the *khazn* in the performance of his religious duties. The *meshoyrer* system, whereby young boys would be apprenticed to older, experienced *khazonim*, also found a parallel in the klezmer world, where children would be inaugurated into local *kapel-yes*, who played in the back row while they learned, slowly moving to the front.

Using instruments popular in their particular region, klezmorim played fiddle, flute, bass, *baraban* (drum), *tsimbl* (hammered dulcimer), and *tats* (cymbals). By the nineteenth century other instruments such as clarinets, trumpets, and tubas were also added. The repertoire reflected the wide diversity of classes and communities with which the klezmer interacted.

Music was heard at weddings, balls, market days, village inns, and other celebrations. The Jewish repertoire was characterized by a large number of tunes tied to the *khasene* (wedding). General dances such as the *sher* (scissors dance), which closely resembles an American square dance, the *hora* (or *krimer tants*, "limping" dance, so called because of its $\frac{3}{8}$ limping rhythm) and *freylekhs* (lively) were joined by ritual dances, such as those for the bride (*badekn*), the groom (*khusnmol*), and the mothers-in-law (*broyges tants*, "dance of anger and reconciliation"), among others.

Jewish musicians would also learn local peasant dances like the polka (*karobishke, kamariske*, or *oberek*) and in fact these non-Jewish dances were often played at Jewish weddings; for that matter, Jews and gyspies, both at the bottom of the Eastern European social scale, would often play together. For the more cultured patrons, *klezmorim* would be expected to play salon dances, such as the gavotte, quadrille, or lancers, or even light classical overtures. It was through the forum of klezmer music—more than any other medium—that Jews and Gentiles could share their art and economics.

In addition to playing dance music, the musicians would accompany the improvisatory rhymes and songs of the *badkhn*. The *badkhn* combined the talents of a poet, satirist, Talmudist, and social critic. His pithy and sly insights into the nature of life and religious responsibilities made him an integral part of any Jewish wedding. The vocal style used by the *badkhn* was also derived from the religious chanting heard in the synagogue, while the *klezmorim*, in accompanying him, adapted a Rumanian musical form called *doina*, a free-metered rhapsodic form exfasizing improvisatory skills within a set mode or scale. *Doina* was favored by star soloists as a showcase for their virtuosity and usually also contained a *hora* followed by a *freylekhs.*

The life of the klezmer musician was far from easy or honored. In addition to the rabbinical dictates against the "excessive frivolity" that dance music produced, there were also numerous restrictions placed against Jewish musicians throughout the many non-Jewish municipalities through which the klezmer traveled. The enforced second-class status of Jews was clearly seen in the laws passed against Jewish musicians. Limitations on when, where, and how many klezmorim could play in certain towns were common, and in some cases Jewish musicians were banned entirely.

By the 1870s a new development was taking place in the burgeoning Yiddish world. From the wine cellars of Jassy, Rumania, came the Yiddish theater of Abraham Goldfadn (1840–1908). Until Goldfadn's time, the rabbinate discouraged any kind of theater as antithetical to proper Jewish behavior and only tolerated amateur plays that were presented on certain holidays. (On Purim, *purimshpilers*—or schoolboy actors—through song, dance and skit, presented the story of the foiling of a plot against the Jewish community of Persia.) By borrowing from all the sources available to him in the late nineteenth century from grand opera to biblical tale, Goldfadn crafted a musical theater whose future influence was little imagined in its humble birthplace.

Within a few years of the theater's inception, a number of traveling companies had sprung up, bringing Yiddish variants of everything from the works of Shakespeare to contemporary plays based on the pages of daily newspapers, as well as episodes from the annals of Jewish history and popular and trendy music-hall performances. Singers, comics, composers, artists, and musicians joined the growing numbers of these traveling theater troupes. Like their fellow performers, the *klezmorim*, acting companies too suffered at the hands of belligerent local and national governments that instituted restrictive measures against their performances.

Motivated by social and political upheavals in Eastern Europe, some three million Jews emigrated between 1880 and 1924. The ultimate destination for many of these Jews was the United States and among them were numerous musicians, composers, singers, actors, and dancers. They and their children would soon provide the creators, performers, and audiences for the Yiddish-American cultural experience. Chief among them was Dave Tarras.

FROM OLD WORLD TO NEW: THE LIFE OF DAVE TARRAS

Early Training

We were a family of musicians; we knew we were good musicians. My cousins were, my father, my brothers. One was a concert master in the Philharmonic—he played in Leningrad by the sympho-

ny. My grandfather was a fiddler; I had an uncle, a fiddle player . . .
one of the greatest. In our town, Teplik, was a Count Pototski, the
large landowner. So he played for him an affair. Count Pototski told
him to come and take wood and pick himself a spot and build himself a house for nothing. He built a two-story house, when there
were no two-story houses in Teplik. And he had four sons, also
good fiddle players, and clarinet; they played all instruments. They
were in my time. My father was the second generation.

Dave Tarras was born in the Ukranian *shtetl* (town) of Ternovka, where
the family had only recently moved from the nearby town of Teplik. The family's professional involvement with music went back several generations by
the time Tarras was born, in 1897: When Tarras was nine, his father, a trom-
bonist and a *badkhn,* taught him to read and write music. At the same time,
Tarras began instrumental lessons, first on the balalaika, then on the man-
dolin and flute. The following year his father took him to play his first wedding.

The first lesson I got was the notes: a, b, c . . . There was a flute player in my father's band, so he started teaching me a little. And then
he got himself a girl in town, so he stopped teaching me because he
was afraid if he teaches me to be a flute player, he wouldn't have . . .

What he "wouldn't have" was a corner on the flute market and a more secure
way to support himself and his bride-to-be. What he would have, and recognized it, was a competitor in the talented young Tarras.
This incident, and the fact that the sound of the instrument did not
express his musical ideas, caused Tarras, at age thirteen, to become dissatis-
fied with the flute.

I went to [the city of] Uman for three, four weeks and . . . a certain
clarinet player taught me how to play a little bit—just three weeks.
So I come home from the holidays, I went to play already a *goyishe
khasene* [non-Jewish wedding], my father, on the clarinet, and then
I just picked up by accident a nice tone. He was very impressed.

The training that the young Tarras received as a member of the family
kapelye would also be the underpinning of his later success in New York: the
willingness to travel, the technical ability to produce both the repertoires and
correct style of various genres of music, and a dignified and professional
mien. That the family's *kapelye* was obligated to perform the repertoires of
diverse communities—secular and Hasidic Jews as well as non-Jewish peasants and aristocracy—and was able to play them in a convincing stylistic

manner presupposed a meticulous attention to technical skills and deep knowledge of the repertoire.

> My father kept ten men: two fiddles or three, one was a *secunda* (chord-playing second fiddle) flute, clarinet, trumpet, trombone, tuba, and drums with the tats in the right hand and another played a small drum. We traveled for a hundred miles . . . those days landowners, the Poles, counts, barons. We used to go play weddings, banquets, they used to make every time balls, you already had to play different music: waltzes, mazurkas, and once in a while an overture like [von Suppé's] "Poet and Peasant." So my relatives were good musicians and they were prepared. And I learned from them to read music and I played with them.

They were successful in learning the art and salon music repertoire from music published in the big cities, such as Kiev; the Jewish music was an entirely different matter:

> Mostly on Jewish weddings we didn't need arrangements: we knew hundreds of waltzes by memory, *shers, freylekhs, bulgars.* Each instrument knew exactly what they should do, how to fill in.

The ugliness of the anti-Semitism rife among the peasantry, and always just beneath the surface in most day-to-day relationships, did not emerge in their dealings with the Polish nobility:

> They had for us the greatest respect: they used to come for us with a wagon with four big horses, and give us good seats, and take us. After two or three days (at the wedding) they gave us along a sack of potatoes, and chickens, and bread, and brought us back to the door. Maybe they were anti-Semites, but it never came out. They had respect.

With his future as a musician in his father's *kapelye* all but assured, the outbreak of World War I dramatically changed his plans. Though Tarras was conscripted into the Czarist army, he was luckily recognized as a musical talent and transferred to the military band, where he continued to sharpen his musical skills. In 1917 the Bolshevik Revolution eliminated Russian involvement in the war. In the chaos and confusion, Tarras returned home to Ternovka to find the war, the revolution, and the subsequent counter-revolution (all with their attendant anti-Jewish pogroms) overwhelming. In 1921, after having written to his older sister, who lived in New York with her husband, he left for America, his clarinet in his satchel.

On to America

His arrival at Ellis Island, however, was less than auspicious:

> From the ship we walked off, I had my clarinet with me in a satchel. They wanted to fumigate and I wanted to tell them that I had a clarinet, but before I started to explain what I want, the clarinet was fumigated and was to pieces.

Nevertheless, even had the instrument not been ruined, Tarras would initially not have been disposed to playing music in America. Instead, the recently married Tarras had his brother-in-law find him work in the fur trade.

> I thought that in America to be a musician one has to have—he must be something—I didn't think I'm good enough to be a musician. I went to work in a factory and I swept the floor. I got ten dollars the first week, I figured it was worth twenty rubles in Russian money. They taught me to be an operator; I got fifteen, twenty, fifty dollars a week with overtime I worked fifty hours. I was happy with it.

Tarras worked at that job for almost a year before he bought a new clarinet and began taking small wedding jobs booked through his cousin, a trumpet player.

Tarras's First Big Break

Soon word began to spread about the new clarinet player who worked weddings. Tarras's first important break came through the drummer Joe Helfenbein, who remembered a job they worked together in 1923:

> I heard this guy play and I said "This guy is terrific." So I says: "I played a job the other day and I worked with a player he plays Jewish beautifully. And a gentleman!"

Helfenbein arranged an audition for Tarras with Joseph Cherniavsky, a composer and conductor who led the popular Yiddish vaudeville act "The Oriental-American Syncopators." Tarras recalled:

> I had an appointment to see Cherniavsky. His wife was a very fine pianist and [I] brought my clarinet and played for her. "Very good. Could you read music?" "I try." So she put out a couple of songs and I swallowed it down. So Cherniavsky booked me for a job in Philadelphia.

Tarras's first outing with Cherniavsky was a success. The fact that he was a fast and accurate reader who had both a great command of the Yiddish style and a clean "legitimate" sound made him a natural choice. At the conclusion of the concert, Cherniavsky made Tarras an offer:

> "I have one week to play in the Bronx, next week all I can pay you is $110." He thought I would ask for more and when I heard $110, I nearly fainted. So I accepted and saw that I can make a living here. I went to my brother-in-law and his two partners in the furriers and I said: "Thank you very much for giving me a job—I'm quitting." He was glad too, to see that I'm doing good.

"I went, I make": On the Stage and in the Recording Studio
The Yiddish theater that Tarras came in contact with in New York was a far cry from the simpler one Goldfadn had founded back in Rumania. By the time Tarras arrived in the United States there were over fifty theaters in the New York City area alone—with dozens more peppered across the United States, making for a widely rooted circuit for traveling performers—each presenting its own brand of show from high art to low music hall. For a while, the Yiddish theater eclipsed its non-Jewish uptown cousin, Broadway, as the preeminent showcase of cutting-edge theater. Non-Jewish patrons and critics flocked to Second Avenue (called the "Jewish Rialto") to witness the latest Yiddish plays in addition to American premieres—albeit in Yiddish—by such contemporary playwrights as Ibsen and Strindberg and to witness the introduction of modern acting techniques, such as the Stanislavsky Method.

Though there were many "art" theaters that played these highly dramatic plays, it was the musical theater that was closest to the hearts of its patrons. Many of the composers who wrote for the stage had studied to be *meshoyr'rim* and brought with them not only a knowledge of the broad spectrum of Jewish musical modes and scales but also a profound understanding of the spirituality inherent in the music and sense of community experienced by Jews who attended the synagogue. By recontextualizing the prayer modes into popular songs, the composers—and the singers and musicians—encouraged a deep response from their enthusiastic and loyal audiences.

One of the other by-products of Tarras's association with Cherniavsky and the "Oriental-American Syncopators" was his introduction to the recording world. In the spring of 1924, Cherniavsky was approached by a representative from the Pathé record company.

Pathé, like Columbia, Victor, and other major labels of their day, produced a wide assortment of records. In addition to the pop and classical titles these companies maintained large catalogs of foreign and domestic traditional musics. Yiddish records had been recorded in the United States since the earliest days of commercial recording in the early 1890s.

It may have been due to the success of his first recording with the Cherniavsky orchestra that word got out about Tarras and his studio skills. The Columbia record label approached Tarras about recording for them. Tarras was contacted by Moe Nodiff, the A & R (Artist and Repertoire) man for foreign recordings:

> Nodiff calls me up and books me to play a record . . . four sides, two recordings. He says, "Mr. Tarras, I'm giving you forty dollars and make me a session. And then if it's all right I'll give you more."
>
> Forty dollars? I would've done it for nothing. I was so . . . I was making a record!
>
> "Can you play a Russian session?"
>
> "Yeah."
>
> "Good, so you'll come down next week and make a Russian session."
>
> So I went; I make. Two weeks later I make another Jewish session with Schwartz; whatever Nodiff gave me: Russian, Polish, Greek. . . .
>
> A recording session consisted of four records—eight songs—so writing the songs was no problem for me. They'd let me know, "Two weeks from today we'll need . . ." I sat down for a day or two to write the numbers; I wrote for the piano the chords, the violin or trumpet melody. The drums he knew; I didn't write. My part, I knew by heart. I had the four numbers in a couple of days. But the names, I had with them trouble; I gave family names: my daughter, my grandfather . . .
>
> We never rehearsed. All the music was done in the studio. The whole pay was fifteen dollars a musician to play three hours and make four sides. We came in at nine and by twelve o'clock we were out. If we had to stay later, he paid us overtime. We played through the number, and if anything we needed to change—so the engineer took a test and he played it back right away, he played through the test. If the test was good, we went through to the next.

As soon as it became clear that Tarras was a rapid sight reader who could coolly improvise a stylistically appropriate musical accompaniment on the spot, his rank as a session musician rose. Listen to CD Track 3 for an example of Tarras playing with Abe Schwartz. In 1927, Tarras was invited to join the "Boiberiker Kapelle," a popular Yiddish music act that made broadcasting history in 1929. Together with Molly Picon, Irving Grossman, and other stars of the Yiddish theater, Tarras appeared on the newly created CBS radio network's "The Jewish Day Radio Concert," the first—and last—network Yiddish radio show.

It was about this time that Tarras met Irving Gratz, who would be his longtime drummer. Gratz, who was sixteen when he came to the United States in 1923, was encouraged to become a musician by his father. Before joining Tarras, Gratz, a classically trained percussionist, gained experience with other New York Jewish bands, including that of fiddler Abe Katzman, with whom he began his career. Gratz and Tarras would continue to work together on and off until Tarras's death.

The haphazard scheduling of jobs in the Jewish music world required a willingness to travel and an ability to play various repertoires—those same skills Tarras had learned in Ternovka. His description of a Saturday night from the mid-1930s, when he played with bandleader and composer Alexander Olshanetsky, illustrates this point:

> I played with Olshanetsky a job for the Baker's Union in the Bronx till about five o'clock in the morning . . . so we went from that job to his hotel where we showered and he had to finish one of the arrangements for the "Forverts Hour" at WEVD. And we go straight to the radio to make rehearsal, and I got through with the job at twelve o'clock. I went from the radio, I went to the Paramount in the Bronx—I had an afternoon there—and at night I had at the DeLuxe Palace on Howard Avenue back in Brooklyn. See what I mean?

The Catskills

By the time he had established himself as a full-time professional, another venue for his performing had established itself as well. The Catskill region of New York State was transformed from a series of former farmhouses that sheltered tubercular Jewish New York sweatshop laborers at the turn of the century, to one of the most developed and influential resort areas in America.

By the 1920s, the Borscht Belt, as it later came to be called, boasted scores of hotels that catered to a Jewish clientele; hotels in other parts of the Catskill region routinely restricted the admission of Jews. The Hotel Majestic, the Pineview, the Normandie Hotel, and Echo Lodge, among others, competed to bring to the newly emerging Jewish leisure class a full palette of cultural and culinary offerings.

Though many of the professionals in the Yiddish theater would vacation in the Catskills during the theatrical off-season, entertainment was not the original attraction at these resorts. Later, however, as resort culture came of age, so too did stand-up comedy, now a standard fare of American entertainment. Like the *badkhn* of old, who was hired to liven up Jewish weddings, so too was the *tumler* at Jewish hotels. The *tumler* (literally someone who makes a *tuml*, a big racket) was supposed to be quick, inventive, and above all, funny, anything to divert the guests, who, in a generation, had gone from "recuperation" to "recreation." In time, the *tumler* was transformed into the modern emcee, who epitomizes the contemporary "stand-up" comic. Well-known entertainment personae Jerry Lewis, Sid Caesar, Joan Rivers, Buddy Hackett, and dozens like them, took the styles they originally perfected in the Jewish resorts during the 1930s and adapted them from the small cozy stages in the Jewish hotels to the more gaudy—and lucrative—stages of Las Vegas and television.

For musicians, the development of this new performance context was not as profound as it was for the comics. For them, playing the Borscht Belt was just another gig. At its peak, the Catskills circuit required a combination of the rigor of playing for the theater and the flexibility of a wedding reception—and sometimes the worst aspects of both. What made the comics so successful was the dream of all performers: to cross over into the American mainstream. And for a brief moment the crossover dream was possible for Dave Tarras.

The Rise of "Jewish-Jazz"

When the Yiddish theater season reopened in 1932, Tarras was there too, featured as a soloist in the Yiddish musical "I Would If I Could." Despite billing top actors and actresses and a wonderful score, it closed after a few weeks. One of the songs from this show, "Bay Mir Bistu Sheyn," was sold for forty dollars by composer Sholem Secunda and in 1938 became a huge hit for the newly formed non-Jewish Andrews Sisters vocal trio. The immense popularity of this song meant that this was the first Jewish tune to become popular in American music, thus beginning a short but furious fad of "Jewish-Jazz" hits.

In an age when "making it" in American entertainment meant that the children of immigrants would change their names, such personalities as Detroit Tiger star Hank Greenberg and swing clarinetist Benny Goodman were heroes to the immigrants for not changing their names. Proclaimed the King of Swing, Goodman used jazz to create a bridge between black and white performers and audiences. Though Jewish, Goodman had no interest in playing klezmer style, preferring the newly emerging jazz coming up in his Chicago hometown. When Goodman wanted a "Jewish" solo he would turn to trumpeter Harry ("Ziggy") Elman (born Finkelman), as he did on their recording of "Bei Mir Bist Du Schoen". The first solo record Elman was to make upon entering the studio in late December 1938, was a tune that would push the Jewish/jazz crossover even farther along.

Elman crafted an imaginative and thrilling arrangement of a solid old Yiddish dance chestnut that had earlier been recorded under the title of "Der Shtiler Bulgar" (The Quiet Bulgar). Calling it "Frailach in Swing" (And the Angels Sing)," Elman's version wove back and forth between sophisticated swing trumpet skills and the driving meat-and-potatoes style of Yiddish dance music, exhibiting his experience in both genres. Once again, Goodman saw the potential of a crossover, and two months later, in February of 1939, recorded "And the Angels Sing" with Martha Tilton as the vocalist and with words by Johnny Mercer. And again, there was a big "Jewish" hit, a trend that would continue for several more years.

If Dave Tarras was the improved, Americanized version of the rougher-hewn, old-country klezmer, then Goodman represented the next generational development. Because of this inevitable comparison, Tarras was considered redundant and dubbed the "Jewish Benny Goodman," a term he found bizarre but complimentary nonetheless.

On the Air: Radio Reaches Out

It was also in 1939 that the piano-playing son of a Yiddish theater veteran approached Tarras about appearing in his radio orchestra. Young Sam Medoff—whose father was the Yiddish-Russian recording pioneer David Medoff—was impressed by the great success of using Jewish music as a wedge into the popular mainstream and saw his opportunity. Medoff recognized that his generation—those born in America of European parents—felt a cultural allegiance to both communities; and the show effectively addressed that loyalty in its choice of musical repertoire and its mixed English-Yiddish script. Although radio station WHN had a regular orchestra, Medoff's agreement with the station allowed him to bring in his own band. Tarras was his first choice.

Accelerating the assimilation of foreign-born Jews while simultaneously engaging younger American-born Jews in older Yiddish culture was a formidable and seemingly hopeless task. The program continued on the air long after swing ceased to be the cutting-edge music for the younger generation (and saw its orchestra shrink from eleven to five musicians). Tarras's long-term involvement with the show ended when "Yiddish Melodies in Swing" went off the air in 1955.

This was not Tarras's only outlet in broadcasting, for at the same time he was the music director at the small WBBC ("The Brooklyn Broadcasting Company"), a competing Brooklyn station, and at WARD and WLTH, housed in the Yiddish Second Avenue Theater.

THE HOLOCAUST AND THE NEXT GENERATION

The postwar years brought a decline in Jewish audiences despite the small, temporary influx of Yiddish-speaking Holocaust survivors. American anti-immigration laws aimed at eastern and southern Europeans in the middle 1920s effectively shut the doors to Jews attempting to flee Hitler in the 1930s. The genocide of six million European Jews meant that the fertile birthplace of Yiddish culture was forever destroyed and now only its offshoots—like the one in America—would continue the traditions of the older Jewish communities.

Yet despite this shrinking of venues for performance, the 1920s' American-born generation of clarinetists who had grown up emulating Dave Tarras were now ready to enter the fray full-time. Among them were Danny Rubinstein,

Rudy Tepel, Howie Leess, Marty Levitt, and Sid Beckerman. Chief among them, however, was a tenor-sax player in the Gene Krupa band: Sammy Musiker.

In the postwar years, Musiker, who was born in 1916 and whose name means *musician* in Yiddish, worked with Dave Tarras regularly. He developed a sound that was so much like Tarras's that when he wanted to, he could play so that no one could tell them apart. But Musiker's strong ego would not let him merely imitate someone else's style or sound, and he pushed further to explore his own interpretation, incorporating all the lessons he had learned from both Tarras and from Big Band drummer and bandleader Gene Krupa, in whose orchestra he played. The results were extraordinary. More recording opportunities were in store for Tarras and the young Musiker.

In 1946, Savoy, a jazz and popular label, contacted Dave to record for them:

> Savoy came to me. They wanted a band that mixed Jewish and jazz
> . . . And I arranged for a big band and I made Sammy do the
> arrangements. He made beautiful arrangements.

The two sessions, in 1946 and 1947, produced five discs. Musiker effectively constructed arrangements around Tarras's strengths—and avoided his weaknesses. Knowing Tarras's jazz playing to be virtually nonexistent, he had him play in the ensemble (or sit out) until the arrangement blossomed forth in the "Jewish" section—where he soloed brilliantly.

This ternary sectional form (ABA)—jazz, Jewish, jazz—is based on the structure used by Ziggy Elman on his ". . . Angels Sing" recording. Yet, as Tarras recalled,

> The stores said: "It's a good record, it's beautiful, but if jazz we
> want, we got Benny Goodman." It's not Jewish 'cause it's mixing in
> too much jazz, and it's not jazz 'cause it's mixing in too much
> Jewish. It's what killed it.

They were just too late. "Hot" swing had finally surrendered its place of honor to the "sweet" bands, whose lush orchestrations became the standard for mainstream pop music until the unexpected phenomenon of rock 'n' roll in the 1950s.

The postwar period engendered an immense upheaval in the Jewish community. The Holocaust ended forever the fertile source of new Yiddish-speaking audiences and performers, with a definite shift of focus from European Jewish culture to Israeli Jewish culture. With the founding of the State of Israel in 1948, the increasing popularity of all things Israeli also meant that for the first time in his playing career, Dave Tarras—and many of his contemporaries—would be approaching a form of Jewish music as a stranger. Tarras neither liked nor was challenged by the pseudo-folk music coming out of Israel, as much of it was a merely a simplification of the music he already played and mastered.

This was also the time of the rising Jewish middle class: the emergence of the suburbs with its attendant easy access to assimilation—a generation that forsook the Catskills for the Caribbean, the Yiddish theater for Broadway.

If, however, bourgeois assimilation was happening in some quarters of the American Jewish community, at the same time a separatist ultra-Orthodoxy was rising in others. The Hasidic communities, which had for the most part not migrated to America before the war, did come en masse after the destruction of the European towns from which they originated. Early on, the growing Hasidic communities sought out Dave Tarras to play for them. But he was not long for this scene because of its rigorous physical requirements (weddings usually lasted all night) and his growing disinterest in the current simplified repertoire demanded by this community.

"Tantz": The Klezmer Supernova

In 1956, Epic records, a budget label at Columbia, brought Dave into the studios. The album "Tantz!" was conceived by Sammy Musiker, and it emerged as the most musically sophisticated fusion of Yiddish and American music forms to that time. Musiker's brilliant arrangements, played in a masterly fashion with their foreshadowing of melodic elements and precise attention to interesting voicings, are matched by a unity of overall construction, giving this record a thematic coherence that puts it many years ahead of its time. He utilized a wide variety of harmonies culled from modern jazz, show music, and classical and traditional Jewish music sources, creating a unique bridge between the styles. To achieve that, he needed the best players.

In spite of the presence of some of New York's top Jewish musicians ("Red" Solomon on trumpet; Seymour Megenheimer on accordion; Moe Wechsler, piano; Mac Chopnick, bass; Irving Gratz, drums; and Sam and his younger brother, Ray Musiker, on clarinets and saxophones), CBS did not pursue an aggressive outreach with "Tantz!" and sales foundered. Within a few years it was impossible for the record-buying public to find a copy. (Its rarity, sadly, continues to this day: although there have been several inquiries to CBS to produce a rerelease, at this time there are no plans to reissue "Tantz" on CD.)

Though this was the era of be-bop, rock 'n' roll, and folk music, there were still young Jewish musicians who found themselves gravitating to the Jewish music world. Chief among them was reed-player-turned-pianist Pete Sokolow.

In 1959, three years after he had turned professional, Pete Sokolow played his first job with Dave Tarras. They were co-occupants in the sax section of the Ralph Kahn big band at New York's swanky Hotel Astor. Sokolow recalls:

> At this time Tarras had a tremendous reputation, he was the absolute king of the Jewish world—an icon. People spoke to him in deferential tones. Kahn had him there to play a specialty: go out on the floor,

play a *doina,* a *bulgar.* He introduced himself to me: "I am Dave Tarras: I am teacher of clarinet." As if I weren't intimidated enough!

As the demand for klezmer music waned, so did its major proponent, Dave Tarras. He kept active with occasional gigs in hospitals or old-age homes, and music union "Trust Fund" jobs with his old sidemen. Now and then he would hear a record of his played on radio station WEVD, or receive an occasional fan letter. Fewer and fewer people were stopping him on the street to ask if he was indeed Dave Tarras.

After the death of his wife, he reacted by throwing out many photographs, records, and memorabilia from their early days together in America—much of it related to his career—a response to grief that he later regretted. He was, by his own account, at the lowest ebb of his life.

THE REBIRTH OF *"KLEZMER"*: MY OWN REAWAKENING

Nevertheless, while Tarras thought that recognition of his work was all behind him, another event outside his control was taking shape. Almost as gradually as the postwar interest in Yiddish culture faded, a renewed interest in it emerged in the 1970s.

Figure 3.2. KlezKamp: The Yiddish Folk Arts Program 1985 shooting a scene from the documentary film "A Jumpin' Night in the Garden of Eden" (1987). Left to right: Hankus Netsky, sax, Joel Rubin, clarinet, Henry Sapoznik, banjo, Marc Smason, trombone. Photo courtesy of Living Traditions, Inc.

In the early 1970s, I played Appalachian string-band music ("old-time music") in a group called "The Delaware Water Gap String Band," spending part of each year collecting traditional music and playing with local older musicians in the Blue Ridge Mountains of North Carolina.

But what was I doing there?

I didn't come from six generations of Scots-Irish settlers. My family were Holocaust survivors who came over after World War II and were steeped in Eastern European Yiddish culture. My father was not a renowned square-dance fiddler and caller but a renowned *khazn* in whose choirs I began singing at the age of six, learning the time-honored modes, scales, and vocal skills required for the traditional synagogue services.

In my quest as a child of immigrants, I resolved to become even more conscious of authentic American music than many Americans. I came to old-time music through folk music that was generated by the anti-Vietnam war movement. From there it was not very difficult to make the transition to the rural music that inspired urban folk singers like Pete Seeger and Bob Dylan.

It was through the generosity and help of the veteran Appalachian music collector Ray Alden that I was introduced to the world of the music of the Blue Ridge Mountains, and veteran fiddle and banjo players Fred Cockerham and Tommy Jarrell. These older men were hospitable and gracious hosts and guides who, taking me under their wings, shared the accrued artistry of their family's musical heritage as if I were one of their own.

Yet, they were also a bit puzzled. I was not the only one who had beaten a path to their doors seeking insight into one of America's most exciting musical forms. Others preceded me, and not a few of them were also Jews from urban areas. At one point, several years into my trips to Tommy Jarrell's home and knowing I was Jewish, he asked "Don't your people got none of your own music?" I was surprised but intrigued. Did we have a music as simple and powerful as the fiddle tunes Fred and Tommy played? Was there an unbroken line in Yiddish music that was as easily definable as the one Tommy bridged from his fiddle-playing father, Benjamin Franklin Jarrell, to his fiddle-playing son, Benjamin Franklin Jarrell? I did not know. But I was determined to find out.

The Old Records Have Something New to Say

Consulting the renowned folklorist Barbara Kirshenblatt-Gimblett, I was introduced to the holdings of period 78 rpm records at New York's YIVO Institute for Jewish Research. Collected but never listened to here—I would have to bring in my own turntable to play the records!—were hundreds of Jewish 78s recorded from the turn of the century up to the post–World War II era. I was, for the first time, able to hear the records that were made in my community at the same time that Tommy's father had made his recordings in the mid-1920s. And there it was. That same directness. The same ease of understanding about how to play simple and powerful music and project a sense of the moment. But instead of "Charlie Poole and the North Carolina Ramblers" or "Uncle Dave Macon and the Fruit Jar Drinkers," I was listening to "Abe Katzman's Bessarabian Orchestra" and "The Boiberiker Kapelle." What I had loved about the singularity of old-time music, I was now discovering in the music I grew up with; it was there in klezmer. (Interestingly, during its heyday, this music was never referred to as *klezmer,* but as *tants muzik,* dance music; *khasene muzik,* wedding music; *freylekhs;* or simply "Yiddish music." In many ways the term *klezmer* was a demeaning one, connoting either *shtetl* "hick" music of a crude and untutored character, or a romantic image of a wandering, passionate, tragic artist. In either case, the revivification of the music form in the 1970s also elevated the term *klezmer* to a new and respected status.)

Though I had never before heard these old records, there was a strong sense of familiarity about them. Apart from the reassuring hiss of the 78 rpms with their sepia-toned sound of yesterday, the music, the voices, and the presence all jumped out at me at once. And none more so than those of Dave Tarras. There was something about his records that seemed even more familiar than the others. I asked my father, who, as a professional *khazn,* had sung at all the major synagogues and hotels, about Dave Tarras. Tarras, my father reminded me, was an old friend of his, whom we knew from the hotels where my father conducted the religious services. It was a standard situation: during the days my father led the singing of prayers in the synagogue, I sang in the choir and Dave was one of the members of the congregation. At night, Dave played onstage and everyone listened and danced to his music.

I Meet Dave . . . Again

That was Dave Tarras? As a kid, he seemed older than music itself. This was the guy I dubbed "a round man playing square music"? How could I have missed the power in his playing? I had been so intent on becoming part of American culture, so adept at ignoring and dismissing my heritage, that I had blocked out my own primary and deep interaction with a living folk culture. It was the rediscovery of Dave's 78s—and the man himself—that reminded me what I had very nearly thrown away.

Through my father, I began visiting Dave and thus began a rich and mutually enlightening relationship. Dave, like Tommy Jarrell, was a genial host, allowing me into his home and life. Unlike Tommy, Dave had seen me grow up and could not resist reminding me of just that fact. He had a profound sense of self and had, in many ways, been waiting years for someone to come to him to get "The Story." He was ready and so was I.

The most interesting adjustment for me was to learn how to do field-work in my own community. Even though I already understood the language (I had spoken Yiddish before English), I had to learn to make myself a stranger in order to ask and understand basic questions and to assume nothing. Through Tarras, I was able to contact many of the surviving veteran klezmer musicians in New York, such as Joe Helfenbein, Irving Gratz, and

Louis Grupp, all of whom were generous and equally startled that anyone, let alone a young American-born kid, would take an interest in music that had ceased being relevant in the Jewish world years ago.

It was at this time that I created and then directed the Archives of Recorded Sound at the YIVO, building the collection in thirteen years from several hundred to several thousand discs, the most important collection of its kind in the world. (The vast number of 78 rpms that Dave recorded—somewhere over five hundred—have given me the pleasure of reuniting Dave with recordings of performances that he had forgotten.) Soon, the work that I was doing at the YIVO—reissuing these classic recordings, lecturing on and writing about the history of the performances of Andy Statman, who was a student of Tarras's, and The Klezmorim—began to stimulate an interest in this music. Part of the impetus was the location and identification of authentic old-time klezmer players. No one fit that bill better than Dave Tarras.

Tarras's home in the Coney Island section of Brooklyn became a klezmer mecca. It was now not unusual for TV or documentary filmmakers to set up shop in his living room and record this last of the old-world klezmorim. Klezmer was hot and Dave Tarras was its Godfather.

A steady stream of well-wishers and klezmer fans came to him bearing recordings, publicity kits, and videos of their groups, looking for insights (and endorsements) from this man whom many had known only through his 78s or hard-to-find LPs. His influence, once so powerful for earlier generations of musicians, was again transforming the young players who came to klezmer from rock, jazz, country, classical, and other ethnic musics—from musics an earlier generation had sought out in order to get away from klezmer. He was real continuity—to be in his presence was to be part of the historic transmission of tradition, a chain of transmission that was growing more and more fragile. He was a 78 rpm come to life.

Enter Kapelye

During this time in 1979, I formed Kapelye to feed my passion for mixing Yiddish music research and playing hot dance tunes. For a performance by Kapelye, refer to CD Track 4. The group was instantaneously acclaimed—making four records and two Hollywood film scores and touring the United States. Buoyed by the general influence of the "Roots" movement, we were in the vanguard of a resurgence of interest in secular Yiddish culture that generated a community-based desire to re-establish a link with this cultural heritage.

In 1984, Kapelye had the singular distinction of being the first band to bring traditional Yiddish music back to Europe. Among the countries we played were France, Switzerland, England, Belgium, and Germany. It was in Germany that I experienced some of the most profound and unsettling feelings I have ever felt. Here, in the birthplace of the most massive campaign of organized genocide in history—where Yiddish culture was born and very nearly destroyed—Yiddish music found a new and enthusiastic audience. The stark contrasts of wanting to share my music with those who loved it as much as I did was tempered by a belief that cultural ownership might claim certain boundaries. Could the children and grandchildren whose community orchestrated the Holocaust take part in the revivification of a culture that was almost obliterated? Had they abrogated their right—or, as I've also thought, who better—to make cultural amends for the mass murder by reanimating this nearly annihilated civilization? It is a conflict that I still harbor.

Dave's Last Years

In 1984 Tarras received a National Heritage Folklife Award from the Folk Arts Division of the National Endowment for the Arts. The significance of the award profoundly moved Tarras, but the happy moment was marred by near tragedy. While performing at the awards ceremony in Ford's Theater in Washington, D.C., Tarras was stricken on stage with a massive heart attack. It was because of this near-death experience that Dave and I stepped up the documentation of his life and thus, among other things, produced our seminal CD-biography *Dave Tarras: Father of Yiddish-American Klezmer Music*.

The following year I founded "KlezKamp: The Yiddish Folk Arts Program," which was dedicated to reviving the "apprentice" environment. We created an intergenerational intensive workshop of music and cultural activities, including language, folklore, poetry, dance, visual arts, song workshops, instrument classes, history seminars, all in a supportive atmosphere of learning and performance. What started as a modest local event of 125 people soon blossomed into an international outpouring of hundreds from around the world. (As of 1995, nearly five thousand people have participated.) In December 1988, Dave Tarras was selected as the first recipient of the newly inaugurated Lifetime Achievement Award from KlezKamp. Due to his ever-weakening condition, however, he was unable to attend KlezKamp to accept his award.

Dave Tarras died on February 14, 1989, but the music scene that his masterful music helped inspire shows no signs of slowing down. Tarras was the necessary element common to all in the Jewish world—from the glorified performers of the Yiddish stage, screen, and radio, to the factory worker who hired him for his daughter's wedding—the career of Dave Tarras is the history of the Yiddish-American culture. It is a testament to the power of Tarras's great gift that a man born in the nineteenth century and who blossomed in the twentieth might extend his influence into the twenty-first century.

GLOSSARY

(NOTE: KH sounds as "ch" as in "Bach")

Ashkenaz (ASHkenaz). Yiddish: literally, Germany (pl. ashkeNAZim). Those Jews of Western and Eastern Europe who are descendants of Jews who originally settled in Germany and then migrated elsewhere, as well as any others whose language and basic cultural forms derive ultimately from the old German Jewish settlement.

Ba'al Koyre (ba'al KOYRE). Heb.: literally, "Master of Reading." Lay reader of the Torah in the synagogue.

Ba'al Tfile (ba'al TFIle). Heb.: literally, "Master of Prayer." Lay leader of prayer in the synagogue.

Badkhn (BADkhn). Heb./Yid.: Improvisatory poet and emcee at traditional Jewish weddings.

Bar Mitzva (bar MITSva). Heb.: Confirmation of Jewish thirteen-year-old boy. *Bas Mitzva* (fem.)

Freylekhs (FREYlekhs). Heb./Yid.: "Lively." Group of Yiddish dance tunes played in $\frac{2}{4}$ time.

Haftora (hafTOra). Heb.: Selection from the Prophets, which is read after the Torah portion on Sabbath and holidays. Thirteen-year-old boys and girls will generally read it at their *bar* or *bas mitzva.*

Hasid (HASid). (pl.: hasIDim) Heb.: Follower of Hasidic movement.

Hasidism (HASidism). Heb.: Eighteenth-century Jewish charismatic religious movement.

Haskala (hasKAla). Heb.: Enlightenment. Nineteenth-century Jewish reform movement.

kapelye (kaPELye). Yid.: Band.

khasene (KHAsene). Heb./Yid.: Wedding.

khazn (KHAzn) (pl.: khaZONim). Heb.: Synagogue liturgical singer.

kheyder (KHEYder). Heb.: Primary Jewish day school.

klezmer (KLEZmer) (pl.: klezMORim). Heb./Yid.: Traditional instrumentalist.

meshoyrer (meshOYrer) (pl.: meshOYr'rim). Heb.: Apprenctice cantor; also chorister.

nigun (NIgun) (pl.: niGUnim). Heb.: Wordless song associated with Hasidim.

pogrom (poGROM). Yid.: Organized mass violence against Jews.

Purim (PUrim). Heb.: Holiday that celebrates the foiling of the plot to destroy the Jews of Persia in the fifth century C.E.

shtetl (SHTEtl) (pl.: SHTETlakh). Yid.: A small town.

COMPANION CD SELECTIONS

Track 3. Abe Schwartz, "Unzer Toirele."

Track 4. Kapelye, "Berditchever/Mazel Tov."

ADDITIONAL SOURCES

Discography

(All historic recordings contain extensive notes)

Historic Recordings

Klezmer Music, 1910–1942. Smithsonian-Folkways FSS 34021.

Dave Tarras: Yiddish-American Klezmer Music. Yazoo 7001.

Klezmer Pioneers: 1905–1952. Rounder 1089.

Naftule Brandwein: King of the Klezmer Clarinet. Rounder 1127.

Contemporary Recordings

Dave Tarras

Master of the Jewish Clarinet. Ethnic Folk Arts US 1002.

Kapelye

Future and Past. Rounder FF249.

Levine and His Flying Machine. Shanachie 21006.

Chicken. Shanachie 21007.

On the Air. Shanachie 67005.

Klezmer Plus

Klezmer Plus: Featuring Sid Beckerman and Howie Leess. Rounder FF 90488.

Films

A Jumpin' Night in the Garden of Eden. 1988. Directed by Mikhl Goldman.

Fiddlers on the Hoof. 1992. BBC. Directed by Simon Braughton.

BIBLIOGRAPHY

Idelsohn, A. Z. 1967. *Jewish Music in Its Historical Development.* New York: Schocken Edition.

Sapoznik, Henry. 1998. *Klezmer! A Very Social History of 100 Years of Yiddish Music in America.* New York: Schirmer Books.

———. 1990. *The Klezmer Plus Folio.* New York: Tara Publications.

———. 1987. *The Compleat Klezmer.* New York: Tara Publications.

———. 1986. Dave Tarras. *New Grove's Dictionary of American Music,* edited by H. Wiley Hitchcock and Stanley Sarlie. London: Macmillan.

———, ed. 1992. Yiddish Music. *Encylopedia of Jewish-American History of Culture.* New York: Garland Publishing, Inc.

Slobin, Mark. 1984. The Neo-Klezmer Movement. *Journal of American Folklore.*

———. 1982. *Old Jewish Folk Music: The Collections and Writings of Moshe Beregovski.* Philadelphia: University of Pennsylvania Press.

Spottswood, Dick. 1990. Ethnic Music on Records: 1895–1942. Urbana: University of Illinois Press.

CHAPTER 4

The Music of Arab Detroit

A Musical Mecca in the Midwest

Anne K. Rasmussen

*A*nne Rasmussen is an ethnomusicologist and musician who has specialized *in the music and culture of the Middle East. Although she has done research and fieldwork within the Arab American community throughout the United States, the focus of this chapter is the multilayered and diverse Arab American community around Detroit, Michigan. With her focus on Arab Detroit, Rasmussen makes the point that ethnic groups that seem homogenous to outsiders are in fact multicultural and multifaceted themselves. Following an historical survey of the musical life of the Arab community in the United States, the author turns her attention to three wedding celebrations in Yemeni, Lebanese, and Iraqi subsections of Detroit's Arab American community. She then takes us to a large city festival and a formal concert as she considers how music patronage works differently on the family level, in the larger community, and with arts agencies who are supported by national funds. The analysis of ethnographic scenarios demonstrates how aspects of ethnicity, class, region, religion, tradition, and innovation are played out through the process of musical performance. Rasmussen views the musicians of Arab Detroit as the cultural and ritual specialists of a community, transporting their family and friends to a time and place that is distinct from that of mainstream America through the powerful medium of music and dance. While giving us some very practical and specific guidelines for understanding and appreciating this "Arab sound," she also suggests a number of points that are crucial to understanding the relationship between music making and community life in any context.*

■   ■   ■   ■

INTRODUCTION

Arab American music culture, a socio-musical complex, has been a part of American life since at least the beginning of this century. In spite of the hegemony of American popular music, Arab music continues to thrive in the many Arab American communities of the United States. This chapter opens with an historical overview of the cultivation of Arab music in the United States over the past one hundred years and then focuses on the dynamic contemporary musical life of one region of the United States, Detroit, Michigan, where the Arab American population is most highly concentrated and multifaceted.[1]

Today the Arab American community, which numbers around two and a half million, is among the fastest growing minority population in the United States. People of Arab heritage trace their family ties to the Arab World—a collection of twenty-two nations that spans from Morocco through Egypt and east through Saudi Arabia and the United Arab Emirates, north through the Levant to Syria and Iraq, and south to the Sudan. The term *Arab world* is a collective term, coined to facilitate social and political solidarity. Although Arabs may differ in their ethnicity, their religious beliefs, their race, and their nationality, people from the Arab world are unified by language and various aspects of culture, such as food, folklore, and music. Arab Americans are, by background, Jews, Christians, and Muslims, and may be highly educated professionals in white-collar jobs, university students, owners and operators of family businesses, or unskilled laborers in industrial plants. Large concentrations of Arab Americans live throughout the United States, most notably in California, New York, Texas and the South, New England, and around Detroit, Michigan, where the community numbers close to a quarter of a million people.[2] It is important to note at the outset that Arab Americans are all individuals and there is a certain danger in discussing them as a group of people all of whom are passionately involved in the music and culture of their heritage. In fact, many Americans whose families originally came from the Arab world may be completely uninvolved and disinterested in Arab expressive culture as it transpires here in America or in the Arab world itself. Nevertheless, it is the ambiance of exuberance during contexts for musical performance that originally pulled me into the Arab American community; many people of Arab heritage in America are involved in a thriving and exciting musical subculture.

The ethnographic scenarios discussed below are intended to show that Arab American musical life, a small piece in the mosaic of multicultural America, is in itself multicultural and multifaceted. Although the descriptor *Arab American* indicates that this population is an homogenous group, Arab Americans themselves make multiple distinctions among each other. These distinctions may be based on such obvious qualities as nationality ("I am from Lebanon, and you are from Egypt"), on religious orientation ("I am

Christian, you are Muslim"), on generation ("My family has been in America since 1915, and your family just arrived"), or on regional provenience ("We are from the north and you are from the south"). Such cultural distinctions, which are often completely invisible to the outsider, may be of paramount importance inside a particular community. Furthermore, and of particular interest for this endeavor, such cultural distinctions may actually be heard, played, sung, and danced during the course of a music event.

Musicians of various heritage—Lebanese, Palestinian, Yemeni, Syrian, and Iraqi—are showcased in this chapter in an attempt to emphasize the central role of individuals as they bring to their community the sounds of culture. In an immigrant or subcultural setting, where the invasion of the mainstream America knocks at every door, the proactive efforts of musicians to learn, teach, perform, and create the repertoires that amalgamate their communities have a phenomenal impact on the expressive culture of a community. Individual musicians are the lifeblood of any music culture.

I hope my work begins to convey that whether recorded or live, music has the power to move people to different times and places and is thus one of the most compelling agents in the definition of community and individual identity.

A BRIEF HISTORY OF THE MUSICAL LIFE OF ARAB AMERICANS

We know from family memoirs and photo albums that, at the beginning of the century, music making was part of most family gatherings and that no wedding or picnic was complete without singing and dancing. The people who made up the first wave of Arab immigration to this country were, for the most part, Christians from Greater Syria, an area sometimes referred to as the *Levant,* which now comprises the countries of Syria, Lebanon, Jordan, and Israel (formerly Palestine). This first wave of immigrants to "the new world" were looking for a haven from the turmoil of the Ottoman occupation of their homeland, and, when they settled in America their music, along with their cuisine, their language, and to some extent their professions, settled here with them. By 1914 the community numbered about one hundred ten thousand (Hoogland 1987). In the early 1920s the United States government began to control the number of foreigners who could come into the country by instituting a quota system that limited immigration from all parts of the world, including "Greater Syria." Nevertheless, the Arab American community continued to expand with new generations of American-born children, and the consistent, if infrequent, arrival of family and friends from overseas.

The photographs and stories of older musicians and clippings from the Arab American press indicate that it was an exciting time for Arab music in the United States. From the mid-1920s through the early 1960s, two primary contexts for music making developed and flourished in the community: the *haflah* (pl. *haflat*), a formal music party; and the *mahrajan* (pl. *mahrajanat*), a weekend-long gathering to which some people traveled from hundreds of miles away. During my interviews and discussions with elderly professional instrumentalists (all men) and singers (both male and female), they remember how busy their schedules were, when, particularly during the summer, they traveled up and down the East Coast to perform for audiences that sometimes numbered in the thousands. *Haflat* and *mahrajanat* were usually sponsored by church or community groups or by a prominent philanthropist. These large-scale social and musical events were usually organized to raise money for some kind of "good cause," such as the building or renovation of a church or the financial and social support of newly arrived immigrants, orphans, or even family members still living in the Middle East. Although many of the Arab Americans who attended these events spoke English well and were completely integrated into American society, the music, dance, and food at these events was—according to community memory—completely Arab. The combination of aromatic Syrian and Lebanese cuisine, the Arabic language, the sights and sounds of musical performance, and the movement of dance created an ambiance and experience of the homeland. Such celebrations brought the qualities of Arab place and time into American place and time through a process that is certainly not unique to the Arab American community. Yet in addition to being a time and a place where "the old country" was invented in the space of a few hours, *haflat* and *mahrajanat* were also affirmatively Arab American. These music parties and festivals that became such a conspicuous feature of Arab American life were sponsored by social organizations that evolved according to the needs and interests of the immigrant community. The musicians played to an audience that was connected not only by their place of birth but more immediately by their journeys to the New World and the challenges that faced them here.

During this same time period, roughly the first half of the twentieth century, the Arab American music media, an equally dynamic context for artistic expression, developed in complement to the live performance culture of the community. Beginning in the second decade of this century, Arab immigrant musicians began recording their music on 78-r.p.m. discs at the invitation of such American record companies as Columbia, Victor, and Standard. These American record companies were searching for, and found, new musics and new markets in the myriad ethnic communities in America. By the 1940s, however, Arab Americans had taken charge of their own recording industry and several Arab American record labels emerged. Thus, recording music, as both an artistic and a commercial endeavor, made up part of the professional activities of the many musicians of the community. When we listen to these old scratchy three-minute-long Arab songs we can only imagine what the live music scene might have been like. Track five on

Figure 4.1. Musicians on stage at a *haflah* (music party) in New York during the 1950s.

the accompanying compact disc is an excerpt of an early 78-r.p.m. recording by singer Moses Cohen, violinist Naim Karakand, and an unidentified qanun player. (See also *The Music of Arab Americans,* under "Recordings and Music Cited.")

The instruments that musicians brought with them and later created here include:

'ud   A fretless pear-shaped lute with a round belly, a bent neck, and eleven strings, ten of which are in double courses.

qanun   A plucked zither with seventy-two strings in triple courses, which are fine-tuned during performance with a series of small levers that are moved up and down.

nay   A reed flute, heard rarely at first in the United States, but more frequently as professional musicians from the Arab world came to this country to perform.

violin   Formerly an Arab upright fiddle called *rebab;* the Western violin was adopted into the Arab ensemble by the early twentieth century.

riqq   A tambourine with heavy brass jingles, also called *daff.*

darabukkah   A vase-shaped ceramic drum with a single head; sometimes the Turkish/Armenian metal *dumbek* was also used.

mizmar	A double-reed folk oboe usually associated with folk and village music. The *mizmar* is a loud instrument used in combination with the drum called *tabl baladi* for celebrations.
tabl baladi	Literally *country drum,* a double-headed drum played on one head with a beater and on the other with a thin willow branch or stick. One head is thicker than the other, giving the drum two distinct pitches. The drum is suspended from the neck of the player, who is free to roam around the floor and play directly to the dancers. Paired with the *mizmar,* the dynamic performance style of *tabl* players gives the dancers tremendous energy.

This early era of Arab American music featured a repertoire that musicians have described as "traditional," "classical," or "listening" music. The repertoire performed included a mix of urban music from such cities as Beirut, Lebanon; Aleppo, Syria; Istanbul, Turkey; and Cairo, Egypt. Musicians laced their performances of listening music with a sprinkling of folk music for dance and an emergent popular music, which by about the 1960s overshadowed and engulfed the listening music of the past.

SAVORING THE MIDDLE EASTERN SOUND: THE INGREDIENTS IN THE MIX

What makes Arab music sound like it does? As are many musical systems of the Middle East, and Central and South Asia, Arab music is based on a number of melodic modes called, in the Arabic language, *maqam* (pl. *maqamat*). Two examples of *maqamat* are shown in Figure 4.2. In addition to a scale of specific notes, each *maqam* is characterized by particular musical phrases and gestures as well as by a particular emotional character. In performance practice, melodic lines may be played with flashy ornamentation or subtle nuance. Harmony is largely absent from Arab music. Each musician plays the same melodic line, yet each musician embroiders his or her part with trills, slides, turns, the addition of a flurry of notes here, the absence of others there, collectively enriching the sonic texture of a performance, creating what ethnomusicologists refer to as *heterophony*.

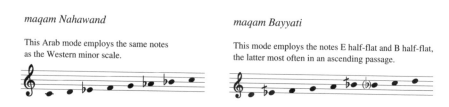

maqam Nahawand

This Arab mode employs the same notes as the Western minor scale.

maqam Bayyati

This mode employs the notes E half-flat and B half-flat, the latter most often in an ascending passage.

Figure 4.2. Two modes of Arab music.

To the uninitiated, Arab music may at first sound "out of tune." It is, however, the tuning system of Arab music that gives it a unique character. While a couple of the *maqamat* have the same notes as the Western major and minor scales, other modes differ in terms of both the collection of pitches and the intonation of each pitch. Arab music uses notes that fall between the cracks of our tuning system. In other words, several modes use what are referred to as quarter tones or neutral tones—notes that cannot be reproduced on Western instruments with fixed pitch, such as the piano. For Arab music to sound Arab, it should be played on traditional Arab instruments, which are built with the capability of playing the pitches of the *maqam* system.

The melodic modes of Arab music are complemented by a set of rhythmic patterns called *iqa'* (pl. *iqa'at*). Rhythmic patterns are recognized by their duration: they may be 3, 4, 7, 8, 10, or 14 beats long (to cite only a few examples), and they comprise a pattern of beats and rests. Two examples of *iqa'at* are shown in Figure 4.3. In performance practice, each beat has a particular timbre, the most important sounds being the *dumm*, a low-pitched tone produced by striking the middle of the head, and the *tek*, a high, dryer sound produced closer to the rim of the drum (or on the jingles in the case of the *riqq* or tambourine). Thus two *iqa'at*, each eight beats long, may have completely different patterns of beats and rests and therefore different names and functions. Like Arab melodies, Arab rhythmic patterns are decorated and varied in performance, producing a musical product that is far more sophisticated and interesting than the theoretical models described on paper.

In addition to metric music, in which rhythmic patterns provide a regular temporal structure in complement to the melody, Arab music features lots of performance in free rhythm, or nonmetric music. Instrumental and vocal improvisation, one of the hallmarks of Arab music, often occurs in free rhythm, and it is this juxtaposition of metric and nonmetric performance, or sometimes even the simultaneous combination of the two, that distinguish-

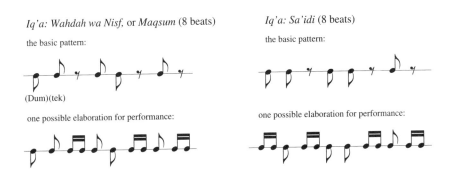

Figure 4.3. Two rhythmic patterns of Arab music.

es Arab music. Track 6 on the CD features Detroit musicians Rana and Naim and myself in an impromptu performance of Lebanese folk genres Mijana and 'Ataba, followed by a lively dance genre, 'Ala Daluna.

Although Arab music of the Levant and Egypt has been accompanied by a written theoretical discourse (see Marcus 1989), it is practiced by many without reference to books and without extensive knowledge of music theory. This is especially true in the United States where musicians learn their craft without the conservatories, music lessons, method books, and other pedagogical institutions and devices that are more readily available in Arab World cities. In spite of the absence of organized music pedagogy, many of the rules of melody, rhythm and form that are written in theoretical works and passionately discussed by musicians, professors, and ethnomusicologists may exist in a musician's practice—the way they play the music—but not conceptualized in their intellectual understanding of the music—the way they explain the music. (See also Davis 1992, Racy 1991, Marcus 1992, and Schuyler 1990.)

When we take the distinguishing features of Arab music together— the unique timbres of traditional instruments; the particular approach to intonation; a melodic texture that foregrounds improvisation, decoration, variation, and nuance; the exciting meters and rhythms of the music and the sounds of the percussion instruments that play them; and the affection for the juxtaposition and combination of metric and nonmetric music—we might begin to understand some of the reasons why we are "turned on to" or "turned off by" the Arab sound. The Arab sound is certainly one that has provided a source of fascination in the West, and this can be heard through the history of Western music. Composers of Western "art music," for example Mozart and Tchaikovsky, have been inspired by music of the Middle East, or the "Orient." In the United States during the early years of this century, the popular music of "Tin Pan Alley" included numerous songs inspired by foreign places and newly arrived immigrants in America, for example "Caravan" and "Lena from Palestina." Music for belly dancing, an American craze of the 1960s and '70s, created by American-born musicians of both Middle Eastern and non–Middle Eastern heritage is a dynamic component of the soundscape of that time (see Rasmussen 1992). And countless Hollywood film scores for movies that depict stories from Biblical epics to James Bond adventures feature music that, through instrumentation, rhythm, and melody, references Middle Eastern music. The contemporary interest in Arab or, more broadly, Middle Eastern music rings out in such "world beat" or "world music" projects as Peter Gabriel's soundtrack for "The Last Temptation of Christ" and the later-released recording "Passion Sources," Yemeni singer Ofra Haza's popular recordings (in a Jewish tradition related to Arab Yemeni music), or Robert Plant and Jimmy Page's recent collaboration, tour, and audio and laser disc recording "No Horse Quarter" with musicians from

Egypt and Morocco. These few examples of contemporary world music demonstrate that the sound of Arab music, with its unique style and performance practice, is meaningful to a population far broader than that of people of Arab heritage.

ARAB AMERICAN COMMUNITY AND CULTURE IN THE DETROIT AREA

There is no place in America, and perhaps in the world, that better approximates the ideological notion of the Arab world mosaic than Detroit and the adjacent city Dearborn. In order to gain insight into the Arab music scene in Detroit, we consider, first, music making at the family level by looking at three wedding celebrations; second, music sponsored by a large community festival in Detroit; third, a concert sponsored by an Arab American cultural arts agency. An appreciation of the interface between contexts for musical performance that are grounded in the "natural" life of the community and those events that are sponsored by larger community, city, or national organizations and institutions is the key to understanding the forces at work behind the Arab American music scene specifically and, by extension, any American music scene in general.

Detroit's Arab American community numbers about two hundred fifty thousand. It is reportedly the largest community of Arabic speakers outside the Arab world. Arab Americans have been in the Detroit area for about one hundred years. Small groups migrated from New York and New England to the area along peddling routes that were established at the beginning of the century. Many more followed with the economic revolution facilitated by the Ford automobile plant and related industry, which created jobs that required few English-language or previous technical training (see Naff 1985). The nature of the Arab American community changed dramatically during the 1960s in Detroit and throughout the United States. First, immigration quotas enacted in 1923 that restricted Arab immigration were lifted in 1965, effecting a surge of émigrés from the Arab world. Second, while the Arab American community had become a relatively stable group, consisting primarily of Christians from Syria and Lebanon and their American-born families, the newly arriving Arabs were from all over the Arab World. Third, while many of these new immigrants sought educational and economic opportunity in the United States, they had also come in order to escape the reverberations of tumultuous conflicts in their home countries, including the Arab-Israeli wars (1948 and 1967), civil war in Lebanon (beginning in 1975), continuing warfare in Beirut and South Lebanon, the Palestinian uprising or *Intifadah* (beginning in 1988), and war in Iraq (1991). In Detroit, many of the first wave of immigrants have moved out to the suburbs. These early immigrants and subsequent generations of

American-born family members are well established and well assimilated. This "old community" stands in sharp contrast to many of the newer communities of people that have immigrated within the past thirty years and are continuously welcoming new members from "back home."

Before turning to three scenarios of music making on the family level, let me place myself in the picture. I began doing fieldwork in the Detroit area during the summer of 1988 as a part of the research for my dissertation in ethnomusicology (Rasmussen 1991). Over the past several years, my original set of contacts has blossomed into an ever-expanding network of musicians, community members, and their families. Since 1988, I have traveled to Detroit nearly every summer, at first owing to professional responsibility, but now also out of social interest.

My point of entrée into Arab American culture in the Detroit area is almost always with musicians. I come to musicians' gigs and meet members of the band; I sit with the band at the musicians' table. Sometimes I "sit in" with the band and play either 'ud or riqq on stage. In the course of the several hours of a music event, I circulate and meet a variety of people: participants, young and old; videographers; caterers; the host of the party; the mother of the bride; festival organizers; a belly dancer. People come to know me in a variety of roles: friend, friend of friend, professor of music, ethnomusicologist, music student, fellow musician, or even "that strange American woman who plays the 'ud." I always ask permission to photograph, videotape, or tape-record and explain that my intentions are for the purposes of documentation and education. Communication transpires in a combination of English and Arabic; although I have a working knowledge of written and spoken Arabic, I am less than fluent in the language. I do not deny that many things may escape my understanding.

In addition to attending weddings, parties, and festivals and dropping in at nightclubs, I visit people in their homes to discuss their musical experience in general and to learn from musicians by playing music for and with them. I have been studying and playing Arab music since 1985 and I believe that this is a source of fascination, curiosity, and pride for many of my "informants." Often when I am invited to someone's home, other family and friends are present, a meal is generously prepared and served, music is played live and videotaped performances are shared, people dance, the television is on, kids come and go, the phone rings.

One of the greatest challenges since beginning my fieldwork among Arab Americans has been to sharpen my perception and understanding of the multicultural Arab music scene in the Detroit area. So, in order to gain insight into the sights and sounds of music making in Arab Detroit on the family level, I offer these experiences—a Lebanese wedding party, a Yemeni wedding party and an Iraqi-Italian wedding party, all having taken place during the summers of 1993 and 1994—as a point of departure.

Figure 4.4. Rana and Naim
Homaidan and Rana's parents wave
goodbye from the porch of their
duplex in Dearborn. The family on
the upstairs porch are also Arab
Americans.

A LEBANESE WEDDING PARTY

We are in a modest but large banquet hall in suburban Detroit. I am seated
at the musicians' table where we are wolfing down our dinner to fuel up for
the three-and-a-half hour set of nonstop music that is to come. The bride
and groom and the bridal party have already ceremoniously entered the hall
to the accompaniment of special processional wedding music supplied by the
band and the singer Mahmoud Beydoun. This special procession, called *zaffah*, knows many variations, but is a prerequisite part of every Arab American
wedding. The bride and groom sit on a raised platform on special thronelike
chairs opposite the band's stage. They do not eat with the guests; rather, they
appear as if on display for the rest of the guests to admire. A group of old
women clad in long *jalabayyahs* (a traditional, straight, long-sleeved, ankle-
length woman's dress) approach the stage and perform *awiyyah*—stylized little poems of welcome and blessing that are called out in a high voice. The
genre of *awiyyah* is probably hundreds of years old. Another guest half reads
and half sings a special poem in the classical or formal Arabic language
(*fusha*) that he has composed for the bride and groom. At our table, the
musicians, including three whom I've known for years and several whom I
am meeting for the first time tonight, eat and visit, paying little attention to
the action in the banquet hall. For them, this is a "gig."

The crowd, especially the women, are dressed in fancy attire. My subtly colored suit pales in comparison. Women wear jeweled gowns and sequined party dresses, many with matching veils. The families of both the bride and the groom come from a predominantly Muslim village of Northern Lebanon. The majority of the attendants are also from that village—many have immigrated recently, some within the past ten years; almost everyone is speaking Lebanese Arabic.

When given our cue, we musicians take our place on the stage. For the remainder of the evening, we provide a kind of temporal structure that frames each set of wedding guests with music, through dance. The musicians take their cue from the master of ceremonies who throughout the evening consults a list of guests, and from the singer, who launches into song after song after song, demonstrating his knowledge of an apparently unlimited repertoire of lively, danceable tunes.

The emcee calls out: "The grandmother and grandfather of the bride and all of their family, please come up, it is your turn." At this point the members of this part of the family come to the dance floor and dance exuberantly. As they dance, money is tossed into the air. A dancer, perhaps a young man or a child, is hoisted upon the shoulders of other dancers. More money is thrown. Young boys, from about five to ten years of age, race around and gather up the bills that are thrown on the floor, stuffing them into cardboard boxes. The throwing of money is both a public display of generosity and a contribution to the new couple. Although the money is tossed into the air in a carefree manner, the bills are fastidiously collected, counted, and later presented to the newlyweds.

At this particular wedding, group after group is called to the dance floor, until every part of the extended family and every guest has been recognized. Sometimes the emcee identifies prospective dancers by their profession. "Let's call up Ali, the engineer!," or "Let's call up the Barda family, the owners of the Caravan restaurant!" Two musicians—Nadeem Dlaikan, who plays the *mizmar,* and Wa'el Yazigi, who plays *tabl baladi*—spend much of their time out on the dance floor playing among the celebrants. The singer, too, often descends from the stage onto the dance floor. He and the other band members whoop and holler, shouting exclamations, calling out the names of the family members who are out on the floor, and urging the dancers on.

The last segment of this wedding evolves into a huge collective line dance called the *dabkah.* Eventually a line of one hundred or more people forms around the perimeter of the dance floor. The line comprises primarily men, who are at the beginning of the line, followed by women and children at the end. Various men take turns leading the *dabkah* line and performing their own fancy variations. Throughout the party, the performance of spirited dancing seems to be almost an obligation of the celebrants in their public expression of joy for the couple.

The singer and musicians are an excellent match for this crowd, whose energy never wanes for even a moment of the long evening. During the *dabkah* segment, Mahmoud Beydoun summons from his memory or invents from his imagination verse after verse and song after song. His tireless singing is supported by Nadeem on *nay* and *mizmar,* Wa'el on the floor with the *tabl baladi,* and Ghassan Shaito, who through his synthesizer can imitate the timbre and tuning of nearly any Arab instrument. The drummers, one on trap drums with electronic pads and one on the traditional vase-shaped *darabukkah,* push the sound system to its limit. Although the musicians complain about the length of the wedding as we are packing up—we played for four and a half hours without a break—they nevertheless seem to enjoy themselves thoroughly as they launch one bomb of musical energy after another into the crowd. In addition to providing a menu of primarily Lebanese folk and pop music for their patrons, they have structured the progression of the evening from the ceremonial *zaffah* procession of the bridal party to the facilitation of kin-group dancing, accompanied by the important financial transaction of gift money to the bride and groom; and they have provided a kinesthetic climax with the long set of *dabkah* music, which is exciting even for those who choose to sit on the sidelines and watch.

Figure 4.5. Tabl Baladi player Wa'el Yazigi plays to the line of dabkah dancers at a Lebanese wedding.

Figure 4.6 Nadeem Dlaikan plays mizmar and Mahmoud Beydoun sings at a Lebanese wedding. Celebrants dance and enjoy themselves in the background; a boy gathers money that has fallen to the ground.

A YEMENI WEDDING PARTY

As we pull into the parking lot of the Crystal Palace Banquet Hall in South Detroit, Sammiah hurries me along, worried that we have already missed the *zaffah*, the initial procession of the bride and groom and their attendants into the public space of the party. Sammiah and her husband agreed to take me along to a Yemeni wedding, just the day before. I had naively anticipated an exotic traditional wedding in a private home, where men and women celebrated separately, each gender dancing their own dances to their own group of musicians. I worried about what to wear and whether to cover my head. I was aware that the Yemeni population in Detroit is considered the most conservative and staunchly Muslim. As we walk into the wedding, I am greeted by the familiar wedding party setting. Round tables, balloons, large platters of green beans, roast beef, chicken, and salad with Italian dressing, pitchers of orange pop and cola: American food at its most mediocre. There are more than three hundred guests in attendance, a typical size for a Detroit wedding party. All but one or two others, like myself, are Arab American, and the majority of these people are of Yemeni heritage. As I become more comfortable with the surroundings and with my new Yemeni-American friend, Sammiah, at my side, my perception sharpens.

Sammiah directs me to the "family side." Here men, women, and children sit together at tables. Women are variously dressed; many wear the traditional head scarf, yet others are attired in sleeveless, tight-fitting evening gowns. Sammiah has led me away from the men's side of the banquet hall. The celebrants on this side of the room are young men who have come to America along the trail of family connections to seek income for their families in Yemen.

At the front of the hall is an elaborately decorated tiered stage where the bride and groom will sit. In the front corner of the family side, a stage is set up for the Lebanese group, the Rana and Naim Band. In the corner of the men's side, the Yemeni band Afrah al-Yemen tunes up. Suddenly, the celebrants move toward the center aisle and crowd towards the door. I have been granted permission to photograph and videotape but am uncomfortable wielding the equipment through the dense crowd.

"Move closer, move up Anne, because you're missing a lot! Just push your way up!" encourages my companion Sammiah. Just then, a booming announcement penetrates the soundscape:

"And now will the beautiful bride and groom enter, they're going to do the *zaffah* with Rana and Naim."

Rana, a Lebanese American artist, is poised at the front of the procession that is about to ensue. She announces the entrants with a traditional wedding song from her country. With her powerful controlled alto voice, Rana belts out the melismatic, nonmetric melody, called *mawwal,* which serves as an introduction to the song that will bring the celebrants into the public space of the party. Naim, Rana's husband and partner, stands behind her, supporting her song on his instrument, the *'ud.* As they lead the procession of bride and groom, bridesmaids, groomsmen, and children and family members, Rana and Naim continue their performance. They work with remote mikes, somehow communicating tempos and transitions through the dense crowd to the rest of the band members, who remain on their stage back in the corner of the hall. As Rana escorts the couple down a sinuous imaginary path between the family side and the men's side of the hall, she sings, claps, and dances with the handsome but naturally shy couple. Two belly dancers, who have been hired especially for this ceremonial *zaffah* procession, assist the musicians by dancing with and around the members of the bridal party. Meanwhile, Naim performs crowd management, directing people in the *zaffah* line, encouraging them to approach the dance floor at the front, all the while playing *'ud.* The celebrants crowd around the couple. Money is tossed into the air and later collected and counted. As soon as there is a critical mass on the dance floor and all the key players of the wedding party are dancing, Rana and Naim "work the tables," greeting the guests, who don't make it to the front, in song. Perhaps twenty or twenty-five minutes after the onset of the *zaffah*, Rana has woven her way through all of the tables on the family side of the hall. Rana and Naim then join the newly married couple on a special tiered stage, where they will sit on thronelike chairs with their "court" of about a dozen child bridesmaids. Rana and Naim wave to all before they leave the couple alone and at the center of attention. In a gesture of closure, the musicians exit the hall, taking the same path the bridal party had traveled during the *zaffah*. There is a break in the action, but their work for the evening is hardly over.

Throughout the rest of the evening Rana and Naim (who bill their music as "Arabic Pop") share the party with Afrah al-Yemen, a group of three young Yemeni men who constitute the only regularly working ensemble of Yemeni musicians in Detroit. Their main singer, Abd al-Nour, plays the *'ud*, the other two play *darabukkah* and bongo drums. As they play their traditional music on the men's side of the banquet room, the men alone dance a graceful line-dance; sometimes they break off into couples and, while supporting each other by grasping their arms, plunge down to the ground and spring back up again without missing a beat (CD Track 7).

The repertoire of Afrah al-Yemen is distinct from that of the Rana and Naim band. The melodies and rhythms they play are Yemeni, their vocal timbre is tight and nasal, their Yemeni dialect and accent different than the pan-Levantine Arabic one hears in much of Detroit. Rana and Naim comment later, while we sit together listening to Afrah al-Yemen, that they understand little of this music. "It sounds like they're just playing the same rhythm all night long," one comments. Although both bands at the party play Arab

Figure 4.7. Afrah al-Yemen (left to right: Mufaddal Yaser, Sal Najar, and 'Abd al-Nour), the only regularly working band of Yemeni Americans, plays on the men's side of the banquet hall. Large rolling video cameras like the one pictured in front are a standard feature at weddings in Arab Detroit.

music, their repertoire comes from two related but very different Arab musical languages. That they are combined in the time and place of this party is worthy of explanation. The Yemeni families who celebrate the wedding have naturally sought out Yemeni music for this auspicious occasion. The band, Afrah al-Yemen, is positioned on the men's side of the hall, and provides the sonic environment for the most traditionally Yemeni aspects of this community of celebrants. The Lebanese and Arab popular music that Rana and Naim perform might be referred to as the musical *lingua franca* of Arab American Detroit. Their songs and musical style are the most commonly heard music in the area. The *zaffah* they lead is beautiful and exciting. Although very few of the hundreds attending this party are Lebanese, they seem to enjoy both styles, and switch between the musical and cultural codes of Yemeni and Lebanese performance.

AN IRAQI-ITALIAN WEDDING PARTY

This evening I am at an exquisite banquet hall in the northern suburbs of Detroit, at the invitation of Majid Kakka and the Bells Band, whose three members, manager, and combination soundman/"roadie"/disc-jockey are of Iraqi heritage. The Bells Band shares the stage with an Italian band whose front man, Pino Marelli, hails from Italy. Among the guests are, not surprisingly, a number of Americans of both Iraqi and Italian heritage. The Detroit Iraqi community is clustered in the Northern Suburbs and is generally quite well off, although there are numerous refugees of the Iran-Iraq and Gulf wars who are less financially stable. The majority of Iraqi Americans in the Detroit area are Caldean (also Chaldean), and their religion is an ancient form of Catholicism. The Italian contingent at the wedding are also Catholic. An Italian-Iraqi mixed marriage makes "sense," one musician told me because their religions are compatible—"both are a brand of Catholicism."

Like the Yemeni community, people of Iraqi heritage in Detroit have unique cultural "products." For example, in addition to the Arabic language, Caldeans speak neo-Aramaic—Aramaic being the language that is believed to have been spoken by Jesus Christ. As a result, contemporary Iraqi music features a repertoire of songs and lyrics that are specifically Caldean as well as rhythms and dances that are completely distinct from the Lebanese/Egyptian traditional and popular music that forms the main staple of Arab music culture in Detroit. Although Iraqis take great pride in the ancient roots of their language and culture, their music is, ironically, the most "modern-sounding" and technically "hip." Very few young Iraqi musicians use any traditional instruments. Rather they represent the sounds of traditional instruments with keyboard synthesizers, drum machines, and sampling devices (CD Track 8).

Unlike Yemeni music, which remains on the margins of the Detroit music scene, the distinctive Iraqi branch of Arab American music is beginning to enter the local musical mainstream. The growing popularity of Iraqi music and dance may be attributed in part to the large number of Iraqis here but also to the fact that these folks are good patrons: they have money to spend on music and dance events for which musicians are hired. As one American-born musician of Palestinian heritage told me: "You've got to play Iraqi [music]. Everybody plays Iraqi. If you don't play Iraqi you starve." My friend's comments reflect the fact that Iraqis pay the piper, as it were, and that the music played by musicians is in part controlled by the audiences and organizations that they serve.

On this particular evening, the Bells Band has already played for the *zaffah* procession as well as performed a set of dance music featuring primarily Iraqi songs with a smattering of mainstream Arab music thrown in. The Bells' front man, Majid Kakka, plays three keyboards, sings, and controls the band's impressive rolling rack of computer and digital technology. Kakka is flanked on either side by two fellow musicians, both of whom play electronic drum pads. Acting as a kind of operations manager, a young man named P-Nice, also of Iraqi heritage, is responsible for getting all of the equipment to the gig, setting it up, running sound, and spinning discs during the band's breaks. While the Bells Band played and P-Nice worked off stage, the wedding guests, holding hands and in a line formation, danced a bouncing Iraqi *dabkah* dance, as well as regular Oriental-style or belly dancing in groups or couples.

But now the energy has shifted. Pino Marelli (on tour from Italy) and his six-piece band are playing a set that includes Italian hits, the *tarantella*, American favorites, and now the ridiculous and fun "chicken dance," in which the participants intermittently act like chickens flapping their wings while moving in a circular procession. The Bells Band, now on break, and myself are hanging out at the side of the stage enjoying the action and the setting. The hall is splendidly appointed. A huge ice sculpture graces the cake table; the cake itself looks like a miniature palace. The dessert table is laden with fruits and *petit fours*. Dinner included seafood and steak and the guests have enjoyed an open bar all night.

I have been captivated by the Iraqi, Italian, Catholic, and American array of expressive culture—music, dance, food, prayer, language, and gesture—that has evolved over the evening. As I try to take in the commentary of my hosts combined with all that I observe, an ethnographic moment occurs that seems to summarize the multicultural essence of this exhilarating scene.

Suddenly, there is a power outage. Pino's sound goes dead. Dancers on the floor gasp but continue to frolic about as we are well into the party. P-Nice checks the Bells' sound on the right side of the stage. Their equipment checks out. The Bells go into standby mode. Then, Pino's sound is back on. "Come on everybody! Let's continue with the Chicken Dance!" calls Pino. But, as soon as the dancing celebrants begin to flap and squawk, the power is out on Pino's side once again.

At this moment, P-Nice springs into action, headphones around his neck, one phone to his ear as he cues up two vinyl discs on twin turntables. He teases the audience with the summer's salsa-flavored hit "Hot! Hot! Hot!" P-Nice scratches the mix and eases into the introduction of another hit of that summer, "Rhythm of the Night." As if they had been rehearsing for weeks, the dance floor shrieks with delight and a wave of free-form disco dancing ensues. P-Nice is in his world, mixing and scratching, choosing up new discs for the rest of his set. But just as the dancers are in the groove of "The Rhythm of the Night," the power comes on again on Pino's side of the stage and the band is up and running. The rhythm reverts to the square and corny chicken dance. The crowd happily complies and continues partying to Pino Marelli's selection of Italian-flavored and international hits. Later the Bells Band steps into the limelight for a last set of their exciting, digitized ethnic sound (CD Track 8).

These three scenes evoke the sound of Arab America in Detroit, all of it virtually invisible to mainstream America. Weddings are the mainstay of a professional musician's livelihood, especially during the summer months when there may be five or six every weekend. Musicians are not only the artistic specialists of their community, they are also cultural and ritual specialists. Through their sound, they provide a regionally specific cultural language that gives meaning and emotional impact to community gatherings. Through the ways in which they arrange their performance, they structure the time of the wedding celebration ritual by directing the sequence of events and the corresponding actions of the participants. In the next two sections of this chapter, we will look at contexts for musical performance that bring together Arabs from all nations, religions, regions, and socioeconomic classes of Detroit in ecumenical events organized by multicultural committees that are interested in presenting Arab American culture.

AN AFTERNOON AT THE ARAB WORLD FESTIVAL

This afternoon we are enjoying a midwestern heat wave in downtown Hart Plaza where the Arab World Festival takes place every summer as part of a series of weekend ethnic festivals in downtown Detroit. The festival has been organized every year since the early 1970s by an ad hoc committee of community members who take an interest in Arab American arts and social causes in general. The festival is free, open to the public, and eminently accessible, and several thousand people, from the Arab American community and the general public, are in attendance today. This year's festival opened ceremoniously with a few words from Detroit and Dearborn politicians and from Muslim and Christian religious leaders of the Arab American community. In the course of the afternoon we are treated to a fashion show featuring traditional Arab dress as well as performances by two dance troupes. One of the troupes comprises about twelve Arab American young men and women wearing coordinated costumes of shiny gold and black fabric. To the accompaniment of recorded music, they dance fancy choreographed variations of a folk dance, the *dabkah*. The second dance troupe, which consists of mostly non–Arab American women, presents solo and group "Oriental" dances. The crowd seems to enjoy everything.

Part of the fun of the Arab World Festival is to wander around and visit the many booths and tables that are set up and around this cement urban fairgrounds. The Arab World Festival also brings great visibility to businesses, social organizations, and clubs, which have set up booths where one may purchase Arabic food and products imported from Arab countries, or simply pick up information about the services available in the community.[3]

Musicians view this as an excellent venue for both established and emergent bands. The singers who are featured in the much-coveted evening time slots are greeted with the cheers and applause of a crowd that matches—in size and volume—that of a rock concert. When evening falls, thousands descend on Hart Plaza and it seems that at least that many crowd toward the front of the performance space to dance and be a general part of the action. The concentration of people (from the newly arrived grandmother who speaks nary a word of English to the wealthy, smartly dressed plastic surgeon), the loud music (pop and urbanized folk music from the Arab world), and the boisterous dancing (usually by young folks who dance variations of the *dabkah*) combine to supercharge the atmosphere of the event with the collective current of the Arab American community.

Today the notion of unity and diversity is honored not only by the myriad groups who participate but also by their musical repertoires and, in some cases, the particular songs that are chosen to represent and recognize all groups. Singers, who are able to perform songs from a variety of countries, carefully string together a medley of songs from Iraq, Egypt, Lebanon, Jordan and so forth. Today, however, one singer, a popular performer at the Arab World Festival, revises the lyrics of "*Ya Saree Saralay*," a Jordanian song about the happiness of the wedding night, to welcome each subset of the Arab community.

Lubnan baladna, Beirut 'asimitna	Lebanon is our country, Beirut is our capital
Filistine baladna, al-Quds 'asimitna	Palestine is our country, Jerusalem is our capital
Urdun baladna, Amman 'asimitna	Jordan is our country, Amman is our capital
Al-Yemen baladna, Sana'a 'asimitna	Yemen is our country, Sana'a is our capital

As they hear the vocalist sing out the names of their countries and capital cities, each section of the crowd cheers and waves.

While Yemeni, Palestinian, Lebanese, Syrian, Egyptian, Jordanian, and Iraqi populations may remain relatively endogamous in their private and professional lives, they *will* come into contact with one another through such civic organizations as the school system and events as the Arab World Festival, at which presumably all sections of the community are represented. The unified Arab world, however, may exist for only a fleeting moment of the festival. In general, Arab Americans, even those who describe themselves as completely Americanized, tend to derive their identity from the unique cultural qualities of their national, regional, and religious heritage rather than from the collective and expansive notion of the Arab world. Music in Detroit references these cultural differences with elegant precision. With respect to Arab American culture in general and music specifically, the Detroit area is in fact unique in its ability to support so many Arab musical subcultures.

FANN WA TARAB: A CELEBRATION OF ARAB AMERICAN ART, MUSIC, AND POETRY

This afternoon we are gathered in a lovely atrium in downtown Detroit's premier art museum, the Detroit Institute of Arts. Waiters serve us wine, and we choose from a colorful variety of Middle Eastern appetizers and snacks. The trickle of the fountain combines with the polite conversation and excited chatter of the eclectic crowd. Several hundred people have already toured a special exhibit in one of the museum's galleries and are now eager to meet and congratulate the six Arab American artists whose paintings are on display. Members of the Detroit arts world, politicians, and Arab American community leaders and their families seat themselves in informal configurations at the iron tables in the atrium or mill about enjoying the refreshments before the concert begins.

　　Attendance at this event is open to the public for the ticket price of twenty-five dollars; the audience seems select. "*Fann wa Tarab,* A Celebration of Arab American Art, Music and Poetry" has been in the planning for more than a year. In this case, the patronage behind the event does not come from a Lebanese or Iraqi family group but from an ecumenical, voluntary civic organization of artists and patrons called the Arab American Arts Council. An excerpt from the sixteen-page program booklet illuminates the mission of the council and sets the tone of the evening.

> Hoping to stimulate creativity and insight, the Council showcases the classical, folk, and contemporary Arab arts in unconventional contexts, for culturally diverse audiences. The Council cultivates young talent and ancient art forms alike. It supports local writers, visual artists, and musicians by encouraging arts programming of the highest quality. The Council also strives, through a variety of collaborative programs, to bridge the distance between Arab

American artists and the larger arts community of Metro Detroit and beyond.

The Arab American Arts Council was created under the auspices of the Cultural Arts Program of ACCESS, the Arab Community Center for Economic and Social Services. The Cultural Arts Program of ACCESS, for many years under the directorship of Sally Howell, has worked to recognize master musicians in the community by commissioning their performance and collaboration for special events. ACCESS's Cultural Arts Program regularly brings in guest artists from other parts of the country and sponsors formal concerts of traditional music and musical fusion projects. ACCESS has organized teaching workshops, research and fieldwork projects, lecture series, and exhibitions. Through all of these activities, and many others, ACCESS aims to bring together various factions of the local Arab American community and non-Arab Americans that might naturally remain separate. Such efforts in Arab cultural arts programming stand in sharp relief to the "natural life" of the music scene in Detroit, which is largely driven by popular and folk music, in the context of private family celebrations, nightclubs, or parties.

The festive reception comes to an abrupt finish, and we are encouraged to take our assigned seats in the adjacent theater. Formal announcements precede a thirty-minute poetry reading by David Williams, who is of Lebanese heritage. Finally, seven musicians, clad in tuxedos, take their seats in a semicircle on the small stage. The selection of Arab classical, traditional, and "serious popular" music has been carefully planned and rehearsed under the authoritative guidance of the New York artist Simon Shaheen, an extremely accomplished and well-respected Arab American who is the premier guest artist of the evening. With the exception of the vocalist, Ghada Ghanem, also visiting from New York, the other musicians have been hand picked by the patrons of the event. All of the musicians are profiled in the program with a biographical paragraph and flattering photograph. Of the perhaps 150 professional musicians in Detroit's Arab American community, these men are considered the most seasoned and the most capable of playing serious music of, in the words of the Arts Council statement quoted above, "the highest quality."

The program proceeds as planned, with the exception perhaps of an encore. The audience, a combination of musical connoisseurs and newcomers to the "Arab sound," responds with enthusiastic appreciation. Although the exuberant dancing, singing, and clapping of the wedding parties and the festival described above is absent, members of the audiences may be heard offering vocal kudos of praise, especially during the long solo improvisations, *taqasim*, which are a hallmark of Arab traditional music performance. For many of those who attend this event, including the musicians, the serious, formal presentation of Arab arts—music, poetry, and painting—is a great source of pride. Normally Arab American musicians depend on the demand of public audiences from within their own ethnic community; the opportunities to formally rehearse a program of serious music for an attentive audience are few. In fact, most of these opportunities come from ACCESS, which has booked these musicians for similar concerts in the past.

The patronage of ACCESS differs in a number of ways from the hiring of musicians by families, nightclubs, and community groups. Cultural programs at ACCESS are carefully conceived and organized. They are always funded in part by moneys from such granting agencies as the National Endowment for the Arts or the Lila Wallace Reader's Digest Foundation, groups that support the arts and artists throughout the country. In order to receive such funds, ACCESS must submit carefully written grant applications describing its plans to present Arab American arts and artists. The application process is fiercely competitive and the language of a grant application must reflect clear vision and purpose. Often, in order to convince granting agencies of the merit of their proposed programs, letters of support are solicited from artists, politicians, cultural leaders, and academics from throughout the country who are thought to be familiar with the people and the arts involved. Because outside supporters have the appropriate credentials, their opinions are usually respected. While it may be unfair to generalize about granting agencies, they tend to fund projects that showcase arts that are considered traditional, classical, or new works. "Pop" music is usually disqualified.

Official support, both financial and moral, for Arab American music fills an important gap in the patronage structure of Arab American musical life. Whereas in the home countries of Arab Americans and other immigrant communities, their music and musicians had the support of local conservatories, theaters, universities, and radio and television stations in the United States, support for their art by such institutions is rare if at all. Thus the health of their musical culture depends to a large extent on the multicultural programming efforts of such agencies as ACCESS and the support of foundations.

There is some irony in this mix because the musicians themselves are rarely involved in the fundraising process. Owing perhaps to their limited language skills, or simply the natural cultural gap between their culture and mainstream America, musicians located in subcultures do not speak the same language as the agencies that might be able to help them the most. Instead, such cultural agents as folklorists, anthropologists, and ethnomusicologists serve as liaisons between the music and the money. In fact, although there may be very little academic prestige attached to work within the public sector (as opposed to pure research and scholarly publication), many people trained in these fields, including perhaps some of the authors of this book, believe that bringing "subcultural" artists into the limelight of mainstream America is our most significant mission.

CONCLUSIONS

What are some of the issues that emerge from the consideration of Arab American music culture that resonate with and extend to other subcultural music scenes in the United States? As mentioned at the outset, Arab American musical culture is in and of itself multicultural and multifaceted. Distinctions, both obvious and subtle, are a feature of many and perhaps all American communities, and it is through music, dance, food, and language that such distinctions are often articulated. In order to "read" social, cultural, and aesthetic issues in music and dance events, it is important to know something of the specific history and contemporary life of the people involved. For immigrant groups, understanding patterns of immigration to the United States, as well as settlement and migration within the country, is crucial to understanding the evolution, flowering, or withering of a particular music scene.

Individual musicians, who both look to their own musical heritage as well as to the artistic currents of the "host" culture in the creation of an expressive voice, have phenomenal impact on the construction and activation of community through performance. By extension, the patronage of sociocultural organizations—from the family to grass roots community centers, religious institutions, and even the national government—directs the path of musical life within a community as they support some artists and art forms and ignore others. It is because of these multitudinous variations in music patronage that some of the activities of a particular musical subculture, such as the neighborhood street fair or the multicultural arts festival, may be easily visible and of great interest to the American mainstream, while others, such as the family wedding, remain completely invisible and/or irrelevant.

It is also important to note that for Arab Americans or, for that matter, any community, the contemporary place of mass media—including, at first, 78 rpm discs and, later, radio, television, records, cassettes, videotapes, and cable television—plays a huge role in collapsing distance between peoples within the same cities, among communities across the country, and between nations separated by oceans, political boundaries, and government travel bans. The idea that culture is something that is grounded in geographical space is completely irrelevant when it comes to issues of expressive culture.

Whether recorded or live, music moves people to different times and places and is thus one of the most compelling agents in the definition of community and individual identity. In the course of a decade-long involvement with musicians and audiences of the Arab American community, I too have been powerfully affected by the sound and spirit of their musical performance. As is the case with any ethnographer, I bring to my work a unique and selective perspective that is dependent on my relationships with friends and consultants in the community and what I have experienced in the process of research and fieldwork. While I may be able to interpret and describe some aspects of this musical subculture, I no doubt remain ignorant of others.

In this chapter, I have attempted to highlight some of the issues that are central to an understanding of the musical life of Arab Americans and the relationship of this musical subculture to music culture of the United States as a whole. Furthermore, I believe that such issues—the power of performance, the initiative of individuals, the relationship of musical performance to ritual structure and social process, the effects of patronage, an understanding of community history, a consideration of mass media, and the rich experience and inevitable limitations of ethnographic fieldwork—are also germane to the consideration of the nearly infinite musical microcosms that constitute our American musical landscape.

NOTES

1. This chapter reflects research and relationships that have been ongoing since 1987. For this particular project I am indebted to many musicians, community members, and colleagues in the Detroit Dearborn area. Among them I thank Pete Arabo, Mahmoud Beydoun, Nadeem Dlaikan, Naim and Rana Homaidan, Sally Howell, Mahsin and Samia al-Jabri, Majid Kakka, Maher Mejdi, Saleh Najar, 'Abd al-Nur, Ghassan Shaito, Andrew Shryock, Wa'el Yazigi, and Mufadel Yaser. Fieldwork focusing specifically on weddings in Arab Detroit was carried out during the summers of 1993 and 1994 and was supported in part by Michigan State University, which featured the expressive culture of Arab weddings at the 1996 Michigan Folklife Festival that was produced by the university.

2. The term *Arab world* was one used by former Egyptian president Gamal 'Abd al-Nasser, beginning in the 1950s. Arab world countries include (starting from eastern coast of North Africa): Mauritania, Morocco, Algeria, Tunisia, Libya, Egypt, Sudan, Jordan, Lebanon, Syria, Iraq, Kuwait, Saudi Arabia, Yemen, Djibouti, Somalia, Oman, United Arab Emirates, Bahrain, and Qatar.

3.The number of clubs and social organizations in the Arab American community is overwhelming. There are church groups and groups from Islamic centers. (It should be mentioned that although there are significant numbers of Arab Americans of the Jewish faith, very few of them live in the Detroit area). Some groups have political agendas and others provide medical or translation services. Some are based around an activity—such as *dabkah* dancing, others around a common affiliation with a region. Some Arab American Organizations—such as the Ramallah Club—have branches throughout the United States and hold huge annual weekend conventions for thousands of people who trace their roots to the Palestinian town of Ramallah. When these clubs and social organizations hold events—often fundraisers—they can be an excellent source of patronage for musicians. *The Palestine Democratic Youth Organization, the Union of Lebanese Women, the American Islamic Institute, the Arab-American Chaldean Council, Beit Hanina Social Club,* and *the Syrian American Council of North America* are just a few of the clubs that might establish a presence at the Arab World Festival. Numerous and varied businesses sell their wares, from calligraphy, to insurance, to *tabouleh* (a delicious salad made with bulgur wheat, parsley, and tomatoes).

COMPANION CD SELECTIONS

Track 5. An excerpt of a 78-rpm recording from the early 1900s. Moses Cohen, vocalist; Naim Karakand, violinist; and an unnamed qanun player, "Ma Hadi Zayeh" (No one was ever so distressed).

Track 6. Rana and Naim Homaidan and the author perform Lebanese folk genres 'Ataba, Mijana, and 'Ala Daluna. Rana's family is heard clapping, dancing, and singing along in this spontaneous afternoon performance in their living room.

Track 7. A brief excerpt of the Yemeni America group Afrah al-Yemen performing at a wedding during the summer of 1994. Group members include vocalist 'Abd al-Nur and Saleh Najar and Mufadal Yaser on percussion.

Track 8. A brief excerpt of the Iraqi-American group the Bells Band at a wedding during the summer of 1995. Majid Kakka is the group's director, lead singer, and keyboard player. Salam Kakka and Johny Sana are on percussion synthesizers.

REFERENCES CITED

Davis, Ruth. 1992. The Effects of Notation on Performance Practice in Tunisian Art Music. *The World of Music* 34, no. 1.

Hoogland, Eric, ed. 1987. *Crossing the Waters: Arabic-Speaking Immigrants to the United States before 1940*. Washington, D.C., and London: Smithsonian Institution Press.

Marcus, Scott. 1989. Arab Music Theory in the Modern Period. Ph.D. Diss., University of California, Los Angeles.

Marcus, Scott L. 1992. Modulation in Arab Music: Documenting Oral Concepts, Performance Rules and Strategies. *Ethnomusicology* 36, no. 2: 171–96.

Naaf, Alexa. 1985. *Becoming American: The Early Arab Immigrant Experience.* Carbondale, Ill.: Southern Illinois University Press.

Racy, Ali Jihad. 1991. Creativity and Ambiance: An Ecstatic Feedback Model from Arab Music. *The World of Music* 33, no. 3: 7–28.

Racy, Ali Jihad. 1981. Music in Contemporary Cairo: A Comparative Overview. *Asian Music* 13, no. 1: 4–26.

Rasmussen, Anne K. 1996. Theory and Practice at the "Arabic Org": Digital Technology in Contemporary Arab Music Performance. *Popular Music 15, no. 3: 345–65.*

Rasmussen, Anne K. 1992. "An Evening in the Orient": The Middle Eastern Nightclub in America. *Asian Music* 23, no. 2, (spring–summer): 63–88.

Rasmussen, Anne K. 1991. Individuality and Musical Change in the Music of Arab Americans. Ph.D. Diss. University of California, Los Angeles.

Schuyler, Philip. 1990. Hearts and Minds: Three Attitudes toward Performance Practice and Music Theory in the Yemen Arab Republic. *Ethnomusicology* 34, no. 1: 1–18.

El-Shawan Castelo-Branco, Salwa. 1984. Traditional Arab Music Ensembles in Egypt since 1967: The Continuity of Tradition within a Contemporary Framework. *Ethnomusicology* 28, no. 2: 271–88.

Touma, Habib Hassan. 1996. *The Music of the Arabs.* Expanded ed., with compact disc. Translated by Laurie Schwartz. Portland, Ore.: Amadeus Press.

Vigreux, Pierre, ed. 1989. *Musique Arabe: Le Congrès du Caire.* Proceedings of colloquium on the documents of the First Congress on Arab Music in Cairo, 1932, held in Cairo, May, 1989, under the direction of Sheherezade Qassim Hassan. Cairo: CEDEJ.

RECORDINGS, MUSIC, AND RECORDING ARTISTS

el-Bakkar, Mohammad. 1957. *Port Said: Music of the Middle East.* Mohammed el-Bakkar and his Oriental Ensemble. Audio Fidelity AFSD 5833.

el-Bakkar, Mohammad. 1958. *The Magic Carpet: Music of the Middle East.* Vol. 4. Audio Fidelity AFSD 5895.

"Caravan." 1937. Composed by Juan Tizol and Duke Ellington, words by Irving Mills.

Elias, Fred. n.d. *Artistic Moods for Dance.* Vol. 2. Ultrasonic IS-2003.

Gabriel, Peter. 1989. *Passion: Music for the Last Temptation of Christ.* Geffen CD 24206–2.

Haza, Ofra. 1988. *Fifty Gates of Wisdom: Yemenite Songs.* Shanachie (World Beat/Ethno Pop) 64002.

Kochak, Eddie "the Sheik." 1970s. *Strictly Belly Dancing: Volumes 1–6.* Ameraba 2500 series.

The Music of Arab Americans: A Retrospective Collection. Forthcoming 1997. A collection of performances by Arab American artists originally recorded on 78-rpm disc. Research and production by Anne K. Rasmussen. Rounder Records.

Page, Jimmy and Robert Plant. 1994. *No Quarter (Unledded).* Atlantic 2 CD 82706–2.

"Palesteena." 1918. Composed by Con Conrad and Jay Russel Robinson. Introduced by the Original Dixieland Jazz Band and popularized by Eddie Cantor.

Passion Sources. 1989. [Music by various artists from India, Africa, and the Middle East used as source material for the soundtrack for *The Last Temptation of Christ,* compiled by Peter Gabriel.] Real World Carol 2301–2.

ADDITIONAL SOURCES

Abraham, Sameer Y., and Nabeel. 1983. *Arabs in the New World: Studies on Arab-American Communities.* Detroit: Wayne State University Press, Urban Studies Center.

Ahmad, Ismael and Nancy Adadow Gray, eds. 1988. *The Arab American Family: A Resource Manual for Human Service Providers.* Detroit: ACCESS (Arab Community Center for Economic and Social Services) and Department of Social Work, Eastern Michigan University.

Fa'ik Ala. 1994. Issues of Identity In Theater of Immigrant Community. *The Development of Arab-American Identity,* ed. Ernest McCarus. Ann Arbor: University of Michigan Press. 107–18.

Hitti, Philip. 1924. *Syrians in America.* New York: George Doran.

Kayal, Philip M., and Joseph M. Kayal. 1975. *The Syrian-Lebanese in America: A Study in Religion and Assimilation.* Boston: Twayne Publishers.

McCarus, Ernest. 1984. *The Development of Arab-American Identity.* Ann Arbor: University of Michigan Press.

CHAPTER 5

"Pan Is We Ting"

West Indian Steelbands in Brooklyn[1]

Gage Averill

Gage Averill paints an exciting picture of the music, dance, food, and language of Caribbean New York. This chapter concentrates on the life of steelbands in Brooklyn as they practice and prepare for performances in competitions at the annual Labor Day Carnival parade. Looking back to colonial Trinidad, Averill traces the development of the steel drum, or pan, and the creation of a repertoire and context for its use in performance. Like many multicultural American musics, the establishment of an ensemble in this country begins with a handful of innovative individuals who possess the expertise to construct and tune the various pans in an ensemble. Today, for youth of Caribbean heritage in Brooklyn, nearly all of whom are American born, steelbands are rich institutions of art, culture, and mutual aid that demand rigorous rehearsal and specific musicianship skills from their players. Averill's interview with the directors of a Brooklyn-based Caribbean organization reveals the positive role steelband plays in giving members a sense of direction, self-esteem, and Caribbean identity—even in requiring members to do well in school and stay out of trouble. Averill, a musician and ethnomusicologist who lives and teaches in New York, has been deeply involved not only in fieldwork and research on steel drum but also in rehearsing in the panyards, judging at competitions, and bringing "Pandemonium," the university–based ensemble that he directs, into the ring of competition.

> We take an empty oil drum and we tune it
> Creating an instrument of beautiful music
> Whenever I hear a pan
> Ah feel so proud of my land
> Pan is we ting [thing], doh [don't] stop jamming.

—"Pan In Yuh Pan," Dennis "Merchant" Williams, 1993

Leaving a record store that prominently advertises (and loudly plays) West Indian recordings (soca, calypso, reggae, dancehall) alongside Haitian *compas,* I head over to the travel agency on the opposite corner of Flatbush Avenue that specializes in booking discount charter flights to Trinidad's Carnival. Around the block, one can stock up on salt fish for *accra,* a kind of fried spicy fish cake, and *dasheen* bush for the popular Trinidadian stew called *callaloo.* Haitian Creole, Jamaican patois, and various inflections of Eastern-Caribbean English are the languages and dialects that rule the street and shops in this neighborhood, where men and women have gathered in small groups to *lime* (hang out and chat) in the early evening. It is still two weeks before Brooklyn's Labor Day Carnival, but banners already flutter over Flatbush Avenue proclaiming the names and locations of nearby Mas' Camps where the Carnival costumes are made. On side streets throughout the neighborhood are parking lots that have been transformed into temporary steelband panyards.

Well away from New York's better-known Latin Caribbean barrios like Loisada (the Lower East Side) and El Barrio (Spanish Harlem), the West Indian and Haitian districts of Brooklyn—concentrated in the Flatbush, East Flatbush, Crown Heights, and Bedford-Stuyvesant neighborhoods—have some of the highest immigrant populations of any area in the country.[2] This fact of cultural geography is partly responsible for the emergence of steel pan as one of the most important instruments in Brooklyn's multicultural instrumentarium. Featuring large ensembles with loud instruments, Brooklyn's outdoor panyards provide little rest for their neighbors during Carnival season, serving as noisy reminders of the presence of so many West Indians. In the North American media and popular culture, the pan has become an icon of Caribbean fun in the sun—an auditory symbol used to sell fruit juices and tropical vacations. The Brooklyn steelband movement, however, reflects a deliberate strategy to maintain cultural links to the Eastern Caribbean and to promote West Indian identity. Steel pan and the Carnival on Eastern Parkway are part of a set of transnational practices joining cultural systems in the Caribbean diaspora to those at home in an ongoing, dynamic fashion.[3]

This chapter examines the role played by pan and steelbands in the West Indian community in New York City. I was intrigued by the ways that steelbands construct ethnic solidarity, transmit values to younger generations, and serve as a locus for ongoing interaction and feedback between Brooklyn's West Indian diaspora and the island nations of the West Indies. My interest in these issues was in part a result of my seven years as a pannist, during which I have had sporadic interaction with the steelband movement in Brooklyn. In 1989 and 1990, I documented Carnival on video and spoke with organizers and Brooklyn Museum personnel. In 1991, I paraded with a Haitian band and videotaped the Carnival parade from inside the road march. The steelband that I directed at Wesleyan University, Wesleyan

Pandemonium, competed against a number of the Brooklyn steelbands at Lincoln Center in 1991 and returned to Lincoln Center to open for Trinidad's Trintoc Invaders in 1992. I served as a judge for the 1994 Brooklyn Panorama, an experience I wrote about in the steelband publication *Pan-Lime,* and I played *mas'* (took part in the costumed Carnival parade) in Trinidad that year. In 1996, I "beat" pan with the Silhouettes Steelband, preparing for the Panorama competition and *jouvay,* the early morning parade on Carnival Monday. I have also interviewed pannists and have continued to document Brooklyn Carnival and the panyards. These forms of participant-observation have helped to reveal otherwise inaccessible elements of the musical world in question and have given me some insight into the debates and even conflicts within the West Indian community over musical issues. The experience of preparing for the Panorama steelband competition in the panyards or of adjudicating the competition has involved me directly in the discourse about these events in ways that simple interviews and observation could never have, and these experiences served to deepen my own cross-cultural dialogue about West Indian music in the diaspora.[4]

WEST INDIANS IN BROOKLYN

West Indians have settled in New York City throughout the twentieth century, but migration reached new levels after American immigration laws were liberalized in 1965. There are no reliable statistics on the number of legal and illegal West Indian immigrants (and their children) residing in New York City or in the borough of Brooklyn, but by extrapolating from available census data, it might be assumed that this figure is larger than half a million for the city as a whole, with perhaps half of that number residing in Brooklyn.[5]

With so many West Indians in such a small urban area, businesses can prosper by catering to an exclusively West Indian clientele; this constitutes a disincentive to rapid acculturation. American race relations also play a role in the resistance to acculturative pressures. While West Indian Americans like Marcus Garvey or even Roy Innis have long been involved in the struggle of black peoples in North America and generally adhere to visions of black solidarity, they are also motivated to differentiate themselves from African Americans (a group that West Indians see as structurally disadvantaged in America) at the level of ethnicity in order to pursue the American dream as Caribbean Americans. Black West Indians have little reason to lose their accents or the other markers of cultural distinctiveness that confer on them a more generous reception by white America than they would have as "unmarked" African Americans.[6]

The first West Indian Carnival balls in New York were held in the 1920s in Harlem. When an outdoor parade was organized in 1947, the organizers chose to parade on Labor Day rather than before Lent to take advantage of the warm summer weather. The calypsonian "Lord Invader" (Rupert Grant) penned a 1950s calypso called "Labor Day" on the theme of this Carnival:

> Labor Day I felt happy
> Because I played Carnival in New York City . . .
> From 110th to 142nd, we had bands of every description . . .
> This is the first time New York ever had
> Carnival on the streets like Trinidad (Grant 1956)[7]

This parade on Seventh Avenue in Harlem was held annually until 1964, when the event sparked opposition from African American neighbors radicalized by the civil rights struggle and wary of the happy, festive image the parade projected. The Carnival idea persisted, however, and in 1969, organizers (later called the West Indian American Day Carnival Association) obtained a permit to parade on Eastern Parkway in the heart of the new West Indian neighborhood of Brooklyn.

Pan pioneer Ellie Mannette was invited to the United States in 1967 at the behest of Murray Narell, the father of famous pan soloist Andy Narell, to build and tune pans for inner city youth groups in New York City, and within five years, he had started over ten bands in the New York area.[8] Narell's idea was to use the steel pan to inspire African American and Caribbean American youth to get involved in positive activities and to help them to avoid gangs, drugs, and violence. Other bands were started by the first-generation of pannists in Trinidad and Tobago who had migrated to New York City in the 1960s and early 1970s. Silhouettes, Sonatas, and Moods were all organized in the early 1970s. By the 1980s, many of the bands had come so far in size and quality that they could perform the complex Carnival "Panorama" competition arrangements. Accordingly, a Panorama competition was added to Brooklyn's Labor Day Carnival in 1985.

Trinidad and Tobago's Carnival provides the model for diasporic West Indian Carnivals. Most Eastern Caribbean Carnival arts are recognized as having been developed in Trinidad and Tobago, but they have become something akin to a multi-island "lingua franca," a more embracing notion of West Indian identity in New York City.[9] As Mighty Sparrow sang in *"Mas'* in Brooklyn,"

> New York equalize you
> Bajan, Grenadian, Jamaican, tout moun [Creole: "everybody"]
> Drinkin' they rum, beatin' they bottle an' spoon
> Nobody could watch me and honestly say
> They don't like to be in Brooklyn on Labor Day (Francisco n.d.)

Sparrow hints that the leveling process comes both from without (from Americans who cannot distinguish between different island peoples) and from within (from the various groups sharing cultural features and celebrating together). This is not to deny a continuing struggle over the "national" character of the event; in response to demands of certain constituencies, a Friday night Jamaican reggae concert and a Thursday night Haitian concert were added in the late 1980s to the roster of official Carnival events.

Annual Carnival celebrations in Brooklyn are only one example of the seasonally accentuated ethnicity that is practiced by many ethnic groups in America. Seasonal ethnic holidays, such as St. Patrick's Day or Chinese New Year or Columbus Day, often feature the invented traditions of nostalgic immigrant communities. West Indians are at a distinct advantage in having a model at home of a seasonal event that is already a peak outpouring of local cultural expression (calypso, *soca*, masquerade, pan). Trinidad's Carnival is rich in the exploration of identity, community, hybridity, and social commentary, and it has proved to be a productive template for seasonal "ethnic" festivities throughout the West Indian diaspora. There are some characteristics that are unique to the diasporic festivals, including the pan-West Indian composition of the Carnival crowd and the summer schedule unrelated to the Catholic calendar. The three largest of these Carnivals are, in order of occurrence, Toronto's Caribana, London's Notting Hill Carnival, and Brooklyn's Labor Day Carnival, all of which take place within the span of a single month. This schedule of events has helped to create a West Indian Carnival "circuit" with opportunities for calypsonians, arrangers, costume designers, and other West Indian Carnival professionals to find work during Trinidad's off-season (see Manning 1990, 49).

Carnival arts play a special role in West Indian immigrant identity by virtue of the cathartic nature of the Carnival experience, allowing participants to *leggo* (let go) or to *breakaway* (lose control), to throw one's *hands in the air,* to *jump up* (join in the festivities), to *wine* the waist (to roll the waist and buttocks in a figure eight motion), to *get on bad,* or to improvise playful dancing that Trinidadians call *dingolay.* The terminology employed in the West Indies for this exuberant, bodily response and surrender of control is strikingly similar to that employed in Haiti and in Brazil (Averill 1994a). Calypsonian David Rudder has sung that calypso music is "a living vibration rooted deep within my Caribbean belly. Lyrics to make a politician cringe and turn a woman's body to jelly" (Rudder 1987). The same respect for the power of music is evident in Lord Kitchener's description of a Panorama crowd in "Pan Dingolay":

> People *jumping up*
> Oh Lord and don't want to stop
> Then as Cordettes start to play

And the whole place *breakaway*
A man say "On Earth
We done get our money's worth!" (Roberts 1990)

The hearing of pan music, calypso, and *soca* in New York is often described by West Indian immigrants in just such ecstatic terms. Their full-fledged participation in the experience, *jumping up* with the music or engaging in *breakaway,* invokes a compelling set of feelings and confirms for many of them their Caribbean identity at a profoundly affective level. These kinds of experiences are often overlooked in the literature on ethnicity and immigration, but I believe they play a critical role in easing the transition of West Indians to different social and cultural systems.

IN A BROOKLYN PANYARD

Members of *Silhouettes Steelband* trickle into the parking lot serving as a temporary panyard on Church Avenue in Brooklyn. Inside the gates, there are still cars left in spaces for long-term storage, but there is enough room to set up the band's racks, the mobile frames that carry the pans through the street and onto the stage. Many of these racks have plywood floors on which the pannists stand, but in others, the pannists walk directly on the ground. The stands are pulled by trucks through the streets and are wheeled on stage by hand.

A Miller Beer banner on the fence advertises the Silhouettes Steelband, but other than the banner, Miller's sponsorship extends only to giving the group beer to sell in the panyard. Without a major sponsor, the group must rely on its members to defray the costs of renting the panyard ($1,000 per month in this case), building and tuning the pans, building racks, buying tee-shirts, and paying the arranger's fee. Brooklyn's steelbands are not commercial enterprises. The pannists play for the love of music, for the thrill of competing against other bands, and for the camaraderie and socialization afforded by a panyard.[10] Here, as in Trinidad, yards serve as gathering spots, as "community centers" where neighborhood pannists and their friends hang out.

There is an undeniable fever for pan in the Brooklyn panyards. Pan's history and its role as a symbol of Caribbean hybridity and creativity help fuel this fever. The instrument known as a steel pan grew out of the yards in urban Trinidad where the poorer classes would prepare for Carnival masquerades and assemble in perambulating musical ensembles. Following the abolition of slavery in the English West Indies in 1834, Trinidadians of African descent helped to convert the European celebration of pre-Lenten Carnival into an Afro-Trinidadian emancipation celebration, replete with African style drumming ensembles, stick fighting, the carrying of burning cane, obscene Carnivalesque parodies, masquerades and stilt dancers, and the singing of topical calypsos. The colonial elite lashed out at this lower-class

jamet Carnival, a derogatory term deriving from the French *diametre*, referring to activity that took place outside the "diameter," or periphery, of proper behavior. The authorities banned many Afro-Trinidadian Carnival components in a series of ordinances in the mid to late nineteenth century that
culminated in the Carnival riot of 1881. Due to the prohibitions, Carnival
musicians replaced their drum ensembles with *tamboo bamboo* instruments,
using different lengths of bamboo tubes struck together and pounded on the
ground to produce tones. Business sponsorship of Carnival activities at the
turn of the century helped to advance the *"fancy mas'"* costume bands and to
move calypsonians onto the stages of commercial "tents" where they competed against each other prior to Carnival.

In the 1930s, *tamboo bamboo* bands began incorporating such
makeshift metal instruments as dust bins, pitch-oil pans, garbage-can lids,
and automotive-brake drums. Eventually, bands made entirely of steel instruments appeared on the Carnival scene. This process accelerated when it was
discovered in the late 1930s that multiple surfaces pounded out of the metal
pans could produce multiple pitches. When Carnival bands took to the
streets after World War II, simple melodies were beaten on these new instruments. Ellie Mannette of the Woodbrook Invaders steelband experimented
using fifty-five-gallon oil drums for this purpose, pounding down the bottom of the drum to produce a concave bowl that allowed additional space for
notes. Over the next couple of decades, more notes were added to the drums;
drums were joined together into sets that were differentiated from other
instruments by their ranges; and an orchestra took shape using a set of oil
drums as its raw material. The steelband spread quickly from Trinidad and
Tobago throughout the Eastern Caribbean. In the 1950s, pannists (formerly
looked on by the upper classes as disreputable *badjohns*) earned a level of
respectability. In fact, the colonial ministries even helped to institutionalize
and sponsor pan competitions and to export steelbands as cultural ambassadors for Trinidad and Tobago. Middle-class school boys (and later girls)
increasingly joined in and identified with the steelbands. With Trinidad's
independence came pan programs in the schools, the Panorama contest at
Carnival, and a pan component within the annual classically oriented
Trinidad and Tobago Music Festival.

Tonight in the panyard, the fruits of the technological development of
the steel pan are in full flower. A line of tenor pans occupies the front center
rack of the band; these pans carry the melody of the arrangement and,
despite their name, possess a soprano register. The tenors have a deep bowl,
a very shallow skirt, and approximately thirty noteheads raised from out of
the bowl for a range of approximately two and a half fully-chromatic octaves
[see Figs. 5.1 and 5.2]. The tenors, like all of the higher pans in the yard, have
been dipped in chrome to help preserve their tuning and to resist rust.
Arranged behind and to the sides of the tenors are a few rows of double

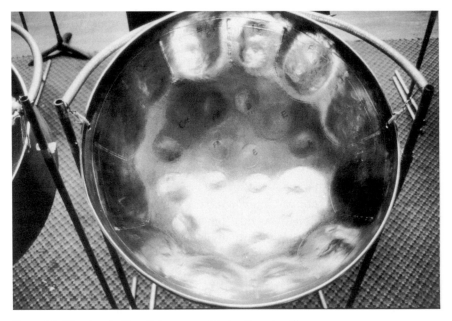

Figure 5.1. The view inside a D-tenor pan. Photo: Gage Averill.

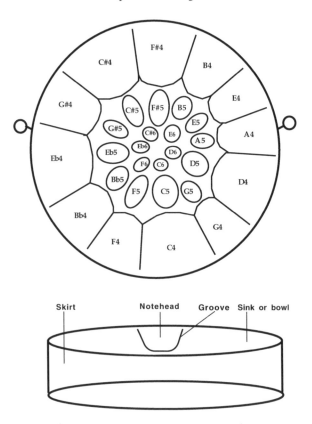

Figure 5.2. Diagram of the tuning and the basic construction of a C-tenor pan.

tenors and double seconds. These are sets of two pans together on a stand with ranges below that of a tenor. The double tenors primarily play harmonizations of the tenor lines, while the double seconds often "strum," hitting two notes on the pans in a rhythmic pattern to fill in the chords in the arrangements. Some lower pans, such as the double guitar pan and the quadraphonic, are also employed primarily in strum patterns. The quadrophonic has four pans, two of which are suspended vertically while the other two are hung horizontally. Bass pans, not surprisingly, carry the bass lines of the arrangements, usually reinforced by the cello pans. The cellos, consisting of low-pitched set of three and four pans—the latter often called a four-pan—can play countermelodies, bass lines, or strums. Basses have the longest "skirts" in order to help their low-pitched notes resonate; these pans are made from entire barrels, and they are arranged in sets of six, nine, or twelve. The "sticks" used to play all of these instruments are merely different lengths of wood and metal tubing with the ends wrapped in varying thicknesses of rubber. A glance at the sea of concave steel playing surfaces in any panyard will confirm that the little former colony of Trinidad and Tobago has succeeded in fashioning one of the world's largest and most complex orchestras. See Figure 5.3 for an example of the layout of the Brooklyn steelband *Pan Rebels* as they arrange themselves on the Panorama stage, and see CD track 9 for their version of "Fire Coming Down."[11]

In the *Silhouettes'* yard, all of the pans are already arranged in the moveable racks that will be rolled onto stage for Panorama. The engine room

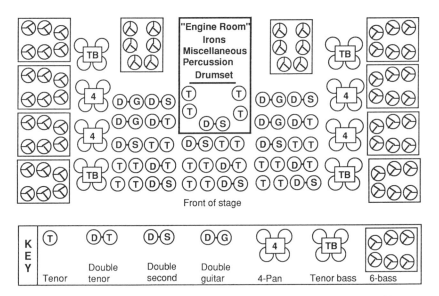

Front of stage

Figure 5.3. The layout of the *Pan Rebels Steelband* on the Panorama stage at Brooklyn Carnival, 1995. This arrangement allows for a heightened spatial awareness of the voices of a pan orchestra on the part of the audience without completely segregating the sections (which would produce an exaggerated stereophonic separation).

(drum set, congas, timbales, and scraped and shaken instruments that provide the band with its rhythmic propulsion) is clustered in the middle of the band. One of the chief instruments of the engine room is the iron, a humble automobile-brake drum struck with iron rods to provide an insistent clanging central to the orchestra's sound. In a steelband, it is the overall layered, composite sound of the engine room that is perceived by listeners as the "rhythm" [see Figs. 5.4, 5.5, and 5.6].

Figure 5.4. Typical hand-held instruments in the steelband engine room include the iron (brake drum), cowbells, scratcher (guëro), tambourine, and maracas. Photo: Gage Averill.

Figure 5.5. Members of the *Pan Rebels'* engine room performing at Carnival 1996. Photo: Gage Averill.

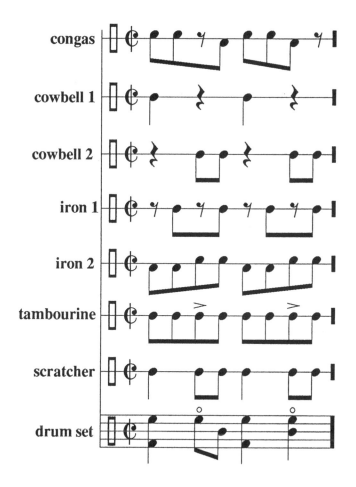

Figure 5.6. A possible layering of parts in the engine room for a *soca*-styled steelband arrangement. The two pitches in the conga transcription refer to the two conga drums (high- and low-pitched) played with mallets. For the drum set, I have chosen to show (from top to bottom of the staff) the high hat, snare, and bass-drum strokes. The small "o" over two of the strokes designates an open stroke on the high hat.

At this moment, the band's tuner, Mikey Enoch, is working on a set of guitar pans, using a small hammer to tighten the metal at the edge of one of the notes. Using a hand-held electronic tuning device, Enoch is "blending" the pan, meaning putting the overtones produced by each note in proper relationship to the fundamental tones and adjusting the loudness of each note to be in balance with the rest. A band's tuner is one of the most important figures in a steelband; in Panorama competitions, a certain percentage of the points are awarded solely on the basis of how well a band's pans are tuned.

The arrival of the band's arranger, Earl La Pierre, marks the start of the formal rehearsal. Many of the points awarded at Panorama are for the quality of arrangement and interpretation, so the work of the arranger is all-important. La Pierre has chosen one of the year's calypsos that adapts well to a steelband arrangement, "Mind Yuh Business," written by the Trinidadian arranger and pannist Len "Boogsie" Sharp (who is, himself, working on an arrangement of this same tune with the *Pan Rebels* a few blocks away). Panorama arrangements are based on commercial recordings by calypsonians that *must* receive airplay and be generally recognizable if the panorama arrangement is to have any chance of success. Without this prior exposure, an audience will be unable to follow the variations on the calypso that the arranger has built into his steelband arrangement. A week before Panorama, La Pierre has nearly completed the ten-minute, multi-part, orchestral arrangement using "Mind Yuh Business" as his raw material. Like all good Panorama arrangements, it is through-composed more or less; although individual sections sometimes repeat, the larger form continues to unfold throughout the piece without large-scale repetition. It begins with an original introduction, followed by a harmonization of the verse and chorus of the calypso. After the basic exposition of the calypso song form, there comes an extensive development section with variations of the calypso's verse and chorus, including a contrasting Latin section. The skill of the pannists is showcased in rapid, chromatic passages and in intricately syncopated strum patterns. La Pierre reprises some of the earlier material before concluding with a rhythmic, high-energy coda featuring pounding chords. Tonight, the double tenors and seconds are running through the introduction, which has a call-and-response dialogue with the basses. This short musical fragment for double tenors and seconds is included as Figure 5.7. Note the syncopation

Figure 5.7. The introduction, as played by the doubles (double tenors and double seconds), to Earl La Pierre's arrangement of Len "Boogsie" Sharpe's "Mind Yuh Business." Note the use of off-beat phrasing (especially the rests at the beginning of measure) characteristic of calypso and *socal* melodies. Each pannist, using two "sticks," is capable of playing two notes simultaneously, either in a single stroke or as a sustained roll. Rolls are shown here with double lines through the stems of the noteheads.

(off-beat accentuation) and the melodic phrasing that begins after the down-beat of the measure, both of which are common throughout this arrangement as they are to the genre of calypso as a whole.

For a winning panorama performance, the pans must be blended sweet-ly, the tune has to be popular and appropriate for pan, the arrangement has to sustain interest over ten minutes, and the playing must be precise and energizing. Tempi are extremely fast (cut-time markings of "half note=132 beats per minute" are not uncommon). In their size, density, and overall form, panorama compositions bear similarities to Western classical sym-phonic movements based on sonata-allegro form, although they draw from theme-and-variation form as well. These similarities to classical structures are not accidental; steelbands were performing pieces from the classical repertory as early as the 1950s, and classical music has exerted an influence on the Carnival competition treatments of calypsos ever since. Figure 5.8 is a short passage from the original arrangement to a 1994 Panorama perfor-mance of "Fire Coming Down," composed and arranged by Robert Greenidge. This is the same song (but in a different arrangement) as the audio example for this chapter. The arrangement starts off in the key of D, modulates to A, then to A minor, back to A major, and finally returns to the original key of D for a coda. The excerpt in Figure 5.8 is taken from the return to A major near the end of the composition. The top three voices—tenor, double tenor, and double second—provide the melody and harmonize it (this melodic motif is taken from the latter part of the verse of the original calypso). The guitar pans provide a syncopated harmonic grounding for the chord progression of B minor to A major. This arrangement was created and taught orally at first and later transcribed for publication (Greenidge 1994).

An arranger seldom comes to the first practice with an entire arrangement in his or her head. Instead, he or she will compose sections day by day, working ideas out with the pannists and revising them as needed. This challenges the memorization skills of even the most virtuosic pannists. Some pannists devise their own notation systems, such as listing the names of the notes in sequence, and some carry tape recorders to capture the complexities of the arrangment, but the most common means employed to memorize arrangements is simply to play them over and over. Anxious arrangers, however, have been known to rearrange extensive sections of the tune only days before the competition.

La Pierre moves over to the basses where he directs one of the players, "No, it's A to E, ba-dum-bum. You've got to hear the melody." From there he turns around, picks up the double tenor sticks and demonstrates the entire double part, and then returns to the middle of the band, taps on a drum to silence the players, and lectures them on stage presence. "I look around the band and I see everybody looking *so serious*. The whole band should be moving and having fun. You are performing, you are presenting something to the people, and you should be *enjoying* yourselves." In the same night, La Pierre composes new lines

Figure 5.8. A four-measure passage from "Fire Coming Down," composed and arranged by Robert Greenidge, transcribed by Steve Popernack, edited by Steve Popernack and Shelly Irvine. Copyright 1994 Ro Gree Publishing (ASCAP), all rights reserved. Published by Panyard, Inc., Akron, Ohio.

for the tenors; admonishes a pannist on his bad panyard manners; tries to lift the band's morale; and sings, talks, and demonstrates many of the instrumental parts. The role of a steelband arranger is, as one can see, extraordinarily complex and demanding in musical, organizational, and personal skills.

A small audience has collected inside the panyard, and they applaud the final two run-throughs of the piece (minus the two minutes of additional material that La Pierre still wants to write for the band). This rehearsal breaks at 11:00 P.M. in deference to the neighbors, but it will be repeated every night until Panorama.

BROOKLYN PANORAMA AND THE ROAD MARCH

In the cool Brooklyn night air, steelband racks roll into the enclosure behind the Brooklyn Museum while a calypsonian on stage sings "On the Parkway, we get down, On Labor Day Monday, we get down." Brooklyn Panorama, 1990. The arriving steelbands position themselves at different corners of the lot to do some last-minute practicing. The growing crowd samples the food for sale in the tents ringing the enclosure, including such West Indian delicacies as doubles, palourie, goat roti, and roasted corn, washing it all down with drinks like Carib beer, Malta, champagne cola, ginger beer, sorrel, and mauby.

The Brooklyn Panorama is a scaled-down version of the competition held at Carnival in Trinidad every February or March. In Trinidad, Panorama is the final stage of weeks of regional and semifinal competitions; eleven bands make it to the finals to compete for the title of Panorama champions on the stage at the Queen's Park Savannah in Port-of-Spain. In Brooklyn, however, there is only one competition with merely enough large orchestras, known as "conventional bands," for the finals [Figures 5.9 and 5.10]. Selected steelband performances at Brooklyn Carnival have been recorded since 1994 by a Brooklyn-based company, Basement Recordings, but these recordings do not have much commercial potential, at least not in the near future.[12] The stakes and media attention may be small in comparison to Trinidad—where an international satellite broadcast carries Panorama to various parts of the world—but New York area pannists take their competition very seriously.

First with its racks on stage is *C. A. S. Y. M. Steelband*, a young persons' steelband, under a banner that reads: "Drugs are a bust, education's a must." The tune is "Pan by Storm," by Professor Ken Philmore, and the banner gives the customary names of arranger, band captain, and tuner. The kids are in

Figure 5.9. Bass pannists from the band *Pan Rebels* on stage for Panorama 1996. Photo: Gage Averill.

Figure 5.10. The front line of the band *Silhouettes Steelband* performing at Panorama with their banner in front and their "flag girl" on the right of the picture. Photo: Gage Averill.

black as are the flag boys and girls. Those carrying flags dance on the front of the stage to entertain and work up the crowd. The arranger sets the tempo with a few taps on the side of a pan, the racks begin to shake, and the metallic fringe on the tops of the racks shimmers in the bright stage lights. Behind the front row of tenors, the engine room plays on a raised central platform, also framed by fringes. The overall effect is of an entire stage—animate and inanimate objects together—dancing, swaying, and sparkling. In front of the stage sit the five judges; behind them, members of the audience raise their arms and dance in place. The climactic final passages, with a shouted part for the pannists, brings the remaining seated audience members to their feet.

Sonatas, next up, unfurls their flags and launches into their own treatment of Philmore's "Pan by Storm." It is not uncommon for a number of bands to select the same calypso for a panorama arrangement. Sponsored by British West Indies Airlines and dressed in yellow, the pannists in *Sonatas* dance their way through the piece, with the audience in tow. And on it goes into the night; every band (*Pan Rebels, Silhouettes, Moods,* and others) has their fifteen minutes or so on stage. Soon after the previous band's final chords fade, another group is rolling onto the stage to take their place. Somewhere just past 4:00 A.M., the last band clears the stage and the judges begin adding up their scores. Panorama judging results are often usually contested by the losing bands and their supporters, and the judges are often booed.

Following the Panorama on Saturday and the calypso contest on Sunday, Carnival hits the Eastern Parkway on Labor Day Monday, routinely attracting over a million onlookers and participants. In 1990 the traditional early Monday parade (*jouvay,* from the French *jour ouvert* or "opening of the day") was still relatively undeveloped, but in recent years, it has become a popular steelband venue. For *jouvay,* the steelband racks are pulled by trucks through the streets from their panyards to join a parade route, surrounded by some of the more traditional (*ol' time*) *mas'* bands. No amplified music is allowed into *jouvay,* and so the steelbands do not have to compete with the stacks of speakers broadcasting commercial calypsos and *soca* songs.

Somewhere around 1:00 P.M., the first wave of the 1990 Carnival road marchers reach the reviewing stand. A group of marchers carry flags of various Caribbean nations; then comes the West Indian American Carnival Association flatbed truck sponsored by Angostura Bitters, which plays a popular road march of the previous year, "Somebody," by Baron. "I want somebody to hug up, somebody to squeeze up, somebody to jump up . . ." It is still early, but behind the blue police barricades and the rows of Port-O-Potty's, the crowds are already filling up the sidewalks of Eastern Parkway. Sailor *mas'* bands with colorful sails unfurled, butterflies, devil bands, and other more traditional *mas'* groups turn the Parkway's asphalt into a sea of dancers *winin'* their hips and taking small, shuffling steps along the parade route, a style of walking called *chipping.* A *mas'* sponsored by an Indo-Trinidadian group plays Native American Indians ("Indian Uprising") to the sound of South Asian drumming. The steelband *Pan Rebels,* dressed in green, is pulled along by friends and volunteers through the crowded streets. The band is playing their Panorama entry, "No, No We Ain't Going Home" by Owen Norville. Many of the iron players walking along behind the band seem to be "sitting in" with the band, and some frequently lose the tempo. But this is road march and there are no judges listening, and the steelbands can hardly be heard over the ambient *soca* anyway.

C. A. S. Y. M. STEELBAND, A "FAMILY INSTITUTION"

The Brooklyn-based community organization *Caribbean American Sports and Youth Movement* (*C. A. S. Y. M.*) is an organization dedicated to improving the situation of West Indian American children in New York. After a long involvement in sporting activities for youth, the organization started a steelband in 1986, and in 1989 they recruited a young Trinidadian pannist, Arddin Herbert, to move to Brooklyn to become the band's musical director. In a few years, the steelband has become the principal activity of the organization, reflecting the attractiveness of pan to West Indian children and teenagers. The *C. A. S. Y. M. Steelband* is one of three youth-oriented community-based steelbands in the Borough. Almost all of the fifty or so members are of school age and were born in the United States of parents who were themselves from the Caribbean. Perhaps 40 percent are of Trinidadian descent, with girls slightly outnumbering the boys. In addition to the musical director, the group also has captains, vice-captains, and a steelband committee.

The *C. A. S. Y. M. Steelband* participates in the Saturday night Panorama competition each year in the Labor Day Carnival on Eastern Parkway. The band moves from their church basement rehearsal space onto an open parking lot for the month of August to practice their Panorama calypso arrangement. After they finish practicing each night, the pannists load their instruments—fifteen tenors, seven double tenors, eight double seconds, one four-pan, three cellos, five guitars, three tenor basses, and about seven six-basses plus engine-room percussion instruments—into the back of a moving van for secure storage.

In our many hours of conversation, William Jones [WJ], founder and executive director of C. A. S. Y. M., and Arddin Herbert [AH], musical director of the *C. A. S. Y. M. Steelband,* repeatedly stressed the role of pan in building a positive identity for West Indian American youths, in developing the discipline and commitment necessary to do well in school, and in building a sense of community. The two community leaders also stressed the involvement of the youths' families as a support network for the band. In the following passages taken from that interview, we discuss the relationship of Carnival and panorama to the band's goals.

GA Tell me a little bit about the early days of *C. A. S. Y. M.* and what you were trying to do.

WJ You may be aware that Brooklyn has a large Caribbean population. My experience, as I came here in 1970, was that the children of Caribbean descent . . . experienced what I would call a culture shock. They were having problems in school obviously at that time. There were four schools in the area: Prospect Heights, Wingate, Erasmus, and Tilden. There was a mixed composition of children there. I was involved in soccer in Trinidad, and I was very much involved in community work also, and I met a lot of children. The Five Borough Soccer League was an adult soccer league and we weren't really dealing with the children. I decided to form the *Caribbean American Sports and Youth Movement* . . . to concentrate on developing the youth in soccer—of course I had a lot of help in that. It was determined that not only should you be playing soccer, but you should be involved in many of the cultural traits of the Caribbean people, and the children love this.

   We had dance and drama, but what caught fire is the steelband. It is very visible. When the steelband performs, people want to bring their children into the group . . . I dare say that *C. A. S. Y. M.* is not an ordinary steelband. The children in this band . . . learn music theory and they have a very big appreciation for the art form. *C. A. S. Y. M.* is very well-developed in a range of music from classic to calypso and we use this as a tool to get the children to understand that education is important. We have a total of about two hundred kids involved both in the schools and outside the schools. The stageside [the performance band] is about fifty. To stay in the stageside, you must be going to school and you must maintain an [good] average. If you have any problems in school, we look for assistance to give to you. I'm very proud to say that in the last three years, 90 percent of our children that graduated from high school went on to college. The band is open to children from five to eighteen, but if you pass eighteen and you are abiding by the rules of the group, we are not going to throw you out. In fact, we have many children who stay in the group and impart the knowledge they have to the younger ones.

GA	When you teach the members music theory, do you use scores and notation or do you do it by rote?

AH	Both. Some of them can read scores and if they can't read scores, I teach them basic note values. When they're in school, we rehearse on Fridays and Saturdays for an average of about two and a half hours. When they're out of school, for the months of July and August, we rehearse from Monday to Saturday, depending on if we have any performances. Most of the players that have left our band—and some were not the best of players—when they went in other bands, they were like really on top there [because of their experience in C. A. S. Y. M.].

WJ	We recruit some children whose parents don't know where to send them. They send them by us and we introduce them to the music. . . .

AH	Steel pan daycare!

GA	Do the parents come to you with problems with their kids?

AH	Usually if the parents have a problem, they will come and say, "Well, this child isn't doing too well," and because I have such a good relationship with most of the kids, I can get through to most of them. If it's something that we can't handle, the parents might say, "You are not going to be able to go to rehearsal for one month," and the kids start to straighten up.

WJ	Whenever a child is being disciplined, one of the things they [the parents] take away from them is the steelband, because they know that they are attached to this art form, so it is used as a form of discipline. As a matter of fact, I was just speaking to a parent whose child disappeared [from the group] and on the order of the captain was suspended from the group. The child was crying to the mother, so she called me. I'm trying to show the type of rapport that we have with the parents and the children in the organization.

GA	Tell me about the generational problems. Are the conflicts pretty intense? Are there pressures on West Indian kids to not look like "jeskummers"—like immigrants—and to fit in?

WJ   In 1970, when I came here, we may have had that problem. You'd find some of my peers not wanting to identify themselves with Trinidad, but over the years, you will find that a Trinidadian will want you to know he's a Trinidadian. He don't try to change his accent—he'll speak his colloquial language—like I do at times! I don't think we have that type of problem anymore.

AH   Back then, because of the colonial scene, those countries were looked down on as Third World, second-class. But now I think most people see the more industrialized countries as having the same problems that we have back home, so we see that they are not much better that we are, so we are proud to be who we are.

WJ   In 1979 and 1980 we had a problem that we attacked in group form. A child coming from Trinidad who had received a quality education, they used to start them all over again. Without testing them, they used to put them some grades lower. And I think it was unfair that they had to stay longer in school to graduate. I don't think you have that problem so much now. How we addressed this is that we had the children themselves help. If you were good in math, you would help the one who was weak in math. We had a kind of common spirit, and I don't ever want that to break from the group, cause it helped a lot . . . each one helping one. We look at this group as a family institution. There are children in this group now aged six and seven whose sisters and brothers were in the band, and it continues. Having had the opportunity to watch the players grow, some of them from age ten, to see the development, it's a joy to behold where I'm concerned. Watching these guys trying to do like Arddin . . . and they have really advanced. It's incredible, it's a thrill.

   To carry on a steelband with young people throughout the year—we go throughout the year—is a difficulty. That's why you get most of the bands operating only during the summer for Panorama. After that they're nonexistent. But it's a painstaking thing, and you have to have the support of the parents, and we do, I must say. We are blessed with having the support of the parents. The children want to come out and practice on Friday night and Saturday, and it's taxing on the parents to come and pick them up.

GA   Do you go on the road for the Monday Carnival parade?

AH   Not in the evening [in the main parade], only in the morning for *jouvay*.

WJ   It's a very ticklish subject. I am concerned, as are most of the parents—remember we are dealing mostly with teenagers of thirteen or twelve—that to have such a mass of children under control in the "heat" of the festival is difficult. So we much prefer to take part in the *jouvay* in early morning.

AH   What I try to maintain is that C. A. S. Y. M. steelband is *not* a Panorama band. If you want to be part of the Panorama, you have to be here for the entire year doing the same thing these kids have been doing, hard work.[13]

WJ   You can't be coming in and out. You have one set of rules all the time. If you have people coming in, they can corrupt what you have going and it's not a good thing. And while you're competing, you want to win, [still] he [Arddin Herbert] doesn't really like to go to Panorama because you're not benefiting anything by it, and you're not improving very much—you spend a number of hours on one particular tune, whereas you could be expanding the knowledge of the children in other areas with the time. Panorama is very time-consuming and very expensive and not that rewarding. So that, in this aspect, I really agree with him. But it has become such a passionate thing with the children—it's hard when you see their faces to tell them no, you know. Economically, we nearly said no this year, as a matter of fact we aren't sure yet [both laugh]. If this thing [a benefit concert] don't turn out right, it's no!

AH I never liked competing with the art form, because I have my view that the art form should be expressed pure on stage. Competition leaves a lot of hard feelings. The only reason why I do it, as he said, is that the kids look forward to it. And right now there isn't a substitute that could equal or surpass Panorama in terms of the hype and the adrenaline. If I could, I would.

WJ We have been trying to get schools involved, and I must say that there's a particular school in Queens. The type of interest that the principal shows encourages you to go out there. We make the tutoring of the pupils free of cost and they purchase their own pans. You know, it's a pleasure to go there when you have a foreigner [a non–West Indian] showing you that type of interest in the art form, so we feel we should expend our energies there, even though sometimes it's inconvenient. Right here on our doorsteps [in the West Indian community], they like the panyard, but for one day alone.

CONCLUSIONS

This chapter has pointed to many paradoxes of steel-pan performance in Brooklyn and throughout the diaspora. For the most part, steel pan in Brooklyn is an amateur, ensemble-based musical form, but it is heavily dependent upon individual professionals who serve as tuners and arrangers and who play a central role in the transmission of the tradition. It is not a commercial music per se; the players are not paid, the instruments are notoriously difficult to record, and there is only a very small market for steelband recordings (one almost never hears them on radio—even on West Indian broadcasts), but steelband arrangers draw on commercially released calypsos as their source material. Panorama performances require extraordinary skill and dexterity, but there are only a few weeks each year in which most steelbands have the opportunity to play. Pan is historically a Trinbagonian art form (it is the "national instrument" of Trinidad and Tobago) that now finds itself embraced as a symbol of pan–West Indian identity. Finally, pan in Brooklyn is a local phenomenon, situated in panyards, on the stage at the Brooklyn Museum Panorama, and on parade along Eastern Parkway; but it is very much a transnational phenomenon too. Pan performances at Panorama in Brooklyn are pegged to the previous winter's Carnival in Trinidad and Tobago by the circulation of calypsos through the diaspora and by the flow of personnel (arrangers, calypsonians, and some pannists) among the various Carnivals. Although the songs may be recycled, the Brooklyn arrangements must be new and different. Steel pan intimately links the Anglophone Caribbean and its diaspora in cultural expression and creativity. Moreover, these paradoxes I have identified—amateur vs. professional, national vs. West Indian, local vs. transnational—are in constant flux precisely because pan is a living, dynamic art form in which so many diasporic West Indians invest their time, energy, and passion.

Pan is in no danger of dying out in Brooklyn. There are a growing number of pan activists ready and willing to keep existing groups together and to organize new groups. Large numbers of young West Indian Americans appear genuinely excited about steelbands and about performing at Carnival. The Brooklyn steelbands almost exclusively consist of West Indians; for them, pan remains a chief form of cultural assertion and an outlet for exploring pan–West Indian ethnic identity. Pan is a "we ting," a cultural expression that symbolizes West Indian cultural creativity and hybridity even as it provides an affective link to the Caribbean. This link has been more or less continuous, involving first and second generation West Indian Americans, but it cannot be assumed that identity issues are somehow consensual or resolved. To the contrary, steel pan becomes a factor in the negotiation of contrasting visions of Trinidadian, West Indian, and Caribbean American identities. Pan is also a vehicle for the display or performance of identities for the benefit of surrounding communities and ethnic groups. At Panorama, in the *jouvay* parade, and in the Carnival road march, West Indians also make pan a "dey ting" (something for "them"), sharing their art with hundreds of thousands of spectators of varied cultural backgrounds.

GLOSSARY

badjohn. Trinidadian slang for a ruffian or hooligan, used to describe early panmen.

beat pan. A more traditional way to say "play" pan.

blend. As a verb, this means to adjust the noteheads of a pan so that all of the overtones are consonant with the fundamental pitches and to vary tone and loudness so that the pan is balanced as an instrument and in relationship to the ensemble.

bomb tune. Among early steelbands, this was a foreign (often Latin) tune worked up secretly before Carnival to impress the other bands when they were unveiled like a "bomb." Bands began using short arrangements of well-known classical and pop tunes set to calypso rhythms for this purpose, and "bomb" competitions have been, off and on, a part of Carnival.

breakaway. This refers to a sudden increase in the intensity of participation, when audiences get worked up and carried away by a song.

broughtupsy. Good upbringing.

cariso/calypso. A broad category (or family really) of Trinidadian songs derived from nine-teenth century *lavways* (Afro-Trinidadian songs accompanying stick fights) and French-Trinidadian *romances*. One division of contemporary calypso would be by function: *tent calypsos* (topical, with an emphasis on the lyrics, sung in the calypso tents and in the calypso monarch competition), *road march calypsos* (rhythmic and tuneful for use by marching *mas'* bands), *steelband calypsos* (related to road march but written with even-tual pan performance in mind, often about pan), and perhaps danceband or party *soca*. Before the 1930s, calypsos were often categorized on the basis of the melodic mode they were written in (for example: *mi minor, la minor*) but most contemporary calypsos are in a major key. Calypsos may also be distinguished by the number of lines of text covered by the basic repeating melody. Old *lavways* and some short *road marches* might comprise two lines (call-and-response), called a *half-tone calypso*; a *single-tone calypso* would con-sist of four lines of text per melodic repeat; and the *double-tone calypso*, eight. Most tent calypsos are of the *double-tone* variety.

calypso monarch. Winner of the annual calypso competition at Carnival (Dimanche Gras).

chipping. Taking small, shuffling steps along a Carnival parade route. Proper chipping con-serves the energy of the masqueraders for the two long days in the Trinidadian sun.

compas. A popular Haitian dance genre and rhythm, originally called *compas-direct*.

Dimanche Gras. A show held on the Sunday night of Carnival that includes the competition for calypso monarch and for king and queen *mas'* costumes.

dingolay. Loose, improvised dance steps of an exuberant nature, executed when sufficiently moved by the music.

engine room. The ancillary percussion section of a steelband, usually comprising a drum set, irons or brake drums, congas, shak shak or shaker, scratcher, cow bells, and so forth.

fete. Party.

iron. A common term for the brake-drum instrument in a steelband engine room, struck with one or two iron rods.

jamet. From French *diametre*. Refers to a set of early Afro-Trinidadian Carnival practices that were considered by the ruling colonial elite and middle classes to be outside of the periph-ery of proper behavior.

jouvay. From the French *jour ouvert* (opening of the day). Used for the early Monday morn-ing Carnival parade that opens the two days of road march. This event tends to have more traditional *mas'* costumes and to be more informal.

jump up. To "join in" with a *mas'* band and enthusiastically participate.

lime. Trinidadian slang for "to hang out."

Mardi Gras. Literally, Fat Tuesday, the Tuesday portion of the pre-Lenten Carnival. Prior to Mardi Gras are Dimanche Gras and Lundi Gras (Fat Sunday and Monday).

mas'. From "Masquerade," this refers to the costuming component of Carnival. *Mas'* bands parade and compete in the Carnival road march. Participants are said to "*play mas'.*"

mas' camp. A space used to build and sew the costumes for a *mas'* band.

pan/steel pan. A melodic percussion instrument made from metal containers (usually fifty-five gallon oil drums). It has been expanded to include a number of instruments of different ranges, for example, tenor/lead, low tenor, double tenor, double second, guitar, quadro-phonic, three-cello, four-pan/four-cello, tenor bass, six-bass, nine-bass, twelve-bass.

pannist. A player of a steel pan. Formerly *panman*.

panyard. The rehearsal space for a steelband, usually a vacant lot out-of-doors.

Panorama. A competition for conventional steelbands at Carnival (in Trinidad and in Brooklyn).

soca. A dance-band ("party") form of calypso, with disco and other international influences pioneered in the 1970s and popular into the 1990s.

strum. A rhythmic striking of two notes on the pan to fill in chords of a composition.

road march. The parade component of Carnival and the form of calypso designed to accompany it.

Savannah. The area of Queen's Park in downtown Port-of-Spain where the Carnival (and Panorama) reviewing stands are located.

scratcher. A scraped percussion instrument used in the steelband engine room.

shak-shak. A shaken percussion instrument with internal rattles used in the steelband engine room. Often simply called a "shaker".

steelband. An ensemble made entirely of pans and ancillary percussion instruments.

> **conventional steelband.** Panorama-sized steelband, usually close to one hundred or more players.

> **stageside.** A smaller performance steelband (perhaps twenty-five to fifty players), often a subset of a conventional band.

> **pan around the neck/traditional steelband.** An old form of steelband designed for marching, with pans carried on straps (one or at most two pans per player), revived in the last decade or so.

tamboo bamboo. A Carnival music ensemble (predecessor to the steelband), largely obsolete, using various lengths of bamboo tubes as percussion and concussion instruments.

tent. The commercial venues for calypso performances in the months prior to Carnival.

tune. As a verb, this means to build a pan and get it into rough tune. The final stage of working the noteheads, to obtain the proper loudness and alignment of overtones, is called "blending."

wine, winin'. A dance move involving a rolling of the hips, often while pressed close to a dance partner.

SELECTED NEW YORK AREA STEELBANDS

Ad-Lib

C.A.S.Y.M.

Desperados, N.Y.C.

Harlem All-Stars

Harmony

Metro

Moods Pan Groove

New Generation

Pan Rebels

Sesame Flyers

Silhouettes

Sonatas

NOTES

1. I would like to thank Arddin Herbert, William George, Caldera Carabello, and members of Silhouettes Steelband for their assistance with this chapter. Amelia K. Ingram and Giovanna Perot-Averill edited the text. In addition, I would like to thank this book's editors, Anne K. Rasmussen and Kip Lornell, for their interest in the subject and for their patience.

2. Although in the United States and Great Britain the term *West Indian* sometimes encompasses the whole of the Caribbean, I am using the term more restrictively to denote the Anglophone Eastern Caribbean islands (including Trinidad and Tobago) plus Bermuda, Grand Cayman, Jamaica, and the Bahamas (in other words, the former—and current—colonies of the British Empire). In Cuba, Haiti, the Dominican Republic, Puerto Rico, and the French Antilles, the term *West Indies* is seldom used as a term of self-reference; instead, these islands employ French and Spanish equivalents of *Caribbean* and *Antilles*.

3. Diasporic carnivals have received sustained attention over the years from researchers, starting with Hill and Abrahamson (1980). Analyses have focused on the transnational circulation of aesthetic practices (Nunley 1988, Manning 1990) between Trinidad and the various diasporic sites and on issues of immigrant identity and politics (Kasinitz 1992; Kasinitz and Fridenberg-Herbstein 1987, and Cohen 1993). Little has been said of the role of pan and steelbands in the diaspora, other than Manning's (1990) misleading dismissal of pan in the Brooklyn and Toronto carnivals (while emphasizing its centrality to London's Notting Hill Carnival).

4. For example, the members of one band with which I had close contact was unanimous in their criticism of Panorama judges for favoring the same small group of bands each year. One group was deeply divided over the decision by the band captain to kick out five pannists only a week before Panorama. The pannists—some of the best players in the group—were playing with more than one band and were missing rehearsals as a consequence. Although this practice is increasingly frequent in steelbands in Brooklyn and Trinidad, the captain held to an older ethos about commitment to a "yard" and about team competitive spirit that was incompatible with the new attitude. In another incident, an arranger and a pannist (with a distinctly American accent and attitude) clashed over a perceived breach of respect and authority, with the arranger complaining publicly, "I'm not paid enough to take this crap. I'm here to do a job, not to be second guessed." The offending pannist said privately later, "I had too much of this shit with those old Trinidadian headmasters when I was a kid at school, you know what I mean? All I did was ask him what it was I was doing wrong. Just, 'Tell me, what am I doing wrong?' This is America—I don't have to take orders and disrespect from nobody." These social dramas revealed clashes of values and worldviews that are revealing of the fault lines that are shaking the steelband movement.

5. See Kasinitz (1992, 54–59) for a summary of available statistics on New York's West Indian population.

6. The positive rewards of asserted ethnicity for West Indians contrast with the situation

historically faced by Haitians in North America, where they encountered an especially virulent form of discrimination based on sensationalist stereotypes of Haitian Vodou, politics, poverty, and disease. Despite two decades of political activism designed to counteract negative attitudes toward Haiti, Haitian youth are far more likely than their West Indian counterparts to attempt to assimilate. See Averill, 1994b; Schiller and Fouron 1989; or Laguerre 1984 for accounts of the Haitian life and culture in New York.

7. Cited in Kasinitz (1992, 141).

8. Ellie Manette was a member of one of Trinidad's first steelbands, the Woodbrook Invaders, and he is credited with being the first to use a fifty-five-gallon oil drum as the raw material for a pan. He achieved his greatest renown as a pan builder and technological innovator, as when he initiated the use of a stroboscope to help adjust the tuning of a pan.

9. In the 1980s and 1990s, younger West Indians gravitated toward the music of Jamaica, especially reggae and forms of dancehall chanting (*bogle, ragga,* etc.) and their various fusions with *soca.*

10. Top Trinbagonian conventional steelbands may make enough money to cover costs by winning prize purses in Panorama, the Carnival "bomb" competition, or the Steelband Music Festival as well as by attracting generous sponsorship. Many conventional steelbands have their sponsors' names preceeding the band name; for example, Carib [beer] Tokyo All-Stars or Amoco (oil) Renegades.

11. This diagram is based loosely on a sketch in *Pro Sound News,* December 1995.

12. Trinidadian steelbands were first recorded in the early 1950s by local entrepreneurs, then by North American audio technician Emory Cook, and eventually by such major transnational companies as Decca, RCA, and Columbia. Few if any of these recordings returned any royalties to the bands. With the rise in popularity of sound systems and of *soca* bands in the late 1970s, steelbands found themselves relegated to a "carnival ghetto;" popular only for a few months of the year and with a declining number of engagements for their smaller, year-round performance bands that Trinidadians call "stagesides." The situation is bleaker in Brooklyn, where few steelbands even bother to organize stagesides; they are literally panorama-only bands with a single arrangement in their repertory each year. Many pannists lament their lack of access to recording studios and to radio and television airplay—in other words, they would love to open up commercial opportunities for pan.

13. Although I have focused on Carnival and Panorama as sites for performance in this chapter, the New York–area stagesides find other venues for performance. One such venue was the 1991 Steelband Festival competition held at Lincoln Center's Avery Fisher Hall, sponsored by small organization called the National Council of Steelbands. Modeled on Trinidad's Steelband Festival ("Pan Is Beautiful"), the competition required that every band perform their own arrangement of the test piece (the tango-tinged "Serenata" by Tin Pan Alley composer Leroy Anderson), a Panorama arrangement, and a classical composition. C. A. S. Y. M. Steelband placed first and my own group, Wesleyan Pandemonium, came in second (a placement disputed by some audience members who felt that the judges had wanted to reward one of the non–West Indian bands). The goals of the organizer of the festival were to provide an opportunity for the Brooklyn steelbands to get out of the borough and into a mainstream, high-status concert setting and to stimulate performance of material other than calypso and soca. C. A. S. Y. M. Steelband has also performed at Symphony Space in Manhattan for World Music, Inc., in the New York schools, and in a touring program called Caribbean Roots and Rhythms that was organized by the New England Foundation for the Arts.

SOURCES CITED

Averill, Gage. 1994a. "Anraje to *Angaje:* Carnival Politics and Music in Haiti," *Ethnomusicology* 38, no. 2: 217–47.

———. 1994b. "*Mezanmi, Kouman Nou Ye?* My Friends, How Are You?" Musical Constructions of the Haitian Transnation. *Diaspora, A Journal of Transnational Studies* 3, no. 3: 253–72.

Cohen, Abner. 1993. *Masquerade Politics: Explorations in the Structure of Urban Culture Movements.* Berkeley and Los Angeles: University of California Press.

Hill, Donald, and Roger Abrahamson. 1980. West Indian Carnival in Brooklyn. *Natural History* 88: 72–84.

Kasinitz, Philip. 1992. *Caribbean New York: Black Immigrants and the Politics of Race.* Ithaca, N.Y.: Cornell University Press.

Kasinitz, Philip, and Judith Fridenberg-Herbstein. 1987. Caribbean Celebrations in New York City: The Puerto Rican Parade and the West Indian Carnival. In *Caribbean Life in New York City: Social and Cultural Dimensions,* edited by Constance Sutton and Elsa Chaney, 327–49. New York: CMS.

Laguerre, Michel S. 1984. *American Odyssey: Haitians in New York City.* Ithaca, N.Y.: Cornell University Press.

Manning, Frank. 1990. Overseas Caribbean Carnivals: The Art of a Transnational Celebration. *Plantation Society in the Americas.* 47–62.

Nunley, John W. 1988. Festival Diffusion into the Metropole. In *Caribbean Festival Arts,* edited by John W. Nunley and Judith Bethelheim. Seattle: University of Washington Press.

Pro Sound News. 1995. Techniques for Recording Steel Drums Live. December: 54, 56.

Schiller, Nina Glick, and Georges Fouron. 1990. "Everywhere We Go, We Are in Danger": Ti-Manno and the Emergence of a Haitian Transnational Identity. *American Ethnologist* 17, no. 2: 329–47.

Stuempfle, Stephen. 1995. *The Steelband Movement: The Forging of a National Art in Trinidad and Tobago.* Philadelphia: University of Pennsylvania Press.

RECORDINGS CITED

Francisco, Slinger. n.d. Mighty Sparrow. *Mas' In Brooklyn.* Recording Artists Productions.

Grant, Rupert. 1956. Lord Invader. *Labor Day.* Folkways Records

Roberts, Aldwin. 1991. Lord Kitchener. *Pan Dingolay.* Soca Hits.

Rudder, David. 1987. Calypso Music. *This Is Soca with David Rudder and Charlie's Roots.* New York: Sire Records.

Williams, Dennis. 1993. Merchant. *Pan in Yuh Pan.*

COMPANION CD SELECTIONS

Track 9. Pan Rebels, "Fire Coming Down." Basement Records.

ADDITIONAL SOURCES

Suggested Bibliography

Aho, William R. 1987. Steel Band Music in Trinidad and Tobago: The Creation of a People's Music. *Latin American Music Review* 8, no. 1): 26–55.

Greenidge, Robert. 1994. Fire Coming Down. Panorama arrangement. Transcribed by Steve Popernack, edited by Steve Popernack and Shelly Irvine. Akron, Ohio: Paynard, Inc.

Hill, Donald. 1993. *Calypso Calalloo: Early Carnival Music In Trinidad.* Gainesville: University Presses of Florida. The accompanying CD contains the first steelband recording ever made.

Hill, Errol. 1972. *The Trinidad Carnival: Mandate For a National Theatre.* Austin: University of Texas.

Kronman, Ulf. 1991. *Steel Pan Tuning: A Handbook for Steel Pan Making and Tuning.* Stockholm: Musikmuseet.

Nunley, John W., and Judith Bettelheim, eds. 1988. *Caribbean Festival Arts.* Seattle: University of Washington Press.

Stuempfle, Stephen. 1995. *The Steelband Movement: The Forging of a National Art in Trinidad and Tobago.* Philadelphia: University of Pennsylvania Press. The best social history of steelband in Trinidad and Tobago currently available.

Suggested Audiography

Note: There are many early recordings of steelbands in existence, but they are generally difficult to find and of only tangential relevance to this chapter. What follows are a few examples of recent recordings that should be relatively easy to locate and that contain compositions similar to those played by contemporary Brooklyn steelbands.

Various. *Panorama: Steel Bands of Trinidad.* Delos 13491 40154.

———. *Pan All Night: Steelbands of Trinidad and Tobago.* Delos DE 4022.

———. *Calypso Season.* Mango Records 539.861-2.

———. *Pan Champs, vols. 1 and 2.* Blue Rhythm Records LP 2430.

Amoco Renegades Steel Orchestra. *Panorama Classics.* Sanch 9203.

Desperadoes Steel Orchestra. *The Jammer.* Delos DE 4023.

Our Boys Steel Band. *Pan Progress.* Mango Records 162 539 916-2.

———. *Pan Night and Day.* Mango Records CCD 9822.

Of special interest are the annual Panorama compilations recorded by Sanch Electronix in Port-of-Spain, Trinidad, (809) 663–1384.

Suggested Videography

Celebration! 1988. Produced and directed by Karen Kramer. Dr. Morton Marks and Dr. Donald Hill, consultants. Ho-ho-kus, N.J.: Film Library. 30 minutes.

Mas' Fever: Inside Trinidad Carnival. 1987. Produced and directed by Glenn Micalleff. Photographed and edited by Larry Johnson. Portland, Ore: Filmsound. 55 minutes.

Moko Jumbie. 1990. Directed by Karen Kramer. Produced by Karen Kramer and James Callahan. Ho-ho-kus, N.J.: Film Library. 15 minutes.

One Hand Don't Clap. 1988. Produced and directed by Kavery Dutta. New York: Rhapsody Films. 92 minutes

Steelband Music in Trinidad and Tobago: The Creation of a People's Music. 1994. Produced by William R. Aho. Akron, Ohio: Panyard, Inc. 32 minutes.

Steelbands of Trinidad (Pan in A-Minor). 1987. Daniel Verba and Jean-Jacques Mrejean. Hurleyville, N.Y.: Villon Films. 49 minutes.

CHAPTER 6

Mexican Mariachi Music: Made in the U.S.A.

Daniel Sheehy

*A*s an arts administrator with the federal government, Daniel Sheehy over-sees a program of financial and technical support for a wide range of cultural pro-jects that sponsor folk and traditional arts throughout the United States. His orig-inal and continuing work as both an ethnomusicologist and a musician, howev-er, is in the area of Mexican mestizo music, including music of the mariachi. In addition to being a well-recognized symbol of "Mexican-ness" for non-Mexican Americans, mariachi remains in important expression of culture of people of Mexican heritage. As such, this music has become part of the curriculum of schools and universities across the Southwest and in a select few other parts of the United States, where Mexican Americans are widely represented. As he traces the evolution of mariachi music in Mexico, Sheehy highlights the ties mariachi has had as with the evolution of Mexican nationalism, a relationship that has been fueled by mass media and one that is perceived not only from within the Mexican American community but by the American population at large. Unlike many of the musics profiled in this book, mariachi is well known in America for a num-ber of reasons. The music (along with a host of other symbols of Mexico) has been featured in countless Western movies, Mexican eateries, and even at Disney World and Disneyland. The use of such Western European instruments as trum-pets and violins in the mariachi ensemble has helped to make this music more acceptable to the mainstream in the United States. And because Spanish is the second most frequently spoken language in the country, the Spanish-language lyrics of mariachi are far more accessible to Americans than any other non-English based musics. Sheehy's chapter on the history of mariachi in Mexico and its transplantation and performance in the United States is especially timely with the recent explosion of popularity and legitimacy of mariachi in the United

States, a phenomenon that may be attributed to the continually expanding presence of Mexican Americans and the performance of mariachi music by such well-known popular singers as Linda Ronstadt.

■ ■ ■ ■

What is mariachi? Many Americans think of it as the stereotype so colorfully portrayed on television, in the movies, or on Linda Ronstadt's "Canciones de mi Padre" tour—a dozen Mexican musicians in big hats and silver-studded pants, playing trumpets, violins, and Mexican guitars, backing up a Mexican country singer crooning beneath a moonlit hacienda balcony. For others, it is a popular music like any other—they buy the latest *música ranchera* (literally, "country music") CD with a well-known singer backed up by a mariachi group, go to large-scale concerts by those same artists, and learn the words to many of the songs. For still others, mariachi music is a potent symbol of their deeply felt identity. As you will read below, over its 150-year history, mariachi has been all of these things and more. It is symbol and stereotype, ancient and modern, glorified and scorned, profession and avocation, a form of musical expression, and a way of life.

The term *mariachi* may mean a single musician, a kind of musical group, or a style of music. In addition to the music itself, three dimensions of mariachi musical life—cultural, commercial, and social—are key to understanding it fully. Since the 1930s, the mariachi ensemble and its music have been a emblem of Mexican identity, a cultural icon to anchor a Mexican culture in transition.

> In contemporary cultural dynamics—dominated by modern electronic communication—particular regional traits are debated in the face of a worldwide homogenizing culture. At the same time a society accepts outside influences, it bases its identity on the perseverance of the values, forms, and rhythms that preceding generations established as their own: the mariachi will continue as the symbol of the Mexican people to the extent that we conserve our national character. (Jesús Jáuregui 1990, 169—my translation)

A similar statement might be made about the symbolic importance of the mariachi ensemble and its music to the culture of many Mexican Americans, particularly those of the recent several generations of immigrants from west Mexico.

For nearly as long, music linked to the mariachi sound has been an important niche in the Mexican popular-music industry and since the 1980s has made important gains among North American consumers as well. And, as long as the mariachi's history has been documented, Mexican middle-class and elite society has been ambivalent in its attitude toward mariachi musicians and their music, which is associated with rural and working-class people. A stanza from Mexican singer and songwriter Cuco Sánchez's classic *canción ranchera* (country song), "No soy monedita de Oro" (I Am Not a Gold Coin), illustrates this attitude:

> In your house they do not want me
> because I live singing.
> They say I am a *mariachi*
> and I don't have enough
> to buy you a wedding dress,
> that I am wasting your time. (my translation)

On any weekend or holiday, particularly during the fair-weather months, hundreds of Mexican mariachi ensembles may be heard performing across the United States. In Los Angeles, San Jose, San Francisco, San Diego, Tucson, Phoenix, Las Vegas, El Paso, San Antonio, Houston, Chicago, Orlando, Washington, D.C., New York, and dozens of other American communities, the sound of trumpets, violins, and guitars enlivens weddings, birthdays, baptisms, parties in homes, festivals, restaurants, bars, and many other social events.

On a Sunday afternoon, musicians Margarito Gutiérrez and his brother Salvador sit on two ramshackle chairs situated comfortably in the shade of the donut shop at the corner of Boyle and First Streets in East Los Angeles. They and most of their immediate family came to the United States from their hometown of Ciudad Guzmán in the Mexican state of Jalisco twenty-five years earlier, looking for greater opportunities for work. Most days of the week, this is where they may be found, passing the time trading jokes and jibes with their fellow musicians. Like most *mariacheros* (another term for mariachi musicians), they are known among their comrades by their nicknames, "Santa Claus" and "Jeremec," respectively. The donut stand sits on a small triangle of concrete and asphalt recently named "Plaza de los Mariachis" by the City of Los Angeles (Fig. 6.1). The Boyle Hotel across the street and several crowded apartment buildings and boarding houses in the surrounding neighborhood are packed with musicians. At peak business hours on weekend evenings, there may be as many as two hundred itinerant *mariacheros,* most dressed in silver-adorned black suits, waiting for clients in need of their services.

An approaching car slows and, like a magnet, attracts the musicians. The elderly driver sees the Gutiérrez brothers, whom he has hired before, and he beckons them over. He wants a group to play at his wife's birthday party in two hours. They agree on a price, number of hours of music, and number of musicians, and the client speeds off to prepare for the festivities. Salvador steps over to the pay telephone and dials the phone and beeper numbers of

Figure 6.1 Members of Mariachi San Matías, posing at the Plaza de los Mariachis in Los Angeles, Calif. Left to right: Gustavo Guitiérrez and the four Gutiérrez borthers—José, Margarito, Enrique, and Salvador. Photo by Daniel Sheehy.

the other five members of their seven-piece group—two other brothers and three nephews—to let them know where to be and when. Their group, Mariachi San Matías—Mariachi Saint Matthew—is named after the Gutiérrez brothers' late father Matías Gutiérrez, also a mariachi musician, as was his father before him. The name is in part an insider, tongue-in-cheek, double entendre witticism. To the unknowing, "San Matías" could refer to a little-known town or to the Christian apostle, but it is in fact a half-humorous, half-reverent gesture at beatifying their late father as a saint. For Mariachi San Matías, this would be a typical Sunday.

Two hours later, the group is at the client's home, shoulder-to-shoulder with a lively gathering of his wife, children, grandchildren, extended family, and friends. Men and women try to outyell one another to request their favorite pieces, and when they recognize the first few notes of a popular *canción ranchera*, the entire gathering erupts in a chorus of *gritos* (traditional yells). When the partygoers feel like dancing, the Mariachi San Matías plays fast *polcas* (polkas) and *cumbias*, as well as slower *valses* (waltzes) and romantic *boleros*. When the two hours of music that they had agreed upon ends, the client negotiates for an additional hour, and all present gather around to sing the birthday greeting song "Las Mañanitas" for the family matriarch. At the end of the final hour, the client pays Salvador a roll of bills, and the musicians return to the time-worn station wagon of one of their members to divide up their pay. Then, since the night is young, they decide to go to a nearby bar to *talonear,* that is, to look for clients who will pay by the song to hear them play (from the word *talón,* "heel," which refers to the walking around from one place to another). At the bar, it's a busy night, and they rove from customer to customer, playing five pieces for two *compadres* out on the town, three songs for a lonely-looking man on a barstool, ten more for two pairs of lovers at a table, and so forth, charging eight dollars per song. After several hours, the crowd thins out, the demand for music is exhausted, and the members of Mariachi San Matías split up their earnings and retire to their homes.

At the moment the client had arrived at the East Los Angeles donut shop, several miles across town at La Fonda restaurant in the more upscale Wilshire District, the thirteen members of Mariachi Los Camperos, led by Natividad "Nati" Cano, were beginning to rehearse several new arrangements for an upcoming show. In a week, they would perform at the annual Tucson International Mariachi Conference before a sellout audience at the Tucson Convention Center. At this year's appearance, they will accompany guest artists Linda Ronstadt and the Chicano music pioneer Lalo Guerrero, both Tucson natives. At their rehearsal, the group's musical arranger, Jesús Guzmán, passes out music for the seven violinists, who begin work on the parts and agree on precise violin bowings; the *guitarronero* (bass player), *vihuelero* (rhythm guitarist), and guitarist coordinate the piece's rhythmic and harmonic accompaniment, and the two trumpet players retire to a corner to practice so that they will not disturb the others. After about an hour, they decide to try the piece out during this evening's performance at La Fonda.

At 6:30 P.M., most of the audience arrives for the first of the evening's five forty-five-minute shows—two busloads of Japanese tourists and a small group of middle-class Mexican Americans and other diners—a typical night at La Fonda. At six forty-five, the Camperos take the stage (Fig. 6.2) and play a forty-five-minute program of tightly arranged medleys of popular tunes. Between medleys, the group's violinist and spokesman says a few words in Japanese and sings the well-known Japanese song "Sakura"—Cherry Blossom—to the delight of the tourists and to the amazement of most of the audience who, before then, had never heard a mariachi sing in Japanese. Near the end of the set, two colorfully dressed folkloric dancers take the stage to perform the "Jarabe Tapatío"—announced as the "Mexican Hat Dance"—the stage lights go out, and the musicians retire to their dressing room. The length of each show and the break that follows is designed to correspond with the time it takes for the diners to order, eat, pay their bill, and leave, so that others may attend the next show. As the night wears on, the audience consists of fewer and fewer tourists and more Mexican American "regulars," many of whom have been coming to La Fonda since it opened in the late 1960s.

Figure 6.2. Mariachi Los Camperos de Nati Cano performing at the restaurant La Fonda de los Camperos on Wilshire Boulevard in Los Angeles, Calif. Photo by Daniel Sheehy.

EARLY MARIACHI: FROM RURAL ROOTS TO URBAN MARKETPLACE

It is remarkable that not until the 1960s did music scholars apply their skills to charting an extensive history of the mariachi, a musical complex that had been a widely accepted icon of Mexican culture since at least the 1930s. Part of the reason for this neglect may have been that during the 1930s, 1940s, and 1950s, when Mexican researchers were intensifying their efforts to discover and to document their nation's rural folk traditions, mariachi musicians and their music had already migrated to urban Mexico City, where it merged with the popular, commercialized *música ranchera* of the radio and cinema, and was consequently outside particular interests of scholars. Since the late 1960s, however, numerous younger Mexican and American ethnomusicologists, ethnographers, historians, and linguists have delved into the origins of the mariachi tradition.

In the United States, the revival of interest in Latin American folksong, the heightened cultural awareness stimulated by the Chicano movement, and the rise of ethnomusicology all invigorated scholarly attention to the mariachi and its music. In the 1960s, UCLA graduate student Don Borcherdt did field-work in Jalisco, collecting ethnographic recordings and cultural history of the mariachi. Building on his work, the Institute for Ethnomusicology at the University of California, Los Angeles, hired mariachi violinist Jesús Sánchez, a native of Zacoalco, Jalisco, who had been working as a farmworker in

California, to lead a student mariachi ensemble at the university. With the volunteer assistance of Professor Timothy Harding, of California State University at Los Angeles, this ensemble thrived and attracted many other young scholars to mariachi music, including Mark Fogelquist (see Fogelquist 1996) and myself. In the period since the late 1960s, dozens of student mariachi ensembles at high schools and universities have emerged throughout the American Southwest, reinforcing the intellectual attention to *mariachi* history and cultural significance. The renewed attention to Mexican folkloric dance that coincided with the Chicano movement beginning in the mid-1960s also reinforced interest in the mariachi music that usually accompanied the dance. Several dance groups cultivated student mariachi groups as part of their companies. Later, in San Jose, California, Jonathan Clark, who had performed mariachi music regularly with the Los Lupeños dance group in the 1970s, began documenting early mariachi history through interviewing living senior musicians and collecting rare historical recordings and photos. His collaboration with the owner of the Arhoolie recording company, Chris Strachwitz, produced three of the most important publications on mariachi music during its years of transition from rural to urban life (Clark 1992; 1993; 1994).

The 1970s and 1980s saw renewed attention among Mexican scholars, as well, to the documentation of regional musical traditions and a sharpened eye toward the anthropological analysis of national cultural symbols. The *Serie de Discos* (Record Series) of the National Institute of Anthropology and History, directed by historian Irene Vázquez Valle, produced recordings of "roots" mariachi music from small towns in Jalisco (Vázquez Valle 1976). Jalisco native and anthropological ethnographer Jesús Jáuregui published the major comprehensive work on mariachi history, *El Mariachi: Símbolo Musical de México* (The Mariachi: Musical Symbol of Mexico) in 1990, highlighting both the music's exploitation by commercial interests and its ongoing folk roots. These three decades of scholarly research have shed much light on the evolution of the mariachi tradition and its place in contemporary life. They have also shown us that there is much yet to be revealed about early mariachi history. The precise origin of the term *mariachi*, for example, is still not clear.

An official letter of May 7, 1852, from the Catholic priest Cosme Santa Anna, of the town of Rosamorada (located in the western Mexican state of Nayarit), contains the first known reference to the mariachi in connection to music. Writing to his archbishop in Guadalajara, the priest complained of the unrestrained music making, drinking, and gambling that occurred outside his church on Holy Saturday, offending his religious sensibilities. He had pressed the local civil authorities to end this type of annual event—called *mariachi* in that region of the country—but the mayor, instead of stopping it, contributed money to bring new musicians for a *fandango* dance party that lasted from Holy Saturday to the following Tuesday (see Jáuregui 1990, 15–16). In his visit to Guadalajara in 1875, General Ignacio Martínez reported the presence of a three- or four-piece orchestra called *mariage* at a serenade in the main plaza, though the musicians may have been from the region's rural areas (see Martínez 1884; Jáuregui 1990, 21). In his book *Paisajes de Occidente* (1908), Enrique Barrios de los Ríos, writing of his observations on life in the coastal region of the territory of Tepic, describes a platform called *mariache*, on which people danced "joyful *jarabes* to the sound of the harp, or of the violin and *vihuela*, or of the violin, snare drum, cymbals, and bass drum in a deafening quartet" (43–44, my translation). The *jarabe* is an indigenous dance form that was first documented around 1800 and seen as an important cultural expression tied to the rise of Mexican *mestizo*—a mix of Spanish, Amerindian, and African—culture and the movement for Mexico's independence erupting in 1810. "Up to four people at once dance on the [mariache], and the loud tapping of the clamorous *jarabe* resounds through the plaza and nearby streets . . . The mariaches are surrounded by a pleasantly entertained crowd absorbed in that joyful and noisy dance" (*ibid.*, 44).

The historical evidence uncovered so far tells us that in the nineteenth century *mariachi* meant more than merely a musical group. It might have described a local festive event with music, or a dance platform, for example, as well as a two-, three-, or four-piece group comprising such string instruments as the violin, vihuela, and harp. Overall, its use circumscribed a varied but discernible widespread musical/choreographic tradition found in the western Mexican states of Jalisco, Nayarit, Colima, Michoacán, and Guerrero and parts of other neighboring states. In the rest of Mexico, the mariachi tradition was little known, that is until several enormously important national trends propelled its rise to national and international prominence in the decades following the Mexican Revolution (1910–1917).

Intellectual and political nationalism, massive migration from rural areas to urban Mexico City, and the growth of a large-scale Mexican electronic media industry were powerful forces directing the evolution of Mexican society, including the mariachi. Before the revolution, the mariachi and its music had begun in a limited way to cross deeply rooted geographic, class, and cultural lines, becoming more widely known. In the late 1800s and early 1900s, piano arrangements of important traditional songs and dance pieces rooted in western Mexico and most likely part of the mariachi's repertoire were published for performance by Mexico's growing middle class. The most prominent of these was the "Jarabe Tapatío," *tapatío* indicating that the dance was from Guadalajara, capital of the state of Jalisco, and the surrounding region. In 1905, Justo Villa's four-piece mariachi was brought from the town of Cocula in Jalisco to Mexico City to perform for the celebrations of President Porfirio Diaz's birthday and Mexican Independence Day on September 16 (Clark 1993, 9). In 1907, on an occasion in Mexico City's Chapultepec Park honoring the American Secretary of State on a good will tour, an eight-piece mariachi ensemble and four folkloric dancers from Guadalajara presented a stage performance of their regional music and dance (October 3, 1907, in the newspaper *El Imparcial*, quoted in Jáuregui, 31). The first-known recordings of mariachi music were made on wax cylinders in 1907 and 1908 by three American recording companies. They were made by Justo Villa's group, called "Cuarteto Coculense" for these recordings (Clark 1993, 9). These emerging roles of the mariachi as a symbol of an important regional grassroots culture, as a part of a staged *espectáculo*, spectacle or show, and a music with commercial potential were early portendings of what would follow.

The Mexican Revolution (1910–1917) brought with it an upheaval in cultural values. While Mexico's elite had looked to Europe for their cultural models and guidance, many post-revolution intellectuals and government officials praised the value of the home-grown cultural accomplishments of Mexico's *mestizo* and Indian inhabitants. Rural, regional cultural traditions were promoted as building blocks for a new, more nationalistic Mexican identity. In 1920, for example, Mexico's Secretary of Public Education José Vasconcelos unveiled a version of the regional folk dance "Jarabe Tapatío"—subsequently known as the *Jarabe nacional* (national *jarabe)*—that was to be taught in schools throughout Mexico. In a massive performance in Mexico City's Chapultepec Park, three hundred dance couples performed a choreography (Saldívar 1937, 9) that had been influenced by the stage production *Fantasía mexicana* (Mexican Fantasy), a production of the visiting Russian ballerina Anna Pavlova in 1919.

In the 1930s the nationalist President Lázaro Cárdenas included mariachi groups in political events, and in 1940 he personally ordered the commander of the Mexico City police "not to bother the mariachis any more" (Gabaldón Márquez, 284) and to lift the prohibitions barring them from performing in the plazas and streets (Jáuregui, 48). At Cárdenas's behest, a mariachi group that came to Mexico City in 1934 from Tecalitlán, Jalisco, led first by Gaspar Vargas and later by his son Silvestre Vargas, destined to be the most influential of all mariachis, was given employment representing the Mexico City police department in public performances that lasted for two decades (Fig. 6.3).

In 1920 Dr. Luis Rodríguez brought the Mariachi Coculense, led by a *guitarrón* player named Cirilo Marmolejo from Tecolotlán, Jalisco, to Mexico City to perform for a group of post-revolution politicians (Sonnichsen 1993, 2). Many of Mexico's new revolutionary elite, who themselves came from rural backgrounds, viewed the mariachi and its music as an important representation of Mexican culture. Marmolejo and his group stayed in Mexico City and found a new, urban clientele for his music, playing for customers in bars and for parties and other special events. His group, "the first mariachi to appear in a stage show in a legitimate theater in Mexico City (the famous Teatro Iris); the first to appear in a 'sound' [Santa 1931] film and, above all, the first to make 'electric' recordings, initiated the era of the dominance of the mariachi style in radio, film and, especially on records, which has endured over fifty years" (3). In 1925 Marmolejo invited another Cocula

Figure 6.3. Mariachi violinist Matías Gutiérrez (far right), father Margarito and Salvador Gutiérrez, pictured with Mariachi Vargas de Tecalitlán, ca. 1940. Photo courtesy of Margarito Gutiérrez.

native, Concho Andrade and his mariachi to alternate with him at the Tenampa Bar located on Garibaldi Plaza in Mexico City, beginning the plaza's longtime popularity as a center for mariachi music. The mariachis led by Marmolejo and Andrade were important pioneers in transplanting mariachi music to Mexico's capital, placing it in a position of significant influence in the enormous societal changes that followed. Little did anyone suspect that this modest seed, planted in the fertile ground of a rapidly urbanizing Mexican society and later transported northward by massive migration, would make its unmistakable mark on the culture of the United States.

The 1920s saw rural musicians from all parts of the country flocking to Mexico City. This movement was part of a large and steady migration that would continue throughout the twentieth century and that would make greater Mexico City the most populous metropolitan area in the world, with well over twenty million inhabitants. At the same time, the capital was becoming more of a modern urban metropolis; the constant influx of rural people who maintained family ties created a demand for music that reflected and renewed connections to their rural, regional identity. Popular media of entertainment—radio, recordings, film, variety shows in major theaters, and live music in restaurants and other public venues—responded to this demand, featuring musics rooted in the provinces. This, in turn, had an unprecedented influence on popular musical tastes throughout the country and beyond.

Mexico's powerful radio station, XEW, inaugurated in 1930 in Mexico City, broadcast live music— including mariachi and other rurally rooted music, along with urban musics more related to international popular tastes—to all corners of the Mexican Republic and neighboring areas. Throughout most of the 1930s Mariachi Tapatío and other groups were heard regularly on XEW and other stations, assuring the mariachi and its music a place in the musical life of the broad Mexican public (Moreno Rivas 1989, 182–83).

In the 1930s, 1940s, and 1950s, Mexico's "Golden Age" of film cultivated noble, idealized images of country life that were epitomized by famous actor-singers performing pseudofolk songs that appealed to the Mexican public's desire to identify with an idyllic rural past. The 1936 film *Allá en el Rancho Grande*, featuring Tito Guízar, was the first of these. Soon, others followed; for example, superstar actor singer Jorge Negrete made his first film in 1941 as a singing *charro* (cowboy) in *Ay Jalisco, No Te Rajes* (Oh, Jalisco, Don't Give Up). Negrete had already launched a career as actor, singer, nightclub entertainer and had worked in New York and Hollywood before he found his lucrative niche in the Mexican counterpart of American westerns. He and such other singer actors as Pedro Infante, Flor Silvestre, and Javier Solís played a major role in bringing mariachi music to national and international attention. These films also circulated among Spanish-speaking communities of the United States, and in fact many became film classics that are still shown regularly on Spanish-language television, especially in the American Southwest. The impact in the United States of over a half century of popularity of the mariachi through film and television has been widespread and profound.

Professional songwriters applied their skills to writing *canciones rancheras* (country songs) and later, the more suave *boleros rancheros* (country *boleros*) that evoked sometimes idealized images and values that struck deep emotional chords in the rural and urban "common man" alike. In the early 1950s, a singer and songwriter from the state of Guanajuato, José Alfredo Jiménez, launched an enormously influential career that endured until his death in 1973. Many of his more than four hundred published compositions have dominated the *canción ranchera* repertoire of mariachis everywhere for decades following his death, and his statue looms over Mexico City's Garibaldi Plaza as testimony to his preeminence. Nearly all of the most fervently requested melodies at the birthday party in East Los Angeles that was described above were written by "José Alfredo," as he is affectionately called by Mexicans and Mexican Americans alike.

Thus, a mutually reinforcing cycle arose, in which rural tastes influenced the popular media, and then in turn were influenced by popular creations appealing to those tastes. As this came about, certain rural musics were successful in breaking into the media mainstream and others were not. Those that were not included often languished or faded away entirely in the shadow of a powerful "mainstream" Mexican life—in both Mexico and the United States— shaped largely by the popular media. Those that were included were inevitably transformed to suit the demands of the commercial market. The mariachi and its music became by far the most universally recognized and commercially dominant of these rurally derived musics. And its expansion through the popular media became the first major step toward the music's widespread acceptance, especially among those of Mexican heritage, in the United States.

THE EVOLUTION OF THE MARIACHI: CREATIVITY, COMMODIFICATION, AND MARIACHI VARGAS DE TECALITLÁN

At the end of the nineteenth century, the mariachi of west Mexico, like most regional mestizo musical ensembles, derived from stringed instruments imported from Spain in the early colonial era (1521–1810). Harp, violin, and different shapes and sizes of guitar were combined in various ways, with particular localities preferring certain combinations. In mariachi culture, the deep-boxed, percussive *guitarra de golpe* and/or smaller *vihuela* were paired with the harp and/or violin. These were the combinations of instruments that were brought to Mexico City in the early decades of the 1900s. The early Mariachi Vargas, for example, embodied the Tecalitlán preference for harp, *guitarra de golpe,* and two or more violins, while the Cuarteto Coculense (from the town of Cocula) that made the first mariachi recordings reflected the local custom of combining the *vihuela* and two violins with the five-string *guitarrón* (later modified by adding a sixth string). In the new context of Mexico City, in which mariachi groups from different local origins intermingled and were in commercial competition with other styles of music, the distinctive local styles merged over time into a more standard instrumentation and, at the same time, incorporated certain innovations that allowed mariachi groups a greater range of musical possibilities.

Early on in the Mexico City environment, violins dominated the melody in the mariachi and the size of the ensemble expanded, both factors diminishing the importance of the harp as a melody instrument in its higher range. The *guitarrón,* preferred in the style of performance associated with the town of Cocula, Jalisco, began to displace the harp as the bass instrument, a trend that continued until all but a few ensembles included a *guitarrón* as the exclusive bass instrument. That the harp has persisted in a small number of urban mariachis is largely due to its inclusion in Mariachi Vargas de Tecalitlán, with its large instrumentation of twelve or more musicians and its roots in Tecalitlán, the area with which the harp has long been associated.

In the 1940s the trumpet's place in the mariachi was established.

Experimentation with nonstringed instruments, the trumpet in particular, had been of interest for decades during the mariachi's transition to urban life. Yet, only when Silvestre Vargas invited Miguel Martínez to become the group's first permanent trumpet player in 1941 (Clark, 6) was the trumpet's destiny as an integral part of the mariachi sealed. Martínez's exquisite technique, tasteful style, and inventiveness in later adding a second trumpet set the standard for the mariachi's future. By the early 1950s the urban mariachi had taken the basic form that today is considered standard—*guitarrón, vihuela,* guitar, two trumpets, three or more violins, and, occasionally, the harp. The standard size of mariachi ensembles ranges from seven to eleven musicians, though major show groups may comprise thirteen or more (customarily adding violins and a guitar), and many groups smaller than seven abound, usually for economic reasons—many clients cannot afford larger groups. In all cases, the *guitarrón, vihuela,* violin, and trumpet are considered to be the minimum-sized core of a genuine mariachi.

A strong influence leading to the standardization of the mariachi's instrumentation was its evolution as a commodity, a commercial product to be packaged, marketed, sold, and consumed by large numbers of people. The expansion of the instrumentation offered greater musical possibilities, but it also allowed the mariachi a broader range of repertoire and thus a competitive edge over other folk-rooted ensembles that did not adapt to the marketplace. The real competition in the urban marketplaces of Mexico and its northern neighbor, undoubtedly, was the Afro- and Euro-American popular music of the United States—dance-band music, popular songs, and their Spanish-language imitation—with "slick" arrangements and aggressive marketing. While the types of music played by the mariachi expanded greatly in the second half of the twentieth century, commodification led to an opposite trend, the standardization of repertoire. The commercial music industry came to dominate musical life, and when music consumers listened to a mariachi, they expected to hear their favorite songs with arrangements like those they had heard over the radio, in the movies, or on recordings. Just as the music in the media of the 1930s and 1940s had eclipsed those that were not included, in the 1950s and afterward, the musical marketplace rewarded a relatively small number of musicians, requiring others to imitate the "stars" in order to please the consuming public so that they might fare well in their profession. Since at least the 1950s, the mariachi that has enjoyed this position of preeminence and influence has been Mariachi Vargas de Tecalitlán, often known—most would agree, with good reason—as "El Mejor Mariachi del Mundo" (The Best Mariachi in the World).

The farsightedness of Silvestre Vargas in adapting his group to urban, commercial, and musical demands, his insistence on a consistently high technical level of performance, his incorporation of extraordinarily talented musicians into the Vargas ranks, and his acceptance of the need for tight, polished, and innovative musical arrangements accounts for much of the success of Mariachi Vargas. In 1937 they appeared in their first film, *Así es mi tierra* (My Land Is Like That), and they would appear in more than two hundred others over the following decades (Clark, 5). Violinist Rubén Fuentes joined the group in 1944 (ibid., 6) and later became the most prominent mariachi arranger and innovator. Mariachi Vargas and Fuentes backed up virtually all of the most famous singers on their major recordings of *música ranchera* and made dozens of their own recordings as well. In the early years of José Alfredo Jiménez's career, for example, the musically unlettered songwriter would sing his melodies to Fuentes, who would then create an arrangement (Moreno Rivas 1989, 194). Fuentes experimented with the mariachi sound, adding such instruments as flutes and French horns, inventing new rhythmic techniques for the *vihuela,* and incorporating contemporary chords and harmonies. He created original compositions with a strikingly new sound. For more than a half century, Mariachi Vargas and Rubén Fuentes have set the standard for mariachi music everywhere, inspiring others to expand its creative possibilities, evolving ever more complex instrumental techniques and precise arrangements, and adapting it to the ever evolving commercial music market, while preserving in it a Mexican musical sensibility.

MARIACHI REPERTOIRE AND PERFORMANCE CONTEXTS

In its earlier rural setting, the mariachi repertoire had at its core the older, lively *sones* and *jarabes* that are imbued with a vigorous rhythm suited for the often percussive footwork of the traditional *zapateado* dance style. The *son* "El Jabalí" (The Wild Boar) exemplifies this style. Other social dance rhythms that rose to popularity in the nineteenth century—the waltz, schottische, and polka, for example—also left their mark on the repertoire of many musicians. A body of instrumental music called *minuetes* (no relation to the minuet) was used exclusively for religious events in western Mexican rural life. When the mariachi moved into the urban sphere, the repertoire and corresponding performance style changed. As the mariachi became more closely associated with *música ranchera,* it increasingly emulated the image of the singer actors of the cinema and the recording superstars. The high intensity, emotion-packed *canción ranchera* and more suave *bolero ranchero* moved to the fore, leaving the *sones* and *jarabes* in a secondary, though nevertheless important, role. The religious *minuetes* did not survive the transition to urban life, although a few of the older style rural groups still remember them.

Today, the common mariachi repertoire still draws from the more stylized forms—*sones, rancheras, boleros,* polkas, and such folkloric classics as "Jarabe Tapatío"—but a wide variety of others have crept into the repertoire as well. The *danzón,* a dance of Cuban origin popular in the first half of the twentieth century; the *cumbia,* rooted in Colombian-Panamanian folk music and popularized in the 1960s and later; folk-based melodies from other Mexican regions, such as "La Bamba" from Veracruz and "Las Chiapanecas" from Chiapas; more recent *baladas* (ballads) crooned by pop singers; novelty pieces, such as "Poet and Peasant Overture," "Orange Blossom Special," and bilingual versions of "Before the Next Teardrop Falls"; the "Macarena" dance craze; and many other kinds of music have been taken up by mariachi groups.

Even as the mariachi repertoire reflects both a deep sense of grassroots Mexican tradition and an adaptation to evolving musical and commercial trends, so do the contexts for mariachi performance. As we observed in the opening vignette about Mariachi San Matías, the mariachi remains an important part of Mexican social life. As they were a century ago, mariachis today are a part of important social occasions—birthday celebrations, wedding receptions, baptisms, and so forth. Notably, another context for mariachi performance is the Catholic Mass. In the several decades since the Catholic Church in the 1960s began encouraging the use of vernacular music in religious ceremony, a new repertoire of music for the Mass has come into existence. The "Mariachi Mass," begun in Mexico and now quite popular in many Catholic churches with large Mexican congregations, offers mariachi arrangements of all the major parts of the Mass, as well as hymns for regular or special occasions, such as the annual celebration of the Virgin of Guadalupe on December 9. This Catholic commemoration of the sixteenth-century apparition of the Virgin Mary on Tepeyac hill in what is now Mexico City is a major event in the calendrical cycle of Mexican Catholicism, as the Virgin of Guadalupe has become an important symbol of Mexican cultural identity on both sides of the border. Mariachi masses often attract large numbers of worshippers and tourists, especially in such large cities as San Antonio or Los Angeles. A mariachi mass has become a popular way of marking a special occasion, and it is not unusual for a mariachi to perform at a mass for a wedding, an anniversary, a funeral, or a *quince años* ("coming-out" party for fifteen-year-old girls) and then move to the church hall or client's home to play at the social celebration that follows.

At the same time that the mariachi expanded into many social and religious contexts, it also made its way into major public venues packaged as a "show." Such groups as Nati Cano's Mariachi Los Camperos of Los Angeles, California, Mariachi Cobre (Copper, after the ubiquitous mineral of Arizona, the state of the group's origin) at EPCOT Center in Florida, and Campanas de América (Bells of America) from San Antonio, Texas, have developed complex arrangements and performance sets fit for such occasions. Consequently, there is a wide range of performance styles and settings for the mariachi. In the United States, the special character of the American cultural and social context have had an interesting effect on mariachi repertoire and performance contexts in recent years.

THE MARIACHI IN THE UNITED STATES: A CHANGING FRAME OF REFERENCE

During the twentieth century, large numbers of Mexican people immigrated to the United States. Particularly in the decades following World War II, a demand for inexpensive labor on the American side and a population explosion and high unemployment on the Mexican side stimulated a dramatic surge of immigration. At the beginning of the century and long before, the United States-Mexican border had meant little in terms of cultural barriers between the two countries. People along the border moved with relative ease back and forth, and as a consequence shared a more-or-less common culture. But culture then was strongly regional, and as the mariachi and its music came from central western Mexico and not from the north, it was not a significant part of border life. When in the late 1930s mariachi music began to be an important part of the growing pan-Mexican experience largely as a result of the expanding media industry, it only then began to play a larger role in Mexican life *north* of the border. Large Mexican American communities in California, Texas, and other parts of the Southwest had long maintained strong cultural ties to Mexico, ties that were further strengthened by the popular media, and one of those ties was the mariachi and its music.

Perhaps the strongest flow of new immigration in the years following World War II was from the agricultural regions of western Mexico, also the traditional stronghold of mariachi music. New immigrants, of course, further bolstered a demand for mariachi music. "As it came to the United States, it was in the *cantina* [a bar that served as the principal gathering place for blue-collar men] that the music first took hold. Musicians followed immigrants and were available to assuage feelings of isolation and loneliness at the end of the work day or week. While major groups in Mexico generated their income from tours, recordings, and the accompaniment of 'star' singers (*artistas*), groups in the United States, like the lower echelon of mariachis in Mexico, were almost entirely employed in the *cantina*, with supplemental income derived from *chambas* ('casuals'): performances at weddings, baptisms, birthdays, and small-scale family celebrations" (Fogelquist 1996a, 3). In general, these two main contexts of mariachi performance—local social occasions attended to by the cantina-based groups and Mexican shows on tour to American venues—were transplanted whole cloth into the American setting and accounted for virtually all occasions for mariachi performance.

Since the late 1960s, though, the American setting has seen many important changes in this pattern, as mariachi music has found a place in school programs and in more genteel middle-class performance settings. At the same time, the changing metaphorical "frame" around the performance—the specific context—has been accompanied by a changing set of meanings about and attitudes toward the music. In the late 1960s mariachi music began to be taught in school settings in the Southwest, a trend that

Figure 6.4. Guitarrón player Raúl Ojeda of Albuquerque, New Mexico's Mariachi Tenampa teaches a student during a 1996 workshop session at the University of New Mexico's Mariachi Spectacular! held each year in Albuquerque. Photo by Daniel Sheehy.

accelerated in the 1970s and 1980s. By the 1990s there were several universi-ty-level mariachi music programs in California, Arizona, New Mexico, and Texas and dozens of middle and secondary school programs throughout the West (see Fig. 6.4). The primary promoters of these programs at the middle and secondary levels were advocates of multicultural education and of the inclusion of music instruction that was culturally representative of Mexican American student populations. One of the first such efforts was in Texas, where multicultural education expert Belle Ortiz of the San Antonio Independent School District launched an ambitious, multischool program of after-school mariachi instruction at both middle and secondary levels. Ortiz's conviction in the educational and human development value of the mariachi-in-schools program led her to organize the first International Mariachi Conference, held in San Antonio in 1979, that combined instruc-tional workshops with a performance by Mariachi Vargas de Tecalitlán. The festival's model of matching youth-oriented instruction with an inspirational concert by the most renowned of mariachi ensembles was a resounding suc-cess. The students, awestruck by the presence and extraordinary musician-ship of the Vargas performers, were highly motivated learners, and in follow-ing years, the San Antonio festival attracted new attendees from as far away as Arizona and California. Festival organizers in Arizona were the first to replicate Ortiz's idea, organizing what came to be the largest of these festivals, followed by many others in California, New Mexico, Nevada, and other Texan cities. Middle and secondary mariachi instructional programs have also multiplied, most of which have been inspired by the festivals themselves or by a greater awareness sparked by the festivals of other model school programs. In any given year, there may be as many as fifteen major mariachi festivals in the United States and many dozens of ongoing school programs nationwide. At the university level, a similar trend, as well as the emergence of several programs in ethnomusicology that emphasized the performance of many styles of music from around the world, was the principal motivating forces for the inauguration of mariachi ensembles. Such programs "have provided unprecedented opportunities for young performers to study with outstanding mariachi musicians, establishing continuity with the roots of the traditions and a forum for the exploration and expression of cultural identity" (Fogelquist 1996, 23). They also led to the formation of new, professional ensembles of American origin. The student group humorously named Los Changuitos Feos (The Ugly Little Monkeys) from Tucson, for example, evolved into the Mariachi Cobre that has performed at the Epcot Center in Florida for over a decade.

At the same time, during the late 1960s, a second development took place: in Los Angeles, Natividad Cano and his Mariachi Los Camperos established La Fonda, the first night club where mariachi music was presented on a stage as a dinner show (Fogelquist1996a, 3). The restaurant-dinner show context provided an inviting environment to middle-class non-Mexicans and others who did not frequent the male-dominated (primarily first-generation immigrant) *cantinas*. The idea caught on and by the 1990s, there were numerous similar situations in Los Angeles, Tucson, Albuquerque, Denver, Houston, San Antonio, and many other cities in the Southwest. These contexts played upon the notion of a Mexican music "show," but they foregrounded the mariachi itself, in contrast to the longstanding tours of big-name Mexican singers in which the mariachi was relegated to the role of an anonymous backup group.

Through the years, these changing frames of reference in the learning, performance, and appreciation of mariachi music have had many noticeable effects—social, contextual, musical—on mariachi musical culture. The social view of music is changing. In Mexico, mariachi musicians were often victims of class prejudice. In the words of one senior musician,

> I know that they say "the mariachi is the heart of Mexico"; and that's an odd thing, because I've also seen that in Mexico there are people who scorn us. . . . I understand from my years as a child on the ranch, how the rich scorn the poor, but it is impossible for me to accept that they feel that way about us, who are the music and the happiness of Mexico. (Gabaldón Márquez 1981, 360)

The change in performance context from the *cantina* to the restaurant and in role from backup musician to featured performer is tied in the minds of some musicians to their desire to elevate the social status of the music and the musicians who play it, distancing them from these old prejudices. Natividad Cano tells of how, in his earlier career in Mexico, there were signs on *cantinas* with the warning "No Dogs, Women, or Mariachis Allowed," and how he is determined to change this form of prejudice through maintaining an extraordinary level of musicianship and through advocating his musical tradition to the widest public possible. Cano has had great success in his efforts; he has performed regularly to sold-out houses in major performance venues, been featured in two national public television shows (including a performance with Linda Ronstadt at the White House), and received a prestigious National Heritage Fellowship from the National Endowment for the Arts.

With the change in performance contexts has also come a change in the social prohibitions governing mariachi performance. In particular, as the schools, dinner-show restaurants, and other public performance venues have moved the mariachi further away from the male-dominated *cantina* context, women instrumentalists have increasingly taken on a role on par with male performers. Historically, while a few all-women mariachis existed, the vast majority of mariachi groups were composed exclusively of men, partly in keeping with the social prohibitions against women participating as musicians in *cantinas* and other libertine circumstances. More gender-equal school programs and stage concerts have changed this, making the presence of women more of an asset to the groups' showmanship. The addition of Chicana violinist Rebecca Gonzales to the ranks of Los Camperos in the early 1970s set the stage for many other female musicians to follow her example and perform with top-notch show-oriented ensembles. Gonzales had previously been a member of Mariachi Uclatlán, the U.C.L.A. student group that had become an independent professional mariachi. As the influence of mariachi school programs and festivals is felt across the Southwest, many more women musicians are becoming professional *mariacheras* (mariachi performers). The "Viva el Mariachi" festival in Fresno, California, has featured the growing role of women in mariachi music, showcasing the all-female groups Mariachi Reyna de Los Angeles (Queen of Los Angeles) from California and Mariachi Femenil "Las Perlitas Tapatías" (The Female Mariachi Tapatía Pearls) from Guadalajara. In addition, a growing number of male and female non-Mexicans, having discovered the music mainly through school and university programs, have played more of a role in both amateur and professional mariachi performance.

Mariachi music's popularity has clearly been on the rise in the United States. An important spinoff of the mariachi festival movement—the Tucson International Mariachi Festival in particular—that added great impetus to this trend was popular-music singer Linda Ronstadt's two recordings, *Canciones de mi Padre* (Songs of my Father) and *Más Canciones* (More Songs), and her national tours of mariachi music. Ronstadt made the recordings following her performance at the Tucson festival, in which she recalled her Mexican American musical heritage during her years growing up in Tucson. The boost in esteem and popularity the music enjoyed both among Mexican Americans and non-Mexicans alike as a result of Ronstadt's efforts were widespread and profound. David Gates, writing for *Newsweek* magazine in 1988, reported that

> [Linda Ronstadt's mariachi album] "Canciones de mi Padre"— Songs of My Father—has gone gold and is at 55 on Billboard's Top Pop album chart: hardly unusual for a Linda Ronstadt LP, but pretty impressive for a record whose words most *norteamericanos* can't understand. (Gates 1988, 66)

Several years later, the late Mexican American superstar vocalist from Corpus Christi, Texas, Selena Quintanilla-Pérez, recorded similar arrangements of several of the "classic" melodies selected from Ronstadt's *Canciones de mi Padre* album, taking mariachi music to still greater audiences and inspiring adoring imitators nationwide.

The show context has had a noticeable influence on the mariachi repertoire. Compared to the *cantina* and other contexts with more social interaction, the musical repertoire performed in the contexts of restaurant dinner shows and major concert performances is significantly more standardized and narrow in range (Pearlman 1984, 7–8). As these new show contexts proliferate, and as young American musicians perform more in these situations and less "*al talón*" (paid-by-the-song) in *cantina* settings or for other social events in which the audience expects the musicians to play the repertoire that *they* request rather than a fixed show repertoire, the overall effect may be to narrow the range of music played. This is not to say that the more intimate and demanding situations in terms of repertoire are destined to fade out; they are not. More likely, the two principal subclasses of mariachi musician and ensemble will be more differentiated, reflecting the particular demands of their respective performance situations. Ideally, many musicians will possess both the technical capability demanded for the show setting and the breadth of repertoire required for more intimate settings and will be equally adaptable to both.

Today, mariachi music is performed frequently in all regions of the United States. New York, New Jersey, Massachusetts, Maryland, Washington, D.C., Virginia, North Carolina, Georgia, Florida, Tennessee, Michigan, Illinois, Kansas, Idaho, Washington, Oregon, Utah, California, New Mexico, Arizona, Texas, Nevada, Utah, Colorado, and many other states are home to mariachi

Figure 6.5. Mariachi Los Amigos performs at a Bolivian family's outdoor birthday celebration in Falls Church, Va. Photo by Daniel Sheehy.

ensembles. And as the mariachi has become more a part of the broad cultural landscape of the United States, so have musicians of many cultural backgrounds taken up the *guitarrón, vihuela,* violin, or trumpet to play the *sones, rancheras, boleros,* and other musical genres at the heart of mariachi tradition.

This Saturday was a normal day for our mariachi, Mariachi Los Amigos, based in the Washington, D.C., area (Fig. 6.5). I had helped organize the group in 1978 when I moved from California, where I had studied Mexican music at U.C.L.A. and played trumpet with Mariachi Uclatlán. Made up of another non-Mexican Californian who had played violin in her university's mariachi in Santa Cruz, two musicians from Mexico who knew the basic repertoire and techniques of *guitarrón* and *vihuela,* a trumpet player from Bolivia, a violinist from Guatemala, and a Chinese-American violinist and ethnomusicologist from Cleveland, our mariachi had committed to memory a repertoire of about two hundred tunes. This, along with our respectably polished style, was more than enough to get by playing for the general American audiences that hired us for house parties, fundraisers, ethnic concert series, and the like. Today, though, we were going to Fredericksburg, Virginia, to play an outdoor Mass and party celebrating the *quince años* (fifteenth birthday) of our friend Rafael's daughter, and we expected that there would be lots of recent immigrants from Mexico who had come to northern Virginia to work in construction and agricultural jobs and who would be requesting plenty of tunes that we didn't know from the *"talón"*-style mariachi's repertoire of at least a couple thousand tunes. Thus, we recruited our friend Pedro, who had arrived a couple years before from El Salvador and who worked *al talón* in the *cantinas* of the Washington area's burgeoning Latino (mainly Central American and Mexican) neighborhoods, to come along with us and fill in as needed.

In a field next to Rafael's mobile home, two Spanish-speaking priests said the Mass as we played the Kyrie, Gloria, Alleluia, Sanctus, and other main parts of the Mass. *Papel picado* (colorful paper cuts) were strung over the altar and platform that would later serve as a dance floor. The reverent audience, about 150 *mexicano* immigrants, mostly men, many of whom wore in Mexican-style Western hats and boots, were reserved and silent. When the Mass ended, the party began, with the unveiling of tables full of *enchiladas, carne asada* (roast beef), *birria* (western Mexican goat stew), and beer. When we started the classic *son* "La Negra" (The Dark Woman), *gritos* (yells) erupted from all sides, and after the final note, we were surrounded by people who requested hits from the latest compact-disc recording by mariachi superstar Vicente Fernández, along with the obscure classic *rancheras* favored by grassroots *mexicanos.* Halfway through the party, the skies opened, and the rain poured down, wilting the *papel picado* and soaking partygoers and musicians alike. But the requests continued, and a few determined men and women kept dancing, until the rain, mud, darkness, and fatigue brought the event to a close and we piled in our cars to return home.

Before we left, we made plans to rendezvous the next day for a performance at a "food fair" that would be put on by local restaurateurs who had hired our mariachi, a German folk music trio, a Japanese *koto* player, and a bluegrass band to represent stereotypes of the ethnic diversity of the Washington restaurant cuisine. As it would be presented in the shallow style of "It's a Small, Small World" there, we would not need Pedro to help us out. The non-Latino public usually asks for the same a dozen-or-so pieces, and we know them all.

■ ■ ■ ■

In the course of time, the people who make music, the audiences for whom it is made, and the contexts in which it is played have a powerful effect on the music itself. As mariachi music becomes more a part of life north of the U.S.-Mexican border, it both changes and remains the same, in order to suit the musical tastes, social needs, and lifestyles of people in its new homeland. This dialectic between tradition and change has brought a particular kind of creative tension to mariachi culture in the United States, resulting in a broad degree of change in the music and its meaning. While mariachi music has changed little in Mexican American communities that are strongly rooted in traditional Mexican cultural ways, some groups have attempted to reach broader audiences through crowd-pleasing pop fusions by playing, for example, arrangements of tunes from the Broadway show "A Chorus Line" (with choreography) or *salsa* music. In the middle are "innovative traditionalists," epitomized by Nati Cano, who embraces both change *and* tradition. "Music is a constant evolution I never cease to enjoy," he once said (Lopetegui, F1). "I can't see why you can't create valuable music while remaining traditional. It is such a rich music." The seeds of mariachi music have been firmly planted in North American culture. The future of mariachi music in the United States and the course of its evolution will undoubtedly be determined by musical leaders like Nati Cano, the enthusiasm of American audiences, the support of educational institutions, and the continuing interest of the entertainment industry.

REFERENCES CITED

Barrios de los Ríos, Enrique. 1908. *Paisajes de Occidente.* Sombrerete, Zacatecas (Mexico): Imprenta de la Biblioteca Estarsiana.

Clark, Jonathan. 1992. *Mexico's Pioneer Mariachis,* vol. 3. *Mariachi Vargas de Tecalitlán: Their First Recordings, 1937–1947.* Descriptive notes to Arhoolie Folklyric CD 7015.

———. 1993. *Mexico's Pioneer Mariachis,* vol. 1. *Mariachi Coculense de Cirilo Marmolejo.* Descriptive notes to Arhoolie Folklyric CD 7011.

Fogelquist, Mark. 1996. Mariachi Conferences and Festivals in the United States. In *The Changing Faces of Tradition: A Report on the Folk and Traditional Arts in the United States.* Washington, D.C.: National Endowment for the Arts, 18–23.

———. 1996a. Mariachi Conferences and Festivals in the United States: A Report. Unpublished manuscript on file with author.

Gabaldón Márquez, Edgar. 1981. *Historias Escogidas del Mariachi Francisco Yáñez Chico, Según los Apuntes de Edgar Gabaldón Márquez.* México City: J.M. Castañón.

Gates, David. 1988. A Rocker Reclaims Her Roots. In *Newsweek,* 29 February, 66–67.

Jáuregui, Jesús. 1990. *El Mariachi: Símbolo Musical de México.* México City: Banpais.

Lopetegui, Enrique. 1996. Still Making Music with a Legendary Enthusiasm. *Los Angeles Times,* 26 December, F1, F4.

Moreno Rivas, Yolanda. 1989. *Historia de la Música Popular Mexicana.* México City: Editorial Patria.

Pearlman, Steven Ray. 1984. Standardization and Innovation in Mariachi Music Performance in Los Angeles. *Pacific Review of Ethnomusicology* 1, 1–12.

Santa. 1931. Director: Antonio Moreno. Producers: Joselito and Roberto Rodríguez Ruelas. Studio: Compania National Productora de Peliculas.

Saldívar, Gabriel. 1937. *El Jarabe: Baile Popular Mexicano.* México City: Talleres Gráficos de la Nación.

Sonnichsen, Philip. 1993. *Mexico's Pioneer Mariachis,* vol. 1. *Mariachi Coculense de Cirilo Marmolejo.* Descriptive notes to Arhoolie Folklyric CD 7011.

Vázquez Valle, Irene, series director. 1976. *El son del sur de Jalisco.* Vols. 1, 2, 18, and 19. Instituto Nacional de Antropología e Historia. Serie de Discos. México: Instituto Nacional de Antropología e Historia.

COMPANION CD SELECTIONS

Track 10. "Las Mananitas." Mariachi Los Camperos.

Track 11. "El Jabali." Mariachi Los Camperos.

ADDITIONAL SOURCES

Canciones de Siempre: Mariachi Los Camperos de Nati Cano. Produced by Linda Ronstadt and George Massenburg. Compact disc. Peer Southern Productions, Polydor 314 519 712-2. Twelve original arrangements of mariachi favorites.

Clark, Jonathan. 1994. *Mexico's Pioneer Mariachis,* vol. 2. *Mariachi Tapatío de José Marmolejo "El Auténtico."* Descriptive notes to Arhoolie Folklyric CD 7012.

Fogelquist, Mark. 1975. *Rhythm and Form in the Contemporary Son Jalisciense.* Master's thesis, University of California, Los Angeles.

———, and Patricia W. Harpole. 1989. *Los Mariachis! An Introduction to Mexican Mariachi Music.* Danbury, Conn.: World Music Press. Twenty-page booklet, illustrations, cassette tape.

Gradante, William. 1982. "El Hijo del Pueblo": José Alfredo Jiménez and the Mexican Canción Ranchera. *Latin American Music Review* 3, no. 1 (spring–summer): 36–59.

Koetting, James. 1977. The *Son Jalisciense:* Structural Variety in Relation to a Mexican *Forme Fixe.* In *Essays for a Humanist: An Offering to Klaus Wachsmann.* New York: The Town House Press. 162–88.

Más Mariachi: Mariachi México de Pepe Villa. Compact disc. Mediterráneo MCD-10130. Contains twenty-three classic polkas, *pasodobles,* folk dances, and songs.

Ronstadt, Linda. *Canciones de mi Padre.* Arranged and conducted by Rubén Fuentes. Compact disc recordings with Spanish texts and English translations. Asylum 9 60765-2.

Vargas de Tecalitlán: "El Mariachi." Compact disc. Polygram Discos, Polydor 839 332 2. Contains mainly new arrangements of older mariachi favorites.

CHAPTER 7

Cultural Interaction in New Mexico as Illustrated in the Matachines Dance

Brenda M. Romero

*R*omero *is an ethnomusicologist who has long-standing involvement with American Indian and Hispanic traditions. In her essay on matachines, a music and dance performance complex with significant spiritual and historical overtones, she examines the cultural interaction between two of the most influential minority populations in the United States—the native Pueblo and Mexican American citizens of New Mexico and southern Colorado. A unique cross-fertilization of their cultures has produced a complicated genre that integrates both music and dance. Romero traces some of their musical forms to eighteenth-century Mexico and even further back, to twelfth-century Spain, through a complex musical and cultural history of tune families. Implicit in this discussion is a quest for that which is "authentic." Romero concludes that authenticity is defined not by the scholar, who searches for the ultimate original version of a tune or a tale, but by the community itself, which imbues the performance, however fresh its elements, with the weight of tradition and authenticity. The long and complicated history of matachines music is further heightened by the role of Romero as insider and outsider. As a scholar and a musician, who now plays an active role in the perpetuation of the matachines fiddle repertoire, Romero demonstrates the potential of the scholar to both objectively "study" a cultural phenomenon and to positively affect its course.*

■ ■ ■ ■

When North Americans talk about Latino musical culture in the United States, they are most likely to mention the Norteño tradition of the Texas-Mexican border area, or the salsa music of the sizeable Cuban and Puerto Rican populations in New York City. Yet, the longest continuously Latino-populated areas in the United States are Northern New Mexico and Southern Colorado, where music has always been an integral part of the daily life of the Hispanic population who traditionally describe themselves in Spanish as *Mejicanos*,[1] the term that is used in this chapter. Although initially colonized by Spain under Don Juan de Oñate in 1598, the area has also been continuously inhabited by American Indian Pueblo[2] peoples, who have sung and danced sacred ceremony into the earth and sky for over forty thousand years. The greatest significance of this rich cultural area lies in the close interaction of Spanish, then Mexican, peoples with the Pueblo people and, more recently, the interaction of these groups with other Americans of various heritage.

New Mexico, the "Land of Enchantment," continues to captivate outsiders with its rich heritage, both ancient and recent, and with the strong sense of Pueblo and Mejicano pride in its political and social life. The state capital, Santa Fe, has emerged in this century as a center of architectural beauty, a place where builders have developed the possibilities inherent in adobe pueblo and Spanish/Moorish forms. With inspirational blue skies, mystical sunsets, and the allure of traditional culture, Santa Fe and Taos have become international centers of fine art. Santa Fe hosts one of the premier opera houses of the world, and the hundreds of art galleries and numerous festivals in New Mexico attract art afficionados and tourists year round.

Why do we group Mejicano and the Pueblo in this chapter? Simply because they share the same space and have for hundreds of years. The reality of the American experience is that we cross over each other's cultural spaces every day. While daily newspapers report water and land disputes between Native Pueblo peoples and local governments, only minutes away from the large cities and towns, the Pueblos open some of their ancient ceremonies to their neighbors and to the mainstream American public. Among these public ceremonies, one of the least known is the matachines dance drama, unique by virtue of being the only Pueblo ceremony that uses European instruments and music. Almost as an accident of fate, the matachines—a performance complex involving music, dance, story, and ritual—took on a devotional quality in both cultures and survived in Mejicano and Pueblo settings, where it was associated with Catholic saints' days. Its profane origins in Old Spain originally gave the matachines a certain autonomy, allowing the ceremony to be in the hands of the people rather than the clergy. For this reason, the matachines is an excellent medium through which to observe the processes of cultural interaction that have defined New Mexican existence for centuries (see Rodriguez 1996).[3]

ETHNOMUSICOLOGICAL METHOD AND APPLICATION

Traditional Western musicology has focused primarily on questions relevant to the understanding and development of Western art music. Since membership or identification with a Western European world view is implicit in this discipline, musicology has not concerned itself with questions of cultural significance, for the most part. Ethnomusicocology differs from traditional musicology in that it is "studying the music of our time" (Porter 1995, 26). The emphasis is synchronic, with diachronic or historical study as a means of better understanding the present musical phenomenon. The discipline requires first-hand observation and experience, and thus fieldwork is an essential aspect of ethnomusicological methodology.

The importance of fieldwork as a tool for understanding more clearly what happens in Pueblo music is undermined by Pueblo resistance to passing their spiritual knowledge into the wrong hands. Pueblo cultures, like many other American Indian cultures, believe firmly in witches and the power of those who are capable of taking sacred knowledge and using it for their own interests, with potentially devastating consequences for others (see Toelken 1995). One does not, then, enter the Pueblo with notebook, camera, and tape recorder in hand. It is essential to direct a written request to conduct fieldwork research to the governing body of the tribe. Additionally, it is essential to contact each newly elected governing tribal body to keep them informed of what you have done and what you are now doing. In every case, in order to continue to conduct research, verbal information must be formalized in a "letter of request."

Most Pueblo families own a camera, including video cameras in some cases. Photographs adorn the walls of the front room of most households. Usually, only Pueblo members are allowed to photograph ceremonies, and sometimes not even they are allowed to do so. Outsiders are in danger of having their equipment and film confiscated should they be ignorant of this general rule. Exceptions to the rule may be made when ceremonial dances take place outside of designated sacred spaces, such as the Pueblo plaza. Usually one is allowed to take pictures only after purchasing a permit, and even then, only in some Pueblos, of particular ceremonies, and during certain years. One is most likely to be allowed to take pictures in such public settings as the state fair or a cultural center. Asking for permission is a common courtesy here as well.

Among the Mejicanos, it is easier to conduct fieldwork, as the culture is predominantly Spanish acculturated (despite the blood mixing of Europeans, Natives, and sometimes Africans). In general, the Mejicanos seem to be as open to field workers as the Pueblos are closed to them. Very few persons are barred from documenting the public matachines in Mejicano settings. One example of a *persona non grata* is a local photographer who has photographed matachines dancers and masks, then displayed and sold his photographs internationally without compensating the groups from whom he profits. Pueblo influences are being felt in places like Bernalillo, where recordings are no longer allowed except by designated individuals.

For both cultures, issues of appropriation for commercial profit are significant concerns. A desire to control the outcome of outside research so that the pueblos benefit is clearly seen in recent Pueblo tribal rulings. While Mejicano community organization does not compare to Pueblo government, there is a growing awareness of a need for community guidelines that will help to protect community and individual rights to cultural property. In both cases, cultural appropriation is potentially tied to religious desecration.

I was born in Santa Fe and am a Mejicana. Much of my childhood was spent in close proximity to the Pueblo peoples, who have influenced rural Mejicanos for centuries. I began to conduct fieldwork on the matachines in 1987 as part of a desire to understand how the matachines dance functioned as a medium for cultural interaction. The folk violinist with whom I wanted to work, Adelaido Martinez, was terminally ill. After his death, I gained assurance from the governors of the Pueblo of Jemez that if I learned the repertoire, I could play in the ceremony, which might then continue. Since I was trained primarily as a composer and guitarist, learning to play the fast pieces on the violin was a challenge. As a result, the fieldwork situation was thrown into turmoil; now, much of my time at the pueblo was spent as a participant who concentrated on being a credible violinist. I was fortunate to be able to keep the rhythm going despite occasional involuntary variations in the melody. The Pueblo elders encouraged me often and praised me highly for good performances, for "without you we cannot dance," they said.

While my role as the necessary and trusted musician was accepted by the elders, my role as an academic researcher was viewed with suspicion. The unethical use of Pueblo religious information by such anthropologists as Elsie Clews Parsons in the 1920s is still fresh in the minds of the elders. I felt gratified to be able to do something for the Pueblo while I grew in my understanding of the culture and its music. I began to view myself as an applied ethnomusicologist, a scholar who identifies the needs of a culture and responds to them. It is important for the Pueblos to see that scholarly work may benefit their people.

Among my questions were the following: In what ways have Mejicano and Pueblo mediated hostility over time? How have these cultures that are in close proximity negotiated difference? What defines identity? What constitutes authenticity when cultures perform borrowed or received ceremonies? Before exploring the matachines, let us acquaint ourselves with the musical cultures of Pueblos and Mejicanos (see Romero 1993). As a preface, bear in mind that the cultures under discussion have been engaged in a constant struggle to overcome poverty over the course of this century. Significant economic gains have been achieved with the commercialization of cultural art forms. Music and dance, however, have resisted commercialization, in large part because of their spiritual importance to the people involved. This essay alludes to Pueblo cultures in general terms but focuses specifically on two tribes: the Tewa-speaking peoples who live in six pueblos north of Santa Fe along the Rio Grande—San Juan Pueblo is the largest of these—and the Towa-speaking peoples of the Pueblo of Jemez, who live in a pueblo about fifty miles northwest of Albuquerque. The Mejicano people live in small towns in close proximity to both tribes, and this general area as a whole best represents the oldest aspects of both cultures.

THE SIGNIFICANCE OF MUSIC AMONG THE PUEBLOS

The sense of place is of central importance for the Pueblo cultures. Ideals of world view, such as that documented by San Juan Tewa anthropologist Alfonso Ortiz (1969), delineate the pueblo as a special place in the universe. This place is defined by sacred hills and mountains on which special shrines mark places for spirits to come and go between this world and an unseen place of origin that is also the individual's ultimate spiritual destination. Tewa Pueblo society is traditionally stratified into three distinct social classes. Those with the highest status, including the medicine men and women, conduct the business of the ceremonial societies and thus carry the greatest responsibility for the physical and spiritual well-being of the pueblo. Secondary status is assigned to those who define the core of the Tewa political organization. The lowest status is assigned to those who serve no official capacity in the political or ceremonial system. After death, a person's spirit enters a spiritual reality commensurate with his or her earthly position (Ortiz 1969, 17).

The ceremonial cycle follows regional ecological patterns, functioning in part to regulate the irregularities of the ecosystem with regard to subsistence, thus assuring the survival of the entire population. Food sharing is a regular feature of public ceremonials; and, not surprisingly, ceremonies are most frequent during the times of the year when fresh food is least available (Ford 1972, 11–12).

Song is the medium of communication with the spiritual forces that govern life, among whom ancestors are included. Kachinas[4] are intermediaries between this reality and non-empirical reality. When particular individuals dress as kachinas, they transform into those kachinas and their participation in ceremony is highly desirable. Songs accompany all aspects of ceremony, representing an active force that can affect the order of things in the universe. Thus, the pueblos emphasize formulas, ritual, and repetition (Ortiz 1972, 143). Functioning as the heartbeat of the deities, it may be said that the drumbeat brings the deities to life in ceremony (Romero 1993, 166). For some tribes, rattles recall the sound of falling rain, accompanying the drum with upbeat and downbeat accents; together they establish the tempo. Against the steady beat, singers must be able to sing seemingly independent rhythms and pulsations. The vocal text does not align itself in an exact correlation with the rattle or drum beat. This soundscape is a complex and subtle weaving, and most importantly, it is alive. The engaging of the unseen forces assures a plentiful harvest and prosperity for all. For this reason, the term *embodiment* is more useful than the term *symbolism* to describe the process of spiritual representation in the pueblos.

Music is always sung and almost always paired with dance, an essential component of communal ceremonies. Dance helps to demonstrate the interdependence of man, nature, and the spiritual world. The corn plant is considered a model for this concept of interdependence: all parts of the plant work together to produce the corn that brings life to the people. Participation in communal ceremonies is imperative to the well-being of the group, and precision is necessary to ensure the participation of the Unseen.[5] Except for cures and society initiations, Pueblo ceremonies do not call much attention to individual-centered rites (Ortiz 1972, 140). As a result of this emphasis on group cooperation, traditional Pueblo song is typically monophonic, accompanied by a single drum, with rare exceptions. It is the men's job to provide a well-rehearsed chorus, which sings tightly, as if in a single voice. Unless they are dancing communal dances, the women are busy with many other aspects

Figure 7.1. Randolph Padilla, 1996 governor of the pueblo of Jemez, and his wife, Nora, dressed for the Corn Dance on August 2, 1995. Photo by Brenda Romero.

of ritual organization, including the all-important job of food preparation and distribution.

Roberts (1972, 251) categorized the Rio Grande Pueblo dances into six basic classifications: kachina dances, maskless kachina dances, animal dances, corn dances, borrowed dances, and social dances. Due to the prohibition of the masks by the Spanish colonial government, which viewed them as idolatrous, masked kachinas are largely missing from most of the Rio Grande Pueblo dances. Masked kachinas do, however, continue to be prominent in the Zuni and Hopi Pueblos, where the Spanish theocracy exerted less influence. Animal dances honor the human relationship to birds and animals, at the same time as they function as sympathetic prayer magic for the perpetuation of species important for subsistence (Romero 1993, 161). Corn dances are essentially fertility dances. Like most public communal dances in the pueblos, the Corn Dance takes place on Catholic feast days and is the best known of the public dances. Hundreds of men, women, and children dance, sometimes under intense sun, usually barefoot, to a well-rehearsed male chorus and drum.

MATACHINA AS A RECEIVED OR BORROWED TRADITION

The matachines is actually a performance complex that was introduced to the Pueblos first by the Spanish colonists and later by the Mejicanos. In fact, there is a long-standing tradition of borrowing or receiving songs and ceremonies among the Pueblos (Ellis 1964, 57; Humphreys 1984, 29–56; Ortiz 1972, 147; Romero 1993, 148, 154). Whether from other native tribes or from the Spanish, borrowed traits were usually adapted to existent patterns and tended to add rather than substitute religious traits (Ellis 1964, 57). This is a crucial point in understanding American Indian world view, which underscores respect for the power inherent in song, dance, and ceremony per se. Recognizing only one Creation composed of a myriad of peoples and languages, American Indians in general perceive no conflict between different tribal belief systems. Tribes were eager in the past to acquire from another tribe a song or ceremony known to be powerful in hunting, healing, or other ritualized activities. The tribal society responsible for the new ceremony took great care to perform the new ceremony and all its attending requirements as closely resembling the original as possible. This is why the Pueblo peoples have a Buffalo Dance, received from Plains tribes, for whom religious ideology revolves around the buffalo. Such adoption of a new ceremony from an outside tribe would normally be accompanied by reciprocal sharing or payment of some kind.

The Spanish matachines is one of the most recently received music/dance forms among the Pueblos, who call it *matachina,* the term used in this chapter when referring specifically to Pueblo versions. It is not known when the Spanish first introduced this pantomime, and it remains the only

Figure 7.2. Pueblo of Jemez
Matachina dancer, Andy Loretto,
assisted by his wife, Geri, in prepara-
tion for the danza at the Los Angeles
Festival, September, 1990.
Photograph by Brenda Romero

pantomime (that is, it has no song texts or lyrics, only gestures) performed in the pueblos. But, while the Spanish may have believed that they were replacing traditional beliefs by allowing matachines as the only masked dance, the Pueblos most likely believed that they were being given the source of spiritual power that the matachines ceremony gave to the Spanish. Today, the matachina is also an example of how a music/dance ceremony received from a highly divergent foreign source may be reinterpreted, or tailored, to fit existent ceremonial Pueblo formats. It is the only ceremony in the pueblos that uses European music and instruments. Like the Corn Dance, the matachina dance in some pueblos evokes a heavily peopled and highly charged atmosphere. Friends and relatives visit at this time, and food, as well as arts and crafts vendors, line the peripheral areas of the sacred plaza in evergreen-shaded booths. In other pueblos, the matachina is not an occasion to which vendors are invited.

Social dances often have "home" contexts and are part of the general festivities at special times of the year, such as Christmas or New Year's Day. While an atmosphere of merry-making, including burlesque, dominates such social dances, they seem to conform to certain ritual requirements of producing an atmosphere of well-being and happiness—assuring all good things during the forthcoming year. Alfonso Ortiz (1972, 147) describes this world view thus:

> Among human beings the primary causal factors are mental and psychological states; if these are harmonious, the supernaturals will dispense what is asked and expected of them. If they are not, untoward consequences will follow just as quickly, because within this relentlessly interconnected universal whole the part can affect the whole, just as like can come from like.

The matachina performance in front of the Infant's House (described below) on New Year's Day incorporates a great deal of burlesque. As such, it closely resembles home dances on that particular occasion.

Songs, in general, use both words and vocables. Among the Tewa, words tend to be arranged in highly rhetorical forms that reflect the process of mediation of such opposite forces as day and night, youth and old age, male and female. Words are polyvalent and multisemous, reflecting different aspects of meaning and beliefs in various ways. For example, the word *old* might imply age, wisdom, eternity, and the like. While commonly described by non-Indians as "meaningless syllables," vocables are often laden with connotations; because of this characteristic, vocables are best described as words without a dictionary or lexical meaning. Sometimes they originated as words in ancient languages that are no longer spoken and which are preserved only in ceremonies. In other instances, vocables serve a variety of functions, including framing texts to enhance musical forms or recalling the sounds of the "animal nations." Vocables also make it possible for different tribes to join together in song even when they do not speak the same language. Sometimes vocables announce, if not evoke, particular deities or a particular ceremony—as, for example, in the San Juan Turtle Dance (LaVigna 1980, 86)—as if recalling the sacredness of sound itself.

Humor is an essential aspect of ceremonial life, for in order to be effective, a ritual must be undertaken with the right heart. Thus, all ceremonies include one or more clown figures, who are among the most sacred of the kachinas. This belief and practice influences daily life, and humor tends to be a regular aspect of everyday interactions. A good example of Pueblo humor may be found in Harold Littlebird's contemporary *Navajo Love Song* (Littlebird 1985, side 1). Littlebird is from the Acoma and Laguna Pueblos. The Navajos were the traditional enemies of the Pueblos in the past, so Littlebird's use of Navajo phrasing, place names, and falsetto (a thin, high tone important in Navajo song) are humorous jabs. For the punch line, the song cleverly uses the well-known fact that Navajos are a matriarchal society, with female prerogatives in courtship and divorce. The song is in English so that Pueblos, Navajos, and non-Indians alike might enjoy it.

Navajo Love Song, by Harold Littlebird
(with permission)

I'm goin' to Holbrook, darlin', *weya-heyaah.*
> [in falsetto] Why you goin' to Holbrook, sweetheart? *Weya-*
> *heyaah, he-yo.*

I'm goin' to Window Rock, darlin', gonna get me 'nother squaw, *weya-*
heyaah.
> [falsetto] Why, sweetheart, ain't I good enough for you? *Weya,*
> *heyaah, he-yo!*

It isn't that sweetheart, it's just I don't like beans and fry bread, *weya, heyaah.*
> [falsetto] Ah, don't leave me sweetheart, just 'cause I ain't no
> damn cook, *weya-heyaah, he-yo!*

I'm goin' to Window Rock, darlin', *weya-heyaah.*
> [in falsetto] Why you goin' to Window Rock, sweetheart?
> *Weya-heyaah, hey-yo.*

I'm goin' to Window Rock, darlin', gonna get me 'nother squaw, *weya-*
heyaah.
> [falsetto] Why, sweetheart, ain't I good enough for you? *Weya,*
> *heyaah, he-yo!*

It isn't that darlin', it's just you can't steer the wagon, *weya, heyaah.*
> [falsetto] Ah, don't leave me sweetheart, just 'cause I ain't no
> mule driver, *weya-heyaah, he-yo!*

I'm goin' to Lukachukai, darlin', *weya-heyaah.*
> [in falsetto] Why you goin' to Lukachukai, sweetheart? *Weya-*
> *heyaah, he-yo.*

I'm goin' to Lukachukai, darlin', gonna get me 'nother squaw, *weya-heyaah.*
> [falsetto] Why, sweetheart, ain't I good enough for you? *Weya,*
> *heyaah, he-yo!*

It isn't that sweetheart, it's just you get saddle sore, *weya, heyaah.*
> [falsetto] Ah, don't leave me sweetheart, just 'cause I got a soft
> ass, *aweya-heyaah, he-yo!*

I'm gonna stay Darlin', *weya-heyaah.*
> [in falsetto] Why you gonna stay sweetheart? *Weya-heyaah,*
> *he-yo!*

Since you asked me, darlin', *weya-heyaah.*
> [falsetto] That's before I met him and he's coming over. *Weya,*
> *heyaah, he-yo!*

Ah, don't leave me Darlin' just cause I told you all those lies, *weya, heyaah.*
[falsetto] It's too late, sweetheart, I already married him.
Weya, heyaah, he-yo!

While radio, television, and video might be absent during the two weeks a home is converted into the Infant's House, they are part of most Pueblo households. Country and western styles are popular in Pueblo households; yet, as more Pueblo and American Indian music in general is available commercially, it forms a significant part of individual recording collections. *National Geographic* videos that feature animal life are a big hit in the Pueblos. For the most part, electronic media is low-key in the pueblos, where community life is still an imposing force. Telephones are not a part of all Pueblo households, and only a few have electric instruments and amplifiers. Only recently have the Pueblos begun to use synthesizers. Many outsiders are highly critical when this happens, as mainstream Americans prefer to think of American Indians, in particular, in rather limiting ways. Although many American Indian recordings are now available that demonstrate a heavy use of synthesizers and other electronic equipment, the *Taos Pueblo Round Dance Song* (Rainier, et al 1992) demonstrates that innovation in one area of American Indian music today often implies innovation in other areas as well. The round dance is a friendship dance usually danced in a circle. While danced by both men and women, it is most often sung by a male chorus, unlike this recording, which features both men and women singers.[6] Further, the voices sing vocables, alternating with the flute, an instrument traditionally played by men in their courtship of women. Finally, a synthesizer is used, sounding Western harmonies in a dronelike effect. Both harmony and the use of a drone are absent in traditional Pueblo and American Indian music in general. Recording the music is itself an innovation, which in many cases also implies the equally innovative idea of concert performances.

THE ESSENCE OF PUEBLO MUSIC

Pueblo Indian life revolves around the idea that the pueblo is a special and unique place in the universe. Song and dance accompany ceremonies that assure the Pueblo's harmony with the natural world, which is continuous with the world of the Unseen. In this belief system, the combination of music and dance embody spiritual forces, which in turn give life to the people by ensuring abundance of all good things. Community participation in ceremonies, reflecting the cooperation of all parts of the corn plant, is important in order to gain the goodness of the Unseen. The ideal chorus sings together in a single voice, accompanied by a single drum whose steady, heartbeat-like accents are not strictly tied to downbeats and upbeats in the melody. Since American Indians honor ceremonies for their inherent spiritual power, dances from foreign sources, such as other tribes or peoples, form part of the ceremonial cycle. Words in songs embody beliefs about the living world, and vocables reinforce the idea that sound itself is sacred. Humor assures the right heart, an essential element of ceremony, and accompanies all aspects of everyday life. Like music everywhere, American Indian music responds to contemporary life. This means using performance and recording technology and bringing music to concert venues.

THE SIGNIFICANCE OF MUSIC AMONG THE MEJICANOS

Much of the folk music of the Mejicanos was already old when the Spaniards settled New Mexico in the early seventeenth century. Some of the songs collected here from 1930 to 1960 date back to the twelfth century and some are still older. They represent many different genres, including narrative ballads (*romances*), topical songs (*canciones*), and children's game songs. For centuries, folk singers took out their *cancioneros* (song books) in the evening hours, after the day's farmwork. They entertained themselves and taught songs to their children and relatives in extended family structures. Among those who continue to perform the old music today, this style of musical transmission is much the same as it used to be. It is not unusual to find similar transmission, from parent to offspring or sibling to sibling, of such nontraditional music as rock and roll, and many local bands reflect kinship ties among members. While the prevalence of older Spanish/Mejicano music has declined since the advent of electricity and the availability of radio and television, traditional Spanish/Mejicano music is still the musical foundation for many contemporary styles.

One of the oldest Mejicano genres is the *romance* (pronounced roh-máhn-seh), or ballad, which features two rhyming sixteen-syllable lines, each a complete thought. In the past, the *romance* featured many verses with much detail and could last a long time, for this was popular evening entertainment, long before the days of televisions or CD players. The *romance* is often set in the royal courts of medieval times, preserving significant historical accounts. The oldest *romance* recorded in New Mexico, *Gerineldo, Gerineldo, Mi Camarero Aguerrido* (*Gerineldo,* My Veteran Steward), dates back to 950 C.E. in the Carolingian Era in Europe. "*Gerineldo*" is a story of forbidden love between the *infanta*, the princess (Emma, the daughter of Charlemagne), and the king's chamberlain (Eginhard). The king cannot bring himself to execute them and instead allows them to marry (Mendoza 1986, 134; Espinosa 1985, 85). Undoubtedly, it is the symbolical bridge between nobility and commoner that made this song so popular for centuries, even far from its original setting.

The most widely disseminated *romance* in the New Mexico and Southern Colorado area was *La Delgadina* (The Thin Maiden, Track 12). Like *Gerineldo,* the song is set in the European royal courts. It is the tale of an incestuous king who locks his daughter in the castle tower when she refuses his indecent advances. The bell-like *estribillo* (refrain) is a play on words, idiomatically mocking the *don*, usually a term of honor for a man. The first few verses as I sing them, incorporating two of the many melodic variants found in New Mexico and Colorado (Robb 1980, 31, 38), are shown in Figure 7.3.

La Delgadina

Delgadina se paseaba,	Delgadina was walking
en una sala cuadrada,	in the great hall,
Con una mantona de oro	Wearing a mantle of gold
que la sala relumbraba	which made the room shine.
Y le dice el rey su padre,	And the king, her father, said to her,
"Aye, que linda Delgadina	"Ah, my most beautiful Delgadina,
(Que din, que don, que don, don, don)	

Figure 7.3. Two melodic variants of La Delgadina (Robb 1980, 31 38) [Transcriptions 1 and 2]

Aye, que linda Delgadina	Ah, my most beautiful Delgadina
puede ser me hermosa dama."	You will be my lovely mistress."
"No lo permite mi dios,	"May God not permit it
ni la reina soberana,	nor the sovereign queen,
Ofensa para mi dios,	It is an offense to God,
Agravio para mi nana."	and an affront to my mother."
"Aprontense aqui mis criados,	"Make haste my servants
de la sala y la cocina,	of the hall and the kitchen,
(Que din, que don, que don, don, don)	
Aprontense aqui mis criados,	Make haste my servants
encierren a Delgadina."	and imprison Delgadina."

In the end Delgadina dies, surrounded by angels, while her father's bed is tormented by devils for the rest of his life and beyond. Still performed in the 1950s, this ballad functioned to discourage incest in the isolated Spanish-Mexican villages. Remnants of Jewish versions of *La Delgadina*, found in New Mexico (Romero 1993, 217; see also Benmayor 1979), reveal another ethnic and religious influence on this culture, reminding us that the Sephardim (Sephardic, or Spanish Jews) lived in Spain continuously since the first century C.E. until their expulsion in 1492 and that many came to the New World as *conversos* (converts). Some converted in order to escape the Inquisition and continued to practice Judaism clandestinely (often a female-centered activity) in colonial New Mexico (see Jacobs 1995, Tobias 1990).

Among other genres that survived the colonial period were hundreds of *canciones*, soulful lyrical songs, such as *Palomita Que Vienes Herida* (Little Dove that Comes to Me Wounded). The dove is a symbol of love, in this case wounded love. The third verse was reconstructed for contemporary performance by myself from verse fragments collected by John Donald Robb (1980, 216).

Palomita que vienes herida	Little dove, that comes wounded
por las manos de un buen tirador,	at the hands of a good hunter,
anda y dile que rinda sus armas	go and tell him to lay down his arms
mientras duerme y descansa mi amor.	while my love rests.
Allá duras y tristes montañas	The distant mountains over there
son testigas del mal que sufrí,	testify to my suffering,

y me dicen y me responden tristes,	and they tell me and sadly answer,
"Ya tu amado no existe aqui."	"Your loved one is no longer here."

¿Donde se halla mi amado, querido,	Where is my true love,
donde se halla esa flor del querer?	where is that flower of my desire?
Pero tu ni siquiera un instante	But you do not even for an instant
ni un momento recuerdas de mi.	nor a moment remember me.

Songs like those discussed above were transformed into songs that reflected life in New Mexico and southern Colorado. They often retained an ancient modal structure, reinforced by Gregorian chant, which was used in the Mass, in New Mexico at least, until the 1960s.[7]

Gradually, the *copla* (also referred to as *verso*) became the most pervasive form in both Mexican and New Mexican folk song. It utilized four eight-syllable lines with an abcb rhyme or assonance scheme (Robb 1980, 869). The *copla* is the form preferred for lyric songs and was traditionally a popular form for improvised song duels, although a more complex ten-line form, the *décima,* was also used in such *trovos* (song contests). For an idea of what these contests sounded like, one might listen to such contemporary song contest traditions as those of the Basque peoples of Spain, whose song styles are reminiscent of the old Mejicano styles of New Mexico (for the New Mexican texts, see Robb 1980).[8]

Most notably, the copla is the form of today's *corrido,* a contemporary ballad that describes events in detail, typically beginning with the date and often the time and place of the event. The *corrido* is often commemorative, commissioned in memory of an important person or event, and frequently

Figure 7.4. Transcription of Palomita Que Vienes Herida (Robb 1980, 216).

appears following a tragedy, as if in protest. The oldest archival example of a New Mexican *corrido* is the *Corrido de la Muerte de Antonio Maestas* (Corrido of the Death of Antonio Maestas), composed by Higinio Gonzales in 1889 (Robb 1980, 523). It fits the textual characteristics of the Mexican *corridos* but is markedly modal, unlike contemporary *corridos,* which are usually in a major key. This *corrido* also exemplifies a typical practice of irregular metrical divisions that is common to the old Mejicano music.

The *corrido* emerged in Mexico in the latter half of the nineteenth century and has not diminished in importance since then. The *corrido* is popular in New Mexico as well, for the political boundaries between the United States and Mexico have not prevented a continuous musical exchange. The ready availability of radio since the 1950s has also aided the process.

To a degree, isolation from the rest of the Spanish-speaking world was a condition of the Spanish-Mexican colonies that became New Mexico and Colorado. Such isolation was reinforced when political boundaries were formed between Mexico and the United States in 1848. Consequently, many song types that developed into more modern, major-minor key styles in Mexico, continued in an older modal style in New Mexico until the introduction of radio and television in the early 1950s. Contemporary Mejicano *corridos* in New Mexico follow the Mexican styles more closely. These include one about the Challenger disaster that killed seven astronauts, *El Corrido de los Astronautas,* which appeared on the radio only one week after the accident and, more recently, *El Corrido del 720,* which is dedicated to the members of the 720th Transportation Company and their families. The latter aired in 1991 during Operation Desert Storm in the Persian Gulf, where the 720th

Corrido de la Muerte de Antonio Maestas (Robb 1980:523)

Figure 7.5. Transcription of *Corrido de la Muerte de Antonio Maestas* (Robb 1980, 527). Note the changing meters from $\frac{3}{8}$ to $\frac{6}{8}$.

was stationed. Both *corridos* were written by Roberto Martinez and recorded by Los Reyes de Albuquerque, his local mariachi group.

The Mejicano song genre referred to as the *indita,* which is indigenous to the New World and emerged during the nineteenth century, also utilizes Indian musical or textual themes. An example of this genre is the *Indita de Manuelito,* which is in the Dorian mode (Robb 1980, 434). The words, which mention the English names Charles and Captain Grey, reflect intercultural conflict following the Anglo-American colonization of this area.

Indita de Manuelito

¡Indita, indita, indita,   Indita, indita, indita,

con que sentimiento estás!   what grief you must feel!

Que en el ojo de la gallina   That, like true cowards,

te dieron muerte de paz.   they gave you the peace of death.

No te mataron peliando   They did not kill you fighting,

ni tampoco bien a bien.   nor in a decent way.

Te mataron a traición   They killed you by treachery,

Charles y el Capitán Grey.   Charles and Captain Grey.

Figure 7.6. Transcription of *La Indita de Manuelito* (Robb 1980, 434). In Dorian mode, sung here with G as the tonic note. The chords provided are those I use in performance. The D7 is used in the second and last lines because in early European art music it was common to raise the seventh tone of the scale, a practice that eventually led to the development of the European major/minor system.

Yo soy el indio Manuel,	I am the Indian Manuel,
hermanito del Mariano,	little brother of Mariano,
que con mi flecha en la mano	who with my arrow in my hand
empalmo de dos a tres.	pierce two or three at a time.
Yo soy el indio Manuel	I am the Indian Manuel
que tenía mis ovejitas,	who herded my ewes,
les tenía dada querencia	who felt affection for them,
en el ojo de Lemitar.	at the spring at Lemitar.

Many other vocal genres existed in the past and survived through the 1950s, including children's game songs that taught numbers or colors or that added a new animal or event in the same style and format as *Old McDonald*, the children's nursery rhyme. In celebrations, however, it was the dance music that took center stage. The *baile*, or social dance, originally was set in the front room of a large house, in which furniture was rearranged to create a large space for dancing. Young women were always accompanied by chaperones, and the virtue of women was protected even in the dances, where men and women often held opposite ends of handkerchiefs rather than each other's hands. Most of the dances were group dances, some of which originated in the Spanish courts before the Conquest. They included quadrilles, pavannes, schottisches, waltzes, and other dances of pan-European origins. *Inditas* were sometimes played as dance pieces; today their words, occasionally vulgar, are usually not sung or are lost. The following melody was provided by Arsenio Córdova of Taos.

Figure 7.7. *La Indita de Taos.* Transcription by Brenda Romero.

Today most Mejicano households have telephones and greater access than do the Pueblos to electronic media. Radio, television, and even VCRs are part of most Mejicano households. Moreover, Mejicanos show a marked preference for Spanish-language stations. Electric instruments and amplifiers have been in common use since the 1950s, and many popular Mejicano dance bands, such as the family-oriented Blue Ventures, also own synthesizers. Technology typically enhances traditional and popular forms rather than dominating them. The matachines, an outdoor ceremony, is one example of this, since the guitar and violin are often amplified.

THE MATACHINES DANZA

While ritual dance dramas are common among the Pueblos, the masked matachines dance is the only such ancient form among the Mejicanos. A symbiotic relationship between the Pueblos and Mejicanos developed, however, as a result of the need for Mejicano musicians in the pueblos and the need for an organizational role model with regard to ritual dance dramas, among the Mejicanos. Over the years, each culture reinforced the continuing performance of matachines and influenced each other's beliefs and practices in different ways.

The Matachines *danza* is an ancient pantomime that enacts the spiritual victory of a king, although the specific details of this interpretation vary depending on the religion of the interpreter. The word *matachines* may derive from an obscure Arabic term for masked dancers; it is more easily associated, however, with the Italian term *mattaccino,* meaning jester or strolling player. Each part of the play features one or more dance sequences, each of which is accompanied by a particular melody played on the violin and guitar. Some of the melodies bear likeness to those of Arbeau's *Buffons* and *Morisque,* documented in 1543 (Romero 1993, 28–39; Arbeau [1588] 1925, 156–62). The earliest ancestors of the matachines in the Old World were Roman sword dances, which had evolved by the thirteenth century into ceremonial dances for religious processions and public festivals. Burlesque elements that accompanied such profane dances as the matachines often served as vehicles for social commentary (similar to the function of ritual clowns in Pueblo ceremonials). For this reason the church, which was then also the state, censored such displays as early as the sixteenth century; and even as late as 1780 they were prohibited in church processions (Romero 1993, 76). A sacred version without burlesque elements, known as the *auto sacramental,* or religious play, survived in the New World as a symbol of the subduing of the Turks and the Moors, both major historical events for Christian Europeans. The *auto sacramental,* developed in Spain and transported across the ocean, survived in the New World, where it eventually reincorporated burlesque elements. In New Mexico, it is this matachines, comprising both sacred and secular aspects, that has survived.

The matachines *danza* (which shall hence refer to the entire dance drama, as opposed to the individual dances of which it consists) features four central characters, the *Monarca*, the *Malinche*, the *Abuelo*, and the *Toro*, as well as from eight to twelve matachines dancers in a double file. The *Monarca*, or king, struggles toward spiritual conversion; he symbolizes Moctezuma.[9] *La Malinche* symbolizes the first Indian convert to Christianity, or Christ's Virgin Mother as a child. The *Abuelo* symbolizes the wisdom of old people. He assists the *Monarca* and the *Malinche* during the *Monarca*'s struggle. The *Abuelo* also cues the musicians, who play a different dance melody (in Mexico generically called *son*) for each sequence of the *danza*, and he helps to control the unruly *Toro* (Bull), who distracts the *Monarca* and the *Malinche* from their spiritual mission. *Toro* symbolizes man's lower nature. The central characters dance between and around the double file of matachines, who symbolize Christian foot soldiers, or Christ's twelve apostles, although the masked headdress also identifies them as subdued Turks or Moors. An *Abuela* (Grandmother), usually a man dressed as a drunk old woman, often features in the burlesque, serving to exemplify socially unacceptable behavior, through symbolic reversal (the opposite of what is intended).

THE MATACHINES AMONG THE MEJICANOS

The matachines was introduced in Mexico as a means of evangelizing the Indians. Because the Indians resisted Spanish attempts at complete coloniza-

Figure 7.8. Fructoso "Toso" Medina, in burlesque costume as the *Abuela* in Alcalde, 1988. Photograph by Brenda Romero.

tion, the matachines dances of New Mexico often include obscure sequences that can only be explained through Mexican indigenous symbolism.[10] A strong Mexican indigenous influence is also apparent in the character of the *Malinche,* one of the first New World converts to Christianity.[11] Formerly, women did not dance the matachines; thus a boy, usually dressed in a white dress, enacted the part of *La Malinche* in both Pueblo and Mejicano versions. Social roles of men and women have gradually become less rigid, and today women are seen dancing along with men in Bernalillo and other Mejicano villages, or as the *mayordoma* (steward), who is appointed by the community to be responsible for the *danza* on any given year.

For most Mejicanos, the matachines *danza* no longer implies the conversion of the natives, but rather, it is perceived as a dance honoring saints (each village celebrates its own saint's day throughout the year) or the Holy Child during the Christmas season.[12] The Catholic Church no longer governs everyday life and local priests do not spend their time organizing community activities. Neither does the mayor of a town organize the matachines dance merely because he is mayor. Charles Aguilar, who is the mayor of Bernalillo, happens to organize the matachines dance there, but he was a matachines dancer and violin player long before he became mayor. The matachines dance has gained importance through survival. Always through the efforts of individuals, faith is renewed by dancing or by helping to preserve the tradition. Much as the Mejicano culture itself has survived in spite of colonization, matachines has survived to become a symbol of resistance to outside

Figure 7.9. Musicians Melitón Medina (violin) and Joe Segovia (guitar), facing the Alcalde Matachines dancers in December, 1988. Photograph by Brenda Romero.

hegemony. But, more importantly, matachines is an emblem of the pride of a people struggling for freedom from imposed external colonization as well as the colonized mentality.

MATACHINES IN THE PUEBLOS

Because the Pueblos have sovereign status, they have their own governing bodies and laws, which are separate from the New Mexico state authorities and laws that apply to non-Indians. Within the Pueblo structure are both ancient and civil forms of government. The head of the ancient governing body is the *cacique,* who is also the spiritual leader of the tribe. The head of the civil government is the governor of the tribe, who is usually assisted by two lieutenant governors. Although it is an honor to serve, there are many social and religious obligations attendant to holding office.

Social and ceremonial obligations are regulated in part by dividing the pueblo into moieties (halves). The Tewa Pueblos, along the Rio Grande in northern New Mexico, are unique in that they elect both a summer chief and a winter chief, who is also the hunting chief. In most other pueblos the two moieties are designated as belonging either to the Pumpkin (Squash) or Turquoise *kiva,* a term used to refer to the underground chamber that is the center of ceremonial activity. The kiva is served by a war chief, whose responsibility includes organizing the public ceremonies for the year. It is the war chief who appoints dancers, notifies them about rehearsals, and makes sure that everything is done and at the right time. In the Pueblo of Jemez, the war chief organizes all aspects of the matachina. In San Juan Pueblo it is the responsibility of the civil authorities, or governor's office. In either case, organizing the dance is part of a systematic and coordinated effort supported by Pueblo social structure. A man demonstrates honor by dancing the matachina; becoming a civil authority is often preceded by participation in the matachina dance. In San Juan Pueblo, dancing in the matachina is so closely associated with civil government, which was imposed by the Spanish in the early seventeenth century, that it seems almost to constitute a prerequisite for civil office. While in office, however, pressing responsibilities preclude dancing in any ceremony.

CROSSING INTO EACH OTHER'S CULTURAL SPACES

For New Mexican Mejicanos and Pueblos, crossing into each other's cultural spaces has historically been limited to social dance and church contexts. Throughout the early colonial period, Indians mostly observed the *bailes,* or social dances, when they occurred in church contexts on saints' days, at trade fairs, or as a result of being laborers for the Spanish-Mexicans. In the postcolonial period, prominent Anglo-American settlers, such as Kit Carson and Charles Bent, were known for inviting Indians to their fiestas, for which Mejicano musicians provided the music. Over time, the Indians grew familiar with the dances, which utilized group-dance choreographies similar in many ways to Indian ceremonials.

Indian resistance to outside cultural hegemony—including the Catholic Church—has been the rule, so that once Spanish control of the missions began to wane, the Pueblos abandoned the polyphonic liturgical Latin music they reportedly learned so well.[13] Like most Euro-Americans, the Mejicanos held to superstitions regarding Pueblo traditional religious beliefs. For the most part, they observed Pueblo ceremonies with little, if any, understanding or appreciation of them. In spite of this, matachines survived in Mejicano and Pueblo settings as an expression of Catholic devotion in the honoring of the saints. Its lively dances have been visibly influenced by the old *bailes,* and its ritualized character made the ceremony easier to assimilate into Pueblo formats, so much so that it was adopted and maintained by many. The strength of ceremony in the Pueblos no doubt helped to reinforce the matachines among the Mejicanos after 1848, when their culture was severed from Mexico following the takeover of the area by the United States.

Because the matachines is performed to honor Catholic saints in both cultural settings, the *danza* provides an ongoing context for the interaction of Mejicano and Pueblo musicians and peoples. Because saint's day celebrations tend to be big events and immediately follow the mass, many Mejicanos attend the Pueblo matachina and vice-versa. And, although the two cultures live largely separate existences, a great deal of visiting and feasting at each other's houses occurs when the matachines players dance. At first the music required Mejicano musicians. Gradually, Pueblo musicians began to play the violin and guitar; nevertheless, there are few who play today, and Mejicanos are still hired to play in most pueblos. In the Pueblo of Jemez, Adelaido Martinez, a Mejicano from the nearby town of Ponderosa, played the violin for the matachina for thirty years before his death in 1988. For the last eighteen of those thirty years, he was accompanied by Daniel Culacke on the guitar. Daniel was a member of the Jemez Pumpkin kiva, but played for the Turquoise kiva matachina. He continued to play the guitar, accompanying me on the violin, until his death in 1994. The accompanying recorded examples are from the Pueblo of Jemez Turquoise kiva matachina repertoire. First is the *Son de la Malinche,* featuring Adelaido Martinez on violin and Daniel Culacke on guitar in a recording collected on December 29, 1979, by John Donald Robb (Track 13). The following performance is also the *Son de la Malinche,* featuring Gabriel Casiquito, a member of the Pumpkin Kiva at Jemez Pueblo, on January 1, 1993 (Track 14). This is followed by the *Son del Toro*—a favorite of Adelaido Martinez—which again features Martinez, violin, and Culacke, guitar, from the same recording collected on December 29,

1979, by John Donald Robb (Track 15). The Malinche and Toro melodies are related motivically in that they both use the same fast ornamental slide. In the *Son del Toro,* the gesture expresses the mischievious nature for which the *Torito* (little bull) is known. The final example, "The Fast Monarcha," or "The Jemez Man Song" (Track 16), features myself on the violin and Daniel Culacke on guitar, performing at the infant's house on January 1, 1993.

Figure 7.10. *La Malinche* sequence of the *danza* in the Pueblo of Jemez. Transcription by Brenda Romero.

Figure 7.11. *El Toro* sequence of the *danza* in the Pueblo of Jemez. Transcription by Brenda Romero.

Moving beyond the components of performance, matachines allows a glimpse into the ways that the Pueblos negotiate difference and define identity. A few Pueblos perform two different versions of the matachina. A "drum" version, said to have originated in Santo Domingo Pueblo, substitutes male chorus and drum for the "Spanish" version, which uses violin and guitar. The choreography remains almost exactly the same, although the ceremonial dress is completely Indian. Instead of dress trousers and leather boots, for example, the dancers wear traditional Pueblo leggings and moccasins. Instead of a prepubescent *Malinche* in a white holy communion dress, she is a young teenager, who wears a traditional Pueblo maiden's dress, with one shoulder bared. She is more a symbol of latent fertility than of virgin chastity. The song that is sung for her is in the Keres language of the Santo Domingo tribe; the words describe the ceremonial dress she wears. In the Pueblo of Jemez, the Spanish version is done by the Turquoise kiva and the drum version is done by the Pumpkin kiva, the more conservative and traditional of the two kivas. One group immediately follows the other in the same ceremonial space on the sacred plaza. The *danza* has been effectively reinterpreted into the male-chorus-and-drum format in one kiva, which reinforces the resistance to foreign cultural hegemony, while obvious ties to Mejicano culture are maintained in the other kiva, perhaps in recognition of the intermixing of blood lines through the centuries. Both versions are performed to honor the Virgin of Guadalupe on December 12, as well as St. Manuel, whose feast day happens to be on January 1. On January 1, many Pueblo women participate in humorous parodies and burlesques simultaneously with the serious matachina.

While some may say that matachina is not authentically Pueblo, time and circumstances, as well as its ritual practice, have authenticated the ceremony. Most Pueblos are aware that the ceremony was brought by the Spanish-Mexicans but believe it is theirs now, incorporating into it various general ceremonial practices common to the more traditional Pueblo dances and adapting Spanish-Mexican practices in unique ways. In San Juan Pueblo, the matachina dancers dance to fulfill a sacred *promesa* (promise), a practice introduced by the Spanish, but which was highly compatible with traditional Pueblo ritual obligations that ensure sufficient rain and a plentiful harvest. In contrast, the Mexican *Malinche* is strikingly similar in concept to the idea of the White Corn Goddess, the female Winter deity for the Tewas. White Corn Goddess is highly mystical and is only impregnated by the sun, much as the Virgin Mary is believed to be impregnated by spirit. Various mystical Pueblo beliefs surround the matachina and its characters; for instance, in San Juan Pueblo when the *Malinche* is from the Winter moiety, she is believed to bring snow to the village.

Mejicanos who participate as matachines musicians often feel a spiritual calling, perhaps because of the extremely cold conditions in which one is usually required to perform. Adelaido Martinez never required payment from the Jemez for playing on December 12, when the Pueblo celebrated the feast day of the Virgin of Guadalupe, although he did charge them on New Year's Day. When I became the violin player at the pueblo, I received a dream from Adelaido after his death—although I was not aware then that he had died. I interpreted that dream as a sign for me to learn the repertoire and play for the Pueblo—and the Pueblo agreed to allow me to do so. Pueblo influences are felt among Mejicanos most strongly in a sense of renewal that accompanies the entire ceremony, from the simple rituals of making their own ceremonial crown (*corona*) to the repetitive dance steps on the cool, sacred earth. The concept of *tierra sagrada,* or sacred earth, is perhaps the most profound reflection of the Indian influence on Mejicano beliefs.

Among the Mejicano musicians who play in the pueblos, one is moved by the ritual of sprinkling sacred corn meal—sacred because of the ancient provenance of the seed used to grow it—in the prayers for life. Many Pueblo practices serve to teach a simple yet magical humanity. The warmth and caring of family relationships in the pueblos is significant, especially obvious in the largess displayed on feast days, which belie the fact that few are wealthy. In the Pueblo of Jemez, for two weeks, from December 24 to January 6, one house is designated the Holy Infant's House, in which food is served every day from dawn until 2 A.M. the following day. Everyone in the pueblo who is able to do so contributes a delicious dish every day. No one goes hungry, all are welcome. The Infant's House is also lavishly decorated: scarves and blankets cover the ceilings and walls, which are adorned with paintings, baskets, and ceremonial items of various kinds. Tinsel and fringe suspend from above in colorful synergy, suggesting the falling rain.

IN CONCLUSION

When two communities cross over and share each other's cultural spaces, opportunities are provided for interaction that may alter how they feel and think about each other. Mejicano and Pueblo have interacted in limited, yet profoundly spiritual ways over the past five hundred years. Negotiating differences has not meant abandoning ethnic and cultural identities. Rather, the two cultures have maintained a ceremony in common, sharing its music and its musicians freely, learning from and gradually influencing each other. Authenticity is subject to change, for what gives musics authenticity is not open to quantification, as much as to cultural and spiritual intent. The matachines in New Mexico illustrate a profound sharing of spiritual intent that is mutually expressed in musical/artistic forms, and which helps to bridge cultural distance.

NOTES

1. *Mejicanos* is the term used by the older generation to refer to themselves in Spanish. They do not use the English equivalent, *Mexican*, which was used pejoratively by the Anglo setters (see also Briggs 1988). Older culture members might refer to themselves as "Spanish," which reflects Spanish ancestry and governance of this area until 1821, or Mexican-American, which reflects Mexican governance from 1821 until 1848. Many of the younger educated generation refer to themselves as "Chicanos," a politicized term coined during the civil rights movement in the late 1960s. The term *Chicano*, literally "children of the earth" in Nahuatl, denotes the same respect for the indigenous contributions to the *cultura* as has always been given to the Hispano contributions.

2. *Pueblo* is the Spanish word for *village*, widely used as a designation for the apartment-style adobe villages of the Native peoples in New Mexico and the Hopi in Arizona. There are nineteen pueblos, all of which have sovereign rights and thus their own governing bodies, as do all recognized Native tribes in the United States.

3. Other kinds of Chicano music in the United States exemplify the crossover between cultures: Tex-Mex and Norteño styles have incorporated the German and Polish polka styles with Mexican, and more recently with Cajun musical styles. Afro-Cuban and Puerto Rican styles reflect the mixing of black and white musical styles. Such satisfying musics belie the presence of intercultural hostility, yet interracial violence in the cities accelerates daily.

4. Most non-Indians are familiar with the doll-like kachina representations sold commercially throughout the Southwest. These small representations, usually carved out of cottonwood, serve to preserve the features associated with particular kachinas. When displayed at home, the kachina dolls are considered spiritual guardians. The Jemez artist Jose Rey Toledo has this to say about kachinas: "They are creatures in that [spiritual] world that are very much like creatures here that act as negotiators and mediators. It's so precious to people, [kachinas] are considered very special and very much a part of [us] and should not be watered down to where it has only fun value and not sacred value. The tourist is always looking for appetites that he has of fun and fantasy . . . They look more for something theatrical all the time. That's where we differ in our religious concept" (unpublished manuscript 42).

5. Ed Valandra, Lakota political sciencist, objects to the use of the words *supernatural* and *deities,* since the Lakota world-view and indigenous world-views in general, do not distinguish between natural and supernatural phenomena.

6. Traditionally, American Indians have well-specified gender roles. The reason men dominate ritual is not necessarily because they consider themselves superior to women. In societies that focus on human harmony with natural forces, women are considered to be naturally in greater harmony. Evidence for this is seen in women's ability to bear children, and by monthly purification cycles. Men, who are most often in touch with forces in opposition to life, through war or hunting, for instance, constantly need to be reaffirmed in the cycles of life, and thus require ritual intervention. This is not to undermine the fact that women in the Pueblos may have become, in some instances, victims of imposed Eurocentric ideas of male domination.

7. With changes initiated by Pope John and Vatican II in the early 1960s, the liturgy of the Mass gradually became dominated by vernacular musics. A new wave of local and regional church compositions arose, modeling or using folk melodies, mostly Mexican. In 1996, the

Church is again trying to revive the use of Gregorian chant in the Mass, although the effects of this trend have not yet reached rural New Mexico.

8. Song duels, called *Zajal,* are also currently practiced in many places in the Arab world, from Lebanon to Saudi Arabia. The practice is thought to have originated in the Moorish courts at Córdova and Granada during the Arab occupation of Spain from 711–1492 (Anne Rasmussen, personal communication).

9. *Moctecuzoma* is the original spelling in the Spanish codices. It subsequently changed to Moctezuma (the *z* in Latin American Spanish is pronounced like the English *ss*). *Montezuma* is the English spelling and pronounciation (Salvador Rodriguez del Pino, personal communication, 1996).

10. An example of this is the *Monarca's* (Monarch's) sequence, in which he extends an ailing leg to the *Abuelo* (Grandfather). A possible explanation is that this part of the dance was taken from an Aztec dance that honored Tizoc, who ruled the Aztecs in the late fifteenth century. Tizoc was known for bleeding his leg with cactus spines, for which the Spanish named him *Pierna Enferma,* or Sick Leg. One recalls that the Aztecs had many self-bleeding practices to ensure order in the universe. No doubt the Spanish tried to reinterpret the sequence in order to give strength to the Aztec conversion to Christianity.

11. In Mexico, Maliche is maligned as a traitor to indigenous cultures, but she is not perceived this way in New Mexico.

12. In the town of Bernalillo, the matachines commemorates the return of the Spanish to New Mexico following the great Pueblo Revolt of 1680. Here the *danza* honors an ancient *promesa* (promise) to dance on August 10, the feast day of San Lorenzo, and the day on which many Spanish colonists were killed or fled New Mexico (Lamadrid 1989).

13. Polyphony and the use of European instruments were both eventually resisted by the Pueblos. There is no evidence that European music influenced traditional Pueblo formats (Roberts 1972, 243) except for its use in the matachina.

REFERENCES CITED

Arbeau, Thoinot. (1588) 1925. *Orchesography.* London: Cyril W. Beaumont.

Briggs, Charles. 1988. *Competence in Performance, the Creativity of Tradition in Mejicano Verbal Art.* Philadelphia: University of Pennsylvania Press.

Ellis, Florence Hawley. 1964. A Reconstruction of the Basic Jemez Pattern of Social Organization, with Comparisons to Other Tanoan Social Structures. *University of New Mexico Publications in Anthropology,* no. 11. Albuquerque: University of New Mexico Press.

Espinosa, Aurelio M. 1985. *The Folklore of Spain in the American Southwest.* Norman: University of Oklahoma Press.

Ford, Richard. 1972. An Ecological Perspective on the Eastern Pueblos. *New Perspectives on the Pueblos,* 1–17.

Humphreys, Paul. 1984. The Borrowing and Adapting of Songs among the Pueblo Indians of the Southwest United States. *Pacific Review of Ethnomusicology* 1: 29–56.

Jacobs, Janet. 1995. Unpublished manuscript.

Lamadrid, Enrique. 1994. *Los Tesoros del Espiritu: A Portrait in Sound of Hispanic New Mexico.* Bilingual, with set of three compact discs or cassette recordings. Researched and written by Enrique Lamadrid. Recorded and produced by Jack Loeffler. Photographs by Miguel A. Gandert. Embudo, N. Mex.: El Norte/Academia Publications.

LaVigna, Maria. 1980. Okushare, Music for a Winter Ceremony: The Turtle Dance Songs of San Juan Pueblo. In *Selected Reports in Ethnomusicology* 3, no. 2, edited by Charlotte Heth. Los Angeles: Regents of the University of California. 77–99.

Mendoza, Vicente, and Virginia R. R. de Mendoza. 1986. *Estudio y Clasificación de la Música Tradicional Hispánica de Nuevo México.* México: Universidad Nacional Autónoma de México.

Ortiz, Alfonso, ed. 1972. *New Perspectives on the Pueblos.* Albuquerque: University of New Mexico Press.

Ortiz, Alfonso. 1972. Ritual Drama and the Pueblo World View. *New Perspectives on the Pueblos.* 135–61.

———. 1969. *The Tewa World.* Chicago: University of Chicago Press.

Porter, James. 1995. Eth-no-mus-i-co-lo-gy. In *Rhythmmusic* 4, no. 5: 22–26.

Robb, John Donald. 1980. *Hispanic Folk Music of New Mexico and the Southwest: A Self-Portrait of a People.* Norman: University of Oklahoma Press.

Roberts, Don. 1972. The Ethnomusicology of the Eastern Pueblos. *New Perspectives on the Pueblos.*

Rodriguez, Sylvia. 1996. *The Matachines Dance, Ritual Symbolism and Interethnic Relations in the Upper Río Grande Valley.* Albuquerque: University of New Mexico Press.

Romero, Brenda M. 1993. *The Matachines Music and Dance in San Juan Pueblo and Alcalde, New Mexico: Contexts and Meanings.* Ph.D. diss., University of California, Los Angeles.

Tobias, Henry J. 1990. *A History of the Jews in New Mexico.* Albuquerque: University of New Mexico Press.

Toelken, Barre. 1995. Enlightened Fieldwork. In *Parabola* (summer): 28–35.

Toledo, Jose Rey. Forthcoming. Morning Star, *The Autobiography of a Jemez Pueblo Indian Artist.* Unpublished manuscript in collaboration with Susan Scarberry-Garcia. Albuquerque, N.M.: University of New Mexico Press.

COMPANION CD SELECTIONS

Track 12. La Delgadina.

Track 13. Malinche no. 1.

Track 14. Malinche no. 2.

Track 15. Son del Toro.

Track 16. Monarcha.

ADDITIONAL SOURCES

Champe, Flavia W. 1983. *The Matachines Dance of the Upper Rio Grande.* Lincoln: University of Nebraska Press.

Campa, Arthur L. 1979. *Hispanic Culture in the Southwest*. Norman, Okla.: University of Oklahoma Press.

Dozier, Edward P. 1970. *The Pueblo Indians of North America*. New York: Holt, Rinehart, and Winston.

García, Nasario. 1987. *Recuerdos de los Viejitos: Tales of the Río Puerco*. Albuquerque: University of New Mexico Press.

Gutiérrez, Ramón. 1991. *When Jesus Came, the Corn Mothers Went Away*. Stanford, Calif.: Stanford University Press.

Sweet, Jill. 1985. *Dances of the Tewa Pueblo Indians: Expressions of New Life*. Santa Fe, N. Mex.: School of American Research Press.

Weigle, Marta and Peter White. 1987. *The Lore of New Mexico*. Albuquerque: University of New Mexico Press.

Yeh, Nora. 1980. Pogonshare: The Cloud Dance Songs of San Juan Pueblo. In *Selected Reports in Ethnomusicology* 3, no. 3, edited by Charlotte Heth. Los Angeles: University of California:1.01–45.32

RECORDINGS CITED

Littlebird, Harold. 1985. Navajo Love Song. *A Circle Begins, Poetry and Song by Harold Littlebird*. Santa Fe, N. Mex.: Littlebird Studios.

Martinez, Roberto. 1991. *Ayer y Hoy, New Mexico's 720th Bound for War*. Dedicated to the members of the 720th Transportation Company and their families. Los Reyes de Albuquerque. MORE Records 0814.

———. 1995. *Treinta Años de Grabaciones*. Los Reyes de Albuquerque. MA-0827.

Ranier, John Jr., with Lillian, Verenda, Howard, and John Ranier, Sr., and P. J. McAfee. 1992. Taos Pueblo Round Dance Song. *Music of New Mexico: Native American Traditions*. Liner notes by Edward Wapp Wahpeconiah. Smithsonian/Folkways. CD SF 40408.

Romero, Brenda M. Forthcoming. *Canciones de mis Patrias; Early New Mexican Folksongs*. With explanatory notes. Produced by Emotional Logic Studio, 4312 Tennyson, Denver, Colorado 80212.Telephone 1-888-300-4CDS

ADDITIONAL RECOMMENDED LISTENING

Cipriano con Música Folklórica. 1994. Cipriano Vigil. Catalina Records, P.O. Box 747, El Rito, N. Mex. 87530; (505) 581-4520.

Ditch-Cleaning and Picnic Songs of Picuris Pueblo. 1972. Indian House. 1051-C.

Lamadrid, Enrique. 1994. *Los Tesoros del Espiritu: A Portrait in sound of Hispanic New Mexico*. Bilingual, with set of three compact discs or cassette recordings. Researched and written by Enrique Lamadrid. Recorded and produced by Jack Loeffler. Photographs by Miguel A. Gandert. Embudo, N. Mex.: El Norte/Academia Publications.

Martinez, Roberto. 1993. *Lo Mejor de Lorenzo Martinez y Sus Violines*. CD-MO 0823.

Talking Spirits, Native American Music from the Hopi, Zuni, and San Juan Pueblos. 1982. Liner notes by David P. McAllester. Music of the World Recordings. CDT-126.

The Tewa Indian Women's Choir of San Juan Pueblo, Songs from the Tewa Mass. 1994. Tewa Indian Women's Choir, P.O. Box 27, San Juan Pueblo, N. Mex. 87566.

The Trujillo Family. 1996. *New Mexican Colonial Folk Dances.* Trujillo. Denver, Col., telephone (303) 986–6821.

Turtle Dance Songs of San Juan Pueblo. 1972. With explanatory notes. Indian House. 1101-C.

CHAPTER 8

Waila: The Social Dance Music of the Tohono O'odham

James S. Griffith

Griffith is an anthropologist and folklorist with strong interests in topics as
diverse as Uncle Dave Macon and mariachi music. The factors that he discusses
in relationship to the development and performance of waila *music, also called
"chicken scratch," in southern Arizona, include the physical and cultural isolation
faced for decades by the Tohono O'odham (also known as the Pima Indians).
Modern (post–World War II) waila *music, largely unknown outside of its hearth
area, has been shaped by several musical forces, both Native and non–Native
American. As an example, Griffith describes the influence of religious continuity,
specifically the Catholic Church, in shaping the lives and rituals of Tohono
O'odham. Similarly he explores the role of educational institutions, and boarding schools in particular, in their lives and music (in the "Indian School" marching bands). In the light of these disparate factors, it is not surprising that many
members of Waila bands are members of the same, often extended families. This
sense of community and family is reinforced by the standard performance contexts for* waila: *local dances and the religious ceremonies around which they are
often built.*

■ ■ ■ ■

SETTING THE SCENE

It is dusk on the Arizona desert, about one hundred miles west of Tucson. We
are in a small village on Tohono O'odham Nation, an almost three-million-acre
tract of land formerly called the Papago Indian Reservation. The village, which

could be any one of twenty or more similar settlements, is about twenty miles north of the Mexican border, and we have traveled for almost two hours from Tucson by paved and dirt roads in order to reach it. Although the village normally contains perhaps ten families, there seem to be at least one hundred fifty people gathered here, standing around the church, saying a Rosary in the chapel, eating in shifts in a nearby outdoor dining room. In front of a small white-painted Catholic chapel is a cement dance floor festooned with paper streamers suspended from wires overhead. To one side of the floor is a small, three-sided house. The side facing the dance floor is open to the elements.

Five Indian men in Levis and T-shirts enter this building. One sits behind a drum kit, the others pick up their instruments: electric guitar and bass, saxophone, button accordion. The tuning process over, the accordion player nods to the others and the band bursts into a recognizable polka. The music is strictly instrumental and promises to remain that way; although the group is amplified, no voice mikes are in evidence. Couple by couple, the people who have been standing and sitting nearby move onto the floor and start to dance, moving with small steps around the floor in a counter-clockwise motion. The dance—the *waila*—has begun and will probably last until dawn the next morning. The following essay is an attempt to explain *waila* music and dance and to show how these art forms arrived in Tohono O'odham culture and how they fit into the world of the O'odham.

REGION, PEOPLE, AND HISTORY

The American Southwest is a very large region consisting of Arizona, New Mexico, and west Texas; it extends north into Utah and Colorado and west into California. Physically it is marked by extreme dryness and a warm climate; its most important cultural characteristics stem from the fact that, long before it became the southwestern portion of the United States, it was the Northwest. By the end of the eleventh century, it had become the northwest-ernmost extension of the high native cultures of Central Mexico; from the 1540s on, it was northwestern New Spain, and after 1821 it was northwest Mexico. This "northwestishness" has marked the region strongly and provides many of the cultural features that make it seem exotic and fascinating to the rest of the country.

The Southwest is not, however, a unified region, either physically or culturally. This fact may be difficult to discern from a distance, for its shared characteristics—dryness verging on desert conditions, warm climate, a large Native American population that has preserved many aspects of its traditional cultures, and a strong Spanish, and later Mexican, presence—tend to obscure the intraregional differences.

Yet the Southwest is in fact a region of highly distinctive subregions. The major cities of the region, notably Albuquerque and Santa Fe in New Mexico,

El Paso, Texas, and Phoenix and Tucson in southern Arizona, differ from each other in environment, history, and character. Northern New Mexico is ecologically and culturally distinct from southern New Mexico. The Arizona deserts are separated from Arizona's high plateau by several thousand feet of elevation and the White Mountains. The Native American peoples of these different regions have distinctive cultures. The Pueblo and Navajo people of the Four Corners area (where New Mexico, Arizona, Colorado, and Utah meet) are very different from the O'odham and Yaquis of the Arizona borderlands (Byrkit 1992, Griffith 1996, Wilder 1990).

These subregional distinctions are important to bear in mind, for this essay will focus on a kind of music which, though related to other musics of the Southwest, is unique to Southern Arizona. This music—*waila* (pronounced to rhyme with "pile-a")—is played by Native peoples whose home is in the desert and river country stretching from approximately Phoenix to the Mexican border. It is *a* Southwestern music but by no means *the* or even the best known Southwestern music. *Waila* is the traditional social-dance music of the Tohono O'odham and the Akimel O'odham—the peoples who since their first contact with Europeans have been called by outsiders the Papago and Pima Indians but who now prefer to be called by the traditional names of their own language. While this essay will deal primarily with the music of the Tohono O'odham (Desert People, formerly the Papago Indians), the music and dance traditions are much the same for the Akimel O'odham (River People) or Pimas as well (Fontana 1981, Russell 1975).

O'odham means *people* in a language that is spoken throughout much of south central Arizona and in small pockets in the Mexican states of Sonora and Durango. The earliest known contact between O'odham and Europeans occurred when the Spanish explorer Cabeza de Vaca arrived at a village of those people in the Sonora River valley in 1539. The earliest permanent contact between Europeans and the northern O'odham—ancestors of today's Pimas and Papagos—occurred in 1687, when Father Eusebio Francisco Kino, S.J., arrived in what was then called the *Pimería Alta,* Upper Pima Country, to start his labors as a Catholic missionary and emissary of the Spanish crown.

Kino and the missionaries who followed him—members of the Jesuit order until 1767 and of the Franciscan order from then to the 1840s—brought a series of profound changes to the peoples of the desert. The region and its people ceased being independent units and became connected with ever-tightening political, economic, and cultural bonds to Mexico, to Europe, and eventually to the entire globe. This process of connection to the outside world continues to this day as the region becomes steadily evermore integrated into the life of the "global village."

The missionaries, who initially came from many different parts of Europe, brought with them new crops and domestic animals, such as wheat and cattle. They brought membership in the Spanish Empire and in the Catholic religion. They brought European architecture, European dress, European world views, and European music.

Most of these commodities were brought only to the river valleys in the eastern portions of O'odham country. In these valleys—the Santa Cruz, in what is now Arizona; and the Magdalena, Concepción, and Altar, in what is now Sonora, Mexico—the newcomers erected mission churches and established a continuing presence among the O'odham. Many of these churches still stand, and one, San Xavier del Bac, just south of present-day Tucson, is still surrounded by its O'odham village.

The rest of the O'odham did not survive as well in their mission communities, however. Ravaged by new diseases and subject to the forces of acculturation and intermarriage, the native peoples slowly disappeared from all the mission communities save San Xavier. Only in the north, along the Gila and Salt Rivers, and in the desert to the west—both areas where permanent missions were never established—did the O'odham remain undisturbed on their traditional lands. And finally, by the 1830s, the missionaries had withdrawn as well and the remaining O'odham, along with their Mexicano neighbors, were left in semi-isolation to work out their own destinies. This did not mean that the O'odham were isolated in an idealized kind of static, traditional culture. O'odham and Europeans had been in some sort of contact since the 1680s, and such imported foods as wheat and cattle were well established in O'odham country. Rather, the O'odham were sufficiently isolated and could select the concepts and practices that made sense to them and adapt them to O'odham culture.

This gradually changing scene lasted until a new people appeared on the horizon, this time speaking English and coming from the north and east. Following the Gadsden Purchase of 1853, an international border was drawn from east to west across O'odham country and the area north of that border became a part of something new—the American Southwest.

Change, though still slow, inevitably accelerated in O'odham country, especially after 1886, when Geronimo's final surrender ended two hundred years of warfare between the Apaches and their European and Indian neighbors. By around 1915, two institutions were in place that would bring the Desert and River People closer than ever to the mainstream of American life. One of these was the United States government–sponsored boarding school. Beginning in the late nineteenth century, it had become U.S. government policy to separate Native American children from their parents and culture and raise them in English-speaking boarding schools, usually organized along military lines. This policy was to have the effect, believed to be salutary and possible at the time, of turning Native American children into mainstream American farmers and laborers. As has been the case with many other acculturation schemes, however, things simply did not turn out the way the government expected. Human cultures do not change on demand, and the plan of efficiently turning members of one culture into full participants of another failed.

The other institution was the modern-day Franciscan mission. Setting out from Phoenix, Franciscan missionaries, many of whom were German-Americans, worked among the O'odham, initially the River People and then, beginning in 1909, among the Desert People south of Phoenix and west of Tucson. By 1913, Franciscan missionary priests had taken up residence in Tohono O'odham villages. These men said mass, offered religious instruction, set up day schools, and mediated with outside state and federal agencies on behalf of the Papagos, the Desert O'odham. In fact the very shape of the Papago Indian Reservation—which was established in 1916, and nowadays is called Tohono O'odham Nation—and the fact that its organization reflects at least some of the realities of O'odham culture, is due to the intervention of sympathetic missionaries.

When the twentieth-century Franciscan missionaries first came to many of the Papago villages, they were surprised to discover what appeared to be Catholic chapels (see Fig. 8.1). During the late nineteenth Century, many O'odham on both sides of the border had absorbed a kind of folk Catholicism

Figure 8.1. Tohono O'odham musician, by the front wall of an unidentified chapel in the 1920s. From the Franciscan photo files at Mission San Xavier del Bac, Arizona.

from their Mexican neighbors—a Catholicism that had developed along specifically O'odham patterns, with emphasis on the maintenance of the health of people and animals in the village. This health maintainance was, and is, accomplished through the accumulation of power-charged holy pictures and statues, annual trips to the great regional pilgrimage center at Magdalena, Sonora, and the holding of village saint's day feasts. These feasts include such activities as praying, marching in processions, feasting on special foods, and couple-dancing to European-style music (Bahr 1988; Griffith 1992, 67–93).

O'ODHAM MUSIC THROUGH TIME

Where is O'odham music in this historical portrait? The Jesuit and Franciscan missionaries of the eighteenth and nineteenth centuries took pains to teach their Indian charges how to play such European instruments as the violin, the guitar, and the European bass and side drums. This was done so that the Indians could provide music for the mass and other church occasions. Thus there were probably violinists, guitarists, and drummers in such communities as the one at San Xavier, south of Tucson, through which the American "49'ers" traveled on their way to the California Goldrush and camped in order to repair their gear and "water up" before embarking on the brutal desert journey ahead. It may have been in this sort of context that O'odham musicians learned such new, fashionable dances as the polka, mazurka, and schottische. By the late 1860s, an O'odham band consisting of fiddles and guitars was playing at Tucson's annual Fiesta de San Agustín. Here is how the band looked and sounded to John Spring, a pioneer Arizona educator. In this passage, Spring remembers a fiesta from around 1869:

> In the middle of the square stood a wooden platform, an improve-
> ment over the earth floor and here the rabble danced as of yore,
> and to the same music and tones I had first heard twelve years
> before. In fact, the music, which was for years produced by the
> same Papago Indians upon their home-made fiddles, consisted of
> only two recognizable airs. One did service for polka, schottische,
> waltz, and quadrilles [sic] by simply adapting its "tempo" to the
> faster or slower movements of each dance. The other was the so-
> called "pascola," a distinctively Papago dance. What these active
> musicians lacked in tuneful accomplishments, they made up by
> perseverance, for they daily played these two tunes consistently
> from four P.M. until long after midnight, during the nineteen days
> that the feast lasted. Upon the platform only low-caste Mexicans,
> half breeds and Indians danced, and only women of questionable
> (or rather unquestionable) reputation. (Gustafson 1966, 301)

It is extremely likely that Mr. Spring's perception that only one tune was played in different tempos for different dances may reflect his personal view of the music rather than what the musicians were actually playing. One frequently hears such comments as "it all sounds the same" from those who describe music that is unfamiliar to their ears. Aside from Spring's casual remarks about the music itself, this is a valuable description of a performance of an old-style *waila* band.

According to older O'odham musicians, ensembles such as that described by Mr. Spring remained active until after the Second World War, when they were gradually replaced by modern *waila* bands. These groups have instrumentation modeled after that of the popular *conjunto norteño* of the Mexican-American borderlands: button accordion, saxophone, guitar, bass, and drum kit (Peña 1985). During the 1960s most reservation villages had electricity, and electric instruments became practical. As a result, most *waila* bands use electric guitars and bass guitars, and accordion and saxophone players play into microphones.

One impetus for the new instrumentation, in addition to the highly popular *norteño* music that was flooding Southern Arizona at this time, may well have been the boarding school program mentioned earlier. Bands were important features of these schools, and apparently many students enjoyed playing in them. In fact, in the decades after the Second World War, all-Indian marching bands composed of boarding-school veterans appeared in many of the Southwestern cities that were adjacent to reservations. The saxophone may well have entered O'odham culture via this route. If so, it would confirm that modern *waila* music derives from the two great historical acculturative programs that have been directed at the O'odham: the Spanish mission system and the Indian boarding school of the late nineteenth and early twentieth centuries.

WAILA TODAY

This brings us back to where we started—the band is warming up to play polkas at an all-night dance in a village on Tohono O'odham Nation. The music is called *waila,* from *baile,* the Spanish word for "social dance." More specifically, *waila* means *polka* as well as the whole genre of music. Another name for *waila* is "Chicken Scratch," which is a reference to an older dance in which the dancers kick up their heels behind them like chickens scratching in the dust. The name is more accepted by the River People than it is by the Desert People, many of whom feel that the term *chicken scratch* is slightly derogatory and used only by whites. A guitar and saxophone player, Philip Miguel, recently remarked at a workshop, "We are not chickens; we're O'odham, and this is O'odham *waila* music" (Miguel 1995).

The line-up of a contemporary *waila* band consists of button accordion, saxophone, or both, as lead instruments supported by bass guitar, electric guitar, and drum kit. All of the musicians are males, with very few exceptions. The music consists of three main music and dance genres: the polka (*waila* in O'odham), two-step (*cho:di*, in O'odham; *chotis*, in local Spanish), and the *cumbia*, a Caribbean genre that originated in Colombia but that has been extremely popular in the U.S.–Mexico borderlands since the 1970s. *Mazurkas* or fast waltzes and tunes in $\frac{6}{8}$ are also heard, although more rarely.

The button accordion and saxophone function as the melody or lead instruments. Not all bands have both; in some there is only an accordion, in others, the accordion player doubles on second sax, and in still other bands there are two saxes. But in all cases, these instruments supply the melody. Sometimes they play together in unison, sometimes in harmony; occasionally they will trade solos. The guitarist usually plays a strum on the off-beat. The drummer maintains a steady, heavy beat on the bass drum and may drop occasional "bombs" on his other percussion instruments to accentuate the rhythm.

Waila tunes come from many sources. A large number are borrowed from the *norteño* repertoire and from the repertoires of other Mexican musical traditions. Many are popular mainstream American pieces, old and new. I have heard tunes from American popular and vernacular music, such as "Blue Tango," "Turkey in the Straw," "The Beer Barrel Polka," "Clementine," and "It's a Small World," all played by *waila* bands. One veteran *waila* musician told me that there are three ways of inventing a "new" song: revive an old-time tune that no one plays anymore; play a well-known tune in a new key, thus changing its character; or take bits of other songs and recombine them into a new tune. The *waila* repertoire is highly eclectic and constantly expanding (Enis, Mike 1974–80, Joaquin 1976–80).

Waila tunes do not necessarily have titles. The best way to request a certain tune from a band is either to hum a few bars or to refer to some memorable occasion on which the band played that tune. This system of tune reference serves dancers and musicians perfectly well until a band has cut a tape and needs to assign titles to each song for liner notes. Under these circumstances, the group will usually work out titles by suggestion and consensus. Occasionally, someone will remember a name for the tune in English or Spanish, or, if not, the tune frequently takes its name from a member of the band or some other person who especially likes it—as, for example, "John's Special"—or after a village where the piece went over particularly well, as in the case of the "Pisinimo Two-Step." Both of these titles appear on an LP recorded by the band the American Indians in March, 1974 (The American Indians 1974, A-3, A-5).

Several years ago, I accompanied the Enis Company from San Xavier Village to the National Folk Festival at Wolf Trap Park outside of Washington, D.C. The band felt that one of their polkas was especially well received during the festival, and so the tune was known thereafter among band members as "The D.C. Polka." At about the same time, in the mid-1970s, I was in the habit of requesting the Mexican waltz "Las Nubes" of the band whenever I danced to their music. I learned later that this tune, which had previously been known as "That Old Waltz" had started to be called "Jim's Waltz" (Enis, Marvin 1976).

Waila is almost entirely instrumental. One musician, Virgil Molina, who played with a *waila* band in the 1970s and '80s, recorded a few vocal numbers that included one of his one compositions in the O'odham language; but he stands alone (The Molinas 1972, A-1, B-1; 1976, A-3, A-5, A-6). Few other singers have yet followed his lead, although I have occasionally heard musicians say that they were thinking about working up some songs in O'odham. On August 25, 1996, at the Tucson Historical Society's San Agustín Fiesta, I heard the Cisco Band from Sells, the capital of Tohono O'odham Nation. They featured harmony duets sung in English—but this is only the second time in more than twenty years that I have heard a band sing.

Waila is primarily dance music. On those occasions when *waila* bands played at folklife festivals and other culturally mixed events, some attempt has usually been made to accommodate dancers. The average *waila* tune is certainly much longer then the traditional three-minute-plus duration of the record single or LP cut. Once a band has started to play a tune, there is little change. Musicians seldom "take off" in solo variations; the melody is simply played over and over by one or both lead instruments until the band is finished. This may be slowly changing, as in the case of contemporary groups like Southern Scratch, who are more accustomed to playing for non-O'odham audiences, but it still seems to be the rule more often than not.

Waila is very well integrated into and contained within O'odham culture. Although a number of commercial recordings are available on the Phoenix-based Canyon label, *waila* is not often played over the air, and *waila* bands are seldom invited to appear at culturally mixed occasions. But this is changing also. Since 1974, a *waila* band has been featured at the annual Tucson Meet Yourself Festival, and, more recently, *waila* bands have become regular additions to other multicultural celebrations. Since 1994 a group of Tucsonans who are interested in various kinds of traditional dance has sponsored annual *waila* dance workshops. Finally, since 1989 an annual *waila* festival, conceived and organized by a Tohono O'odham, has been sponsored in Tucson by the Arizona Historical Society (see Fig. 8.2).

Waila, as I have said, is first and foremost a dance music. Moreover, at an O'odham *waila,* everybody dances—elders, little children, teenagers, young adults. The local version of the polka is, however, quite different from the two-step used by many immigrant European communities, and even farther from the athletic one-two-three-HOP favored in other parts of the United States. Throughout the borderlands, the regional polka step is a walking one-step, in which the dancer moves a foot with each beat of the music.

Figure 8.2. The Tohono O'odham *waila* band at the 1993 *Waila* Festival at the Arizona Historical Society, Tucson. From left, Francisco Antone, saxophone; Sylvester Oliver, guitar; Ervin Lopez, drums; Philip Miguel, tenor saxophone; Richard Garcia, accordion; and Homer Marks Sr., bass. Arizona Historical Society, photo by David Burkhalter.

Within this general style, which is practiced by Native Americans and Mexicanos alike, there seem to be certain distinctly O'odham characteristics. Where a Mexicano male dancer will balance on the balls of his feet, leaning forwards into the dance, an O'odham man will have his weight centered on his heels, leaning even slightly backwards. A Mexicano couple's polka stance seems to dramatize a traditional set of gender-based expectations, with the man assuming an aggressive stance and the woman leaning either slightly away from him or crushed against him. Left-arm positions may accentuate this sense of tension. O'odham couples, on the other hand, often dance close to each other, with a more passive, cooperative body language.

Movement around the floor is inevitably counterclockwise. (This is the same direction taken by the traditional O'odham *keihina*, or circle dance, and opposite from the direction used by many other Native American peoples.) Couples move lightly around the floor, taking small steps and turning to the left and right. Rarely, if ever, will an O'odham couple separate and promenade side-by-side or engage in hand swings, as Mexican-American couples will. The dance, like the music, is solid and matter-of-fact. The visual aesthetic, as it is all along the border, is one of smoothness, with little or no vertical movement.

Performance of the *cho:di,* or two-step, in the O'odham context reveals fewer variations, although I have seen O'odham couples deliberately dance the "step-close-step-pause" pattern *across* the phrasing of the tune. The *cumbia* is danced in couples, each partner dancing alone, with hands raised above the waist and fists lightly clenched. Once again, the O'odham *cumbia,* in both music and dance, is a little more solid, a little heavier, than it usually is in its Colombian home.

Finally, *waila* tends to be a family music. It is not uncommon to find three generations of male musicians in the same family, and many *waila* groups comprise brothers or cousins who play together. In fact, at a recent workshop designed to bring together teenaged *waila* novices and seasoned veteran musicians, not only did all of the youngsters have parents who were *waila* musicians, but also, almost without exception, did the veterans![1]

THE VILLAGE FEAST, A CONTEXT FOR *WAILA*

Although *waila* is featured at all kinds of celebrations—weddings, graduations, birthday parties, first Holy Communions, and the like—perhaps the most typical setting for *waila* is still the village feast. These feasts occur on the assigned day that a particular saint is venerated in the village. If possible, the priest will come by and say the mass in the morning. (There are currently three misionary priests serving about forty active villages on the nearly three-million-acre main reservation of Tohono O'odham Nation, second only in size to the 19.7 million-acre Navajo Nation. They visit outlying villages by automobile on a regular monthly schedule.) Before or after the mass, a procession will form at the Catholic chapel, and men, women, and children of the village carry all of the holy statues and pictures from the chapel to a stationary cross that stands some distance to the east or south of the chapel door. As they walk along, they sing religious songs in O'odham and Spanish. After a pause by the cross, during which each participant establishes a personal contact with each sacred object, the procession returns to the chapel.

After the mass and procession are over, the feasting starts. One or more steers have been slaughtered, butchered, and cooked in an outdoor kitchen near the chapel. The cooking is done in huge pots over a series of adobe firepits, under a *ramada* (see Glossary).

Traditional feast foods include shredded beef stewed with red chile, beef and beef bones cooked with corn, squash and other vegetables, pinto beans, potato salad, locally made flour tortillas and wheat bread that has been baked in a communal, outdoor oven, and Kool-aid, coffee, and cake. Other, optional dishes include *menudo* (a stew of tripe, hominy, and cows' feet), the local flat enchiladas (fried cakes of corn meal and chile, served in a red chile sauce), and sometimes macaroni salad.

Interestingly enough, none of these foods, except for some of the vegetables in the beef stew, were eaten by the O'odham before the missionaries arrived. This is almost a completely borrowed diet, even as the occasion is a borrowed, Christian celebration. Beef and wheat were brought to the O'odham in the seventeenth century by Spanish missionaries; tortillas, pinto beans and coffee were also introduced during the Spanish period, and potato salad, Kool-aid, and iced cake are all twentieth-century contributions (Bahr 1988).

Guests are fed in shifts through the night until shortly after dawn when the dance concludes. The men and women of the village serve the food, clean and reset oilcloth-covered tables after each group finishes, and place serving bowls along the middle of the table. The guests sit at long, homemade benches to eat their food, getting up to thank the cooks and servers when they are finished.

During the feast day, some of the celebratory activity takes place in the chapel. This sacred activity may include the recitation of a rosary or other prayers in Spanish or O'odham, which is led by a villager who specializes in reciting sacred Catholic texts. Unlike Roman Catholic churches, the Tohono O'odham folk chapels have the specific purpose of protecting the village supply of holy pictures and statues. These sacred objects have been acquired during the annual October pilgrimage to Magdalena de Kino, a colonial mission town on the main north-south highway, about sixty miles south of the border in Sonora, Mexico. The objects are placed next to a particularly miraculous statue of St. Francis Xavier, which, it is believed, charges them with spiritual power. The acquisitions from the pilgrimage are then brought back to the village, spiritually aligned with the needs of the villagers and their animals through a ceremony of baptism, and placed on home altars or in the village chapel. Here the pictures and statues serve to maintain the balance that protects villagers and livestock from illness and misfortune.

This religious and philosophical system, with its emphasis on healing and the maintenance of health and spiritual balance, is as much, if not more, O'odham than it is Catholic, and has over the years been called "Sonoran Catholicism" and "O'odham Catholicism" by Anglos, and *santo himdag*—"saint way"—by O'odham. It is a dynamic religious and philosophical system, changing with each generation of O'odham in order to accommodate their needs. It is in this context—a context rich in ideas and customs that have been borrowed from Mexican and other neighbors and then reinterpreted by the O'odham—that *waila* music may best be understood.

THE OLDER FIDDLE MUSIC: *WAILA, KWARIYA,* AND *PASCOLA*

Related to modern *waila* music is the music played by old-style fiddle-based bands. Related in turn to the fiddle music (and often played by the same men) are two forms of strictly ritual music and dance: the *pascola* and *mata-chinis* complexes. So that *waila* and its place in O'odham culture may be fully understood, a brief explanation of these three violin-based forms of dance music follows.

The older violin-based bands of an earlier period have not disappeared entirely from the desert scene. These groups, which typically consist of two violins, one or more guitars, and a bass drum and a snare drum—each played by a different musician—have undergone a revival since the mid-1980s, when for several years an All-O'odham Old-Time Fiddle Orchestra Contest was featured at the annual Wa:k Pow Wow in March. As a result of the interest generated by these contests, older musicians started playing again, and three bands have produced commercial cassettes. These are the San Xavier Fiddle Band from the San Xavier District, the Gu Achi Fiddlers from the middle of Tohono O'odham Nation (listen to Track 18, "Libby Bird Mazurku" to hear this music), and the Gila River Fiddlers from the Gila River Pima (Akimel O'odham) Reservation. The first two groups recorded for the ubiquitous Canyon label, while the latter tape was self-produced (San Xavier Fiddle Band 1989, Gu Achi Fiddlers 1988, Gila River Old-Time Fiddlers 1990).

Closely allied to the older fiddle band sound is a distinct kind of dance, known in O'odham as *kwariya,* a version of the Spanish *cuadrilla* or quadrille. Oddly, the kwariya is not a quadrille at all, but rather a circle dance in which couples promenade, reverse direction, do a grand chain, and then form into two-couple sets for such well-known Anglo-American square dance figures as "duck for the oyster," "birdie in the cage," and "around that couple you take a little peek." Figures are called by one of the dancers, and the couples are likely to exit the floor by promenading under a bridge of hands.

Music for the *kwariya* is provided exclusively by old-time fiddle bands and consists of various tunes played in $\frac{6}{8}$ time. Each village seems to have its special *kwariya* tune, the one from San Xavier Village being a six-eight version of the tune known to Southeastern Anglo-American fiddlers as "Flop-Eared Mule." This piece is known all the way from Eastern Europe to Arizona. The tempo varies from place to place: in New Mexico, for instance, the tune is played as a schottische, while Southeastern fiddlers play it as a fast reel—but it keeps its general melodic outline and two-key structure wherever it is found.

Another kind of traditional O'odham music commonly played on violins and guitars are the *pascola* tunes that John Spring mentioned were distinct from the European social dances of the mid-nineteenth century. *Pascola* is a loan word from the Yaqui Indian language. The Yaquis, whose homeland is in southern Sonora, Mexico, and who moved to the United States around the turn of the century to escape persecution, have a rich tradition of Native Christian ceremonialism that was developed through several centuries of contact with European missionaries.

In Yaqui, *pahko o'ola* means "Old Man of the Fiesta," and the Yaqui *pascola* is the ritual host of every religious feast and ceremony. Yaqui *pascolas* open and close the feast with speeches, prayers, and fireworks. They act as hosts, passing out cigarettes and water to spectators. They serve as clowns, engaging in humorous dialogue and pantomime. And they perform step dances to two kinds of music—for violin and harp and for flute and drum—both kinds played by one man. Judging from the types of tunes and melodies heard in Yaqui *pascola* performance, the violin and harp music appears to be based upon relatively old European models, preserved in the community through oral tradition since the early eighteenth century. It is this violin music that has been transmitted to the O'odham, along with the *pascola* dance (Griffith and Molina 1981).

At some time in the past, the Tohono O'odham seem to have borrowed the *pascola* dance and its music from the Yaquis. As long ago as the 1750s, a Jesuit missionary described Yaqui *pascolas* dancing at O'odham feasts in what is now northern Sonora, Mexico. Since about the turn of the century, there have been colonies of Yaquis living and performing their traditional ritual dances in and near Tucson and at various sites near Phoenix. At some point, apparently before the 1860s and John Spring's experiences at the San Agustín Fiesta, O'odham learned their *pascola* music and dances.

Unlike their Yaqui neighbors, who wear masks and breechcloths, O'odham *pascolas* wear ordinary feast clothes—Levis and a dress shirt. Each man wears a belt with several metal jingle bells (preferably brass ones) dangling from it. A string of rattles made from the dried cocoons of the giant silk moth (*Rothschildia jurulla*) is wrapped around each ankle. The *pascola*'s feet are bare.

Pascolas usually dance in a small *ramada* erected to one side of the chapel. A small altar with images of one or more saints stands at the rear of the *ramada*. The musicians—one or more violinists and a guitarist—sit to one side of the cleared, swept dance floor. When they commence playing the first *pascola* tune or *son* (pronounced to rhyme with "bone"), the *pascolas* kneel before the altar and cross themselves, quietly reciting a short prayer. Then each *pascola*, in order from the youngest to oldest, takes his turn at dancing. There may be as many as four *pascolas* at any given feast. The dance is an elaborate step-dance performed in a slightly stooped stance, with head lowered and arms hanging loosely at the sides. The leg rattles accentuate the complex rhythm of the *son*, thus allowing the *pascola* to become a third musical instrument.

Pascolas dance at the feasts all night until around dawn, when they close the ceremony by dancing several times in unison up to the altar and back, kneel and cross themselves once more, and recite a closing prayer. The dance music is traditionally regulated by the time of night at which it is played. Typically, there is one body of tunes for the early evening, one for the hours just after midnight, and one for the early morning. In many villages, the instruments are retuned to a different pitch at midnight. Sometimes there is a special *son* for the hour of midnight and another for the dawn.

The other great body of Yaqui violin-based music that has been borrowed by the O'odham is used to accompany the *matachines* dancers. Among the Yaquis, *matachines* are men and boys who perform European-derived contradances as an act of devotion to Our Lady of Guadalupe. Wearing paper crowns and carrying trident wands decorated with feathers, they march and wheel in three lines, going through their intricate figures in time to music played by several violinists and guitarists. Among the *matachin* figures danced by Yaquis is the winding and unwinding of a Maypole (Painter 1986, 157–83).

I know of one group of O'odham *matachines* dancers, based in the Gila River reservation. Once again, their dance and music is very similar to those of the Yaquis, and the Pima (as the River O'odham were formerly known) undoubtedly learned this dance complex from their Yaqui neighbors.

SACRED OR SECULAR DANCE MUSIC?

I have pointed to the most traditional context for *waila* music and dance as being the village feast, itself an occasion for various kinds of European-based behavior, much of which has been modified and reinterpreted by the O'odham to suit their own cultural needs. One more detail should be mentioned. Just as Yaqui and O'odham *pascolas* have the custom of setting aside specific tunings and melodies for specific times of night, so the traditional *waila* bands seem to have had specific songs for such times as midnight and dawn. After midnight, they would retune their instruments in order to play at a higher pitch. One O'odham who discussed this with me added that few musicians know these conventions any more. All tunes are the same for the musicians nowadays, to be used whenever they feel like it. "And that's why," he told me, "you'll sometimes hear some of the old people sitting by the dance floor listen to a song and then say something like 'Dawn is sure coming early tonight'" (Juan 1980). This parallel with the overtly sacred *pascola* music and dance complex suggests strongly that there is an important ritual component to *waila*.

It seems evident to me that, with a music like *waila*, the oft-made distinctions between the sacred and the secular simply do not apply. Yes, *waila* is similar to and derived from a music and dance form that in its original, European-based context is secular. Yes, its use has spread to celebrations other than village feasts—weddings, first Holy Communions, baptisms, birthdays, graduations, even to bars and dance halls outside the reservation. But only one of the family occasions that I have mentioned is itself purely secular, and the lines that may be drawn between the sacred and the secular

Figure 8.3. The Alex Gomez Band playing for a dance at the Arizona Historical Society following the 1995 Young *Waila* Musicians' Workshop. From left: Roger Carlos, guitar; Alex Gomez, saxophone; Rachel Gomez (Alex's daughter), accordion. More and more girls and women are becoming *waila* musicians in the 1990s; the music is still passed down through generations of family members. Arizona Historical Society, photo by Scott Baglione.

do not sit comfortably on O'odham culture. I recall being instructed by an O'odham man of about my age in how to do the *keihina* or traditional round dance. "Stomp your feet hard down on the ground to bring in the rain clouds," he told me, "and get yourself between two big women and dance with your elbows out." So even the courtship and flirtation aspects of European-style social dancing may not appear as secular to O'odham eyes as they do in European-derived cultures, where generations of young people have been told in one way or another that the Devil himself lurks on the dance floor.

At a recent *waila* workshop that offered school-aged musicians an opportunity to work directly with older players, the phrase "make people happy" was used over the over by the older men to describe their function as musicians. In mainstream American culture, this may legitimately be understood as a reference to entertainment, pure and simple. In traditional O'odham culture, with its emphasis on spiritual balance and its need for full cooperation among small groups of people in isolated villages, the phrase may well mean a good deal more. I suggest that *waila* bands operate ideally within O'odham culture as a means of maintaining community health and good feelings. Thus, the *waila* occasion becomes a little less secular than it may appear at first and a little more involved with the sacred purposes of life.

WAILA BEYOND THE O'ODHAM

Waila music has been exported beyond the O'odham community since at least the 1860s, when John Spring witnessed *waila* music and dance at the San Agustín fiesta in Tucson. With the end of the Apache Wars in 1886, however, Papagos (the Desert O'odham) were no longer valued allies of the whites, and in most cases simply stopped being noticed. Over the course of the twentieth century, they increasingly became regarded as providing a sort of local color, and their music, especially music that did not fit the stereotype of Indians singing with drums and rattles, was largely ignored by middle-class, mainstream Arizonans.

Waila music became better known outside of O'odham culture after January 1972, with Ray Boley's Canyon Records Company recording of Tohono O'odham *waila* band, Mike Enis and Company, in the dance *ramada* at San Xavier Village. This resulted in the LP record "Chicken Scratch"—Popular Dance Music of the Indians of Southern Arizona" (The Enis Company 1972).

This was not the first time *waila* music had appeared on record. A 78-rpm single of an old-style fiddle band—Harry Marcus and Orchestra—was produced as a fund-raiser for the St. Johns Indian School at Komatke, Arizona, in 1951 (Marcus 1951). But the 1972 Canyon disc was the first *waila* recording to be made available to the non-Indian world. It also stimulated me to become interested in *waila*, especially as I discovered that members of the Enis band were my next-door neighbors. Thus I became a part of the *waila* scene, at first as a dancer, and later as a writer and a concert and festival presenter.

Since 1974 I have been active in studying *waila* music and presenting it to a wider audience. That first year I was able to secure invitations for the Enis band to the San Diego Folk Festival and the National Folk Festival outside of Washington, D.C. Also in 1974 I produced the first edition of the Tucson Meet Yourself folklife festival, which was to become an annual event until 1994, and which featured a *waila* band (and later on, an old-style fiddle band) each year. *Waila* bands made subsequent appearances at several festivals around the country, including the National Folk Festival and the Smithsonian Festival of American Folklife, and even appeared at Carnegie Hall in New York.

The first Canyon Record was swiftly followed by more LP's and cassettes, as other bands approached Boley and requested recordings. In September 1995, the Canyon catalogue included fifty *waila* tapes—with more new and reissue recordings in production—and three cassettes of old-time fiddle bands. Although there is some crossover trade into the mainstream world, an attempt at marketing *waila* music to Mexican American fans of *norteño* music was unsuccessful. Consequently, most recordings of *waila* music are confined to sales within the Native American market.

All of this recording and festival activity gradually drew *waila* music into the consciousness of the local middle classes and people connected to universities in Tucson and elsewhere. When the Arizona Historical Society revived the San Agustín Fiesta as a cultural event in the 1980s, it seemed only right to feature a *waila* band. Then, in 1989, Angelo Joaquin, Jr., son of the founder of the highly popular Joaquin Brothers band and veteran festival volunteer at national, regional, and local folklife festivals, founded the annual *Waila* Festival, held each Spring at the Arizona Historical Society headquarters and museum in Tucson.

By 1996 *waila* music has moved, not into the mainstream of American culture, but into a state of contact with and recognition by that mainstream. With the exception of one group of New Mexico musicians who studied with the late Elliott Johnson of the Gu-Achi Fiddlers, no non-O'odham to my knowledge have tried to learn *waila* or to form a *waila* band.[2] In 1994 and 1995, workshops were held on how to dance *waila* for the Tucson Friends of Traditional Music, a local contradance and old-time music organization that comprised mostly college-educated, middle-class young adults. People from many cultural traditions attend the festivals at which *waila* is played and dance enthusiastically to the music when the opportunity arises. However, they tend not to seek out opportunities for *waila* dancing at strictly O'odham social occasions.

Waila has also begun to make an appearance in print through the media of scholarly and other writing. Beginning with an article in *Country Music Magazine* in 1976 (Miller 1976), *waila* has sporadically come to the notice of popular music fans (Wilson 1995); occasional scholarly articles discuss the music, usually in the broader context of O'odham Catholic practice. (Griffith 1979, Griffith 1988, 71–84). The archives at the University of Arizona Library's Southwest Folklore Center contain a few *waila* interviews, copies of all commercial *waila* recordings, and tapes of *waila* performances at Tucson Meet Yourself and other public festivals.

Despite this broadening of horizons and audience, however, *waila* continues to be an O'odham music. Most *waila* is still played in a thoroughly O'odham context—at village feasts and personal celebrations, such as weddings, baptisms, and birthdays. (In the 1970s and '80s, a few Tucson bars, catering to a predominantly working-class clientele, featured *waila* for dancing on weekend evenings; however, I am aware of no such opportunities in the mid-nineties.) *Waila* musicians continue to eschew vocals, and continue the O'odham tradition of enthusiastic tune borrowing. Some innovations occur; two or three of the twenty or more *waila* bands have experimented with electronic keyboards, for instance, and in the 1970s and '80s Big John Manuel of "The American Indians" played his button accordion with a wa-wa pedal, somewhat in the style of *norteño* innovator Esteban Jordan. Women are slowly entering *waila*, and there is an all-woman band playing on the reservation.

But these innovations seem to be well within the mainstream of *waila* music, which has long reflected the various kinds of musical influences available to the O'odham. The basic nature of the music—an instrumental dance music played mostly by men, with a repertoire consisting mainly of polkas, two-steps, mazurkas, and cumbias—seems unchanged, nor does it seem likely to change radically. *Waila* lacks the excitement and the high-energy rhythm that might propel it to follow *zydeco* and the various world-beat musics into the floodlight of mass popularity. It possesses a certain conservatism and solidity that seems to ensure that, for awhile, at least, it will remain what it has been—the traditional dance music of the O'odham of Southern Arizona.

GLOSSARY

baile. Spanish word that refers to "social dance."

conjunto norteño. Popular music of Mexican Americans who live along the U.S.-Mexican border.

cumbia. Dance from Columbia that has been popular along the U.S.–Mexican border since the early 1970s.

keihina. Traditional O'odham circle dance.

kwariya. Local version of a quadrille, which is actually a type of circle dance.

mazurkas. Fast waltzes (played in $\frac{6}{8}$ time).

pascola. Religious ritual and ceremony held by the Yaqui Indians.

ramada. Common word in the Southwest referring to a roof that is supported by four or more posts.

son. First tune played at a *pascola* and distantly related to the Cuban dance of the same name.

Sonoran Catholicism. Also called *santo himdag,* or *saint way,* by the O'odam. A religious and philosophical system that blends O'odham beliefs with Catholicism.

NOTES

1. The First Young *Waila* Musicians' Workshop was held at the Southwest Center for Music in Tucson on Saturday, August 12, 1995. It was sponsored by the *Waila* Festival Board and partially funded through a grant from the Folk and Traditional Arts Division of the National Endowment for the Arts.

2. The Anglo musicians mentioned in this sentence are Ken Keppeler and Jeanie McLerie of Albuquerque, New Mexico. Their band, which specializes in various kinds of traditional dance music, is called Bayou Seco, although for their recording of O'odham fiddle tunes they renamed themselves Bayou Eclectico. They have also recorded O'odham music under the name o-a-machetah/Bayou Eclectico. The word *o-a-machetah* is a phonetically spelled O'odham name bestowed on the group by the late O'odham fiddler Elliott Johnson, from whom they learned most of their *waila* music. It means "fry bread," a favorite O'odham food-stuff. For the sake of convenience, their commercial recordings are listed under the name

Bayou Seco. Bayou Seco's recordings are available from 2824 Sierra Vista, N.W., Albuquerque, New Mexico 87107.

REFERENCES CITED

Bahr, Donald. 1988. Pima-Papago Christianity. *Journal of the Southwest* 30, no. 2: 133–67.

Byrkit, James W. 1992. Land, Sky, and People: The Southwest Defined. *Journal of the Southwest* 34, no 2. Entire issue.

Enis, Marvin. 1976. Conversation with the author.

Enis, Mike. 1974–1980. Conversations with author.

Fontana, Bernard L. 1981. *Of Earth and Little Rain.* Flagstaff, Ariz.: Northland Press.

Griffith, James S. 1979. *Waila*—The Social Dance Music of the Indians of Southern Arizona: An Introduction and Discography. *JEMF Quarterly* 15, no. 56: 193–204.

———. 1988. *Southern Arizona Folk Arts.* Tucson: University of Arizona Press.

———. 1991. *Beliefs and Holy Places: A Spiritual Geography of the Pimería Alta.* Tucson: University of Arizona Press.

———. 1996. The Southwest. *American Folklore: An Encyclopedia.* Jan Harold Brunvand, ed. New York and London: Garland Publishing, Inc., 681–82.

———, and Felipe S. Molina. 1981. *Old Men of the Fiesta: An Introduction to the Pascola Arts.* Phoenix, Ariz.: Heard Museum.

Gustafson, A. M., ed. 1966. *John Spring's Arizona.* Tucson: University of Arizona Press.

Joaquin, Daniel. 1976–1980. Conversations with author.

Juan, Blaine. 1980. Conversation with author.

Miguel, Philip. 1995. Public Comment at First Annual Young *Waila* Musicians Workshop, Tucson, August 12.

Miller, Tom. 1976. Papago Indians are Chicken Scratching . . . *Country Music* 4, no. 8: 16.

Painter, Muriel Thayer. 1986. *With Good Heart: Yaqui Beliefs and Ceremonies in Pascua Village.* Tucson: University of Arizona Press.

Peña, Manuel C. 1985. *The Texas-Mexican Conjunto: History of a Working-Class Music.* Austin: University of Texas Press.

Russell, Frank. 1975. *The Pima Indians.* Tucson: University of Arizona Press.

San Xavier Fiddle Band. 1989. San Xavier Fiddle Band. Phoenix: Canyon CR-8085.

Wilder, Joseph, ed. 1990. Inventing the Southwest. *Journal of the Southwest* 32 no. 4.

Wilson, Sule Greg C. 1995. Dancing in their Ancestors' Footsteps. *Rhythm Music* 4, no. 4: 36–38.

RECORDINGS CITED

The American Indians. 1974. *The American Indians Play Chicken Scratch.* Phoenix, Ariz.: Canyon CC-6120.

Bayou Seco. *Following in the Tuneprints.* UBIK UB-25. Cassette and CD, containing seven *waila* cuts.

Bayou Eclectico. *Memories in Cababi.* UBIK UB-27. Cassette; all *waila* music. One cut, "First Choice Two-Step," is no. 21 on Rounder CD-0391, *Old-Time Music on the Air,* vol. 2.

o-a-machetah/Bayou Eclectico. Cut no. 1, on Rounder CD-0379, *American Folkies,* vol. 1, is a *waila* piece named "Squash Fields."

Gila River Old-Time Fiddlers. 1990. *Gila River Old-Time Fiddlers.* Phoenix, Ariz.: Akina Productions, no number.

Gu-Achi Fiddlers. 1988. *Gu-Achi Fiddlers.* Phoenix, Ariz.: Canyon CR-8082.

Marcus, Harry. 1951. *Harry Marcus and Orchestra:* "Honor y Patria" (A), "Nos Fuimos" (B). Phoenix, Ariz.: Komatke ARP 132/133.

Mike Enis and Company. 1972. *Chicken Scratch: Popular Dance Music of the Indians of Southern Arizona.* Phoenix, Ariz.: Canyon C-6085, Side B.

The Molinas. 1974. *The Molinas: Super Scratch Kings Number One.* Phoenix, Ariz.: Canyon C-6128.

———. 1976. *Scratch Encores with Virgil Molina.* Phoenix: Canyon C-6161.

COMPANION CD SELECTIONS

Track 17. Southern Scratch, "First Stop *Waila.*"

Track 18. Gu Achi Fiddlers, "Libby Bird Mazurka."

CHAPTER 9

Triangles, Squares, Circles, and Diamonds

The "Fasola Folk" and Their Singing Tradition

Ron Pen

*I*n his chapter on the "fasola folk," music professor and Sacred Harp singer and teacher Ron Pen narrates the history and contemporary life of an American singing tradition that may be characterized as the quintessential expression of white, Anglo-Celtic ethnicity. Prior to American independence, immigrant colonists developed a musical performance practice for religious worship that was distinctly different from that of their European forebears. Pen traces the development of psalm singing from its first manifestations in New England through the migration of singing schools to the South, the rise of white spirituals, gospel hymnody at camp meetings, and the evolution of revivalism and traditionalism in shape-note singing today. These distinct singing styles and their respective communities of performers are bound to two volumes of sacred-harp music: The Southern Harmony *and* The Sacred Harp. *During each historical stage, the musical tradition has been marked by a particular repertoire of sacred music, an approach to teaching and performing that repertoire, and a uniquely American version of music theory and performance practice. In his analysis of two tributaries of the same stream, Pen points to the continuity of the family- and community-perpetuated tradition of* The Southern Harmony, *in which the "authenticity of practice" is surely, if tenuously, guaranteed by the fragile line of oral transmission dating at least back to 1884. The practice of* The Sacred Harp, *on the other hand, is a vibrant example of a revivalist musical subculture in America, whose proponents may have little or no connection to the family, community, and religious genetics of the authentic tradition. Contemporary Sacred Harp sings, which are held regularly throughout the nation, hold attraction for*

Americans because of the powerful sound and experience of The Sacred Harp
and the creation of a community through musical performance.

■ ■ ■ ■

BIG SINGING DAY IN KENTUCKY

The day dawns bright and beautiful this fourth Sunday in May in the cozy
town of Benton, Kentucky. Located in the far western part of the state in a
remote and rural area known as the Jackson Purchase, Benton, with a population of 3,899, is the seat of Marshall County and home to the venerable *Big
Singing Day*. As you stroll along the quiet, tree-shaded street on the way to the
courthouse, you glance at the bronze marker stating, "The Big Singing in
Benton is the oldest musical tradition in the United States." Then you enter
the red-brick courthouse and climb the stairs to the spacious main courtroom where you see generations of friends, family, and visitors milling about
in animated conversation—a scene that has been reenacted every year since
1884.

At ten-thirty in the morning, with his well-worn copy of the *Southern
Harmony and Musical Companion* grasped firmly in hand, Frank Nichols
strides purposefully to the front of the judges' bench and calls out "Number
103, Holy Manna." Nichols is president of the Bank of Benton and a member
of an extended family that has been intertwined with the singing for generations. His warmly resonant voice sings out the introductory *fa-la-so-la-fa* syllables that provide the singers with the pitch of the opening chord. Slowly
gathering vocal steam, like a train rolling out of the station, the assembled
singers join in, the words resounding round the old courthouse like distant
thunder. "Brethren we have met to worship, and adore the Lord our God. Will
you pray with all your power, while we try to preach the word." It is "Big
Singing Day" again in Benton, Kentucky, and compliant with the 113-year
tradition, the "fasola folk" have met to sing the shape-note hymns whose
roots stretch back to the earliest days of the American colonies.

KENTUCKY SACRED HARP CONVENTION IN
WOODFORD COUNTY

The day dawns bright and beautiful this Saturday in May at the Academy
Building of Pisgah Presbyterian Church in the rolling countryside of
Woodford County, Kentucky. Located in the central Bluegrass region, Pisgah
Church, built in 1784, is the home of the *Kentucky State Sacred Harp
Convention* hosted by the Appalachian Association of Sacred Harp Singers.
As you drive up the country lane to the church you pass the oak-shaded old

graveyard where Revolutionary War soldiers, farmers, and former governors alike now rest. Carrying your copy of the *Sacred Harp* and a covered dish for the noontime "dinner on the grounds," you enter the old stone academy building and see friends and visitors milling about in animated conversation—a scene that has been reenacted every Saturday before the second Sunday in May since 1980.

At nine o'clock, with his well-worn copy of the *Sacred Harp* grasped firmly in hand, the author strode to the middle of the hollow square, welcomed the fifty singers gathered in the resonant meeting hall, and called out "Number 58, Pisgah, in honor of this lovely church where we are meeting today." After pitching the song with the traditional *fa-so-la*, the singers join in with the syllables indicated by the triangle, square, circle, and diamond shapes of the notes. Like the loud rush of a Kentucky mountain stream, the heartfelt words of the hymn gain force and tumble throughout the old hall, "Jesus, thou art the sinner's friend, As such I look to thee." The Kentucky Sacred Harp Convention is meeting again at Pisgah Church, and compliant with tradition, the "fasola folk" have gathered to sing the shape-note hymns whose roots stretch back to the earliest days of the American colonies.

COLONIAL AMERICAN ROOTS

Musical culture in the New England colonies was heavily influenced by Protestant Calvinist theology, which considered the 150 Biblical psalms of David the only proper music for worship. These psalms were intended to be sung simply, in unison with every voice on the same melody, and without instrumental accompaniment so that the words were clearly understood. Because of the general illiteracy and scarcity of books in eighteenth-century America, however, colonists adopted a performance technique called *lining out*, in which communities sang in a call-and-response manner. The leader, or deacon, would call out a line of the text, for example, "When I can read my title clear to mansions in the skies," and the congregation would then slowly echo the line by singing it as a group. Even though the congregation was supposedly singing a single unaccompanied version of the melody, individuals personally ornamented and varied the melody in a musical texture known as *heterophony*. After years of such alteration, the psalm tempos became incredibly slow and melodies were transformed by quantities of added notes. Consequently, psalms took ten times as long to sing as they had formerly and the original tunes were distorted beyond recognition. Thomas Walter, a contemporary writer, described the process as follows: "For much time is taken up in shaking out these turns and quavers, and besides, no two men in the congregation quaver alike, or together; which sounds in the ears of a good judge, like five hundred different tunes roared out at the same time" (Walter 1721, 4–5).

Harvard-educated clerics who were greatly upset by the style of this singing called it "a horrid medley of confused and disorderly noises" and "the uncouth noise of untuned ears." Writers such as Thomas Symmes called for an end of lined out singing and a return to "regular" singing through a return to reading music notation. As a result, in 1721 Boston witnessed the first *singing school* devoted to teaching members of a community how to read music and sing in harmony. Popular as both an educational and recreational experience, singing schools soon spread throughout New England. By the end of the century, singing schools had traveled down through Pennsylvania and west along the Shenandoah Valley into the southern frontiers of Virginia and Kentucky.

SINGING SCHOOLS

Singing schools were taught by a traveling *singing school master* who settled in a community for a period of two or three weeks. Singing masters seldom had any formal musical training, instead they generally apprenticed through participation in singing schools themselves—all that was required was a keen ear, a strong voice, and a burning desire to travel in order to spread this music. In compensation for his instruction, the teacher would customarily be provided with meals and lodging and given a small fee for each student. Amzi Chapin (1768–1835), a singing school master working in Kentucky, had the following agreement: "We the subscribers do promise to pay unto Amzi Chapin nine shillings for each person whom we subscribe to instruct them in the Art of Music. Twenty six days. Payment to be made at the expiration of the term."

Meeting in the evening, after the day's chores were completed, the singing master would begin by instructing the class in the rudiments of music theory, teaching the students how to read rhythms and how to follow steps of the scale by reading the pitches on the music staff. After the class gained enough proficiency in the rudiments, he would then lead them in singing parts to some of the less complex hymns. First, the class would learn the *air,* or melody, which was in the tenor voice, and once they had mastered that, they would begin reading the other parts—*treble* (soprano), *counter* (alto), and *bass.* As the students gained confidence in their ability to read music at sight, they proceeded to learn more challenging music until the final *singing lecture,* a graduation ceremony in which they presented a public concert to demonstrate their achievements. The purpose was pedagogical, the atmosphere was morally uplifting, but it is clear from this Yale student's journal entry of 1782 that the singing school also provided a much-needed social outlet.

> At present I have no inclination for anything, for I am almost sick of the world and were it not for the hopes of going to the singing meeting tonight and indulging myself a little in the carnal delights

of the flesh, such as kissing and squeezing etc., I should willingly leave it now. (Lowens 1964, 282)

SINGING SCHOOLS

The early lined out psalm singing style required only a book with the words of the psalms printed for use by the song leader. Because the congregation merely echoed the leader's line of text and followed the well-known melodies by ear in lined out style, a single copy of a book was all that was really needed for performance. Singing schools, however, required a book for every participant since each singer was sight reading the words and music for their individual harmony lines.

John Tufts (1689–1750) printed the first book suitable for use with the singing schools. His *A Very Plain and Easy Introduction to the Singing of Psalm Tunes* (c.1714) was a short, twelve-page volume containing thirty-seven tunes written for treble, tenor, and bass voice parts. As the book's purpose was to teach illiterate colonists to read music, Tufts sought an innovative system that would be more clear and easy to read than conventional European notation. He placed letters of a *solfege* system on a five-line staff rather than the usual "round notes." Thus, he used the letter *F* for the pitch *fa*, the letter *S* for *so*, *L* for *la*, and *M* for *mi*. Today, we commonly use seven syllables—*do, re, mi, fa,*

Figure 9.1. Melody and bass lines of *Old 100* as printed in *A Very Plain and Easy Introduction to the Singing of Psalm Tunes* by John Tufts. Transcription by Larry Nelson, University of Kentucky.

so, la, ti, do—to teach students how to read music, but Tufts employed an earlier English system that only used the four syllables *fa, so, la,* and *mi* to indicate the pitches of the scale and show the distance, or *interval,* between one
note and the next.

The rhythms were also represented by a simple, yet innovative, system.
The letter alone was worth a quarter note (F), a letter with a period following it was a half note (F.), and a letter followed by a colon was a whole note
(F:). The inventive notational solutions of Tufts were typical of the American
process of cultural adaptation in which we retained aspects of "old world"
British culture and transformed them to suit our new situation. Psalmody
may still have been "music in America" rather than "American music," but the
rise of the singing school soon led to the first distinctive musical expression
of the American colonies.

NEW ENGLAND

Tufts's book opened the floodgates to a whole generation of New England
singing masters who composed their own original music as well as collected
and arranged earlier music in their publications. In addition to the psalm
tunes inherited from Britain, such Yankee singing masters as William Billings
added new *plain tunes,* vigorous *fuging tunes,* and extended *anthems* that
explored the expressive relationship between words and music. Plain tunes
were short "chorale style" works in which all the voices moved *homophoni-
cally* (rhythmically together) to complement metrical strophic texts of
repeated verses. Fuging tunes began with a section in which all the voices
sang rhythmically together in four-part harmony followed by an imitative
section in which the voices chased each other as in a "round." Anthems were
more extended compositions with changes of tempo, different rhythms, and
key changes that painted the meaning of the words through musical expression. This was a new American music suited to the temperament and needs
of a new American people.

This new singing school music clearly reflected the important question
that was at the heart of America's experiment in participatory democracy—
how was this country going to reconcile the tension between individual freedom and the constraints of social order. Each vocal line was fiercely independent in following its own path. William Hauser, author of *The Hesperian
Harp,* stated that each part should be "so good a melody that it will charm
even when sung by itself" (Hauser 1848, xviii).

Tenors, trebles, counters (altos), and basses all possessed their own
melodic direction that coexisted with the other independent parts in a loose
confederation of harmony. The bass was not content merely to plod sub-
serviently below the soprano melody and the counter refused to be relegated
to the supportive role of doubling harmony notes. Each part had its own dis-

tinct melody that contributed a unique perspective to the total sound. Democracy can sometimes be a messy process, and occasionally the independent vocal parts clashed discordantly or tripped over themselves as they crossed paths with another part, but they always did so within a framework of collective order.

SHAPED NOTES

Despite the efforts of John Tufts to develop a clearer system of music notation, musicians continued to use the conventional round notes for all singing school tune books through the eighteenth century. In 1798, however, William Little and William Smith of Philadelphia invented an entirely different way of indicating pitches, using various shapes to represent notes. Taking the four syllable fasola system used earlier by Tufts as the basis, Little and Smith substituted differently shaped note heads for the letters as a visual aid in reading music. Thus, a triangle was used for *fa*, a circle for *so*, a square for *la*, and a diamond for *mi*.

Unlike the common *do-re-mi* system where each of the seven pitches of the scale corresponds to a different syllable, this shape-note fasola system has to repeat three of the syllables and their corresponding shapes twice within a scale; thus the entire scale would be sung *fa, so, la, fa, so, la, mi, fa*. This is not really confusing, however, since the note shapes are placed on a five-line staff

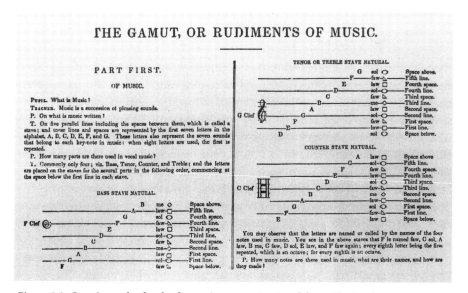

Figure 9.2. C-major scales for the four voice parts. Reprinted from *The Southern Harmony and Musical Companion*, edited by Glenn Wilcox, copyright © 1987 by the University Press of Kentucky, by permission of the publishers.

and it is easy to distinguish the pitches by their *relative* height on the lines and spaces of the staff. It is also important to remember that the shapes only indicate the relative placement in a scale and the interval between tones. The shapes do not represent fixed pitches as do notes on a piano. For instance, *fa* is the root and fourth of any major scale—in the key of C major, the *fa* corresponds to the notes *C* and *F*, while in the key of D major *fa* corresponds to the notes *D* and *G*. Rhythms were indicated the same way as with round notes, with hollow or shaded note heads and stems and beams.

The combination of fasola syllables and the shape-note notation proved to be highly successful. Between the printing of Little and Smith's *The Easy Instructor* in 1798 and the publication of *The Social Harp* in 1855, there were at least thirty-eight different tune books in circulation that all used the four shapes. Singing masters compiled and printed books for use in their own schools that typically included an assortment of the most popular hymns excerpted from other books as well as original compositions and arrangements of vernacular melodies that were matched with sacred texts and adapted for hymn use. In this way, the collective compiling work of various singing masters increased the singing school repertoire beyond the original British psalm tunes through the inclusion of original American compositions and adaptations. Like a living organism, shape-note repertoire evolved in response to the changing tastes of musical America. Now as singing school masters followed the growing tide of migration to the southern and western frontiers, another rich layer of new shape-note hymnody, known as white spirituals, would further enrich the repertoire.

WHITE SPIRITUALS

During the first decades of the nineteenth century, musical life in New England was altered by the rise of public school music education, an emphasis on European "classical" music, and the immigration of trained professional European musicians. Singing schools and their folksy home-grown music became an endangered species in the urban centers of New York, Boston, and Philadelphia. Such reformist musicians as Lowell Mason, who condescendingly called shape notes "dunce notes," established more formalized organizations—the Boston Handel and Haydn Society, for example—and forced the singing schools to retreat to rural areas of New England and down through Pennsylvania into the wilderness areas of Virginia, North Carolina, and Kentucky.

Kentuckians were especially receptive to singing schools. The first school was recorded in Lexington in 1797, and shortly thereafter subsequent singings spread throughout the bluegrass region and into the mountains to the east and the Purchase area of the west. Southern singing-school masters also began compiling and publishing their own tunebooks. Incorporating the contributions of Lucius and Amzi Chapin, who were living in Fleming County, Kentucky, John Wyeth published the *Repository of Sacred Music* in 1810. Six years later Ananais Davisson, who lived in the Shenandoah Valley, printed his *Kentucky Harmony,* and the following year Samuel Metcalf of Shelbyville, Kentucky, issued the *Kentucky Harmonist* in Lexington.

These first southern books were important because they introduced a whole new type of shape-note hymn based on indigenous music. Called *white spirituals* by scholar George Pullen Jackson, the new hymns married sacred texts of such authors as Isaac Watts, John Newton (author of *Amazing Grace*), and Charles Wesley with melodies drawn from secular ballads, fiddle tunes, and lyric songs. For example, the hymn "Sawyer's Exit," found in the *Sacred Harp,* couples the words "How bright is the day when the Christian receives the sweet message to come" to the bouncy Irish jig called "Rosin the Beau (Bow)." White spirituals blurred that fine line between sacred and secular since the same tune sung at Saturday night's frolic might be heard at Sunday morning's worship as well.

The tunes are pungently striking, with melodies often based on five-note *pentatonic scales,* or *modal scales,* that impart a high, lonesome sound reminiscent of the sound of Scottish bagpipes. Often composed for only three voice parts, by eliminating the counter line, they have a distinctively "hollow" quality that sounds more "ancient" than the rounded chordal sound characteristic of classical harmonic practice. White spirituals were enthusiastically embraced by the fasola folk because the words contained vivid and colorful imagery, the tunes were exciting, and the melodies were already familiar to many southerners through square dances or back-porch singings.

CAMP MEETINGS

At the turn of the century, a religious fervor known as the *Great Revival,* or *The Second Great Awakening,* swept through the country. In 1801 approximately twenty-thousand people flocked to Cane Ridge Meeting House in Bourbon County, Kentucky. Twenty thousand people drawn by wagon and mule and on foot along dirt roads, praying, loudly singing, barking like dogs, dancing wildly, weeping, and jerking uncontrollably in the throes of religious ecstasy—the Woodstock of its day. Presbyterian, Methodist, and Baptist ministers gathered and preached fire and salvation to the crowds from wagon beds and tree stumps. The excitement kindled by this first huge camp meeting spread throughout the south and carried with it a new type of gospel hymnody that was added to the constantly expanding repertoire of shape-note music.

Singing was an important means of exciting the passions of the crowds at a camp meeting. The rhythmic propulsion and melodic surge of repeated refrains had the effect of simultaneously reinforcing key ideas as well as

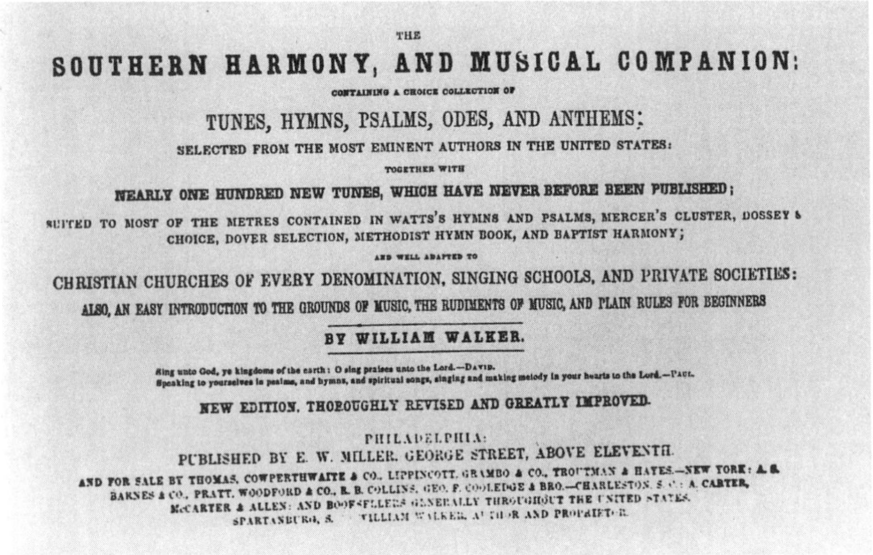
THE

SOUTHERN HARMONY, AND MUSICAL COMPANION:

CONTAINING A CHOICE COLLECTION OF

TUNES, HYMNS, PSALMS, ODES, AND ANTHEMS;

SELECTED FROM THE MOST EMINENT AUTHORS IN THE UNITED STATES:

TOGETHER WITH

NEARLY ONE HUNDRED NEW TUNES, WHICH HAVE NEVER BEFORE BEEN PUBLISHED;

SUITED TO MOST OF THE METRES CONTAINED IN WATTS'S HYMNS AND PSALMS, MERCER'S CLUSTER, DOSSEY'S CHOICE, DOVER SELECTION, METHODIST HYMN BOOK, AND BAPTIST HARMONY;

AND WELL ADAPTED TO

CHRISTIAN CHURCHES OF EVERY DENOMINATION, SINGING SCHOOLS, AND PRIVATE SOCIETIES:

ALSO, AN EASY INTRODUCTION TO THE GROUNDS OF MUSIC, THE RUDIMENTS OF MUSIC, AND PLAIN RULES FOR BEGINNERS

BY WILLIAM WALKER.

Sing unto God, ye kingdoms of the earth: O sing praises unto the Lord.—DAVID.
Speaking to yourselves in psalms, and hymns, and spiritual songs, singing and making melody in your hearts to the Lord.—PAUL.

NEW EDITION, THOROUGHLY REVISED AND GREATLY IMPROVED.

PHILADELPHIA:
PUBLISHED BY E. W. MILLER, GEORGE STREET, ABOVE ELEVENTH.
AND FOR SALE BY THOMAS, COWPERTHWAITE & CO., LIPPINCOTT, GRAMBO & CO., TROUTMAN & HAYES.—NEW YORK: A. S. BARNES & CO., PRATT, WOODFORD & CO., R. B. COLLINS, GEO. F. COOLEDGE & BRO.—CHARLESTON, S. C.: A. CARTER, McCARTER & ALLEN: AND BOOKSELLERS GENERALLY THROUGHOUT THE UNITED STATES.
SPARTANBURG, S. C.: WILLIAM WALKER, AUTHOR AND PROPRIETOR.

Figure 9.3. Reprinted from *The Southern Harmony and Musical Companion,* edited by Glenn Wilcox, copyright © 1987 by the University Press of Kentucky, by permission of the publishers.

inducing an out-of-body trance experience. Since people could not read words or music notation from books at a camp meeting, songs that were easily learned had to be chosen so that people could immediately participate. Therefore, camp meeting gospel music had limited vocal ranges, catchy tunes, infectious dancelike rhythms, short verses, and choruses that could be repeated forever. Often the same verse could be repeated over and over simply by changing a few words. For instance, "Hebrew Children," found in *The Sacred Harp,* has a repeating line, "Where are the Hebrew children," that may be changed to "Where are the twelve apostles" or "Where are the holy Christians," to stretch out the song for numerous verses.

SOUTHERN HARMONY AND THE SACRED HARP

Approaching the middle of the nineteenth century, when Southern fasola singing was at the zenith of its popularity, two shape-note tune books, *The Southern Harmony* and *The Sacred Harp,* appeared. Although similar in appearance and contents, they were destined for very different fates. The *Southern Harmony* would become frozen in time, preserved in a single traditional annual performance, Big Singing Day at Benton, Kentucky, while *The Sacred Harp* would become a living history told through various revisions and editions performed in hundreds of contemporary singings held throughout the United States to this very day.

SOUTHERN HARMONY ORIGINS

The two books had curiously intertwined origins. William "Singin' Billy" Walker and Benjamin Franklin White, both of Spartanburg, South Carolina, were brothers-in-law through their marriage to the Golightly sisters. The two men compiled *The Southern Harmony* together, but in 1835 Walker evidently took the book to New Haven, Connecticut, to get it printed and somehow failed to credit White with his share of the authorship. The story may merely be fiction, but to this day the legend is still the source of good-natured bantering back and forth between adherents of the different books as though the schism between Walker and White were just a recent family unpleasantry.

Walker was much in demand as a singing-school teacher and his *Southern Harmony* was the most popular tune book of the nineteenth century, selling approximately six hundred thousand copies, with a revision in 1847 and a final revision in 1854. Unfortunately, the book's further development was disrupted by the Civil War and Walker's subsequent decision to publish a new book, *The Christian Harmony*, in the seven-shape solfege system that was supplanting the four-shape notation. The life of a singing is tied to the life of a book. With the final *Southern Harmony* published in 1854, the book would have become extinct were it not for a single community event sparked by the enthusiasm of James R. Lemon, editor and owner of the Benton *Tribune*.

As a child, Lemon traveled from North Carolina with his family over the Blue Ridge and Cumberland Mountains to Marshall County, Kentucky, in 1852. Packed away in the family's covered wagon was a copy of the *Southern Harmony*, perhaps acquired directly from a singing school led by William Walker himself. Lemon began teaching in singing schools as a young man and maintained a lifelong devotion to fasola music. Observing that the music of his youth was rapidly disappearing, Lemmon used the public forum of his paper to propose a general gathering in Benton that would be devoted to singing from *The Southern Harmony*. Following that first Big Singing Day in 1884, the countywide family reunion, coupled with the *Southern Harmony* singing, has become a local tradition tenaciously maintained in the face of many cultural changes that have threatened its existence over the years.

One of the greatest challenges to the survival of the tradition was the scarcity of books. By the 1930s there were scarcely thirty of the precious and tattered 1854 editions still available. Many people were singing from memory. In 1931 George Pullen Jackson noted:

> The *Southern Harmony* singings at Benton are probably the last of their kind anywhere and dissolution stares them in the face. The only thing that can lengthen their life is a new supply of the song books with which the tradition is inseparably bound up. Will some worshipper at the shrine of "old-time songs" provide that supply? (Jackson [1933] 1965, 67–68)

Fortunately, that "worshipper" appeared close at hand. The book that is the lifeblood of the tradition was reissued in 1939 by the Young Men's Progress Club, and subsequently local singer Dr. Glenn Wilcox published his Pro Music Americana edition in 1966. The book is still in print today through a 1987 facsimile edited by Wilcox and published by the University Press of Kentucky.

SACRED HARP ORIGINS

B. F. White moved to Georgia and collaborated with Elisha J. King to publish his own tune book, *The Sacred Harp* in 1844. White's book shared many of the same tunes as Walker's with the usual representation of New England composers, such as William Billings and Daniel Read, and white spirituals by Davisson and the Chapins. In addition, nearly a quarter of the tunes in the book were written by, or at least attributed to, Georgia singers including White, King, and White's nephew J. T. White. The success of a book depended on the compiler's ability to choose the best and most popular hymns for inclusion. Obviously White chose well, for *The Sacred Harp* has enjoyed a 150-year publishing history marked by the appearance of various revisions and many printings. The popular 1991 edition is currently in its third printing of three thousand copies.

Popular in its time but nearly extinct today, *The Southern Harmony* would come to represent fasola as it was in mid-eighteenth-century South, while *The Sacred Harp*, with its continuous history of growth and change, would evolve to reflect the state of fasola singing at the end of the twentieth century. Folks at Benton talk of the "purity" of their singing and complain about *Sacred Harp* innovations, such as "those ragtimey rhythms" and "that added counter part," but it is exactly that element of change that doomed *The Southern Harmony* to museum status and contributed to *The Sacred Harp*'s role in the rise of shape-note revivalism.

For that reason, a comparison of Big Singing Day and the Kentucky Sacred Harp Convention represents a comprehensive portrait of community *traditionalism* and *revivalism* characteristic of shape-note singing in American culture. Let us briefly define *tradition* as culture that is "bred in the bone," passed on through oral transmission within an identifiable community. *Revivalism* consists of participation in a tradition by people who are not born into the traditional community yet who consciously choose to participate in that community.

BIG SINGING DAY

The day dawns bright and beautiful this fourth Sunday in May as you enter the red-brick courthouse and climb the stairs to the spacious wood-paneled courtroom. At about ten o'clock folks dressed in their Sunday finery begin to gather. Soon, excited knots of people form, catching up on all the news and stories since they were last together. Patriarchal figures, such as Dr. Ray Mofield and Dr. Glenn Wilcox, are busy with last-minute organizational details, making introductions and drawing up a list of the morning's song leaders. Mrs. Tula Nichols and Miss Margaret Heath, resplendent in their "go-to-meeting" hats, are engaged in conversation with a young graduate student who is making her first visit to Benton. Young children dart between legs of parents, a sound engineer from Texas is adjusting microphones, luncheon plans are discussed, area politicians shake hands with potential voters, recipes are traded, golf games recounted, and family and visitors alike are drawn into the social fabric woven at that first singing gathering of 1884.

It is a tight social fabric, woven from a narrowly circumscribed geographic region and limited social context. The community is defined by a common evangelical Protestant heritage—chiefly Primitive Baptist, Church of Christ, and Baptist. The singing itself is a secular event and is not associated with any church, although there is a strongly moral foundation since all the song texts are scriptural, and invocation and benediction prayers frame the day.

Members of the singing represent a homogenous ethnic stock that is almost exclusively Anglo-Celtic in origin. Most of the singers are members of families that have been associated with the singing for generations, such as the Nichols family. Marshall County is essentially an agricultural economy with

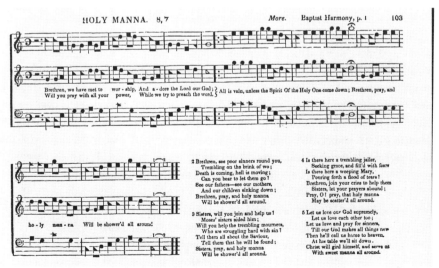

Figure 9.4. Reprinted from *The Southern Harmony and Musical Companion*, edited by Glenn Wilcox, copyright © 1987 by the University Press of Kentucky, by permission of the publishers.

little industry capable of either retaining younger residents or luring new inhabitants to the area. As a result, few singers who did not grow up with the tradition are permanently integrated into the Big Singing Day community.

As is characteristic of farming communities, home and family are at the core of the values system. The concept of homeplace is itself firmly rooted in the Big Singing. Family members may be dispersed far beyond the region, but on Big Singing Day they religiously return home for the weekend, drawn by the bonds of family, community, and identity. Big Singing Day is actually more of a family reunion than a musical event. The singing would surely have died off years ago if it had not been closely intertwined with homecoming and community identity.

THE DAY CONTINUES

You walk over to the benches on the left hand side of the judge's chair and sit with a group of men that look as though they might be basses. Shortly after ten-thirty, the singers have seated themselves in their accustomed places in the area before the bar while community members and visitors who are present merely to listen have arranged themselves in the audience area. The courtroom looks crowded with approximately fifty singers and several hundred audience members. It is hard to imagine how the building and square outside would have looked back in the 1920s and 1930s when ten thousand people regularly attended the event.

With his well-worn copy of *The Southern Harmony* grasped firmly in hand, Frank Nichols rises and an expectant quiet settles over the gathering. After a short greeting, Nichols announces *Holy Manna* (Track 19), pitches the song by ear, and exclaims "by the note," directing people to sing the syllables. Beating time simply with his right arm, he cautions the singers to observe the two beats of rest at the beginning by calling out "down left." With books open on their laps and rapt expressions on their faces, the singers slowly and gravely make their way through the syllables. After the shapes have been sung through once, Nichols says "by the line," which signals the singers to sing the music with the words. Following *Holy Manna*, an invocation is delivered that is always succeeded by the singing of *New Britain*, more commonly known as *Amazing Grace*. The hymn always concludes with the verse beginning "When we've been there ten thousand years," which are the only words sung by the Benton community that are not printed in *The Southern Harmony*.

Each year a senior and highly respected member of the singing community is charged with convening the sessions and moderating the day's activities. In recent years this role has been entrusted to university professors Ray Mofield and Glenn Wilcox, both now deceased, and Frank Nichols, who is currently president of the Society for the Preservation of *Southern Harmony* Singing. The decorum, tone, and organization of the entire day are

Figure 9.5. Glenn Wilcox leading at Big Singing Day at Benton, Kentucky, 1979. Photo courtesy of Helen Wilcox.

set by the moderator, who is a link in the unbroken lineage stretching back all the way to Walker himself.

The rest of the morning is structured according to a simple, recurring pattern. Each singer who is willing to lead comes forward and chooses two of his favorite tunes. Calling out the number and title of the song, and perhaps prefacing it with a few comments—such as "Raymond Lay always loved this song. He was a fine gentleman and a wonderful singer"—the leader pitches the song and sets the tempo with simple conducting gestures. In between songs, there may be a little conversation among singers commenting on the tempo or sharing an anecdote from past years, but the orderly process of singing proceeds almost like clockwork until noon.

After all the experienced community members have had an opportunity to lead, younger singers and visitors are encouraged to come forward and participate. In this way, novices have the opportunity of first observing the model of veteran singers before participating themselves. The singers are supportive of these unfamiliar leaders, but if one chooses a fast tempo, beats with an unclear pattern, or chooses a difficult and unfamiliar number, the singing can quickly disintegrate and even cease altogether. If this happens, the singers feel perfectly comfortable with starting again by altering the pitch or gently correcting the tempo. The day is viewed as a singing school and not a polished performance. They are singing with one another, not performing for the public, and the courtroom audience is merely an extension of the singers themselves.

By tradition, only men are permitted to lead. This has caused quite a bit of controversy in recent years, but tradition is a strongly conservative force, and the weight of one hundred and thirteen years of custom have defined the role of men and women at Big Singing Day. Women are certainly treated as equals in all other respects, in fact, they hold many of the elected positions within the Society for the Preservation of Southern Harmony, but they never lead the singing itself. Leadership within the community is based on singing ability, knowledge, experience, and family relationships without respect to gender, but the leadership role on Big Singing Day is reserved for the men of the community.

THE AFTERNOON SESSION

At noon, the singers quickly disperse and head for various homes where dinner is served. At one time, Courthouse Square was the scene of a huge "dinner on the grounds," with family picnics sprawling out in all directions. In recent years, most families gather at home to eat, although several picnics are customarily held upstairs in the court building itself. Since it is Sunday, most of the restaurants in town are closed, so guests are cheerfully welcomed into various families for the "potluck" meals. The hospitality of Mrs. Tula Nichols is legendary, and after a dinner of the wonderful vinegary barbecued mutton accompanied by an array of vegetable casseroles and a host of home-baked desserts washed down by gallons of iced tea, it seems scarcely possible that people will be able to sing again that afternoon.

By one-thirty people have returned to the courthouse. Frank Nichols rises and opens the session again with *Holy Manna*. Following a welcoming address that notes the history of the singing, eulogizes prominent singers who have passed away during the year, and acknowledges visitors, the singing commences. The afternoon session is more formal than the morning, with a printed program listing the probable song choices for likely leaders. There are 341 songs in the book, but singers usually choose from a core repertory of thirty-seven tunes that are most familiar to the community—songs with evocative titles like *Happy Land, Thorny Desert,* and *Sweet Rivers*. In the same way that *Holy Manna* has become identified with the entire Big Singing Day, certain hymns become strongly associated with certain leaders or families who may have led the song for years. It is considered a mild breach of etiquette for a song leader to knowingly "trespass" on another person's song. Songs are not repeated, although the same song may be chosen at both the morning and afternoon sessions.

The tempos are characteristically slow and deliberate, as though the participants are lingering with a cherished friend whom they won't see again for at least another year. The balance features strong tenor and bass sections with fewer penetrating treble voices than might be found at a Sacred Harp singing. Singing style is full and natural, complemented by the pitching, which is low, often as much as a third below the note indicated on the music. The overall sound is haunting, powerful, and unhurried.

Figure 9.6. Pisgah Curch, Woodford County, Kentucky, site of the Kentucky Sacred Harp Convention. Photo by Ron Pen.

The afternoon passes in much the same way as the morning session with each leader rising to lead two songs. As you glance down at your watch, you realize that you have been lulled into a timeless moment that has all too quickly passed. At three-thirty Frank Nichols calls for the final song in the book, *The Christian's Farewell,* which traditionally closes the singing. There is a final benediction, and then you find yourself wandering through the crowd, saying good bye to new friends and promising to return again next year. Another Big Singing Day has passed into history, but the gathering has again served to bind the community together with the shared song of an unbroken lineage stretching back into the past and forward into an uncertain future.

KENTUCKY SACRED HARP CONVENTION

The day dawns bright and beautiful this Saturday in May as you drive down twisty Pisgah Pike leading to the old Presbyterian Church in the heart of rolling Kentucky bluegrass horse country. As you enter the stone Academy Building, you encounter a beehive of activity. There are folks standing by a front table registering and chatting, another group of people is gathered in the kitchen sorting out covered dishes and desserts for the noon dinner on the grounds. Moving into the meeting hall, you see other folks moving

Windsor chairs into the traditional hollow, square configuration that allows singers to really hear one another. Resonant with bare wood floors and ceilings, and graced by an unadorned nineteenth-century ambience, Pisgah is exactly the sort of singing space favored by Sacred Harp singers. Just as Gothic cathedrals are suited to the quality of Gregorian plainchant, so do resonant meeting halls enhance the intertwining melodic lines of fasola singing.

In quick snatches of conversation, old friends are greeted and visitors are made to feel welcome as the singers move into the hall and begin to take their seats. Tenor voices sit closest to the door, basses on their left by the windows, trebles on the tenors' right, and counter voices are seated across the room. More experienced "front bench" singers generally occupy the first row of chairs, and visitors or people who merely wish to listen usually gravitate to the back seats. There are no accomodations for an audience since Sacred Harp singing is intended for active participation rather than passive consumption.

By nine o'clock there are approximately fifty singers, the majority of whom are members of the Appalachian Association of Sacred Harp Singers, an organization that meets for monthly singings and hosts the annual convention. While most of the singers are from the central Kentucky region, there are also visitors from the eastern and western portions of Kentucky as well as out-of-state guests from Tennessee, Ohio, Indiana, Illinois, Missouri, and Virginia.

It is a fairly homogenous gathering. Many of the singers are urban professionals, and there is a particularly large contingent associated with the nearby University of Kentucky. There is little ethnic or religious diversity—the majority of the singers are Caucasian and belong to mainline Protestant or Catholic faiths. The only exceptions are several Jewish participants who have been drawn to the sound of the music despite the fundamentalist Christian theology of the words. Unlike the Benton gathering, which is essentially a family affair, most of the Kentucky Convention singers have been drawn to *The Sacred Harp* by interest and not birth.

REVIVALISM

Most of the singers are "baby boomers" with an average age of forty-five. There are a few young children, several college-age students, and a handful of more mature participants, but the vast majority of the singers are in their forties and fifties. This age profile is characteristic of revivalist singings. In fact, the development of the sixteen-year-old Kentucky Convention itself parallels the involvement of many revivalist singers who were introduced to Sacred Harp singing in the 1970s. There is a core of singers who have grown up with the Benton singing or been introduced to shape-note singing through church backgrounds, but the majority of the singers may be identified as revivalists.

Figure 9.7. Singers in the hollow square at the Sacred Harp Convention in Kentucky. Photo by Ron Pen.

Urbanization, mobility, and the rise of media technology separated most of a generation from participation in singing schools. Only the most rural and isolated areas of the deep south retained their Sacred Harp singings and passed them on to the next generation. Ironically, the same media and technology that threatened the existence of fasola singing also reintroduced the revivalist generation to Sacred Harp music through recordings, radio, and television exposure. The same mobility that drew families from their homeplace roots also facilitated travel to singings. The same urbanization that fragmented communities throughout migration has provided a favorable climate for singings in large cities of the northeast and midwest. The very same cultural changes that severed a generation from traditional fasola singing have also served to reconnect that generation to the Sacred Harp community.

THE SINGING BEGINS

Seated in your chair in the treble section, you observe the moderator striding into the middle of the square to convene the morning session of the singing. After some brief opening remarks welcoming folks and familiarizing singers with local customs, he cradles his *Sacred Harp* in the crook of his left arm and calls for number 103, *Pisgah*. Sounding pitches of the opening chord, the leader starts the singing by beating time with a simple up and down motion of his right arm. Tentative at first with the syllables, the music gains in confidence and volume by the time the singers begin the words. Soon the old meeting hall is ringing with the loud, rushing sounds of *The Sacred Harp.*

PERFORMANCE STYLE

The style of performance is very different from that of the Benton gathering. Songs are taken at brisk tempos—not as fast as the deep southern Georgia and Alabama singings, but in many cases, twice the speed of Big Singing Day. The tempo emphasizes the surge of the rhythm and, noticeably, many people are tapping their feet or beating time with their hand in unison with the leader. While pitch is different according to each leader (there are no tuning forks or pitch pipes), pitches tend to be higher than those at Benton in order to emphasize the tension between the tenor and treble parts. The intonation is not absolute and is shaded towards modal inflections in which the pitch notated in the music is not the pitch that is actually sung (for example, note the raised sixth that is sung instead of the D♭ that is notated in the melody line of *Wondrous Love*).

Voices tend to be wide open, without vibrato, somewhat nasal, and strained at the top register. The sheer volume of the sound is striking. If the Big Singing can be characterized as a nostalgic reminiscence, then the Kentucky Convention is an exultant shout. There is little dynamic contrast except for a few places where the singers customarily grow quiet, as in the second emotional utterance of "Oh my son" in *David's Lamentation*. The musical force of *The Sacred Harp* is manifest in the words and in the rhythmic drive of the melody lines—there is little desire for the expressive subtleties found in art music.

The morning unfolds in a pattern similar to Big Singing Day. The leadership rotates, with each person, in turn, guiding the singers through two songs. However, unlike Benton, the women and men are both encouraged to lead. The relationship between gender and power is not really an issue at the singing. Women and men share the leadership as well as kitchen duties equally, and while the two moderators for the convention have both been male in recent years, the elected song leader of the Appalachian Association of Sacred Harp Singers is currently female. Female and male leaders are judged according to the same criteria—their ability to lead a song by pitching it correctly, to set an appropriate tempo, and to lead the singers through difficult passages and problematic repeats through the strength of one's voice and personality. (Listen to Track 20, "Promised Land.")

Before the noon recess for dinner, there is a Memorial Lesson at which time deceased members of the singing community are remembered with brief comments and a song dedicated to their memory. One especially emotional Memorial Lesson at a Kentucky Convention involved the observance of a longtime female member who had been brutally murdered. The song

Figure 9.8. Dinner on the grounds at the Kentucky Sacred Harp Convention. Photo by Ron Pen.

given in her memory was *Stockwood,* whose words have been permanently etched in this community's memory of the young woman.

> Sister, thou wast mild and lovely,
> Gentle as the summer breeze,
> Pleasant as the air of evening,
> When it flows among the trees.
>
> Peaceful be thy silent slumber,
> Peaceful in the grave so low;
> Thou no more wilt join our number,
> Thou no more our songs shall know.

AFTERNOON

At noon, *Old 100* is sung as a blessing and the session adjourns for dinner on the grounds. Sacred Harp singing provides an excuse for cooks to parade their favorite recipes, and soon plates are piled high with home-baked bread, sweet potato casserole, spring garden salads, countless variations on fried chicken and corn bread, and a host of home-baked pies and fresh strawberry shortcake. Nothing forges a community more tightly than shared song, conversation, and a good meal.

At one o'clock the afternoon session is convened and the singing continues in the same vein as the morning. Approximately forty hymns, fuging tunes, and anthems are attempted before the afternoon draws to an end with *Parting Friends,* the song the Appalachian Association traditionally uses to conclude its singings.

> Farewell my friends, I'm bound for Canaan,
> I'm trav'ling through the wilderness.
> Your company has been delightful.

It has been a long day. Empty casserole dish and *Sacred Harp* in hand, you climb in your car and head back down Pisgah Pike. Fragments of songs, bits of stories, a haunting melody, a new face, and the taste of fresh strawberries, are all woven together in a memory quilt that accompanies you down the highway home.

FINAL THOUGHTS

Big Singing Day and the Kentucky Sacred Harp Convention are tenuous survivals of the past that have lingered into the end of the twentieth century. The original function and context of singing schools has been permanently altered by contemporary culture, but the infusion of revivalist energy flowing into the steady stream of tradition has invested this uniquely American heritage with meaning and vigor. In a fragmented modern society, family has been preserved and community established through shared song.

Singers in Benton are born into shape-note singing early in life through a traditional family background. Singers may chose to become involved in Sacred Harp singing later in life, through a revivalist introduction. Either way, at some point the singer must make a conscious choice to identify herself or himself with the tradition, and in so doing, they become yet another voice in the unbroken lineage of fasola singing stretching back to the American colonies.

GLOSSARY

air. The principal melody in a shape-note hymn that is sung by the tenor voice.

anthem. An extended vocal work with a through-composed text. Anthems often contain changes of key, rhythm, or meter to illustrate the words and provide variety.

bass. The lowest singing part, usually sung only by men.

Big Singing Day. Held annually on the fourth Sunday in May since 1884, Big Singing Day in Benton, Kentucky meets at the Courthouse in a morning and afternoon session to sing from *The Southern Harmony*, a shape-note songbook by William Walker.

counter. The voice part called the alto today. This is the lowest part for female voices.

fuging tune. Originating in eighteenth-century America, the fuging tune is a musical composition in two sections—the first is a homophonic, sung in "chordal" style; the second, with imitative entries, is similar to a "round."

heterophony. A musical texture in which all voices are singing a single melody, but each voice personalizes the melody through rhythmic and melodic ornamentation.

interval. The musical distance between any two pitches.

lining out. A singing technique in which a leader sings out a line of text that is then echoed by a group of singers in call-and-response style. This makes it easy for singers to participate even when they are not musically literate or songbooks are unavailable.

modal scale. Diatonic scales—such as the dorian, for example—that are built on various patterns of half and whole steps but which sound archaic because of a particular interval that differentiates them from the more conventional major and minor scales.

pentatonic scale. A five-note scale. One pentatonic scale may be represented by playing the black keys of a piano.

revivalism. Participation in a traditional culture by individuals who are foreign to that culture but who consciously choose to participate in it.

singing school. Originating in the New England colonies in the eighteenth century, singing schools were designed to teach singing by reading music notation. Typically, they taught the rudiments of theory and instructed students in sight-reading hymns, fuging tunes, and anthems during a three-week period.

singing-school master. Singing masters usually traveled to communities where they stayed for three weeks to instruct a school in return for bed, board, and stipend. Some masters compiled and printed their own tunebooks for use in their schools.

solfège. A method of singing instruction that uses syllables corresponding to music pitches as a means for learning to sing scales and intervals.

traditionalism. Folk culture disseminated through oral transmission within an identifiable community.

treble. The top singing part usually called the soprano today. In fasola singing, men and women sang the treble part in their own register.

white spirituals. Southern-shape note hymns that coupled familiar melodies drawn from such sources as ballads and dance tunes with sacred texts written by such authors as Isaac Watts.

COMPANION CD SELECTIONS

Track 19. The Southern Harmony, led by Ray Mofier, "Holy Manna."

Track 20. The Southern Harmony, led by Ron Pen, "Promised Land."

ADDITIONAL SOURCES

Bibliography

Cobb, Buell E., Jr. 1978. *The Sacred Harp: A Tradition and Its Music.* Athens, Ga.: University of Georgia Press. Paperback, 1989.

Hauser, William. 1848. *The Hesperian Harp.* Philadelphia.

Jackson, George Pullen. 1933. *White Spirituals in the Southern Uplands.* Chapel Hill: University of North Carolina Press. Reprint, New York: Dover Publications, 1965.

Loftis, Deborah Carlton. 1987. Big Singing Day in Benton, Kentucky: Study of the History, Ethnic Identity, and Musical Styles of the Southern Harmony Singers. Ph.D. Diss., University of Kentucky.

Lowens, Irving. 1964. *Music and Musicians in Early America.* New York: W. W. Norton and Co.

Sabol, Steven L. 1996. *Sacred Harp and Related Shape-Note Music Resources.* Published by the Author. Available from Steven Sabol, 5504 Lincoln St., Bethesda, Md. 20817.

Walker, William. 1987. *The Southern Harmony and Musical Companion.* Facsimile of the 1854 edition. With an introduction by Glenn C. Wilcox. Lexington, Ky.: University Press of Kentucky.

Walter, Thomas. 1721. *The Grounds and Rules of Musick Explained: Or an Introduction to the Art of Singing by Note.* Boston: J. Franklin for Samuel Gerrish.

White, Benjamin Franklin, and Elisha J. King. White. 1991. *The Sacred Harp.* Edited by Hugh McGraw et al. Bremen, Ga.: Sacred Harp Publishing Company. Original edition.

Audiography

White Spirituals from the Sacred Harp: The Alabama Sacred Harp Convention. 1992. New World 80205-2. CD remastered from original 1959 recording made by Alan Lomax at Fyffe, Alabama.

Companion CD to *The Southern Harmony* 1987. CD-9354. In *The Southern Harmony,* published by the University Press of Kentucky. This recording presents live performances from Big Singing Day between 1966 and 1992.

Holy Manna. LP recorded by Society for the Preservation of Southern Harmony Singing. Available from Benson Blackie, 1615 Dunn Cemetery Road, Benton, Ky. 42025.

The Social Harp: Early American Shape-Note Songs. 1977. Rounder CD 0094. Performed by singers from Georgia and Alabama, led by Hugh McGraw.

The Colored Sacred Harp. 1993. Rounder CD 80433-2. Performed by the Wiregrass Singers of Ozark, Alabama. Led by Dewey Williams, this is a recording of the African-American Sacred Harp tradition.

Sounding Joy. 1990. CD available from Ted Mercer, 1807 West North Ave., Chicago, Ill. 60622. This recording of the United Sacred Harp Musical Association is representative of current Sacred Harp singing style and features northern and southern singers.

CHAPTER 10

The Memphis African American Sacred Quartet Community

Kip Lornell

*L*ornell is an American vernacular music historian with strong ties to cultural geography, folklore, and ethnomusicology. He teaches in Washington, D.C., and works on music-related projects for the Smithsonian Institution. Based on fieldwork accomplished over a three-year period in Memphis, this chapter focuses on a tradition that had been previously overlooked in the world of African American music in general. Lornell examines the importance of families in maintaining musical continuity and the role of quartet trainers (who are viewed as musical specialists) in shaping the sound of quartets. The importance of transmitting religious values and religiosity in general is another theme explored by the author. The contexts for quartet performances—churches, community halls, and contests—and the relationship (and tension) between this religious expression and popular music provides a backdrop to the entire article. Finally, Lornell discusses the reasons for the decline in popular interest in quartets and why some of the groups have persisted in singing in this style.

■ ■ ■ ■

PROLOGUE

The genesis of this study may be traced back to 1979 when I moved to Memphis to become one of the first students in the newly founded doctoral program in Southern Regional Music and Ethnomusicology at the University of Memphis. With my interest in fieldwork-oriented projects and African American music, I soon decided that it would make sense to choose a local subject for research and, ultimately, as a dissertation topic. I knew Memphis as the focal point for early country-blues activity, rockabilly in the middle 1950s, and the "Stax Sound" of soul in the 1960s (Gordon 1995). Two major, black gospel composers—the Reverend William Herbert Brewster and Lucie Campbell—lived in Memphis and contributed many important compositions to the canon beginning in the 1920s and continuing through the 1950s (Reagon 1992). Such nationally known jazz musicians as pianists Phineas Newborn and James Williams, in addition to the saxophonist George Coleman, were born and trained in Memphis. Important blues figures like B. B. King and Howlin' Wolf made Memphis their home in the late 1940s and early 1950s before moving further north.

I was familiar with the work that had been done on vernacular music in Memphis and felt compelled to conduct research in some area that had been overlooked. My previous work on blues and other related forms of music by African Americans had been expanded by a recent one-year stint in Tidewater Virginia, which has a long and complicated history of sacred quartet singing among its black residents. I had undertaken the modest project of interviewing older quartet singers in Tidewater, and I wondered if this music was, or had been, widely performed in Memphis too. After less than two months of preliminary research—including a quick survey of local black newspapers and some brief conversations with singers—it became evident that the topic of sacred quartets in Memphis was ripe with promise.

The fact is that very little of the history and development of this community of singers had been collected, analyzed, and written about. The singers themselves, or members of their families, held the key to understanding the history of quartet singing in Memphis in the twentieth century. My dissertation and subsequent publications based on this research are largely built on the oral histories and interviews undertaken between 1979 and 1983 (Lornell 1995). In addition to speaking with members of the quartet community, which included not only singers but also radio personalities, record executives, and concert promoters, I attended many rehearsals and some programs in churches.

This essay focuses on not only sacred quartet singing in Memphis but also two of its specific aspects. The introduction presents the historical background of quartet singing; the first part of the essay, "A Family of Singers," looks at the diverse nature and relationships among members of the quartet community; the concluding section, "Training Quartets," will explain how the quartets themselves are formed and directed as well as the types of venues in which these vocal harmony groups performed.

HISTORICAL BACKGROUND

African American sacred quartet singing is a pan-southern tradition that can be traced back to the Reconstruction era that followed the end of the Civil War. This musical phenomenon is most closely tied to the newly founded colleges, such as Fisk and Hampton, that sponsored "jubilee" groups as well as to traveling minstrel shows and community-based groups that emerged near the dawn of the twentieth century. Community-based quartets, in particular, proved to be so popular that they helped to spread this style of singing among the black population in general. In reminiscing about his Florida childhood during the 1890s, the noted African American writer James Weldon Johnson wrote:

> Pick up four colored boys or young men anywhere and the chances are ninety out of a hundred that you will have a quartet. Let one of them sing the melody and others will naturally find parts. Indeed, it may be said that all male Negro youth of the United States is divided into quartets. When I was fifteen and my brother was thirteen we were singing in a quartet which competed with other quartets. In the days when such a thing as a white barber was unknown in the South, every barbershop had its quartet and the young men spent their leisure time "harmonizing."[1]

Such groups as the one described by Johnson were predominately male. They featured four voices, which included a bass singer, two tenors, and one alto. The lead singer was chosen according to the song's arrangement; "Roll, Jordan, Roll," an antebellum spiritual that may still be heard in the 1990s, almost always features a tenor singer. Track 21 is an a capella version of this song from the Harmonizers, a Memphis group. "Wade in the Water," on the other hand, is usually performed with the bass singer fronting the group. These pioneering quartets almost always sang *a capella* (without instrumental accompaniment) and utilized a repertoire that relied heavily upon traditional songs, especially spirituals.

At the beginning of the twentieth century the interest in quartet singing continued to grow, and the music was often incorporated into the everyday lives of many working-class, blue-collar black Americans. This trend continued with great vigor well into the 1920s as sugar refinery workers, railroad pullmen, and family members formed quartets that sang in local Baptist or Methodist churches, for neighborhood gatherings, and at other social functions. Barbershops, as James Weldon Johnson intimated, often served as a center for male blacks' social life in general and for quartet singing in particular (Abbott 1992).

These trends were directly related to the increasingly urban character of the South's black population. Many African Americans were leaving their agrarian roots behind and moving to cities in search of economic advancement. Following the end of World War I, the Hampton Roads section of Virginia, and Jefferson County (especially Birmingham), Alabama, emerged as the best-known centers for gospel quartet singing. Significantly, these were two areas with large numbers of blue-collar jobs that were becoming increasingly available to blacks. In Hampton Roads, the ship building industry was booming, while the burgeoning coal and iron industry attracted nearly one hundred thousand blacks to greater Birmingham between 1890 and 1920. The singing from these two centers was disseminated not only by the quartets that began to tour for performances, but especially through commercial phonograph records by such groups as the Birmingham Jubilee Singers, the Norfolk Jubilee Quartet, the Silver Leaf Quartette of Norfolk, and the Bessemer [Alabama] Melody Boys (Seroff 1980).

Since the 1920s at least, Memphis has been home to a thriving gospel quartet community. In nearly all general respects the development of sacred quartets in Memphis mirrored the trends in other parts of the United States. The earliest documentation of sacred quartet singing comes not from a school or a community-based group but from an ensemble that, along with the Orval Brothers (Construction Company) and the S. and W. (Construction Company), was affiliated through work. The I.C. [Illinois Central Rail Road] Glee Club Quartet was organized around 1927 and lasted for approximately ten years. Haywood Gaines, a retired Illinois Central employee who performed with the second I.C. Quartet in the early 1930s, quite literally sang with the quartet on the trains as they moved passengers from Memphis to points north and south. Performances by quartets helped to attract passengers back to the railroads, which had lost business because of the growing automobile trade and the Depression:

> Folks thought little of the railroad at that time [the passenger service] and to get them to come and ride with us, we had booster clubs and singers. The booster club was . . . an organization that gave different parties or entertainment. They would entertain and invite the general public. When we got them there, we would impress upon them the necessity to use the railroad as transportation. We sang, held dances . . . had five or six hundred people! That brought business back to the railroads.[2]

The overwhelming majority of Memphis quartets, however, were affiliated with neighborhood groups or with specific churches. North Memphis and South Memphis have long been bastions for black residents of the city. The Harmony Four was perhaps the premier sacred quartet from the southern part of Memphis during the 1930s; in the northern section both the Royal Harmony Four and the Old Rose Quartet sang frequently at local churches. Church groups were equally important, as, for example, the Lake Grove [Baptist] Specials and the Middle Baptist Quartet, who performed during the Depression and afterward, into World War II. In the days prior to full-time professional quartet singing, which began around 1938, the members of these and other groups worked at full-time extramusical jobs. These groups generally rehearsed one evening each week and sang publicly in church at least once on Sunday.

Figure 10.1. The Spirit of Memphis Quartette (circa 1953). (Top) Fred Howard, "Jet" Bledsoe, Earl Malone; (bottom) Robert Reed, Silas Steele, "Little Ax" Broadnax, Theo Wade. Courtesy, Kip Lornell.

Without a doubt the best-known group to emerge from the city during the early years of quartet singing was the Spirit of Memphis Quartette (Fig. 10.1). (This "old-fashioned" spelling of quartet was often used by groups in the late 1920s and into the 1930s.) The roots of the Spirit of Memphis are in the T.M. and S. Quartet, a name derived from the initials of the three churches—Tree of Life, Mount Olive, and St. Matthew's Baptist—attended by its founders about 1927. The revamped name came about two years later in honor of Charles Lindbergh's 1927 flight across the Atlantic in the "Spirit of St. Louis." According to founding member James Darling:

> When the group was named . . . it was named after the initials of the churches and when we decided to organized into a quartet we had to bring in some names. The night we had to bring in some names, I hadn't thought up a name until we almost got to [the house at] Looney and Second Street. I had a pocket handkerchief, had the "Spirit of St. Louis" in the corner. That's where the name really originated.[3]

The Spirit of Memphis eventually became the city's first fully professional quartet. After nearly two decades of singing in Memphis and the Mid-

South, the group followed the rapidly growing trend towards full-time professional status that began some ten years earlier. In fact, the Spirit of Memphis routinely booked, through a cosponsorship arrangement, the Famous Blue Jay Singers of Birmingham, Alabama, and the Soul Stirrers, who originated in Houston, Texas. Because the quartet attracted such large audiences and were not a part of the Sunday worship service, their programs were held in one of the large churches or in the downtown City Auditorium. The onset of World War II all but stopped this movement because of wartime restrictions on travel for all citizens of the United States, but after the war, opportunities for performance soared. Spurred by the ability to travel once again and by the evolution of independent record companies willing to take a chance on both the better-known and the obscure groups, many quartets began to hit the road in an attempt to cash in on the widespread interest in four-part vocal harmony singing.

In 1949 the Spirit of Memphis contained all of the ingredients to make the daring leap from a highly respected, semiprofessional quartet to full-time status. It had added two important out-of-town members—lead singers Silas Steele and Wilbur Broadnax, best known as "Little Ax"—who had sung with such well-known groups as the Famous Blue Jay Singers. The Spirit of Memphis also benefited from its first commercial record release, "I'm Happy in the Service of the Lord"/"My Life Is in His Hands," on a small local label. The record had only regional impact, but it led to a contract with the far-larger independent King Records, which was based in Cincinatti and specialized in hillbilly, rhythm and blues, and gospel music. These elements allowed the group to book enough programs to quit their day jobs and become full-time quartet singers. The success of the Spirit of Memphis helped to inspire two other local groups—the Southern Wonders and the Sunset Travelers—to take the same leap.

Around 1950, black sacred quartet singing was at its height of popularity not only in Memphis and the mid-South but across the entire country. The number of quartets performing on all levels—community-based, semiprofessional, and fully professional—was at an all-time high. Professional groups as diverse as the extremely popular "jubilee" ensemble, the Golden Gate Quartet, and the Dixie Hummingbirds (a "hard" gospel quartet featuring the dramatic lead singing of Ira Tucker) enjoyed great success as recording artists and radio performers as well as through live programs. The elite status of these perhaps sixty professional groups was augmented by hundreds of semiprofessional quartets and thousands of community-based groups that formed the backbone of the black vocal sacred-quartet tradition (Abbott 1983).

The music had evolved into two distinctive but related styles. The "hard" quartet style uses alternating lead vocalists, whose arsenals include falsetto, wordless moans, and extended sections of improvised singing drawn from the well of the African American musical vocabulary. This style is perhaps best characterized by the dramatic singing of Claude Jeter of the Swan Silvertones, the Dixie Hummingbird's Ira Tucker, and Silas Steele of the Spirit of Memphis Quartet. The jubilee style, on the other hand, featured an even more syncopated style, with a prominent bass part, a *cante-fable* (half spoken–half sung) lead vocalist, and texts often taken from the New Testament of the Bible (listen to Track 22). The Golden Gate Quartet is the archetype jubilee quartet, and from the late 1930s through the early 1950s they became the model for other groups—particularly in the Southeast and Middle Atlantic States—who wish to explore this style (Grendysa 1976).

While the professional quartets that toured both locally and nationally may have gained the greatest attention, it was the community-based groups that continued to provide most black Memphians with the music they heard each week. The community quartets in Memphis, to some degree, followed the lead of their professional counterparts; identical uniforms often replaced the neatly tailored suits of an earlier era, and by 1950 most groups had added at least a guitar to a genre that began *a capella*. In addition to the traditional stockpile of songs, local Memphis groups were sometimes able to introduce the new compositions Lucie Campbell and Reverend Herbert W. Brewster who—as mentioned earlier—published many gospel songs between the early 1920s and the early 1960s (Reagon, 1992). Among local quartets, Reverend Brewster's compositions, in particular "Old Landmark" (1948) and "Surely, God is Able" (1950), are long time favorites. Lucie Campbell's most popular and widely performed composition was undoubtedly "The King's Highway" (1923), which continues to be performed by quartets and other religious ensembles in the 1990s.

Local community-based quartets—for example, the Campbellaires (named after Lucie Campbell), the Friendly Brothers Quartet (fronted by John and Robert Maddrie), the True Friends Gospel Singers, and such female groups as the Golden Stars (Fig. 10.2) and the Harps of Melody—performed regularly in local churches during the 1940s and into the 1950s. They existed as an outlet for Memphis singers who had talent and commitment as well as a desire to sing for other black Christians who attended the same mainstream Protestant, primarily Baptist and Methodist, churches. These quartets served the community well and could be counted on to provide sacred vocal harmony singing whenever it was called for.

While quartets usually sang during the Sunday worship services, they also performed at special song programs that were typically held early Saturday evening or late Sunday afternoon. Such programs, which proliferated in the early 1950s, offered not only quartet enthusiasts but everyday church-goers an opportunity to hear the music they loved. It also provided black Christians with another occasion to worship the Lord in song.

The popular interest in quartet singing began to fade in the middle 1950s. Some of the more conservative church members felt that the music

Figure 10.2. The Golden Star Quartet (1945): Mary Ruth Youngblood, Clara Anderson, Mary Louise Wilson, Hazel Cole, Sylvia Anne Garret, Courtesy, Clare Anderson.

and culture was become too secular. Harry Winfield, a Memphis keyboard player who was active in the 1950s, suggested that the quartet singing

> was traveling more towards rock and roll music. They were chang-
> ing their style and they were dancing on stage. They were now,
> more or less, giving performances. They were now walking on
> benches and getting sort of ridiculous. Quartet singers were now
> processing their hair and riding in Cadillacs, doing very much of
> the things that the gospel people attributed to the world, you know,
> drinking. We see you now on stage, can't hardly stand up . . .
> Church people [soon] felt that they were being deceived. Lots of
> things happened that started people totally against what was hap-
> pening in the gospel field, as far as quartets was concerned.[4]

This sea change in the popularity of quartets was by no means restrict-ed to Memphis. Even such popular groups as the Pilgrim Jubilees and Soul Stirrers fell upon financial hard times. Among Memphis groups, the Spirit of Memphis were on the road full time into the late 1950s, several years longer than the Sunset Travelers or the Southern Wonders remained fully profes-sional quartets. Local semiprofessional groups, such as the Jubilee

Hummingbirds, the Dixie Wonders, and the Southern Jubilees, began to de-emphasize harmony singing and perform even more contemporary gospel songs to the accompaniment of a full rhythm section. In spite of new trends, older community-based groups have continued to perform, with everchanging personnel, for several decades. Today, the roots of at least three community groups—the Royal Harmony Four, the Gospel Writers, and Harps of Melody—extend back to the 1940s and continue to represent the quartet tradition in its oldest form.

A FAMILY OF SINGERS

Since its inception in the 1920s, the community of African American gospel quartet singers in Memphis has evolved into a highly complex social unit analogous to the so-called extended family—a family related through birth, marriage, geographical proximity, religious affiliation, social values, and economic status. The group encompasses not only the singers themselves but disc jockeys, preachers, record-company officials, and fans. The singers themselves, the organizers of local gospel quartet unions, and those who train quartets constitute the core of this unique community, and it is the interaction among these groups that will be described in the rest of this essay.

In the course of my fieldwork among the Memphis gospel quartet singers, the term *family of singers* took on literal meaning. Of the forty-five singers interviewed for this study, 60 percent were married to others who had been affiliated with quartets. Cleo and Louis Satterfield, for instance, first met in 1941 at a gospel quartet program; Louis sang with the True Friends Gospel Singers, while Cleo sang with the Union Soft Singers (in Memphis, the word *Soft* designates a quartet as female). Both in their early twenties, the singers married within two years. Another couple in the Memphis family, Elijah Jones and his first wife, Jimmie Martin, became acquainted in the late 1930s when he led the Gospel Writers and she performed with the Gospel Writer Junior Girls (Fig. 10.3). Some of the most influential singing couples in Memphis—for example, Jethroe and Shirley Bledsoe, James and Elizabeth Darling, Floyd and Florence Wiley—were involved with gospel quartets both before and after their marriages.

Patterns of kinship within the gospel quartet community are not limited only to married couples; many siblings have also been involved with singing. Willie and Rochester Neal began their careers in the late 1940s as members of the Gospel Writer Junior Boys, which was under the direction of their stepfather, Elijah Jones. The brothers have continued to sing together throughout most of their lives. During the 1950s their first group became the Dixie Nightingales, but when the group switched to secular music in the middle 1960s, they left to join the Pattersonaires with whom they remain today. Clara Anderson, founder and leader of the Harps of Melody in the late

Figure 10.3. Gospel writer Junior Girls (late 1940's), were led by Elizabeth Darling (far right). Courtesy, Kip Lornell.

1940s, began singing with her sister, Essie, around 1935 in the Busyline Soft Singers, then briefly with a neighborhood quartet until Essie's death in 1938.

Familial involvements in black gospel music has certainly not been limited to quartets or to Memphis (Burnim 1985; Heilbut 1985). The Staples Singers, for example, is a family group that began in Mississippi and later moved to Chicago; and one of the most popular groups from the 1980s, the Winnans, are led by the sisters Bebe and Cece Winnans. Nevertheless, it is in Memphis that kinship systems are most strikingly pervasive.

Despite its size, its position as a transportation hub, and its importance as a destination for migrants in the Mid-South, the quartet community in Memphis remains largely insular and thus free of outside musical influences. This may be attributed not only to the factors previously cited but also to the continued importance of families in shaping the sound of indigenous quartets. As most of the in-migration consisted of people who had moved to Memphis from nearby counties in the Mid-South—in particular, from northern Mississippi, eastern Arkansas, and west Tennessee—the familiar styles of singing and the favorite songs in the repertoire of quartets tended to remain intact.

QUARTET UNIONS

Beyond the kinship systems described above, the formation of unions helped to cultivate and promote quartet singing in Memphis. The National

Convention of Gospel Choirs and Choruses, Inc., founded in 1932 by the famous composer, entreprenuer, and performer Reverend Thomas A. Dorsey, worked with vocal ensembles, which included some quartets, to promote gospel music across the United States (Harris 1992; Stebbins 1972). In the late 1930s the first quartet organization in Memphis, the City Quartette Union, was established by "Doctor" Frost, who was not a singer himself but simply a man who loved singing and was friends with many of the community's members. The City Quartette Union, a cooperative and nonprofit venture, helped to organize and promote weekly programs in and around Memphis with Frost himself often serving as the master of ceremonies (see Fig. 10.4). After Frost migrated to Detroit in 1943, he was succeeded by James Darling, one of the early members of the Spirit of Memphis Quartet, and then by another local singer, Huddie Moore, who held the job until its dissolution in 1953. Moore explains that the idea behind the City Quartette Union was "to get a lot of singers together and cooperate, and have more people participate on your program. When you had the City Quartette Union and the quartets, you had your program—all you had to get [was] the church and render your program. We had the City Quartette Union [chorus] open the program and let the quartets come on later."[5]

Two other organizations, the South Memphis Singing Union and the North Memphis Singing Union, briefly augmented the work forwarded by

SPIRITUAL SINGERS
By the City Quartett Union and Chorus

Figure 10.4. This ad (circa 1940) was used to promote the activities of the City Quartette Union. Courtesy, Kip Lornell.

the City Quartette Union. They existed in the early 1940s but were so short-lived and ephemeral that nothing more than their names remain. Directly after World War II, Lillian Wafford organized the United Singing Union, which quickly emerged as a significant force in organizing Memphis quartets. Although it nominally existed until the early 1980s, the United Singing Union was strong for only its first decade. With Mrs. Wafford's death in 1982, the city's last gospel quartet cooperative disbanded.

Quartet unions served several important functions: to encourage solidarity among its members, to assist groups in booking their programs, and to promote quartet singing. While the goals of the unions were concrete and their leadership stable, the organizations themselves were less stable. According to Mary Davis, cofounder of the Majestic Soft Singers in 1944, the ranks of the United Singing Union was always in flux: "The original group was the Majestic Soft Singers plus the Spiritual Pilgrims. Then came the Wells Spirituals . . . then the Morris Special Singers . . . [and] four or five years later, the Brewsteraires. Then we had the Walker Specials to join in. In other words, we had several groups to going in, but several of them didn't stay too long."[6]

During its prime in the early 1950s, the United Singing Union served a useful and an important function for members of the Memphis gospel quartet community. Mrs. Wafford devised a simple formula for splitting the monetary honoraria, or "donation," between the group and the church that hosted them. (Quartet musicians prefer these more neutral sounding terms because they suggest that their motivation for gospel singing is not tainted by the lure of money.) Basically, for programs held in Memphis, 50 percent of the money went to the group(s) and an equal amount was donated to the church. Programs held outside of Memphis or in neighboring Shelby County were split differently, with 60 percent going to the musicians and the rest helping to fill the church coffers.

This spirit of cooperation and mutual assistance that characterized these cooperatives was emblematic of a more general sense of a synergetic partnership that permeated the black American gospel quartet community in Memphis. Although singing remained the focal point for their energies, nearly all of the union members were also involved in service to the community at large. In this sense, the quartet singers were simply fulfilling their role within the family, extending their role to encompass the city's entire black population, not merely those in their own nuclear family or in their own neighborhood (Burnim 1980, Dyen 1977, Jackson 1988). The city's black religious community—the church and its many allied support services—in fact, had served as the unofficial center of black social and community life long before President Johnson's presidency passed the so-called Great Society bills with its more highly codified welfare system and Aid to Dependent Children.

Cleo Satterfield spoke an length about the importance of the union within the community at large:

Frost [founder of the City Quartette Union around 1939] was the type of person who could keep a program so alive that everybody wanted to hear him talk after the singing. He was nice about helping someone if he know they were sick or somebody in the group of the church was sick. If somebody tell him about it, he would raise an offering for them . . . they would always reach out and give a helping hand. We never had that much, but what we had, we'd give it freely.[7]

Huddie Moore echoed these sentiments and recalled that the City Quartette Union "would do a program for somebody who had gotten burned out or something like that. We would put on programs to raise money to help that family . . . or for somebody who was in necessity."[8]

This aid included spiritual sustenance as well, particularly in the form of free programs presented in rest homes and senior citizens' centers where the word of God could be preached to a captive, and often willing, audience. Some quartets even performed in local prisons and jails, the idea being simply to spread the ministry of God in song. Etherlene Beans explains how she and her group, the Willing Four Softline Singers, worked:

They contacted us because they found that we were just a group that liked to sing. We didn't sing for finances... [but because] we like to sing and we always want to share what we had with other people. We was really a spiritual group [that] like to sing and get happy and let other people get happy [reaching an ecstatic state of direct communication with God]. We would go to the workhouse and sing . . . also sing for sick people, cripple[d] children's hospitals, and to help people.[9]

The relationship between quartet singing and spirituality cannot be overstated. Since most quartet singers are devoutly religious, their intent is clear; to provide their fellow singers and their audience alike with a Protestant Christian message through words and songs. In this regard quartet musicians and preachers share similar roles—that of delivering the message of God's love and salvation. Instead of preaching a sermon, quartet singers deliver their message through song (Allen 1992, Franklin 1982, Jackson 1988). Hershall McDonald, of the Harmonizeers, told me,

We believe that we carry the gospel in a number of ways. One is the direct teaching of principals, which we carry through in our songs. In singing, our work is twofold—to edify and serve as inspiration for those who are members of the body and as a source of inspiration and a way to draw those who are not members of the church.[10]

TRAINING QUARTETS

Sacred quartet trainers help to shape musical direction, they are agents of both continuity and change. Their role in shaping the sound of sacred quartets in Memphis is unique and their influence is profound. To the best of my knowledge, there is no parallel to quartet trainers in any other form of black American vernacular music, either sacred or secular.

At first glance, the primary role of gospel quartet trainers appears quite simple: they teach songs. Quartet training, however, is very demanding, requires extremely specialized skills, and is critical to the preservation of the genre because it is one of the principal means by which repertoire, style, and innovation are transmitted. By preserving specific aspects of performance practices traits—most importantly vocal timbre, and the approach to rhythm and harmony—quartet trainers also provide a crucial link between one generation of musicians and another, as well as links among groups within the city.

The functions of trainers in a community are actually quite complex, and they have long been regarded by quartets as specialists. A quartet trainer is asked by groups to indoctrinate new members and to help them to learn new songs or to change an arrangement that needs a complete overhauling, updating, or merely tinkering. If a trainer develops an innovative arrangement that proves popular, other local groups will often ask him to provide a similar service for them, tailored to their particular strengths. Trainers have sometimes been called upon to locate new singers for groups, though most groups will recruit members themselves. Elijah Jones, who worked with Memphis quartets for forty years beginning in the middle 1930s, served as the unofficial coordinator for local groups looking for new singers.

Although they are very busy assisting quartets in a variety of ways, trainers are usually not motivated by the prospect of financial gain. The most influential Memphis trainers—Elijah Jones and his mentor, Gus Miller—sang with several local quartets but supported themselves through other means: Miller survived with the help of a veteran's pension that was given to him after he was severely wounded in World War I; Jones worked at a series of blue-collar jobs. Trainers were occasionally offered money for their services, however this was strictly a free-will offering or an honorarium. Etherlene Beans notes that Jones "never did get money from us. Now [in the late 1970s, just before Jones's death] we give him a little transportation money, but he never made money off us. He just likes singing . . . and he was always willing to assist us in singing."[11]

This observation provides the key to understanding the motivation of quartet trainers—these talented men [nearly all of them male] not only loved harmony singing, they freely shared their special abilities with their fellow singers. George Rooks, who knew and sang with Elijah Jones off and on for nearly forty years, stated that Jones always stood at the nexus of the quartet community. Most weekends found him singing or attending a quartet program or a rehearsal. During the week he might receive a telephone call asking him to help a group to locate a new tenor singer or to judge an upcoming quartet contest (see discussion below).

Recognition by one's peers as a trainer denotes a special status within this closely knit musical community. Gospel quartet trainers are thought to be blessed with unusually perceptive ears and keen minds as well as the ability to communicate their knowledge. That groups regularly come to certain individuals asking for assistance acknowledges and underscores the community's respect for talents that have been honed through years of practical application rather than formal education. Elijah Ruffin, who worked with about a dozen groups throughout a career that stretched from the early 1930s into the middle 1980s, considered his training ability a natural gift.

Males have dominated quartet training in Memphis, but it is not precisely clear why this trend is so pronounced. Except for a handful of women—such as Clara Anderson, who trained her own groups, the Harps of Melody and the Golden Stars—female quartet trainers were an anomaly. The number of women who have participated in quartet singing in Memphis is less than the number of men. None of the female groups became fully professional, only the Songbirds of the South reached semiprofessional status. The rest of the female quartets were either community-based or affiliated with a local church. From the 1920s through the 1950s, women were expected to assume the responsibility for child rearing and other obligations that tended to keep them close to home, and this may be the reason why fewer women than men participated in quartet singing.

The fundamental process of training quartets appears straightforward: the trainer merely sings each part to the singers in turn and then they blend the parts in four-part harmony. This means, though, that the trainer must take upon himself the difficult task of learning and remembering all four parts. Jack Miller, of the Royal Harmony Four, who trained a dozen or so groups during a career that spanned nearly five decades, offered these general tips:

> The first thing is the voice. Check the voice out; see if it is fitted for a tenor, baritone, lead, or bass . . . You have four voices to get the pitch of the song, to teach it. Then you work on the time of the songs, how long you should go with it. Some people are quick to catch on, some are not. If they got the talent to catch on and the voice, then you can train them in a couple of months.[12]

Although the basic process sounds simple, it demands an unusual knowledge as well as specialized skills. First the trainer must be able to sing each of the four voices. Many trainers, in fact, fulfill the role of "utility" singer in their own quartet, as does the utility player in baseball, who fills in as a shortstop, left fielder, or catcher with equal skill. The trainer also intuitively conceives harmonies, rhythms, and tempos, a process that is refined and then adjusted as the parts are taught to the group. Finally, because they do not use musical notation, trainers work entirely through oral means, relying entirely upon tonal memory and sheer repetition. Training a quartet requires not only an immense amount of skill but also a willingness to invest a great deal of time, concentration, and energy.

The most renowned and influential trainer in Memphis, Elijah Jones, worked with countless groups during his career. Etherlene Beans describes how Jones helped the Willing Four Soft Singers during the late 1940s:

> He would train you how to control your voice, how to keep your voice with the next singer, not to get too loud for the next singer, not to get too loud for your music [instruments], not to get your music too loud for you . . . He always teach you to sing words distinctly, and . . . you cannot really sing a song unless you know it. He helped us a whole lot; it was just remarkable what he could do with singers.[13]

Memphis trainers are also notable for giving suggestions about vocal and tonal qualities or techniques. For instance, a trainer might advise that the featured singer affect a more raspy timbre or sing in falsetto. The trainer might also make the arrangement of a song distinctive by altering the tempo during the chorus or by having the background sung more staccato. Working with a new song or rearranging a well-known quartet piece could take several evenings of work, or at least several hours of exhausting work.

The role of quartet trainers has diminished since the 1960s; people who might have trained quartets probably now work with choirs or choruses. Many of the first generation of trainers retired, moved from the area, or died. With the diminishing interest in quartet singing, fewer people stepped forward to take their places and fewer groups sought the help of a trainer. The era when quartet trainers flourished corresponded with the height of interest in quartets. By the 1990s, the art of quartet training has all but been lost in Memphis.

Performance

Live performances—usually called programs—provide the most common forum for the public to hear and see these singers. On Sundays and nearly every Saturday since the 1920s, Memphis gospel quartets have appeared in churches and auditoriums throughout the city. Although all quartets have some direct affiliation with churches, either as church-related groups or simply as members of a church, they have not always appeared as part of the worship service itself. More often, it is congregational singing, choirs, or choruses, rather than quartets, that present the musical offering during the regularly scheduled church service.

In Memphis, quartets usually perform on special musical programs that are held during the afternoons or evenings and feature more than one ensemble. Quartet programs are similar to the Sunday morning worship service, the difference being the programs' emphasis on music. These programs are promoted within the black church community by way of placards, posters, notices in the church bulletins or newsletters, announcements from the pulpit, over the radio, during other programs, and by word of mouth (Cantor 1992).

Programs have almost always been held at local churches in the predominately black sections of Memphis, such as Orange Mound, North Memphis, or Whitehaven. Occasionally programs are held in private homes, usually by groups just beginning to sing together—though this was more common in the past. Huddie Moore describes the early appearances of the Spiritual Four in the late 1930s:

> When you first getting started, you be a little shy about going out and facing public. We would rehearse and set up programs at different one's houses. Just say you gonna have a program, we invite other groups and set up chairs and sing in the house. We would get ready to get out on the stage at the church. We used to have a nice time at a house program.[14]

All quartet programs feature at least one local group, but it is not uncommon to have one or more quartets from outside of the city—especially if the program is held in a larger venue, such as a community hall. Programs featuring non-Memphis quartets fall into two categories. The first comprises nonprofessional, community-based groups much like nearly all of the quartets from Memphis. These ensembles are nearly always from the mid-South or more northern towns and cities, such as St. Louis, Chicago, or Milwaukee, to which Memphians have migrated. These quartets frequently "trade" appearances back and forth, especially when groups celebrate their founding through an anniversary program that may last up to ten hours. The other category encompasses performances by well-known professional groups that are held in larger venues such as the City Auditorium or Mason's Temple. In years past, the Soul Stirrers, Pilgrim Jubilees, or Golden Gates drew thousands of people; in the 1980s and 1990s the Mighty Clouds of Joy or the Jackson Southernaires attracted hundreds of listeners to one of the large churches in the city.

Performance events by groups in either category are not radically different, and all ceremonies by quartet singers have religious praise as their primary goal. Such events are complex and are structured according to a clearly established format with three essential "players": the MC (master of ceremonies), the quartets, and the audience. The programs usually open with a well-known song that is led by the emcee, a minister, or a quartet member and performed by everyone in the audience. This helps to establish a feeling of fellowship among the participants. A prayer offered by one of the ministers then follows (Allen 1992).

The job of the MC is to move the program along so that each group has a chance to sing. This person is also responsible for making certain that the quartets appear in the announced order and providing proper introductions. The MC (who is often, but not always, male) also fills in the time between groups—while the equipment is being changed and the quartets are getting set up—with announcements about future programs, family-oriented jokes, recognitions for people attending the program, and general observations about life. He makes it as friendly and downhome as possible, partly in deference to previous role models but mostly because the MC knows most of the other participants quite well. Emcees, especially for anniversary programs or ones featuring major out-of-town groups, are specialists. They are usually disk jockeys who host one of the local gospel musical radio programs or have some other type of media connection. For strictly local programs, one of the group members or a clergyman may serve in this capacity.

Song Battles

In Memphis, two related types of programs, known locally as quartet contests and song battles, emerged as early as the middle 1930s and continued for twenty years. Such contests, which simply pit one group against another, have also been reported in Birmingham, Alabama, and the Hampton Roads section of Virginia. These programs, featuring local ensembles, were held in local churches and billed themselves as "quartet contests" in order to build interest in a specific program. The format called for each group to perform from four to six selections, whereby the quartet giving the finest performance was declared the winner. Judges for these contests, who were chosen from the ranks of veteran and respected singers not participating in this program, evaluated the finer points of singing and then determined the winners by assigning points to each group. Although the criteria were inherently subjective, they usually included rhythmic precision, enunciation of words, inventiveness, accuracy of harmony, and the ability of the singers. Elijah Jones, who served the quartet community as a trainer, singer, and judge, talked about his experiences in the 1930s:

> I always liked judging 'cause so many folks didn't know singing. You got three judges that know singing, then you got fairly seeded [rated]. They would look for time, music, don't miss no minors or

sharps. The one that makes the most points, that's the one that wins. During that particular time, we didn't have but four voices: leader, tenor, baritone, and bass, and we would listen to each voice.[15]

Money was, he added, the impetus for local churches to hold a quartet contest. The winning group received a modest share of the donations collected at the door, but perhaps more importantly, the quartet members' performing ability was acknowledged by their peers. To be the champion of a local contest meant both prestige and greater respect, which is one of the reasons why—along with fund raising—the contest gained in popularity into the 1940s. During the late 1940s, quartet singing became even more popular, more groups turned professional, and a shift occurred in the format and style of these competitions: they became known as "song battles" and were frequently staged in large auditoriums.

In Memphis, most of the major songs battles took place in the Mason's Temple or in the City Auditorium. These performance events were a manifestation of popular culture and a local evolution of the earlier contests. The audience's applause, rather than a small number of specialists, decided the winner of the song battle. Elijah Jones observed that "we started having audiences judging in the fifties. Then you just get out there hoopin' and hollerin' and if they like that, then you be the man."[16] Jones's dislike for the event reflected a clear movement from a program overseen by the quartet community itself to one dominated by popular trends and opinion. Julius Readers, who was most active as a semiprofessional quartet singer during the 1950s, told me:

> It sort of worked like the group that get the most shouts of the most applause—you know what the favorite group was. You didn't need judges then because if you were tough, when you hit the floor you knowed who had it then, because two to one if you were a favorite in town, when they call your name, everybody go wild! Then you get up there, their hands clap, and you know who was the winner![17]

Quartet programs tend to start slowly and build in intensity, similar to the momentum gained as the spirit moves those in the church during the delivery of a chanted sermon or a Pentecostal service. Much of the success of this kind of musical performance depends upon the interaction between the quartet and the audience. By the 1950s, almost all Memphis quartets, and certainly each of the more highly regarded out-of-town ensembles, stressed their stage presentation along with a well-choreographed and well-planned performance. Seemingly small things, such as a singer's gesture towards the audience or a particularly well-chosen spoken-aside commentary—perhaps about a topical event, such as a tragic plane crash or the unexpected death of a community member—could help to ignite a performance. The possibilities brought on by this type of interaction is vividly recalled by Tommie Todd, who sang with the Gospel Writers in the decade following the close of World War II:

> When we would go and render our programs, a lot of times we'd get converts. A lot of times people would join the church on our singing. That's the reason I liked it, because there was something in it I could feel, that other people could feel. So many people would come to hear us because we would give them something that was a help to them. We would have our prayer service just like a revival, then we'd go from there. When we got into our singing, people would be shouting. One time they got shouting so bad until a lady got hold of the wrong end of my tie and pulled and choked me! When we got singing like that they'd be shouting and throwing pocketbooks and like that.[18]

Before such black popular singers as Little Richard or James Brown gained the limelight in the middle to late 1950s, professional quartet singers like Silas Steele and "Jet" Bledsoe of the Spirit of Memphis Quartet were highly respected for their ability to "work" an audience. Their performances combined a dramatic stage presence and singing calculated to motivate and engage the crowd (Allen 1992, Burnim 1988). It became acceptable for singers to crawl along the floor or walk on the floor—behavior that strongly contrasted with the more sedate programs held in the 1920s or 1930s, before full-time professional groups began touring the United States.

The frantic and colorful nature of post–World War II professional quartets sometimes bothered older quartet singers, such as Leon Moody, who began singing in the late 1930s and had a different sensibility regarding the performance of sacred music:

> Every song we sung, we tried to tell a message. We figured that in every song we sung, if we couldn't give them something to think about, that song wasn't worth singing. But some people just get up and go for a lot of "Hallelujah." Most generally they go for guitars and a whole lot of noise. They do a lot of performing, a lot of show. I think if it is supposed to be a religious program, it should be a service.[19]

It would be easy, however, to simply dismiss certain on-stage mannerisms as mere stylized antics. Professionalism undeniably changed the character of black gospel quartet performances, but the singers still draw some of their inspiration and role models from older traditions. Unquestionably, some of these characteristics—dramatic body gestures, emotional vocal styles, and flamboyant behavior—may be partially attributed to the Pentecostal movement, in which holy dancing and speaking in tongues is part of worship. Memphis has been home to the Church of God in Christ, one of the largest black American pentecostal churches since the early 1900s (Burnim 1989). The ecstatic speech heard in ring shouts, which remain part of a few of the West African-based religious services of the coastal islands of Georgia and South Carolina, provide another probable role model for Pentecostals.

Despite the controversies regarding performance practices and song battles in the 1950s, even the most conservative members of the quartet community agree that singing comes from the spirit and helps to promote religious feeling. These spiritual impulses are, in fact, at the core of the community of quartet singers from Memphis. Gospel quartet singing, after all, helps to express religious convictions and is one of the many ways that Christians communicate their message of salvation through a belief in God. Etherlene Beans of the Willing Four Softline Singers spoke for many of the community members when she told me that "we like to sing and we always want to share what we had with other people. I like to sing quartet singing because I am a Christian person and I believe in feeling spiritually. I sing until I feel good and feel like I've helped somebody. I want to try and save a soul through my singing [and go where] the spirit is needed."[20]

NOTES

Much of this essay first appeared as parts of three chapters in *"Happy in the Service of the Lord:" African-American Sacred Vocal Harmony Quartets in Memphis* (second edition). Copyright © 1995 by the University of Tennessee Press. Used with permission.

1. James Weldon Johnson, "The Origins of the 'Barber Chord,'" *The Mentor* (February 1929), p. 53.

2. Haywood Gaines, interviewed by Kip Lornell, June 24, 1982. Unless indicated otherwise, all interviews were conducted by the author in Memphis, Tennessee. Transcript copies and tapes are on deposit at the Mississippi Valley Collection, Brister Library, University of Memphis.

3. James Darling, telephone interview by Kip Lornell, July 21, 1982.

4. Harry Winfield, interviewed by Kip Lornell, July 14, 1982.

5. Huddie Moore, interviewed by Kip Lornell, February 2, 1982.

6. Mary Davis, interviewed by Kip Lornell, May 10, 1982.

7. Cleo Satterfield, interviewed by Kip Lornell, June 7, 1982.

8. Huddie Moore interview.

9. Etherlene Beans, interviewed by Kip Lornell, July 3, 1982.

10. Herschall McDonald, interviewed by Kip Lornell, February 22, 1982.

11. Etherlene Beans interview.

12. Jack Miller, interviewed by Kip Lornell, February 1980.

13. Etherlene Beans interview.

14. Huddie Moore interview.

15. Elijah Jones, interviewed by Kip Lornell, October, 1979.

16. Ibid.

17. Julius Readers, interviewed by Kip Lornell, May 28, 1982.

18. Tommie Todd, interviewed by Kip Lornell, August 11, 1982.

19. Leon Moody, interviewed by Kip Lornell, February 8, 1981.

20. Etherlene Beans interview.

REFERENCES CITED

Abbott, Lynn. 1983. *The Sproco Singers: A New Orleans Quartet Family Tree.* New Orleans, La.: National Park Service.

———. 1992. "Play That Barbershop Chord": A Case for the African-American Origin of Barbershop Harmony. *American Music* 10 (Fall): 289–326.

Allen, Ray. 1992. *Singing in the Spirit: African-American Sacred Quartets in New York City.* Philadelphia: University of Pennsylvania Press.

Burnim, Mellonee. 1980. The Black Gospel Music Tradition: A Symbol of Ethnicity. Ph.D. Diss., Indiana University.

———. 1985. Cultural Bearer and Tradtion Bearer: An Ethnomusicolgist's Research on Gospel Music. *Ethnomusicology* (Fall): 432–37.

———. 1988. Functional Dimensions of Gospel Music Performance. *Western Jounal of Black Studies* 12: 112–21.

———. 1989. The Performance of Gospel Music as Transformation. *Councilium: International Review of Theology* 2: 52–61.

Cantor, Louis. 1992. *Wheelin' on Beale.* New York: Pharos Books.

Dyen, Doris. 1977. The Role of Black Shape-Note Music in the Musical Culture of Black Communities in Southeast Alabama. Ph.D. Diss., University of Illinois.

Franklin, Marion Joseph. 1982. The Relationship of Black Preaching to Black Gospel Music. Ph.D. Diss., Drew University.

Gordon, Robert. 1995. *It Came From Memphis.* New York: Faber and Faber.

Grendysa, Pete. 1976. The Golden Gate Quartet. *Record Exchanger* 5: 5–9.

Harris, Michael. 1992. *The Rise of Gospel Blues: The Music of Thomas Andrew Dorsey in the Urban Church.* New York: Oxford University Press.

Heilbut, Tony. 1985. *The Gospel Sound: Good News and Bad Times.* 2nd ed. New York: Simon & Schuster.

Jackson, Joyce. 1988. The Performing Black Sacred Quartet: An Expression of Cultural Values and Aesthetics. Ph.D. Diss., Indiana University.

Lornell, Kip. 1995. *"Happy in the Service of the Lord": African-American Sacred Vocal Harmony Quartets in Memphis.* 2nd ed. Knoxville: University of Tennessee Press.

Reagon, Bernice Johnson, ed. 1992. *We'll Understand It Better By and By: Pioneering African American Gospel Composers.* Washington, D.C.: Smithsonian Institution Press.

Seroff, Doug. 1980. Brochure notes, *Birmingham Quartet Anthology.* Clanka Lanka Records CL 144.

Stebbins, Robert. 1972. A Theory of the Jazz Community. In *American Music: From Storyville to Woodstock,* edited by Charles Nanry. New Brunswick, N.J.: Transactional Books.

COMPANION CD SELECTIONS

Track 21. The Harmonizers, "Roll, Jordan, Roll."

Track 22. Spirit of Memphis, "I Saw John."

ADDITIONAL SOURCES

Selected Audiography

Broadnax, Willmer. *So Many Years.* Gospel Jubilee RF-1403.

Fairfield Four. *Standing in the Safety Zone.* Warner 9 26945-2.

Golden Gate Quartet. *Travelin' Shoes.* RCA 66063-2.

Paramount Singers. *Work and Pray On.* Arhoolie CD 382.

Pilgrim Travelers. *Best Of.* ACE CDCHD 342.

Soul Stirrers. *Jesus Gave Me Water.* Specialty SPCD 2802.

Spirit of Memphis Quartet. *When Mother's Gone.* Gospel Jubilee 1404.

Spirit of Memphis Quartet. *Traveling On with the Spirit of Memphis.* High Water LP 1005.

Trumpeteers. *Milky White Way.* Gospel Jubilee 1401.

Various Artist. *Bless My Bones: Memphis Gospel Radio—1950s.* Rounder 6032.

Various Artists. *Happy in the Service of the Lord: Memphis Gospel Quartet Heritage in the 1980s.* High Water LP 1002.

Various Artists. *San Francisco Bay Gospel.* Gospel Heritage HT 314.

CHAPTER 11

Sansei Voices in the Community

Japanese American Musicians in California

Susan M. Asai

*S*usan Asai is an ethnomusicologist with a long-standing interest and first-hand experience in the music cultures of Japan and of people of Asian heritage in the United States. Asai's essay problematizes the entity "Japanese American music" as she investigates the notion and practice of music making among three generations of Japanese Americans, focusing most specifically on sansei, *or the third generation. Working from a framework that highlights theories of ethnicity and identity formation, Asai asks what has been inherited, what has been forgotten, what is relearned, and what is invented for each generation of Japanese Americans. The author addresses the role of cultural intrusion and the devastating effects of the internment of Japanese Americans during World War II. She, furthermore, considers the interface of Japanese American musicians with mainstream American artistic and cultural trends, such as jazz, swing, and the civil rights movement. To exemplify some of the forces at work in the creative processes of* sansei, *a group of which Asai herself is a member, the author provides biographical profiles of three* sansei *artists who speak for Asian-American communities.*

■　■　■　■

INTRODUCTION

The relationship of music and identity is of interest at a time when Americans of color choose to retain aspects of their forebears' cultures as a positive way to reinvent themselves in countering their marginalization within American society. Such populations have discovered that one's ethnicity is important as both a social identity and a political force. Among the numerous studies of Japanese American identity, few have used the parameters of music in discussing the construction of identity. The emergence of a substantial repertoire of compositions in the past few years now make it possible to study identity as expressed in abstract musical forms. Asian American literature written in the past ten years or so explores "finding a way home" or building a sense of self by returning to one's ethnic heritage (Thornton 1992, 165–74). Many Asian American musicians choose to follow that path and create innovative work.

Very few Americans know anything about the four generations of Japanese Americans now living in the continental United States. The first generation, or *issei,* perpetuated the musical tradition and practices that they had brought with them from Japan. Many maintained traditions of the culture they had left behind as a source of well-being from which they could draw as they faced discrimination and alienation here in the United States. Musical activities in San Francisco and Los Angeles serve as examples of *issei* music making in urban centers. *The Japanese American Yearbook,* published in 1914, indicates that a variety of music instruction was offered in San Francisco at that time: *koto* (thirteen-stringed zither), *shamisen* (three-stringed plucked lute), *shakuhachi* (bamboo end-blown flute), piano, choral music at the YWCA, *yōkyoku* (*nō* drama recitation), and Satsuma *biwa* (four-stringed plucked lute). The *issei* were exposed to Western music primarily in the form of Christian hymns. Learning hymns appealed to the pro-Western attitudes of those who wanted to become Americanized as quickly as possible (Asai 1995, 432–33).

Issues of a Japanese newspaper, *Rafu Shimpo,* from 1926 to 1941 provide information about musical performances in and around Los Angeles. Reports of traditional Japanese music mention *sankyoku* (chamber music featuring *koto, shamisen,* and *shakuhachi*), *jōruri* (narrative *shamisen* music for puppet plays), *biwa* music, *utai* (*nō* theater songs), *shigin* (Chinese poems set to music), *nagauta* (narrative songs for kabuki theater), *ha-uta* (a genre of short *shamisen*-accompanied songs), and *naniwa-bushi* (popular-style narrative *shamisen* music) (Asai 1995, 430).

Music of the second generation, or *nisei,* reflects the increased assimilation of Japanese Americans in the United States. *Nisei* maintained continuity with the past by sustaining musical traditions that had been passed down to them; many continued performing traditional instruments, theater music, and folk styles. They also, however, looked to American musical styles, such as "swing," in moving beyond the traditional music of the first generation. Because *nisei* were American born, they naturally acquired the English language, leading toward greater interest in American music. Members of this generation also made seminal efforts toward mixing Japanese and American musics that the next generation, following in their footsteps, would further explore and extend (Asai 1995, 432–36).

Music of the third generation, or *sansei,* embraces American mainstream and innovative, experimental styles. *Sansei* music encompasses traditional Japanese music styles, nearly every form of Western and American music, and syntheses of Japanese and American music (particularly jazz-based idioms). The joining of Japanese and American musical elements links *sansei* to a Japanese past while also functioning as a statement of their social and cultural identity as Americans (Asai 1995, 449).

The great concentration of Japanese Americans in California provides a fertile environment for music making. Additionally, a consideration of the social, political, and economic discrimination endured by Japanese Americans in California provides the background for understanding the retention of ethnicity among *sansei.* The inhospitable attitude of Californians toward first and second generations shaped "Japanese ethnic solidarity," an identity that Japanese Americans shared as "countrymen" holding "common cultural values." Japanese ethnic solidarity in turn provided an economic basis that reinforced "ethnic cohesiveness" (Takaki 1989, 180). The retention of cultural traditions, such as music, became an expression of that ethnic cohesiveness.

The varied backgrounds and musical development of the artists discussed below illustrate a spectrum of music making among *sansei.* This discussion does not attempt to define *sansei* music making in all of its stylistic permutations. Rather, it searches for the relationships among music, ethnicity, and community. The distinct musical voices and socialization of the three artists exemplify these relationships. This study also represents my personal quest as a *sansei* musician who is interested in exploring the way music reflects my socialization and upbringing, as well as the varying ways in which we *sansei* perceive ourselves and our music.

IN SEARCH OF AN IDENTITY

Theories of identity formation developed primarily by sociologists form the framework for investigating the relationship between *sansei* music and ethnicity. Ethnomusicologist Gerhard Kubik describes ethnicity as a social response of a particular population who have experienced "cultural conflict and aborted transculturation." He discusses the concept of ethnicity and the rise of ethnic movements as an ideologically programmed response to "outside aggression, deprivation, discrimination, and holocaust . . . the traumatic collective experience of a group" (Kubik 1994, 41). The internment of 110,000 Japanese Americans on the West Coast during World War II is an example of cultural conflict turned into complete social, economic, and political isolation. The existential trauma of first- and second-generation Japanese American internees continues to affect the consciousness and identity of the third generation.

The idea of ethnicity as a process, rather than as a state of being, was originally developed by the historian Oscar Handlin (1951), whose work with European immigrants led him to declare that ethnicity was "shaped as much by processes that occurred in the New World as by the cultural content they brought with them from the Old World" (as cited in Fugita and O'Brien 1991, 20). This idea progressed into the concept of an emergent ethnicity, describing how the "specific cultural content will change as the ethnic group faces different structural exigencies" in an evolving identification (Fugita and O'Brien 1991, 21). Ethnicity is presented as having a built-in flexibility and bring sensitive to historical events that have shaped or influenced the development of a particular ethnic group.

The signficance of Stephen Fugita and David O'Brien's research in *Japanese American Ethnicity: The Persistence of Community* is that the emergent-ethnicity perspective allows for greater play between being structurally assimilated and retaining ethnicity. The perspective proposes that individuals in varying degrees "transform the nature of their ethnicity" rather than negate it completely. The proportion of assimilation and retention varies and changes according to the exigencies that an individual or community faces in society (Fugita and O'Brien 1991, 22).

A second theoretical framework for this study is Marcus Hansen's sociological thesis, called "the law of the return of the third generation." He posits that the third generation of any immigrant group, who are in a more secure position in terms of socioeconomic status and identity as Americans, is more inclined to reclaim their ethnic heritage than the second generation, who strove to become part of the dominant culture in their "efforts to overcome discrimination and marginality" (Montero 1981, 829). Sociologist Stanford Lyman further explores Hansen's idea by proposing that the third generation may also experience a certain ambivalence or dilemma. He states that *sansei* "do exhibit a certain 'Hansen effect'—that is, a desire to recover selected and specific elements of the culture of Old Japan—but in this endeavor itself they discover that their own Americanization has limited the possibility of very effective recovery" (Lyman 1971, 63). Despite the large-scale assimilation of many *sansei,* it is still useful to consider Hansen's effect as applied to musicians whose work exhibits aspects of the music of "Old Japan." The strong influence that traditional Japanese music has had on some *sansei* musicians may be interpreted as artists reclaiming their ethnic heritage.

A SENSE OF COMMUNITY

Cohesive Japanese American communities in California are a manifestation of the marginality and isolation experienced by the first and second generations. Fugita's and O'Brien's research explores the sense of community cultivated among Japanese Americans based on traditional Japanese social and kinship relationships. Ronald P. Dore describes local community life in Japan as one of cohesion, of carefully constructed social relationships that preserve law and order, and concepts of duty and obligation to the broader community; all are necessary in order for individuals to maintain the honor of their family (1958, 22). Even though Japanese American families live scattered throughout California, quasi-kin social relationships continue to bind individuals to their ethnic community.

The relationship between community and individual identity is explored in Wendy L. Ng's "Collective Memories of Communities." Ng discusses "community memory" as the catalyst that links past and present generations to a particular community in which individuals "derive a sense of belonging, identity, and meaning in their lives" (Ng 1991, 104). Community memory encompasses the history and collective memories of individuals and the community as a whole. She suggests that

> History has played an important role in shaping the Japanese American community, and today, past actions have taken on new and reinterpreted meanings in the context of justice and civil rights. (1991, 103)

In the 1980s, the call for redress and reparations, addressed to the United States government, prompted Japanese Americans to exercise their civil rights and become more politically active. The political activism of Japanese American communities is important in understanding the basis for the creative work of some *sansei* musicians.

SANSEI: A BROADENED MUSICAL LANDSCAPE

Sansei form a diverse group. The music they play includes European classical and contemporary styles, traditional Japanese music, Broadway musicals, jazz, soul, pop, assorted rock styles, country, funk, and various fusions of popular music. The story of music making among *sansei* is not very different from the mainstream population of the United States. Nevertheless, there is a growing musical landscape fostered by *sansei* who center their creative efforts on music that explores and fulfills their ethnic well-being as Americans of Japanese descent.

A broader Asian American music that served to express the political motivations and aspirations of the Asian American movement in the 1970s preceded Japanese American music. The political origins of Asian American music imbue it with a certain revolutionary character. The movement continues to function as a platform for greater sociopolitical consciousness and empowerment of Asian Americans. The civil rights movement and the ensuing black-power movement provided the impetus for the new political power Asian Americans feel.

Asian American activists involved in the movement realized the need for cultural forms that would provide a means to express their newly emerging identity. Certain artists within Asian American communities developed work in response to the growing political consciousness raised by the movement. William Wei outlines "two competing but interrelated approaches to Asian American culture: political and aesthetic" (Wei 1993, 64). The political approach was shaped by Marxist cultural theory, which emphasized making art responsible to the people and, by extension, Mao Tse-tung's belief that "art must meet first a political requirement and only secondarily aesthetic criteria" (Wei 1993, 64).

In finding a voice, many Asian American artists turned toward their own history and experience (Wei 1993, 54). In the late 1960s and 1970s, folk music, inspired by the socially conscious songs of Woody Guthrie, Pete Seeger, and Bob Dylan, served to express the struggles and prejudices faced by Asians in the United States. Motivated by increasing political and social awareness, music groups that comprised members of various Asian ethnicities emerged. Recordings within this genre include those by Chris Iijima, Joanne Miyamoto, and Charlie Chin (of New York City) and Yokohama California (of San Francisco) led by Peter Horikoshi. Both groups performed in a folk style, expressing their identity as Asian Americans and their move toward effecting positive social change. The political approach to art has appealed to certain *sansei* musician-composers for whom music is an artistic expression of sociopolitical and psychological responses to being Japanese American. Music in this context functions as a form of social commentary and ideology, defining who people of Japanese ancestry are and how they can foster positive change. Japanese American music in this vein is an expression of group social and political solidarity within the larger context of Asian America. As an art form, it expresses the values, cultural identity, and awareness of people of Japanese descent in America.

Not all *sansei* musicians, however, choose to be explicitly political in their art. In their artistic development, the concerns of many artists are not political and their energies are directed toward achieving a more broadly conceived musical vision. Some may still incorporate themes of identity, cultural conflict, and alienation in their work, but the work itself does not have a political agenda. Reaching wider, more diverse audiences and attaining some commercial success are greater priorities in their quest for "art for art's sake."

EMERGENCE OF A TRANSCULTURATED MUSIC

The study of traditional Japanese music is currently one avenue taken by many Japanese Americans who seek sound referents for their own work. The study and performance of Japanese music directly connects *sansei* to the "musical memory" of past generations. The exploration of "authentic" Japanese music appears to be the first stage in many a composer's creative journey. The sonic offerings of traditional music include the timbre and idiomatic playing styles of various Japanese instruments as well as its indigenous pentatonic melodies, rhythms, forms, or stylistic and aesthetic aspects. An example of an aesthetic concept is *ma,* or the "silent beat," employed in classical music styles, whereby the silences between notes are as integral to a composition as the sounding of notes.

Japanese court music, or *gagaku,* is one source of inspiration for *sansei* traveling the traditional music route. The former Japanese Imperial Household court-dancer Suenobu Togi is solely responsible for the dissemination of court music in the United States. From 1960 on, he taught many seminars in Boston; San Francisco; Los Angeles; Austin, Texas; and Boulder, Colorado. In Los Angeles, Togi established *gagaku* groups at the University of California, Los Angeles, as one of the music ensembles in the ethnomusicology program, and at both the Senshin Buddhist Church and the Tenrikyo Temple. Today, under the tutelage of Togi, the San Francisco Gagaku Society, directed by the pianist and *koto* player Miya Masaoka, continues the court music tradition. Masaoka points out that *gagaku*'s pan-Asian origins— Chinese, Korean, Indian, and Southeast Asian—make it an ideal music for bringing together musicians of various Asian backgrounds. The San Francisco Gagaku Society reflects the spirit of the broader Asian American cultural movement. Pan-Asian thinking grew out of the sociopolitical realization that to become part of mainstream American society and "to interact with others on equal terms," ethnic groups had to first distinguish themselves as a separate and empowered population" (Schulze 1992).

Other forms of traditional music from which musician-composers draw include Japanese folk *taiko* drumming music (Fig. 11.1), regional folk songs, and the classical repertories of the *koto, shamisen,* and *shakuhachi.* These musical genres are combined with a wide spectrum of contemporary musical styles. The American aspect of the Japanese American music equation may be found in the use of such genres as folk music (as described earlier), jazz-based music, jazz fusion, or pop songs with lyrics that express ideology or personal statements about what it means to be of Japanese descent in the United States. English lyrics offer an outlet for expressing attitudes about working condi-

Figure 11.1. Japanese folk *taiko* drumming: Kinnara Taiko performa at Senshin Buddhist Church in Los Angeles for the O-Bon Festival, July 1995. Photo by Susan Asai.

tions, prejudical treatment, social alienation, and the political, racial, and economic injustices of the internment camps during World War II.

DISTINCT *SANSEI* VOICES

This section is a journey into the musical and communal life of three contemporary *sansei* musicians in urban California. Interviews with the musicians focused on the following questions: "How would you describe your socialization while you were growing up and do you feel connected to a Japanese American or Asian American community?" and "Does your music reflect how you ethnically identify yourself?"

Nobuko Miyamoto: Tale of a Socially and Politically Active Songster
Nobuko Miyamoto's music within Asian American communities spans a period of more than twenty-five years and includes a number of musical styles. She is a pioneer in using music for raising political and social consciousness and calling to action Asian Americans in the 1970s. *A Grain of Sand: Music for the Struggle by Asians in America* (1973), an album Miyamoto created with Chris Iijima and Charlie Chin, represents some of the first Asian American songs with social and political commentary. The songs on this

Figure 11.2. Nobuko Miyamoto. Photo by Ed Ikuta.

seminal album follow in the footsteps of Woody Guthrie's, Pete Seeger's, and Bob Dylan's socially conscious folk-based music.

Born in Los Angeles in 1939, Miyamoto grew up during the upheaval of the Japanese American internment during World War II. After the war she and her family lived with her aunt and uncle, creating close ties to other Japanese American families for economic survival and moral support. While growing up, Miyamoto lived in three different areas of Los Angeles—Crenshaw, Boyle Heights, and Pico Union—where substantial numbers of Japanese Americans formed communities.

Several musical styles influenced her development as a musician. She has a strong memory of her uncle singing *utai* (a vocal style used in *nō* theater), which formed an interesting cultural juxtaposition to Miyamoto's European classical piano studies. She felt spiritually attached to European classical music—preferred by her mother and father—because it was music that could take her to another place. She was also influenced by the pop music of the 1950s and '60s, in particular the singer Frank Sinatra.

Miyamoto's vocal training led to her involvement in singing songs of the Asian American political movement. At the age of seven, she sang Bach chorales, studying with a teacher who believed that children could sing four-part harmony. Later, a jazz vocal teacher broadened her repertoire with the music of Billie Holiday, Lena Horne, Sarah Vaughn, and other American masters. Her first professional stint as a jazz vocalist lasted for eight months at the Colony Club in Seattle, where Pat Suzuki had performed before heading to New York City. Miyamoto experienced a political awakening when she came under the influence of young people in her audience, who were actively involved in protesting the Vietnam War.

She worked with an Italian filmmaker who documented the lives of black people in the United States. The docudrama, *Seize the Time,* recorded the transformation of a man into a revolutionary nationalist as a result of joining the Black Panther Party. From 1967 to 1968 Miyamoto traveled around the country making films. During this time, the civil rights movement was in full swing and the Black Panther Party was at its height of popularity and influence. Miyamoto's exposure to the black power movement and others' struggle for equality spawned her political awareness and activism. Her role as a songster of the Asian American movement in the 1970s was significant in her search for an identity:

> I had never been around militant Asians before. It was during Vietnam and there were all the news clips of Asians being killed again: World War II to Korea and Vietnam, three wars in which Asians were body counts. So a lot of consciousness was being raised through that, and then there were questions of our own identity. (Noriyuki 1995, 2)

The Vietnam War raised questions about self-identity for Asian American activists as they realized that their heritage as Americans was not acknowledged by other Americans, who instead viewed them as foreigners and, in the context of the war, resented them.

In New York City, Miyamoto came into contact with politically minded Japanese Americans—Yuri Kochiyama and the Iijima family—who were active in Asian Americans for Action (AAA). While working with AAA, Miyamoto and Chris Iijima began to write politically motivated music. During a week-long conference that brought Asian American political groups together in Chicago, the pair collaborated on their first song, "The People's Beat," which was inspired by a speech that had been made by Fred Hampton, a Black Panther who had recently been killed by FBI agents. Before presenting their song, Miyamoto and Iijima showed two films: one of the atomic bomb exploding on Hiroshima and another about the Vietnam war. The films supported their talk about the similarity of attitudes that Americans held toward people of both African and Asian descent. Afterward, they performed "The People's Beat," which called for stronger ties between Asian and black political agendas.

Continuing their musical partnership, Miyamoto and Iijima wrote five songs that were sung for such Asian American community organizations across California as Yellow Brotherhood in Los Angeles, the Japanese Community Youth Council in San Francisco, and the Yellow Seed youth program in Stockton. About 1970, one year after their first performance, the duo was joined by Charlie Chin, whom they had met at New York University. For the three years following, the trio traveled throughout the United States.

Miyamoto, Iijima, and Chin built their reputation as proponents of the political approach to music and served as voices for politically active Asian Americans. Their songs criticized capitalism, racism, and sexism and propagated socialist views that were intended to liberate and empower people of color in the United States. The trio sang at protest demonstrations on college campuses and community-based events across the country, encouraging the emergence of other Asian American music groups.

The group strove to create a sense of unity among people of color, as promoted in the Third World Strike at San Francisco State that lasted from November 1968 to March 1969. They extended their artistic reach by writing political songs in Spanish for the Puerto Rican and Dominican squatters' movement in New York City. Their popularity with this segment of the population resulted in a recording of two songs—"Venaremos" and "Somos Asiaticos," the latter of which was released in Puerto Rico—and a year of singing engagements for Puerto Rican organizations and communities. Their summit performance was at the Puerto Rican Liberation Day celebration at Madison Square Garden in New York City. At The Dot coffeehouse in New York City, they joined *nueva cancion* singers and *cancionero* poets, who were accompanied by *cuatro* (the four-stringed plucked lute) players. The trio's experience with Latino musicians and poets introduced them to the idea of using the arts as a vehicle for expressing the struggles for freedom and equality in Puerto Rico, Peru, the Dominican Republic, Chile, and Cuba; soon songs of the *nueva cancion* movement became part of their repertoire.

As musical ambassadors, Miyamoto, Iijima, and Chin joined forces with people of color in New York City. Yuri Kochiyama, a *nisei* who was involved with both the black nationalist movement and the Asian Americans for Action, invited the three to perform for black political events. They freely traversed Asian, black, and Latino communities, schools, and colleges, bringing their political messages through song.

Returning to Los Angeles in 1973, Miyamoto continued her musical career without Chris Iijima and Charlie Chin. Friends introduced her to Benny Yee, a keyboard player who had just left the band Hiroshima (which is discussed below). Together, they formed Warriors of the Rainbow, a jazz fusion band, with the Japanese American saxophonist Russel Baba and the drummer E. W. Wainwright. The Warriors went through several transformations over a five-year period. Miyamoto and Yee wrote socially aware though not politically direct songs for Warriors.

Miyamoto's work also reflects her connection to the Japanese American community in Los Angeles. As an artist and activist, she chooses "to create in the community something that reflects the community." Her early involvement with Japanese American groups was through dance, and she performed ballet at Nisei Week talent shows for a number of years. From 1975 to 1978, she taught modern dance at the Senshin Buddhist Church in Los Angeles, which brought her into close contact with other Japanese Americans there. Her large classes of twenty to forty people were evidence of the community's strong desire for cultural activities. Her recognition of the community's hunger for cultural events provided the impetus for Miyamoto to form Great Leap, Inc., so that she might produce original work for the stage. From its inception, Great Leap has played an important role in showcasing the work of many Asian American performers (Fong 1995, 1). Great Leap's "Slice of Rice" performance series usually features solo theater pieces that combine music, dance, and drama.

In 1990, turning fifty years old prompted Miyamoto to create an autobiographical one-woman show, titled *A Grain of Sand*—after her 1973 album—which she currently performs in venues across the country. It is an ambitious work that outlines the shaping of Miyamoto's experiences, attitudes, and activism as a Japanese American woman. It is a statement of who she is and how she identifies herself. She has performed *A Grain of Sand* at numerous theaters throughout New England, the Midwest, and the West Coast, targeting college-age audiences.

Miyamoto's support of the Japanese American community in Los Angeles also includes performances that she did for redress-and-reparation movement events, some of which address the Japanese American experience. "Gaman," a song on the album *Best of Both Worlds,* describes the internment experience. The Public Broadcasting System aired a short film of the song, with a series of drawings by Betty Chen, produced by Great Leap. Subsequently, Miyamoto performed "Gaman" with slides or showed the film at various redress-and-reparation events.

Two recently written songs symbolize Miyamoto's close ties to the Japanese American community. "Yuiyo Bon Odori" and "Tampopo" (Track 23 on the accompanying compact disc) are Japanese-style folk songs with verses sung in English and choruses sung in Japanese. The O-Bon festival—a commemoration of the souls of deceased ancestors—at the Senshin Buddhist Church in July 1995 included a live performance of the two songs by the group Friends of the Yagura. Both songs accompanied Japanese folk dancing for the O-Bon festival (Fig. 11.3). The two songs are based on the musical structure, mode, and rhythms of traditional Japanese folk songs. In the traditional manner, the *shamisen* (three-string plucked lute) and *shakuhachi* (bamboo transverse flute) duplicate the main, sung melody and the *taiko* (barrel drum) and *atarigane* (brass gong) accent the rhythm. The American aspect of this music is the text of the verses, which are in English.

Figure 11.3. O-Bon Festival dancing at the Senshin Buddhist Church in Los Angeles, July 1995. Photo by Susan Asai.

Prompted by Senshin's Reverend Masao Kodani, Miyamoto's use of English is an attempt to form a link between generations.

Miyamoto wrote "Yuiyo Bon Odori" on commission from the Southern District Buddhist Education Committee in California. The song was first performed on August 18, 1994, at the Southern District O-Bon worship service and Bon Odori, held at the Japanese American Cultural and Community Center in Little Tokyo, downtown Los Angeles. In creating more music for Bon Odori celebrations, Miyamoto composed "Tampopo" in 1994. The traditional context of the O-Bon festival requires a strict interpretation of Japanese folk music as accompaniment to folk dancing. Within the Japanese American community in Los Angeles, the performance of "Yuiyo" and "Tampopo" for O-Bon festivals represents an American contribution to a traditional Japanese event. The use of a Japanese folk music style and instruments serve to authenticate the songs and reaffirm the community's Japanese heritage.

"Tampopo Ondo"
(Dandelion Ondo)

Tampopo Tampopo Kiotsuke-yo, Moshi Kaze Fukeba Aaa————-
1.) Ah————-
The seed of the dandelion, scatters in the sky—
  Tampopo Tampopo - Hi- Hi
A windblown weed, a wildflower, watch it fly—
  Tampopo Tampopo - Hi- Hi
Dancing on the wind, spinning from a world it leaves behind,
Dancing on wind, new life begins.

Okagesama de	Yare Yare Sore
Okagesama de	Yare Yare Sore
Okagesama de	Through all the forces
Okagesama de	Through the shadows and the light
Okagesama de	The unknown forces - dandelion

  Hi - Hi - Hi - Hi - Hi - Hi - Hi, Hi - Hi
2.) Ah————-
The seed of a dandelion, scatters in the sky.
  Tampopo Tampopo - Hi - Hi
A windblown weed, a wildflower, watch it fly—
  Tampopo Tampopo - Hi - Hi
Dancing on the wind, spinning to a world it leaves behind,
Dancing on wind, new life begins.

Yare Yare Sore	Yare Yare Sore
Okagesama de	Yare Yare Sore
Okagesama de	Yare Yare Sore
Okagesama de	On this special night—
Okagesama de	Past and present are one—
Okagesama de	On this night of O-bon—
Okagesama de	Dandelions return—

  Hi - Hi - Hi - Hi - Hi - Hi, Hi - Hi
3.) Ah————-
The seed of the dandelion, bursting in the sky—
  Tampopo Tampopo - Hi - Hi
A windblown weed, a wildflower, watch it fly—
  Tampopo Tampopo - Hi - Hi
Dancing on the wind, spinning to a world beyond the eye
Dancing on the wind, new life begins—Hey!

Okagesama de	Yare Yare Sore
Okagesama de	Yare Yare Sore

Okagesama de	On this night—
Okagesama de	The old and the young—
Okagesama de	All the dandelions—
Okagesama de	Dance as one—Dance, Dance as one

Okagesama de	Yare Yare Sore
Okagesama de	Yare Yare Sore
Okagesama de	Not a Rose or an Iris
Okagesama de	Not a Bird of Paradise
Okagesama de	Not an Orchid or a Lily,

Just a simple dandelion
      Tada no Tampopo
Just a simple dandelion
      Tada no Tampopo
Just a simple dandelion
      Tada no Tampopo
Just a simple dandelion
Tampopo Tampopo
Tampopo Tampopo

Translation of terms:

kiotsuke-yo: careful

moshi kaze fukeba: if the wind blows

okagesama de: with your help

tada no tampopo: a simple dandelion

Miyamoto's songs have a didactic Buddhist message that is intended as an expression of Japanese American Buddhist culture. The song implies learning to hear and receive the Truth through the practice of "just dancing," as interpreted by the Jodo Buddhist sect. The accompanying notes describing Bon Odori state:

According to Jodoshinshū, Truth and Reality are ours for the receiving. We need do nothing but hear and receive the Truth. But to simply hear and receive is as difficult as it is to just dance. To "just do" anything is extremely difficult, for it involves setting aside one's ego for a moment. Bon odori is an exercise in "just dancing," in "just hearing and accepting," in "being a river forever flowing and changing instead of a riverbank forever watching."

"Tampopo" reflects not only Miyamoto's own spiritual beliefs but also the beliefs and practices of Japanese American Buddhists. Many *sansei* are active members of Buddhist churches in southern California. Buddhism, a religion of their Japanese heritage, plays an important role in reinforcing their ethnic identity.

Nobuko Miyamoto's creative life is a history of the arrival of music that expressed a political awareness and a search for identity among Asian Americans in the wake of the black-power movement and the Vietnam war. Her early work is strongly linked to the broader Asian American movement, while her later work not only connects to the Japanese American community but also gives voice to a number of cultures reflecting the diversity of Los Angeles. The artist's latest recording, *To All Relations*—translated from the Lakota expression *"Mitakuye Oyasin"*—is described by Miyamoto as a "gathering of tribes" and features diverse instrumentation and musical elements. The spiritual and cultural breadth of her work is widely felt, and a number of *sansei* musicians in Los Angeles acknowledge the impact she has had on them as artists.

Miyamoto's ties to the community are both national and local. The songs that she sang on her own and with Iijima and Chin addressed Asian American communities nationwide. Locally, her music, dance, and theater performances, music for O-Bon festivals, and other community events and venues project her identification with the Buddhist Church and the Japanese American community in Los Angeles. The original songs "Yuiyo Bon Odori" and "Tampopo" are a tribute to her Japanese roots; they are intentional in their imitation of Japanese folk music as a way to authenticate and distinguish the Japanese aspect of this Japanese American music.

Mark Izu: Traversing Boundaries

Mark Izu is a central figure in the Asian American music scene in the San Francisco Bay area. For eighteen years he has been active in the Asian American contemporary arts scene as a bassist, composer, bandleader, music curator, and arts advocate. Izu's artistic direction of the annual Asian American Jazz Festival is well respected, both nationally and internationally. His music is a creative hybrid that combines his study of traditional Japanese and Chinese music with a strong interest in the music of avant-garde jazzmen Charles Mingus and Albert Ayler. Izu developed his innovative music over several years, and the vocabulary featured in his work is a mature and subtle synthesis of many musical influences.

Izu grew up in Sunnyvale, a white community near San Jose, California. His varied musical training began in the fourth grade with studies in clarinet. His musical interest broadened to include the music of other cultures—Chinese, Japanese, and Korean—to which he had access at the audio library of the San Jose Public Library. Because of his interest in Asian music, Izu's mother encouraged him to study Japanese *koto* during one summer while he

Figure 11.4. Mark Izu. Photo by Dean Wong.

was in junior high school. During his high school years, Izu moved on to playing the guitar and joined various rock bands. Around that time, he was exposed to the music of John Coltrane, and jazz also became of great interest to him.

Izu talks about early influences that inform his music. He had always been intrigued by the Buddhist funeral services that he and his family attended, at which he smelled incense and heard chanting and the sound of gongs. Izu also listened to his parents' Japanese music recordings and was especially moved by court music. This music created an interesting complement to Coltrane's music and European classical music, which he was learning to play on the string bass.

After only a year and a half of playing bass, he successfully auditioned for the music program at San Francisco State University. For four years, eight hours a day, Izu locked himself in a practice room to practice bass and compose. He also joined the Chinese music group Flowing Stream Ensemble, where he met a master Chinese musician and studied the *ehr-hu* (two-string bowed lute) and the *sheng* (bamboo mouth organ). The Flowing Stream Ensemble was a semiprofessional music group that played Cantonese folk music. By going to informal rehearsals that were, in fact, also social gatherings, Izu managed to learn the idiomatic style of playing the two instruments and musical phrasing.

During his four years at the university he also heard about a Japanese *gagaku* (court music) ensemble led by Suenobu Togi that was part of the

Institute of Buddhist Studies in San Francisco. There, Izu studied the *shō* (bamboo mouth organ) and met innovative Japanese American musicians— Russel Baba, Gordie Watanabe, Robert Kikuchi-Yngojo, Paul Yamazaki, Makoto Horiuchi, and others. Joining the *gagaku* group proved to be a turning point in Izu's musical development; he remarked that "for the first time, I felt like I belonged someplace." The years 1976 and 1977 stand out as a fertile time because everyone in the group was writing his own music. After *gagaku* rehearsals, they would go to Chinatown to eat and talk. From that time on, Izu started playing bass with Baba, Horiuchi, and others. In addition, he would go down to the Mission area of San Francisco and learn salsa in workshops given by Carlos Frederico.

This period also marks Izu's collaboration with Lewis Jordan, a poet and musician whom he met at the Blue Dolphin in San Francisco. The Blue Dolphin was a club that featured alternative music, including music set to poetry. In 1977 Izu and Jordan formed Marrón, an African and Asian American ensemble whose members included Ray Collins (saxophone), Yamazaki (clarinet), Kenny Endo (trap drums), Duke Santos (congas), and Watanabe (guitar). The group ended up as an eight- to nine-piece band that became too large to find jobs, and thus disbanded.

Izu maintained his musical partnership with Jordan by joining Jordan's quartet for a performance in West Germany and forming a recording company with the saxophonist. They started RPM Records because there were very few venues for Jordan and Izu to record their style of alternative, new-jazz music. The release of their first album, *Path of the Heart,* generated more jobs and the recording of several more albums.

United Front, a quartet formed in 1979, was Izu's next band with saxophonist Jordan, trumpeter George Sams, and percussionist Anthony Brown. The quartet's repertoire included music that expressed political ideas. They went to Europe every year and recorded several albums. The quartet, however, never reached the point where all the musicians were able to make a full-time living through music (Yanow 1994, 30). Izu believes the band's music was ahead of its time.

Following this endeavor, Izu played bass on pianist Jon Jang's first two albums—*Jang* and *Are You Chinese or Charlie Chan?*—which were produced by Izu's RPM Record company. The collaboration led to performances with Jang and saxophonist Francis Wong in the annual Asian American jazz festival. Since that time, Izu has recorded at least eleven albums as a sideman with key Asian Improv musicians; written scores for documentaries, theater, and a silent film; and recorded *Circle of Fire,* which was his first session as a leader (Yanow 1994, 33).

Izu's bass playing engages the eclectic influences of Japanese court music, Cantonese folk music, and jazz-based music. When interviewed, he spoke about the difficulty of learning different musical styles and instruments (bass, *ehr-hu, sheng, shō*), but, in the course of time, all of these styles became part of his musical vocabulary. An important concept in Izu's music is the concept of space—*ma*, in Japanese. Izu described *ma* in the following way: "It's the space around the notes that define what the note is and how the note sounds and feels." He applies this concept to many of his pieces, including "Scattered Scars"—which is about his parents' internment experience—and "The Shadow," on his *Circle of Fire* recording. He learned the concept of *ma* while learning Japanese court music.

Izu's compositional process varies depending on the piece. For example his collaboration with musician Jin Hin Kim provided the opportunity for him to become familiar with the idiomatic style of the Korean *komungo*. He could then use a rhythmic approach for a composition that successfully incorporated that style. When he studied Japanese court music, Izu learned that music was "a matter of shaping the whole performance, not its individual components" (Ahlgren 1992). Instruments from different cultures find their way into many of his compositions. In reference to their use, he said, "My philosophy of fusing different cultural instruments is that you don't just add [them] to music that already exists; you build . . . from the ground up." (Ahlgren 1992).

Izu's music is eclectic and is self-described as "new jazz." He is most interested in experimenting with musical timbres and textures. One direction he takes is to create pieces that feature *taiko* drumming and work around the rhythms associated with this instrument. Three of his recent sketches are dedicated to people in the community who have been committed to the arts for many years. The music of the African American pianist Horace Tapscott and conversations with him inspired Izu to write musical vignettes about people. Izu says that he is motivated to write such pieces because he believes that it is important for musicians to acknowledge each other's music.

When asked "Who is the audience for your music?" Izu explained that it depended on the concert's venue, location, and where it is advertised. He mentioned that, in general, his audience runs the gamut. He talked about the annual Asian American Jazz Festival—the venue that draws the largest crowds for Asian American jazz-based music—and its current twofold goal to build Asian American participation and audiences at large. He stated that it is important to develop audiences from both Asian and non-Asian populations in order to cultivate future support. Illustrating what he considers ideal, Izu cited the audience who came to see the film "The Dragon Painter," for which he composed and played the musical score, at Chicago's Walker Art Museum: a mix of Asian and non-Asian film buffs, jazz afficionados, and people interested in his current work. He feels satisfaction when he can attract such a group.

Izu's various jobs have put him in touch with the Bay Area's Asian American community. In 1989 he became the director of the Kearny St.

Workshop, which started out as an Asian American grassroots organization supporting the tenet that art is a vehicle for bringing about social change (Wei 1991, 87). A division of the workshop, the Isthmus Press, published two photo journals called *Pursuing Wild Bamboo,* which contain photographs that narrate episodes in the lives of artists. In the visual arts, the workshop started out as a community resource and service center by making silk-screened posters for community events; then people started doing their own work, and now an exhibit at the Yerba Buena Arts Center is underway. Today the main performance event of the workshop is the Asian American Jazz Festival. Izu's role as both artistic director and resident bassist of the festival joins his musical world with that of the Asian American community.

The Japanese American population is also a focus of Izu's musical efforts. He worked as the transportation coordinator at Kimochi, a Japanese American senior citizen center in San Francisco's Japan Town. Izu also served as artistic director and composer for the Day of Remembrance concert in February, 1995, in San Francisco. The music for this event was intended to convey a portrait of the lives of internees in concentration camps during World War II. The music celebrates the resilience of Japanese Americans who survived the humiliation and degradation of the camps. The hope was that the audience would gain more understanding and appreciation of what happened in this dark period of American history. The concert featured guest artist Janice Mirikitani, a poet who was chosen for her ability to "capture the moment" and to express the anger, the spirit, and compassion generated by the camp experience. Her poem about ten children who died while interned at Tule Lake was accompanied by music composed by Izu and modern dance performed by Judy Kajiwara (*ImprovisAsians!* 1995, 4).

Izu also served as the artistic director and composer for the Concert of a Thousand Cranes, which concluded the 1995 Asian American Jazz Festival at the Asian Art Museum in San Francisco's Golden Gate Park. His piece "HIBAKUSHA! Survivors" (Track 24 on the accompanying compact disc), a commemoration of the atomic bomb survivors in Hiroshima and Nagasaki, incorporates chants of the Karok Indians' Healing the Earth ceremony. In the final movement, the Karok chants are performed in tandem with Izu's composition, representing the more integrated approach of his latest compositions (*ImprovisAsians!* 1995, 5).

Izu composed "HIBAKUSHA! Survivors" for a commission by Asian Improv aRts, an Asian American arts umbrella organization in San Francisco. The decision to write about the atomic survivors was made after he had read about the offspring of radiation victims. He stated, "I realized that the most damage that is done by radiation to the human race is on the genetic level, the altering of our DNA. This literally changes one's past, present, and future." That his father served in the acclaimed all–Japanese American 442nd Battalion and that his mother's family is from Hiroshima further reinforced his decision to write on this somber theme. Izu noted how many *hibakusha*, or survivors, were Japanese Americans who were visiting Japan to connect with relatives or to study at the time the war broke out. He conveyed the moving experience of hearing *hibakusha* tell how their lives changed and how even now they are still trying to be recognized by the United States government for financial compensation.

Izu's idea of incorporating in "Hibakusha" the chants of the Karok's Healing the Earth ceremony occurred to him after he was invited to attend the event. Every year the Karok perform ceremonies to heal the earth; they fast, pray, chant, and dance for two weeks on their sacred grounds. Very few non-Karok people are invited; thus Izu's attendance was an honor. Personally touched by the experience, he asked his Karok friend Julian to perform a healing chant at the end of "HIBAKUSHA!"

"HIBAKUSHA! Survivors," in five movements, is scored for a mixed ensemble of Asian and European instruments. A subtext for the musicians is indicated in the score. The piece is a spiritual, emotional journey. Izu wanted to re-create some of the feelings he had during the Karok ceremony. The subtexts and musical description of the composition are as follows:

    I: numbness/shock/self awareness, starts after the bombing

   II: confusion/anger/realization (the most dense and atonal)

  III: questions/the unborn, past/present/future (begins with strings and evolves into imitative motifs initiated by the trombone; the image is that of a drop of water creating ripples on a still pond)

  IV: understanding/coping/telling the story (based on a Japanese *saibara* song, a vocal piece from the court music repertoire about a fleeting moment of the ocean at Ise)

   V: healing/ritual (a Karok chant to the accompaniment of the Japanese court instrument *shō* and the Chinese equivalent, the *sheng*)

Izu's music and activism represent his affiliation with the larger Asian American community, rather than the exclusively Japanese American one. A Pan-Asian orientation is central to the political, social, and artistic endeavors of many people of Asian descent in the United States today owing to the powerful influence and legacy of the Third-World Strike at San Francisco State and the Asian American political movement. The broader Asian American sphere better serves musicians, like Izu, who collectively endeavor to form a broader base from which to build opportunities and exposure for themselves.

Izu does not limit himself to the influences of his Japanese heritage but is open to traditions that expand his musical vocabulary. With his musical and arts advocacy activities, Izu has helped to build a flourishing landscape for Asian American musicians whose music cannot easily be categorized and is an expression of their individuality. His role as bassist-in-residence for Asian Improv Records and artistic director of the annual Asian American Jazz Festival place him in a prominent position to broaden the musical landscape further.

June Kuramoto: The Japanese Koto Innovator

June Kuramoto's *koto* playing heralds a new direction for the traditional instrument that dates back to seventh-century Japan and even earlier in China and Korea. In addition to being an accomplished traditional *koto* player, Kuramoto is adept at improvising music for the Los Angeles-based band Hiroshima, whom many consider the quintessential Japanese American music group. Hiroshima began as a musical voice for the Asian American political movement in southern California during the 1970s. The group's compositions, particularly their older songs, represent a transculturated form of music. The use of traditional instruments, musical modes, and rhythms projects a Japanese heritage, while a rhythm-and-blues and jazz fusion-based musical style expresses an American identity.

June Kuramoto's background is unusual for a *sansei*. She was born in Japan but moved to Los Angeles with her family when she was quite young. Kuramoto is considered a *sansai* since her father was a *nisei*. She grew up in the Crenshaw area of west Los Angeles and attended Dorsey High School, which was one-third African American, one-third Japanese American, and one-third European American. Kuramoto remarked that "Dorsey High School was a multiracial school, so I got exposed to Jewish, black, and Japanese American students. That helped me sense a true community where keeping your identity was very important as to who you are, but we were all a microcosm of something greater, so we all got along. It was ideal." She felt fortunate to have the best of all worlds to draw on, to share with others, and to observe.

When she was a child, Kuramoto considered herself Japanese and not Japanese American because her impression was that she and her family would go back to Japan. Going back to Japan was her assurance that everything would be better as her family earned a meager living in Los Angeles. As time passed, Kuramoto faced the reality that she would not return and her identity began to alter. People from Japan looked at her differently because she was no longer fluent in Japanese and her mannerisms and appearance had become more American. Because she was born in Japan, however, she always felt a strong connection to that culture. Kuramoto is an example of an individual caught between two cultures; she commented that there are times when she feels that she is a person without a country because she is marginalized by both Japanese and Americans. This is a sentiment more characteristic of *nisei*, second-generation Japanese Americans.

For Kuramoto, the experience of playing the *koto* is closely allied with her perception of being Japanese American. In grammar school she walked ten blocks with her instrument to play at school for Girl's Day, an annual Japanese celebration in March. The *koto* also bound her to the community, and as a youngster she played regularly at Keiro, the Japanese American retirement home in Gardena and for the *"ken"* picnics sponsored by organizations that represented districts—or prefectures (*ken*)—in Japan, from which Japanese American families trace their lineage.

She chose to play the *koto* not only because it connected her to Japan, but because she loved the sound of the instrument. At the age of six she began studies with Kazue Kudo, the leading *koto* teacher in Los Angeles. Since then, Kudo has been her only teacher. She also learned about the history and background of the instrument from Kayoko Wakita at Los Angeles City College. Kuramoto's extensive classical *koto* training has given her a firm foundation for playing the less demanding structures and technique required for pop music. After venturing into pop, rock, jazz, and blues styles, she always returns to the classical *koto* repertoire as her source of inspiration. The alternation between playing Japanese classical music and American popular music illustrates how Kuramoto perceives herself—a mix of both Japanese and American.

A purist, Kuramoto believes in retaining the unique sound of the *koto* by playing in the pentatonic mode traditionally used for the instrument. She superimposes this mode onto whatever key the rest of the band plays in, allowing her the wider range that she needs on the instrument for her improvisations. Kuramoto is most comfortable with the pentatonic scale as her earliest musical training is Japanese, not Western. The challenge of fitting the idiomatic playing style of the *koto* into a contemporary music format by performing over the chord changes is well met by Kuramoto who is given free rein in the band.

Kuramoto's past activity in the Japanese American community also confirms her identity with this population. Before her active involvement with the band Hiroshima, she helped to organize the first health fair for the Japanese American Community Service (JACS). Kuramoto also served as an adviser for students in the Go for Broke program, helping Asian American high school students with problems related to adolescence. In addition, she worked with the Asian American Drug Abuse Program (AADAP), which was originally affiliated with a halfway house. Her community activism also includes participation in demonstrations and marches with Asian Americans for Peace during the Vietnam War, as part of the Asian American movement.

The political ferment of the Asian American movement provided the impetus for the founding of Hiroshima. The band embodied an identity for people of Asian descent at that time. Blacks identified with rhythm and blues, jazz, and soul; Chicanos and Latinos had Santana and Malo as their musical emblem of identity, but there was no music to which Asian Americans felt rooted. Kuramoto had always wanted to include the *koto* in a contemporary musical setting. She approached rock musicians Dan Kuramoto and his brother John because they were performing their own music, separating themselves from Asian American cover bands that were prevalent in the 1970s. The Kuramoto brothers had the concept of a band named after Hiroshima that would represent both the atomic age and the phoenix-like image of that city rising from the ashes. June collaborated with the brothers, and the band Hiroshima was born.

The band's political leanings are associated with bandleader Dan Kuramoto, who served as the director of the Asian American Studies Program at California State University at Long Beach. As an academic, he also helped form the Asian American Studies Central, an umbrella organization that supported the emergence of Asian American groups and activities, such as the film and media organization Visual Communications, the newspaper *Gidra*, and picnics that brought the community together.

From the start, Hiroshima had a reciprocal relationship with the Japanese American community. The group played for community organizations such as Joint Communications, AADAP, Amerasia Bookstore, Little Tokyo Service Center, JACS, and the annual potlucks of the Asian American Studies Program at California State University, Long Beach. Many of their performances were benefits. The community reciprocated by providing support for the group's first album by calling the radio stations to request the music of Hiroshima and purchasing the album.

The band officially formed in 1975 and landed their first record deal in 1979. Hiroshima appeared on the Arista label for their first two albums (*Hiroshima* and *Odori*). They were nominated for the "Best Instrumental" Grammy Award for "Winds of Change," a song from their second album. They recorded their third through seventh albums on Epic/Sony Records. For their eighth and ninth albums they switched to Quest Records/Warner, and the band was voted "Best Jazz Group" by Soul Train (a predominantly black organization) in the instrumental music category. Within the community, Hiroshima has won "Best Image" awards from a Chinese American organization and the Asian American Political Alliance (AAPA). In 1995 the Japanese American Cultural and Community Center in Los Angeles conferred the President's Award on the group and the Pacific American Consortium on Education (PACE) presented them with a recognition award.

In solo concerts, Kuramoto performs mostly her own tunes, which appear on Hiroshima's albums but are never performed live by the group. As a complement, she plays one or two traditional *koto* pieces to demonstrate the flair of the instrument in that style. Sometimes she will also include the compositions of others—such as Kazu Matsui's "Morning Mist Across the Sea." Kuramoto schedules solo concerts not only to motivate herself to practice but to provide opportunities for musicians who need work.

When asked "Who is the audience for Hiroshima?" Kuramoto—like Izu—replied that the audience varies depending on the venue. For example, when the band went on its first national tour, they played in a concert space in Chicago that attracted a black audience, and when they performed in a different part of the city, the audience was white. They only tour major cities that have diverse audiences, but often the demographics of their audience range widely. In general, Hiroshima's audiences are a mixture of Caucasians, blacks, and Asians. Their audiences tend to be intergenerational; families come because Hiroshima presents a "clean show."

Even though they tour, the band continues its mission to promote music as a communal activity among Japanese Americans, especially in Los Angeles. Audiences respond emotionally, or "tune in," to their music because it embodies a specific social identity for Japanese Americans and Asian Americans in general. When they perform at the Greek Theater in Griffith Park, the concert is a reunion for many members of the Asian American community, particularly Japanese Americans, who come out and have a wonderful time.

Among the three musicians presented here, June Kuramoto stands out as having the greatest musical connection to her Japanese heritage. She has the rare ability to play classical *koto* music, and can improvise in a popular-music setting as well. Her strong identity with Japanese culture is reflected in her *koto* playing for Hiroshima, where she retains a traditional *koto* sound by employing pentatonic modes. Kuramoto's musicianship allows her to traverse between the worlds of Japanese classical and American popular music.

Kuramoto's ties to the Japanese American community in Los Angeles are evident not only in her work with community organizations but also in her activities with Hiroshima. The band, from its early beginnings, has enjoyed a reciprocally supportive relationship with the community. She and members of the band are emblems of a Japanese American identity whose music intends to be a voice for not only Japanese Americans but all Asian Americans. Hiroshima strives to convey to general audiences, in Dan Kuramoto's words, that "Asian Americans want a voice, we have things to say and that we are creative people who have great feelings and great passions" (Kubo 1974). Their music attempts to weave a thread of Japanese music, through the timbre and pentatonic sound of the *koto*, with pop music elements. They aim to blur boundaries, so that if you were to listen to them with your eyes closed you might think that you were hearing an American mainstream fusion band. This subtle blending of Japanese and American sounds is metaphoric of the bicultural identity many Japanese Americans experience. Today, many active Asian American musicians—especially those of Japanese descent—point to Hiroshima as their source of inspiration; the band's music continues to be a legacy of Asian American pride.

CONCLUSION

The life stories of these artists illustrate the variety of social processes that each individual underwent in developing their ethnic identity as Japanese Americans. In accordance with Hansen's theory, the *sansei* musician-composers in this study chose to return to their Asian heritage in their efforts to musically innovate. Each artist strikes a different balance between assimilation and retention of ethnicity. As a member of the group Hiroshima, Kuramoto is the most mainstream musician, yet her ties to Japanese culture and the Los Angeles Japanese American community remain strong. Miyamoto draws inspiration and support from the Japanese American community but also embraces other minority cultures, while Izu exemplifies a broader Asian American identity that he has cultivated in a more avant-garde music sphere.

The *sansei*'s stories also reflect the political force and influence of the Asian American movement, which initially formed in response to racism and social inequalities. The sociopolitical activism supports the validity of Kubik's notion of ethnicity as a social response to the aborted transculturation Asian Americans experience in this country. A positive and proactive attitude toward one's Asian heritage as a source of political and social empowerment, rather than embarrassment or shame, is a constructive aspect of the movement. The transformative power of the movement ushered in a newly discovered pride and interest in cultural traditions of previous generations. The creation of a new identity gives Asian Americans a chance to positively define who they are in countering the stereotypes and views American society has of them.

The grassroots level of activities within the Asian American movement in the 1970s created strong connections between individuals and the community. This is certainly true of the artists presented in this study, all of whom have been involved with health, social, or arts organizations and whose music serves as an important communal bond. Miyamoto's "Tampopo Ondo" is an example of music written specifically for the O-Bon festival. The impetus for Kuramoto's music stems from her connection to Japanese American and Asian American audiences, while the eclectic approach of Izu's work mirrors his broader reach to an Asian American and even a new music audience.

Ng's study is pertinent to the association between *sansei* identity and community because of her focus on a collective memory in which the "knowledge of the past is transmitted from one generation to another through culture—traditions, rituals, and folklore" (Ng 1991, 103). For *sansei* musicians, the collective memory serves as a critical source of knowledge and traditions from which they can draw. From this connection one may also infer that if music existed as part of a community's past, it could be considered a shared collective memory—a "musical memory." It then follows that musical memory also may be passed down through the generations and thus exist in the minds of *nisei* and *sansei* generations. This memory perhaps accounts for the compositions of *sansei* musician-composers who synthesize elements of traditional Japanese music in their work as a way to develop their own voice. Kuramoto employs the *koto* and its idiomatic playing style as her Japanese American voice. Miyamoto draws on Japanese folk music as an expression of her heritage, while Izu experiments with aspects of Japanese court music, *taiko* drumming, and aesthetic concepts. By incorporating some aspect of traditional Japanese music, *sansei* musican-composers are able to express their feelings and come to terms with an essential part of themselves.

The musical lives presented in this study give voice to a historically silent population. Those who choose to write and perform music that reflects their ethnicity contribute to our understanding of the relationships between music, ethnicity, and community. By preserving bonds with their communities and building identity through music, Japanese American musicians acquire a sense of place whereby they are anchored and empowered.

REFERENCES CITED

A Conversation with Mark Izu. 1995. *ImprovisAsians* 4, no. 1.

A Grain of Sand: Music for the Struggle by Asians in America. 1973. Liner notes by Chris Kando Iijima, Joanne Nobuko Miyamoto, and Charlie Chin. Paredon Records, P-1020.

Ahlgren, Calvin. 1992. Izu: "Circle" Ready to Get Off Square One. *San Francisco Chronicle,* 23 February.

Asai, Susan. 1995. Transformations of Tradition: Three Generations of Japanese American Music Making. *Musical Quarterly* 79, no. 3: 429–53.

Dore, Ronald P. 1958. *City Life in Japan.* Berkeley: University of California Press.

Fong, Giselle L. 1995. Nobuko Miyamoto—A Grain of Sand Sings to Warriors. *Tozai Times* 11: 128.

Fugita, Stephen S., and David J. O'Brien. 1991. *Japanese American Ethnicity: The Persistence of Community.* Seattle: University of Washington Press.

Jayo, Norman, and Paul Yamazaki. 1986. Searching for an Asian American Music: Robert Kikuchi-Yngojo. *East Wind* 5, no. 1: 11.

Kitano, Harry H. L. 1969. *Japanese Americans: The Evolution of a Sub-culture.* Englewood Cliffs, N.J.: Prentice-Hall, Inc.

Kubik, Gerard. 1994. Ethnicity, Cultural Identity, and the Psychology of Culture Contact. In *Music and Black Ethnicity: The Caribbean and South America.* Edited by Gerard Behague. New Brunswick, N.J.: Transaction Publishers.

Lyman, Stanford. 1971. Generation and Character: The Case of Japanese Americans. *Roots: An Asian American Reader.* Los Angeles: UCLA Asian American Studies Center.

Miyamoto, Nobuko. 1984. Notes to "Yuiyo Bon Odori" (Unpublished).

Montero, Darrel. 1981. The Japanese Americans: Changing Patterns of Assimilation Over Three Generations. *American Sociological Review* 46: 6–.

Noriyuki, Duane. 1995. Nobuko Miyamoto, Civil Rights Activist. *Los Angeles Times,* 19 July.

Ng, Wendy. 1991. The Collective Memories of Communities. *Asian Americans: Comparative and Global Perspectives.* Edited by Hune, Kim, Fugita, and Ling. Pullman, Wash.: Washington State University Press.

Schulze, Margaret. 1992. New Group Devoted to Ancient Japanese Music. *Hokubei Mainichi,* 10 January.

Takaki, Ron. 1989. *Strangers from a Different Shore: A History of Asian Americans.* Boston, Toronto, and London: Little, Brown and Co.

Thornton, Michael C. 1992. Finding a Way Home. *Asian Americans: Collages of Identities.* Cornell Asian American Studies Monograph Series, no.1. Ithaca, N.Y.: Asian American Studies Program, Cornell University.

Trimillos, Ricardo. 1986. Music and Ethnic Identity: Strategies Among Overseas Filipino Youth. *Yearbook for Traditional Music* 18: 9–20.

Wei, William. 1993. *The Asian American Movement.* Philadelphia: Temple University Press.

Yanow, Scott. 1994. Enthusiasm. *Jazziz* 11, no. 2: 28–34.

INTERVIEWS

1987. Telephone interview with Arawana Hayashi, Boston, 28 June.

1987. Telephone interview with Paul Yamazaki, San Francisco, 18 July.

1987. Telephone interview with Brian Auerbach, San Francisco, 18 July.

1987. Telephone interview with Mark Izu, San Francisco, 19 July.

1987. Personal interview with Mr. Seizo Oka at the Japanese History Archives, San Francisco, 21 July.

1987. Telephone interview with Mr. Suenobu Togi, Los Angeles, 22 October.

1994. Personal interview with Miya Masaoka, San Francisco, 3 August.

1994 Personal interview with Mr. Seizo Oka, San Francisco, 15 August.

1994. Personal interview with Mark Izu, San Francisco, 14 August.

1995. Personal interview with June Kuramoto, 18 July.

1995. Personal interview with Nobuko Miyamoto, 25 July.

COMPANION CD SELECTIONS

Track 23. Tampopo. Nobuko Miyamoto. Courtesy of the artist.

Track 24. Hibakusha. Mark Izu. Courtesy of the artist.

SELECTED DISCOGRAPHY

Asian American Jazz Trio. 1993. *Moon Over the World.* King Record Co., Inc. KICJ 163.

Tatsu Aoki. 1994. *Kioto.* Asian Improv Records.

Kenny Endo Taiko Ensemble. 1994. *Eternal Energy.* Asian Improv Records. AIR 0021.

Hiroshima. 1979/1980. *Ongaku.* Arista, ARCD 8437.

Hiroshima. 1996. *Urban World Music.* Quest Records/Warner.

Glenn Horiuchi. 1988. *Next Step.* Asian Improv Records, AIR 0002.

Glenn Horiuchi. 1989. *Issei Spirit.* Asian Improv Records.

Glenn Horiuchi. 1989. *Manzanar Voices.* Asian Improv Records, AIR 006.

Glenn Horiuchi. 1991. *Poston Sonata.* Asian Improv Records, AIR 008.

Glenn Horiuchi. 1992. *Oxnard Beet.* Soul Note.

Mark Izu, Lewis Jordan, Anthony Brown, and George Sams. 1981. *United Front.* RPM Records, RPM 1.

Mark Izu and Lewis Jordan. 1988. *The Travels of a Zen Baptist.* RPM Records, RPM 6.

Mark Izu. 1992. *Circle of Fire.* Asian Improv Records, AIR 0009.

Bob Kenmotsu. 1992. *The Spark.* Asian Improv Records, AIR 0010.

Miya Masaoka. 1993. *Compositions/Improvisations.* Asian Improv Records, AIR 00014.

Nobuko Miyamoto. 1997. *To All Relations.* Bindu Records.

Murasaki Ensemble. 1994. *Niji.* A Murasaki Production. TME 8994.

Noh Buddies. 1984. *Noh Buddies.* Sansei Records, SR 442.

Sounds Like 1996: Music by Asian American Artists. 1996. Asian Improv Records. IEL 0002.

Visions. 1991/1992. *Time to Discover.* Mina Productions, MPCD 75.

Yutaka Yokokura. 1978. *Love Light.* Alfa Records, ALR 6009.

VIDEOGRAPHY

Mabalot, Linda. 1993. *Hiroshima Twenty Years Later.* Los Angeles: Visual Communications.

Zantzinger, Gei. 1990. *Susumu* [about Sumi Tonooka's composition "Out from the Silence"]. University Park, Penn.: Continuing and Distance Education, Pennsylvania State University.

CHAPTER 12

Just Being There

Making Asian American Space in the Recording Industry

Deborah Wong

*A*lthough most of her previous research has focused on Thai court music, performers' rituals, and funeral music, Wong has an ongoing interest in Asian and Asian American music. She is an ethnomusicologist whose interests encompass contemporary, intercultural popular music and culture. This essay examines a crossover that will surprise many people: an Asian American hip-hop group that embraces rap in a most uncompromising manner. Rap is, of course, most closely identified with African American speech, style, and music. The Mountain Brothers, the group discussed by Wong, is based on the East Coast and was formed while each of the group members was attending Penn State University. While their performance art may have African American roots, their politically progressive message sometimes contains underlying Asian American themes. It is somewhat ironic that the ability of the Mountain Brothers to win the ears and minds of a multiracial and multiethnic audience also helped them to capture first place in a contest for a commercial jingle for the soft-drink Sprite. The success of these three Americans of Asian heritage in exploring this black American idiom not only underscores the international appeal of hip-hop but—as does Susan Asai's essay—also raises the question, what are the nature and borders of Asian American contemporary music?

■　■　■　■

INTRODUCTION: THEORIZING HIP-HOP AND RACE

I am frankly daunted by the task of introducing hip-hop culture. Introducing Asian American musics is much easier: to my mind, Asian American musics

287

are any music made by Asian Americans, of any ethnicity. Unlike Asian American musics, hip-hop culture has inspired a huge literature that is unusual for its range of authors—from academics to journalists (Nelson and Gonzales 1991, George 1992).

Rap emerged in the 1970s as an integral part of hip-hop culture—indeed, as its generative center. Yet hip-hop is hard to pin down as a subcultural form and style. That it has moved beyond its origin in African American expressive culture is inarguable; yet that origin raises a number of interesting and difficult critical questions. Rap originated in African American culture and society but is no longer confined to African American performers or audiences. Its text is dense, though its lyrics are not always its most important part. Rap may be improvised or precomposed. Its creation often relies strongly on music technology (as, for example, sampling), but not always. Male performers dominate the tradition, yet quite a number of women performers have also left fundamental marks on its development. Rap performers frequently identify themselves as social critics, but not always. Rap emerged from urban environments, but neither its performers nor its audience are confined to cities.

The culture wars of the 1980s and 1990s have frequently centered on rap, but the intensity of such debates isn't new at all. From the 1920s on, cultural anxieties over jazz had prompted an outpouring of social criticism that similarly linked race and morality to a music framed as African American. The relationship between rap—in particular gangsta rap—and social behavior is a matter of ongoing debate. Does rap incite its listeners toward violence? This question is longstanding and loaded with a kind of cultural critique that ought to, but rarely does, extend to other music. Does the most angry gangsta rap cause its listeners to consider killing policemen and women (see, for example, Ice-T's "Cop Killer," 1992)? Does country western music inspire its listeners to uphold family values or to cheat on their husbands and wives? Has *Tristan und Isolde* incited extramarital sexual activity among opera enthusiasts? Such questions may seem ridiculous, but in fact litigation against rap and heavy-metal artists has been based on precisely such reasoning (Walser 1993, 137–8; Baker 1993a; Dyson 1993, 6). That the music is perceived as threatening by certain sectors of American society is obvious; whether it need be feared is another question. Reflecting on the death of Tupac Shakur, noted cultural studies theorist Michael Eric Dyson has suggested that gangsta rap provides a kind of "redemptive vulgarity" that resists the "artificial optimism" of certain African American cultural narratives. Wondering why Shakur fell "prey to the temptation to *be* a gangster," Dyson wonders if gangsta rap "provides a useful lesson to black kids about the limits of The Real and its relation to The Represented" (1996b). In other words, gangsta rap didn't cause Shakur's violent death; rather, Shakur's own attempts to enact the violence of the ghetto, as rhetorically realized in gangsta rap, blurred The Real and The Represented all too well.

Rap as a voice of social criticism has been substantively redefined as it has moved out of African American culture and into others. Hip-hop is urban vernacular in many parts of the United States and indeed the globe, but it is by no means the only expressive form employed by urban performers. Yet Latino, Asian American, and white rappers in the United States have mostly maintained the close relationship between hip-hop performance, rhetoric, and politics (Cross 1993), and this of course has everything to do with class and the proxemics of urban space as social space. American rappers are mostly young men of color, and they *choose* hip-hop as their means of expression for real reasons, based in historical inequities and the means to speak against them.

Hip-hop culture has spread internationally and may be found in Europe, Latin America, Asia, and Africa (Toop 1991). The reasons for its transnational movement are complex, rooted in what might be viewed as the global hegemony of American popular culture but nevertheless also connected with localized resistance to social and political asymmetries. Hip-hop culture can carry with it certain markers of sartorial style (baggy jeans, baseball caps worn backwards, and so forth) and musical style (a heavy emphasis on text, a rhythmicized delivery style somewhere between singing and speaking, sampling, for example) as well as dance styles (that is, break dancing) and public art styles (graffiti). Or it may not. In Thailand, for instance, the popular music called rap is considered rebellious owing not to its violent or critical lyrics (which it rarely has) but to the oversized clothing of its performers, who are viewed as unkempt and impolite by a middle-class urban society that codes grooming and physical appearance as directly iconic of character.

Rap lyrics have attracted quite a bit of attention (Stanley 1992) but the relation of rap's "musical" elements to affective power has scarcely been examined. Robert Walser (1995) has looked closely at Public Enemy's "Fight the Power," unpacking rhythm, instrumentation, timbre, and dialogic voicing (not to mention rhetoric) to show how the piece enacts political critique *and* celebration.

Some of the most cogent critical work on rap has been written by African American scholars and social critics, such as bell hooks (1994), Houston Baker, Jr. (1993a), and Michael Eric Dyson (1993, 1996a). These writers have recognized and questioned the cultural work of rap and hip-hop culture, celebrating its critique of class and race in America while interrogating its misogynies, violence, and racisms. Baker has advocated rap as a formative site for the new black studies—that is, as an expressive form that might provide a performative, critical model for a new kind of theorized "scholarly noise" (1993a, 103).

This point represents an important development in the rapprochement between popular culture, politics, and scholarship. As the academy has refocused its energies on examining the politicized interrelationships of race, class, gender, sexuality, generation, and so forth, and their implications for understanding history and cultural production, hip-hop has been recognized as a constitutive site of American race relations (Costello and Wallace 1990). In the wake of the Los Angeles uprising in 1992, for instance, scholars have revisited Ice Cube's "Black Korea" and critiqued the song's multivalent roles as prophetic *and* as a site for Asian American refusal and empowerment (Chang 1994, Cho 1993). Houston Baker, Jr., historicizes Rodney King and rap as located in the same "expressive economies" (1993b, 48).

Tricia Rose in particular (1994a, 1994b) has looked at the intersection of technology, postindustrial labor, gender relations, and black cultural expression in rap. She notes that rap's "musical voice is achieved via the constant manipulation of high-tech equipment that will continue to have a profound effect on speech, writing, music, communication, and social relations as we approach the twenty-first century" (1994a, 185). I turn now to precisely those effects as I focus on Asian Americans in the music industry and the role of hip-hop in African American and Asian American social relations.

SETTING THE SCENE

> MA RAINEY: They don't care nothing about me. All they want is my voice. . . . As soon as they get my voice down on them recording machines, then it's just like if I'd be some whore and they roll over and put their pants on. Ain't got no use for me then.
>
> —From August Wilson's *Ma Rainey's Black Bottom*

> Our whole thinking is, if we don't do it, who else will? That's what it boils down to. If you want it done, you have to do it yourself. I'm saying the same thing I say to Asian American film makers who always complain that there just don't seem to be very good Asian American role models in film or TV: Well, you need to become a producer, in one of those positions of power where you can make those decisions.
>
> —Nelson Wong, co-founder and director of AARising Records Corp.[1]

There is a moment in August Wilson's play *Ma Rainey's Black Bottom* when several African American musicians argue among themselves whether to play the version of a song requested by the black, blues singer or by the white manager. It's Chicago, 1927; the entire play takes place in a recording studio run by a white producer. The trumpet player, Levee, says,

> Hell, the man's the one putting out the record! He's gonna put out what he wanna put out!

And the piano player Toledo answers,

As long as the colored man look to white folks to put the crown on what he say . . . as long as he looks to white folks for approval . . . then he ain't never going to find out who he is and what he's about. He's just gonna be about what white folks want him to be about. (Wilson 1981, 37)

Levee and Toledo outline an old but nonetheless complex argument. "The man"—a gendered, racialized stand-in for corporate America—will maintain complete socioeconomic control over the music industry unless American Others can opt out and achieve some measure of cultural self-determination. This, in a nutshell, is the dilemma of reinscription—becoming what the system requires you to be and acknowledging its might even by resisting. Opting out is not easily accomplished: trying to step outside the system in order to regain some kind of cultural authority is another kind of reinscription. As Peter McLaren has argued, "When people of color attack white ground rules for handling disputes, or bureaucratic procedures, or specific policies of institutionalized racism, these are necessary oppositional acts, but insufficient for bringing about structural change" because they assume the dominance of white culture (1994, 61). The postcolonial, postnationalist subject—the subject who inhabits border cultures—does not live through "an inverted Eurocentrism," but rather asserts "an identity that is anticapitalist and counterhegemonic but is also critically utopian . . . an identity that transforms the burden of knowledge into a scandal of hope" (ibid., 65–66).

The Mountain Brothers are a three-man Asian American hip-hop group based in Philadelphia. I've admired their music for some time. In this chapter, I want to create an ethnographic portrait of the group as an up-and-coming hip-hop ensemble, and I quite deliberately hope to play a part in the capitalist system that creates or denies success—that is, by writing about them, I want to give the Mountain Brothers some public airplay. As Cornel West has reminded us, race matters in America, and I speak as an Asian American scholar writing on Asian American musics, with a vested interest in seeing more Asian American performers "make it" in a system that's often stacked against their presence. In short, this chapter is about a particular hip-hop group as well as identity politics and the racialized hegemonies of the transnational music industry.

NOT THE MOUNTAIN BOYS

The Mountain Brothers came together in 1991. Chops (Scott Jung), Peril (Chris Wang), and Styles (Steve Wei) attended high school in various suburbs of Philadelphia and were brought together at Penn State University through friends and common interests. At the time of this writing (summer 1996),

Styles had just graduated from Penn State, Peril was starting his second year as a graduate student in biology at the University of Pennsylvania, and Chops had dropped out of graduate school at Michigan State University to produce the Mountain Brothers full time. All three are Chinese American. I once heard them explain the group's name in the following way. They had just performed for a small group of Asian American high school students at a community empowerment organization in Philadelphia called Asian Americans United. A young woman asked:

> Q   What does "the Mountain Brothers" mean?
>
> Peril   It comes from a Chinese legend. But we're not real familiar with the details. [*laughter*] The Mountain Brothers were a bunch of bandits that lived on a mountain. They stole from the rich and gave to the poor. Each one had special powers—there was actually one hundred and eight of them. . . . They had these powers, and we just liked that. We extended the concept. [*He gestured toward Styles.*]
>
> Styles The mountain is part of the ground, you know, but it's like taking it to a higher level. [*As he said this, he outlined a mountain with his hands, gestured upward, let it go.*] But it's still part of the ground— it's still true to the ground—it still has its roots in the ground.

One of the Brothers' pet peeves is the frequency with which they become "the Mountain Boys/Boyz" when outsiders handle their publicity. They suspect that the slip is part of an American history of infantilizing people of color, and Asians in particular. As a group, the Brothers are keenly aware of their image as Asian American men, and they try to control the ways in which this image is produced and received.

The group has been trying to break into the business for several years now. They assiduously attend industry conventions and have gone through the long process of sending out demos and getting callbacks. They have pursued protracted negotiations with several independent record companies. I believe that they represent a principled attempt to enter the mainstream music industry on their own terms. Their allegiances are to the Asian American as well as to the hip-hop community, and this bifocality lends them a special depth and texture. As one of the Brothers, Scott Jung, explained to me,

> We like to think of ourselves as hip-hoppers first—and not necessarily before we're Asian, because we're Asian no matter what we do—but especially how we're going to be marketed and stuff, as somebody who's serious about their music, trying to be as good as we can be about it, as someone who loves the music. You know, we

bring up certain issues because they're relevant to us, just like any other hip-hop artist would do, and in doing that, we have to bring up Asian American issues.[2]

Unlike some Asian American musicians, though, the Mountain Brothers have chosen not to sign with an Asian American label. The Asian American recording company AARising (for "Asian Americans Rising," discussed below) provides them with a space on its homepage, but the Mountain Brothers are openly after mainstream success and recognition. Such recognition would, in their minds, serve its own purpose, above and beyond their personal hopes: in their view, their mere presence as an Asian American group is significant in its own right. As Chris Wang, one of the Brothers, expressed it, "I think just us *being* there is a big step. I mean, we could talk about nothing, and we'd still make a big statement."[3]

Working toward "being there" has involved strategic choices. The group performs for Asian American community events with some frequency. Still, they are constantly on the lookout for opportunities to reach audiences beyond the Asian American community, believing that this will eventually lead to their getting signed. One of their bottom-line conditions for any recording company is to maintain control over their own "beats," that is, the tracks over which they rap. Scott Jung has taken music courses—theory, sightsinging and sightreading, and basic instruction in several instruments—since grade school. He has spent years creating a particular sound for the Mountain Brothers: he took courses in electronic music as an undergraduate at Penn State, and funnels the group's performance fees back into sound equipment. In fact, the increasing sophistication and accessibility of sound hardware and software gives composer-performers considerable control over their own production, and Jung is determined to maintain that control even after the group is signed. During much of 1996, the Mountain Brothers negotiated a contract with Ruffhouse/Columbia, so this issue was at the front of his mind. As he explained:

Scott Jung   One point that we made early on was that, as far as presenting ourselves, we need to have a big say, because if we don't have a big say—if not final say—it could really hurt, not just us, but other Asian groups that might come along in the future. So that's really important to us. And in terms of artistic control, they're pretty much giving it to us. . . . Some of the other labels we were talking to were suggesting we have other producers make the beats, the music, for us, for half the songs, or a certain number of songs on the album. Which [could be] good, because it [would] lend some credibility—would lend a name producer who would make the music and we'd rhyme over it, and it would help us get in quicker. But that's not something we were really particularly interested in, because we think we have our own sound. And that's one thing [this present company] agrees with, so we're happy.

Chris Wang   You look at a lot of new groups coming out—a lot of them use other producers—use them to try to get in, to try to attract more people.

Scott Jung   So they end up sounding like the other groups the producer does, a lot of times.

As an ethnomusicologist, I have inherited a century's worth of keen interest—and even keener *angst*—over recording technology. Ethnomusicology was made possible by such technologies—witness the thousands of wax-cylinder recordings of Native American and other "ethnic" musics. Who is recording whom is a matter of central importance; for whom is another. Audio technologies and the traditions that they fix on tape, vinyl, or plastic disks are often connected in problematic ways. Recording a performance can help to guarantee a tradition's continued existence, but it can also provide the means for its appropriation or expropriation.

What does an Asian American presence mean in the racial politics of the music industry? I suggest that Asian American performers and recording companies are sites of cultural as well as commercial production—indeed, I want to question the distinctions between politics, ideology, aesthetics, and the commercial, and to suggest that the very existence of Asian American sounds, produced musically and commercially by Asian Americans, offers a kind of critical pedagogy for listening. Much has been written about the power of representations in the media, yet a critique of listening practices has yet to take shape. I have not yet met an Asian American musician or producer who's interested in creating something that is aurally recognizable as an Asian American sound; rather, almost all such cultural workers are interested in the political and artistic potential of Asian Americans who could change social land- and soundscapes with their mere presence. I'd like to explore the possibility of such interventions by considering the relationship between "indie" labels, "the industry," and Asian Americans who make music.

The important historical point is that smaller peoples' musics have almost always been recorded by bigger peoples. Ethnomusicologists who went off to the pueblos with their wax cylinder recorders at the turn of the century and Mickey Hart, who goes into the rainforest with the latest DAT recorder in the 1990s, enact, reflect, maintain, and construct power differentials. I do not mean to suggest that smaller, non- or less-dominant peoples have not generated mass-mediated music industries of their own. They have and they do.[4] Multinational recording companies' interest in World

Beat, however, has created new possibilities for capitalist use of the Third World. If a history of music and imperialism is worth writing, then it's worth noting that small peoples' musics, the musics of immigrants and people of color, have been recorded and disseminated in the United States for over a century. The question is, by whom, for whom, and how? And what are those musics?

In fact, the musics of ethnic enclaves in America have often been recorded by and for their own communities. The great European immigrations of the first half of this century led to lively community-based, entrepreneurial recording industries of Yiddish musics in New York City (Slobin 1982), Polish musics in Chicago and Detroit, and so forth. These industries were similar to community-based newspapers, that is, directed inward or at most to similar ethnic communities in other cities. More recently, Asian immigrations have prompted the growth of local entertainment industries directly tied to large-scale transnational flows of goods and peoples. Cassettes and CDs of Chinese, Korean, and South Asian pop sold in your local Asian supermarket were probably produced in Hong Kong, Taiwan, Seoul, Bombay, and Calcutta. In other words, the very nature of immigrant communities and the flow of capital that sustains them has changed.[5]

Looking at the recording industry as a particular site of political struggle is an exercise in uncovering historical inequities. From the beginning—the 1890s, when the phonograph became commercially available—"the recording industry" has been dominated by a few major companies, which, in the 1990s, have become international conglomerates. Like most humanists, I regard market figures with some skepticism, but consider this: only six international "megacorporations"—BMG, MCA, Polygram, Sony, Thorn EMI, and WEA—control approximately eighty-five percent of the record market (Schreiber 1992, xiii). Nevertheless, the phenomenon of independent labels, now called "indies," has always been central to the music industry. In other words, the creative and economic tension between large-scale, corporate recording companies and smaller-scale independent companies has been part and parcel of musicians' hopes and realities for over a century.

Indies tend to come and go. They may be as small as one person and a garage recording studio, or they may grow over time and have staying power. Norman Schreiber, in his guide to indie labels (1992), outlines several characteristics of independent recording companies. As he puts it, "so much happens" first and last on indies (1992, xiv)—that is, indies often discover and record musics that only later become widely popular (as, for example, Cajun, New Orleans R&B), and often maintain historically significant musics long after their initial popularity has come and gone. Furthermore, indie labels tend to "stand for something"—they are frequently brought into existence because someone believes that a band, a genre, or a heritage should be preserved. Schreiber describes the "indie virtues" as "passion, spirit, hope, dedication, individualism, education, and respect for other cultures" (ibid., 195). In fact, indies' producers usually have a renegade attitude because the might of the multinational recording companies simply cannot be denied (ibid., xvi).

The relationship of any recording company to American peoples of color is fraught with cultural politics. It does matter who's recording whom, and how a market is conceived, defined, and targeted. The phenomenon of race records is a case in point: between 1922 and 1949, records of African American musics (jazz, blues, and so forth) were generically referred to as "race music" by the industry, and were an attempt to tap the African American market (Oliver 1984, 8; Eastman 1989, 30). Only later, as the possibility of a so-called crossover market into white audiences became evident, were other names coined for African American popular musics. Since American popular music basically is African American music, these histories provide a very interesting window on the racial politics of the American recording industry.

I am concerned with the intersection of factors that may seem unrelated but are in fact intimately connected. When aesthetics, racialized bodies, and ideas of capitalist profit are brought into close configuration, you get the twentieth-century recording industry. Though the deceptively transcendent language of modernist aesthetics suggests that matters of artistic quality are somehow divorced from the messiness of the marketplace and the shove and push of racial politics, the global flow of capital and the language of aesthetic quality come from older discourses of imperialism and colonialism that established the political vocabularies of us/Other, here/Elsewhere. It is no coincidence that musical sounds have become part of the transnational movement of capital, that is, that the dominant recording companies are international conglomerates based in particular parts of the First World. Nor is it coincidence that these spatial and racial geographies are reproduced within the confines of the United States.

ASIAN AMERICANS RECORDING AND GETTING RECORDED

Asian Americans have never had a significant place in the American recording industry as either performers, producers, or a market. Whites, African Americans, and Latino/as have long been targeted by recording companies as markets for particular kinds of music; Asian Americans, however, have been nearly absent from these socioeconomic geographies. Between 1902 and 1937, several recording companies recorded Chinese, Japanese, and South Asian musicians in New York City, San Francisco, Hollywood, and Camden, New Jersey (Spottswood 1990, vol. 5:2535–52). Most, if not all, of these records were intended for the Asian or Asian American market: most were of traditional ensembles, though a few featured intercultural performances— for example, a Chinese tenor singing hymns in Mandarin (ibid., 2537) and two Japanese American sopranos singing Verdi, Stephen Foster, and Schubert in Japanese (ibid., 2547–48). For the first half of the twentieth century, no documentation exists for any Asian American recording companies.

Since 1987, at least three recording companies that are owned and managed by Asian Americans and that largely feature Asian American musicians have appeared in the Bay Area. Asian Improv, a nonprofit label, was founded in 1987; AARising and Classified Records, both commercial, were founded in 1990 and 1993. These three companies represent different purposes, different ambitions, different audiences, and different conceptions of Asian American music.

Like many indies, Asian Improv had several predecessors. The group of Bay Area jazz musicians who collaborate on Asian Improv met in the late 1970s, brought together through jazz and the Asian American movement. Mark Izu, Jon Jang, Anthony Brown, and Francis Wong formed the group United Front and began to record in the early 1980s on their own label, RPM, putting out the album *Are You Chinese or Charlie Chan?* among others.

By 1987, United Front and RPM were moribund. As Francis Wong said:

> We were sitting around in Jon's living room . . . and he said why don't we have a label so we can have some identification out there in the industry or in the field? So Jon came up with the term *Asian Improv,* and I think that pretty much says what we're about, trying to bring the African American tradition of improvised music and jazz together with our Asian roots. (Jang, Newton, Zhang, et al., 4)

Wong further notes that "RPM was not functioning anymore, so there was almost no choice. We didn't have a longterm plan; [Asian Improv] was mainly seen as a vehicle to promote Asian American creative music and document our compositions" (Yanow 1994, 31). Nine years later, Asian Improv aRts is now a nonprofit arts organization, supporting a newsletter, symposia, performances, and the recording label Asian Improv. As their mission statement expresses it, Asian Improv

> was formed . . . to work for cultural empowerment, self-respect and artistic excellence. This is achieved through creating, recording, and presenting adventurous, cross-cultural work of Asian American creative musicians; producing art that is born out of the Asian American experience; and bridging artists and community.

To date, they have put out twenty-five albums featuring over twelve musicians, mostly Asian American. Asian Improv's style might be called new music with a strong base in African American jazz; the musicians themselves shy away from categorization, preferring to simply call it "creative music."

Figure 12.1. Album cover: *Never Give Up!*
Jon Jang and the Pan Asian Arkestra (1989)
(Asian Improv, AIR 0007).

For all the Asian American musicians closely associated with Asian Improv, the corporation has served as a safe place from which to make music as Asian Americans, but it may not be the only place in which they choose to record. Asian Improv's distribution is limited: finding their albums outside the Bay Area is difficult. While the label provides a principled Asian American place in the industry, professional success beyond Asian American

Figure 12.2. Album cover: *Self Defense! Jon Jang & the Pan-Asian Arkestra* (1992) (Soul Note 121203-1, 121203-2).

Figure 12.3. Album cover:
*Glenn Horiuchi: Oxnard
Beet* (1992) (Soul Note
121228-1, 121228-2).

audiences may require recording elsewhere. Jon Jang, for instance, issued his
cassette album *Never Give Up!* (1989, see Fig. 12.1) on Asian Improv but has
since ventured out to Soul Note, a major jazz label, and most lately has a
commission from the Kronos Quartet. Jang released three early albums on
Asian Improv but released *Self Defense!* (1992, see Fig. 12.2) and *Tiananmen!*
(1993) on Soul Note. Similarly, Glenn Horiuchi has released seven albums on
Asian Improv and one on Soul Note. He told me that a number of consider-
ations go into such decisions: he put out his first three albums on Asian
Improv after Soul Note rejected them (including *Oxnard Beet,* see Fig. 12.3),
but he has subsequently chosen to release two other albums on Asian Improv
because Soul Note may take up to three years to get a CD onto the market
and will not release more than one of his albums per year. On the other hand,
their advance pay and their distribution are "much better" than Asian
Improv's.[6]

AARising—that is, Asian Americans Rising—is self-consciously different from Asian Improv. Formed in 1990 by two Asian American DJs, Nelson
Wong and Andy Kawanami, AARising is everything that Asian Improv is not:
commercial and explicitly focused on popular musics. I asked Nelson Wong
how he would compare AARising to Asian Improv, and he said:

> [We at AARising] are trying to sell our stuff to as many people as
> we can, because that's the way we make money. [At Asian Improv],
> they're doing it more for an artistic, political sort of means. And
> they're using Asian Improv as a vehicle to promote their beliefs,

their art. Which is different from what we're doing—at least, we're not doing it as overtly as they are. Ours is a little more subtle. Neither is right or wrong—it's just a different approach. Like I said, I've talked with Jon about this many times. We just have a different way of doing things. We're on friendly terms. We both have similar goals, as far as the end goal, which is to get more visibility for Asian Americans in art, in music—but the approaches are different. . . . And they have a different target market, anyway.[7]

Moreover, AARising is self-consciously eclectic and solicits Asian American performers' and composers' work; their "concept" is simply that of Asian Americans performing popular music—of nearly any sort. Their target market is, first, "everyone," then Asian Americans, and especially young women between the ages of twelve and twenty-nine, who—studies have shown—represent 60 percent of the album-buying market.

AARising's webpage (Fig. 12.4) reveals something less obvious about the company, though: although it features links to five groups on its primary page, only one is actually signed to them. The others—such as the 18 Mighty Mountain Warriors, the Mountain Brothers—have no professional connection to the company but are Asian American performance groups who are

Welcome person from SMITHMARG.SAS.UPENN.EDU
using Mozilla/1.1N (Windows; I; 16bit).
It's now Thursday May 16th, 1996 at 3:18PM PDT

FLASH: Alana Dung, a 23 month little girl, is in desperate need of a bone marrow transplant. Find out more info by checking out a web site set up for her at: http://www.hula.net/~idc/alana.html

MAY is Asian Pacific American Heritage Month!

NEWS: Look for a radio interview about Asians in Urban Contemporary music on KALX 90.7 on Monday, May 20th from 7pm to 7:30pm. The show is called AAirtime

click on any of the selections in this menu

AARISING RECORDS   MOUNTAIN BROTHERS   18 MIGHTY MOUNTAIN WARRIORS

TANGOVISION   TWO NEW DOGS   ASIAN AM LINKS

ONE VISION

OTHER LINKS   JOIN MAILING LIST

FEATURED ARTIST OF THE MONTH

or you can make your selection by clicking on these as well
AArising Records | One Vision | TangoVision Productions
Two New Dogs | 18 Mighty Mountain Warriors | Mountain Brothers
Cindy Mestre | in-cite
Asian American Links | Other Links | Join Mailing List
Featured Artist of the Month

Figure 12.4. AARising homepage, http://www.aarising.com (from the World Wide Web).

admired by Wong and Kawanami. In conversation, Nelson Wong makes it clear that he is as much in the business of promoting Asian American performers in general as he is in signing them to his own label. At the moment, AARising only has one group signed, One Vision, an Asian American pop group whose first single came out in 1996.

Nelson Wong freely acknowledged that AARising's main competitor is not Asian Improv but rather a third label called Classified Records. Classified Records was formed in 1993 by Kormann Roque, a Filipino American Bay Area DJ and songwriter whose first experiences in the industry included seeing a song he'd written hit the Top 40 after he had lost the rights to it.[8] He decided to get smart and to form his own company, and Classified has just reached the point where three staff members run the office by day while Roque and his partner hold down other full-time jobs. Classified has one of the snazziest web sites around (Fig. 12.5), not least because the label already has twelve groups signed. Most but not all of its groups are Filipino American. Their up-and-coming group is the Pinay Divas, four Filipina

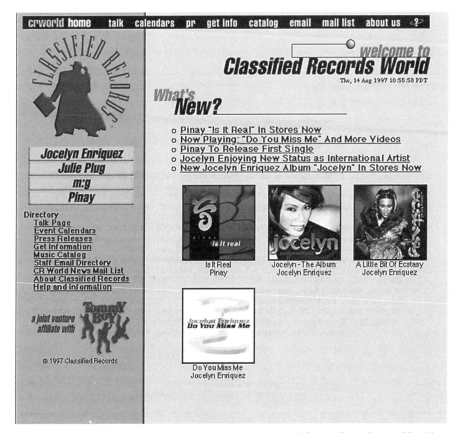

Figure 12.5. Classified Records' artists page, http://www.crworld.com (from the World Wide Web).

Americans whose *a capella* numbers in English and Tagalog have attracted much attention in the Bay Area.

Classified Records' major artist is Jocelyne Enriquez, formerly of the Pinay Divas but now a solo artist. Her first full-length album, *Lovely,* was released last year, and her second will come out in a few months. When she first began to attract attention, some fans assumed she was Latina, and neither she nor Classified initially did anything to suggest otherwise; several musicians have told me that some Latino listeners were then distressed when Enriquez was "outed" as a Filipina. The Classified Records website now includes the statement that "Jocelyne Enriquez is 100% Filipina, is proud of it, and has never claimed otherwise." The politics of ethnic "passing" in the California music scene are complex, to say the least, but all this suggests that Enriquez sounds neither Filipina nor Asian American, and indeed, Classified Records has no interest in developing anything that might be called an Asian American sound. Most of Enriquez's album *Lovely* is straight-ahead dance music, not unlike early Madonna but with occasional brief breaks into Latin riffs and scratching.

Kormann Roque is careful not to characterize his label as Filipino American or Asian American. He insists that they are only after "talent and

---

classified shouts and links   http://www.crworld.com/sh...

our favorite links

classified records
gives loud
shouts to...

AIM 2 PLEEZ, DJ MK2, DJ K-Lau, BIG-O PRODUCTIONS, SOUNDS SO SWEET, ULTIMATE SENSATIONS, LADDA SOUNDS, CREATIVE MADNESS, SYNCHRONIZED SOUNDZ, MISTYK VIBRATION, DJ Bo, P.H.P PRODUCTIONS, UNLIMITED BEATS, ENCORE, SPINTRONIX, RHYTHM IN MOTION, MOBILE WEST, PURE ENERGY, S.B.C., BEAT 2 IMPRESS, 3 STYLE ATTRACTIONS, GENERATIONS, CHUCKLES & CO., AARISING RECORDS, EXPRESSIONS, YOLK MAGAZINE, FILIPINAS MAGAZINE, FREESTYLE FOCUS MAGAZINE, Alvin Caampued, Eric Fructuoso, Alliance Entertainment, Flip Side Entertainment, John Francisco, Strawberry, Jake Da Snake, DJ Jazzy Jim, DJ Mein, Stormin' Norman Poon, Jose Melendez, DJ Backtraxx, DJ Boywonder, Q-Bert, Prince SF, Antonio Guiterrez, J.J Mansalay, Davey D's Hip-Hop Corner, Chuy Gomez, Hugo Gomez, CMC, PASA, AKBAYAN, PACE, BARKADA, MAGKAISA, MGA KAPATID, FASA (Ohlone), PARA SA 'YO, PAA, PACA, PASU, PUSO, SAMAHANG PILIPINO, Jothan Frakes, Chris Campos, Shortkut, D-Styles, Alex Mejia, Glenn Aure, Franzen, Dave Meyer, Edwin Bautista, Latin Prince, Rich Laxamana, Majestchris, Merrill Brodit, DJ Vicious "V", Razor Rob, Slammin' Sam Maxion, Quickmix, Arturo Garces, DJ Ajax, DJ Stevie K, Closed Caption, Eros, Billy Vidal, Prece Hill, Owens Hoady, Ed at Tower Records, Raul at Upstairs, Elvis & JV, The Pro's, BADDA Record Pool, Rico Casanova, SOMA, Richard G., Planet X, "Bad Boy" Jess, Rich Pangalinan

Copyright © 1996 Classified Records, a division of MQ Productions, Inc.

Figure 12.6. Classified Records' "Loud Shouts" page, http://www.crworld.com/shouts.html (from the World Wide Web).

good music, of any sort," and he readily asserts that his goal is for one of their artists to break into the Top 40.[9] Whereas Asian Improv and AARising identify themselves as Asian American, with explicit ideological links to the Asian American movement and activism, Classified Records downplays ethnicity and has no explicit stake in identity politics. When I asked Roque why most of his artists and nearly his entire staff are Filipino American, he explained that he wants to support "Asians" in the industry and to get them out into "the mainstream," so he emphasizes his artists' talents rather than their ethnicities. Several other Asian American producers I've spoken with have expressed some resentment over Classified Records' coyness around its Asian American character; one even suggested that he thinks the label's management has played up ethnicity—which it has—simply to reach a potential market. Self-identifying as Asian American and expressly connecting oneself to the Asian American movement are two different matters, however, and there is quite a bit of room for how ethnicity is displayed electronically, that is, on the Web. At the time of this writing, Classified Records' "Loud Shouts" page (Fig. 12.6) provided a long list of "our favorite links," with hotlinks to more than forty musicians and a few Asian American resources, including *Yolk Magazine* and AARising Records. In other words, there are a number of choices for presenting oneself—openly or subtly or both—as Asian American in the music industry.

BREAKING INTO THE "BIZ"

Most Asian American performers are keenly interested in having their work recorded and commercially distributed. Some also think about their ethnicity and its impact on how they are heard or packaged. Commercial success and control over one's own image do not necessarily go hand in hand; getting ahead in the industry usually requires considerable resourcefulness—but especially for musicians of color and most particularly for Asian American musicians, whose niche in the music industry is largely undefined or even unconsidered.

Unlike Asian Improv and AARising, the Mountain Brothers have sometimes aimed for explicitly mainstream networks for advertising, and in April 1996 they had a big break: they won a national competition for a Sprite commercial. Working out of Jung's home studio, they produced a spot that won first the regional and then the national contest. They were flown out to Los Angeles to receive the prize at the SoulTrain music awards ceremony. Three versions of the spot (30, 40, and 60 seconds) were broadcast nationally on urban radio stations during 1996 and 1997. Here's the text of the sixty-second version (Track 25).

Chops:

> Sippin a Sprite, ya know it's me, flippin the tight poetry,
> upon the mic, obey ya thirst and come check the flavor

Verse One:

> Mountain Brothers gonna need another one-liter
> because we're done with the first.
> image is nothin but bluffin in the city of brotherly love
> we're takin charge right from the west side

Peril:

> yes i'd like a large Sprite with extra ice it might affect my life yo
> this beverage gives leverage, see i'm the man next to mice
> check the cipher up the street, ock, kids rhymin over beatbox,
> time to show my stee rocks the crowd, the texture's nice
> cool & bubbly, gulpin Sprite, i'm provin lovely,
>   spoken bright poetics
> at ease knowin one day, we'll be chokin mics for grands.

Styles:

> it's mad hot my man chops got a jam up at his spot
> he said to drop by and since it's sticky it'd be nice
> to pack a six of Sprite if it's alright, no problem,
> got em in my fridgerator, then later tear the tab
> and engineer the thirst cure
> waitin for the subway train i say hey, talking to a lovely jawn
> sharin Sprites on the platform . . .
> arrivin late at this fellas house, mellow taste in my mouth,
> Chops & Peril give out pounds
> Mountain Brothers downin Sprites all around

This brief moment of hip-hop encapsulates many salient issues around Asian America, the recording industry, and strategies for participation in cultural production. Having decided to feature the Mountain Brothers in this essay, I was torn between focusing on the Sprite ad and discussing any of their longer concert works, which might be seen as free from the tight grip of the corporate world. But the notion of utter creative freedom, exempt from the constraints of a market, is a romantic notion sustained by the objectified values of Western art ideologies; I suggest instead that the relationship between creativity and the market is dynamic and open to manipulations and interventions. Such issues crystallize in the Mountain Brothers' Sprite ad. While I will focus my interpretive energies on these sixty seconds, I urge you to seek out the Mountain Brothers' other work (especially their first album, scheduled for release in 1997).

The advertisement heard over the airwaves was produced not in an industry studio but in a West Philadelphia basement. Scott Jung has single-handedly produced all the Mountain Brothers' demos to date in his home studio. Such studios, usually crammed into a corner of a musician's living room or basement, are important sites of cultural production—simultaneously local but hoping for more, commercial but shaped by a shrewd sense of identity politics. Identity politics are not the special purview of ethnic Americans, of course, but it does matter who's speaking to whom in a postindustrial context like this. In this way, distinctions between literal production (getting particular sounds onto audiotape) and cultural production (making culture, enacting or disrupting ideologies) are less than clear. Consider the startlingly simple movement from basement to national airwaves: that the sounds of this hip-hop site could bridge such disparate levels of production points to what might be called the democratizing aspects of certain technologies. Jung's studio reflects increasingly affordable sound equipment as well as a great deal of resourcefulness. He had his first experiences in a sound studio while in high school, in a professional recording facility, sponsored by an internship program; he later took an introductory electronic music class at Pennsylvania State University. In 1996, his studio contained a digital sampler, a MIDI keyboard, an ancient synthesizer, a double-deck cassette tapedeck, a DAT recorder, a four-track tape recorder; a synch box; a sound module with reverb, delay, compressor, equalizer, and so forth; a mixer; a patch bank; two microphones with homemade pop filters constructed of pantyhose and coathanger wire (to soften explosive consonants); two studio monitor speakers; and two DJ turntables for practicing scratching (Fig. 12.7). Some of the Mountain Brothers' concert proceeds are consistently funnelled into new equipment, as technology is central to hip-hop.

The Sprite ad used four tracks and took the Mountain Brothers six or seven hours to produce, from start to finish. Their compositional process is collaborative yet highlights each individual's personal style. When I asked Chops about the process of creating the Sprite spots, he wrote:

> we write separately, usually. [but] we did that in one day, together. yeah. as soon as we heard the ad on the radio about the contest, i was already writing ideas down (i'm sure steve and chris were too)[10]

Figure 12.8. Photograph of Scott Jung (a.k.a. Chops) in his basement studio (Deborah Wong).

No one member is ever more prominently featured in the Brothers' pieces; instead, the three take turns and each writes his own poetry, though they may make revisions during the recording process, in response to one another. Chops explained that recording the Sprite entry went like this:

> laying down the vocals took maybe an hour or so, max. we generally can record pretty quick these days, since we're used to the recording process. we each laid one track, and then each of us laid a background track for one of the others' vocals. this was all on an old-ass 4-track machine (we have 8 track digital now, thanks to a loan from a good friend).
>
> then doing things like dropping the beat out at certain points, dropping the bass out, around the vocals took me another hour or 2.
>
> mixing down, adding reverb and eq, etc. took me another few hours.
>
> considering the equipment we had, it sounds pretty good. i wish we could have done a little more sound-wise though. over the radio, it's good enough. can't wait until we have some better studio gear though.

The lyrics for the Sprite ad reflect a canny sense for advertising necessities interspersed with references to Philadelphia and hip-hop braggadocio of the best sort. Later, I asked the Brothers to explain the lyrics to me, and although they graciously offered the elaborations provided below, they were a bit reluctant to have their explanations appear here. As Chops noted,

> the slang one uses is something picked up (or made up, if you're creative) over time, and not something to really give away at the drop of a hat. in a way, explaining the meaning of a slang term can deaden [its] impact.[11]

I must emphasize that I include here the Brothers' explanations of their lyrics not to drain them of meaning or deaden their originality but rather to unpack that originality for those not as immersed in hip-hop culture and aesthetics. In "understanding" the Sprite lyrics, it is also important to realize that the power of these poetics lies in their ownership and their placement in particular performers' creative arsenals.

Chops opens by, well, "sippin a Sprite," but then immediately moves into the reflexive oratory of hip-hop, referring to himself, to the well-knit quality of his verse, and to the microphone—the technologically and socially empowering vehicle of the rap artist—before circling back to the soft drink. As he explained to me, *flippin* is "execution with flair," and *tight poetry* is "well-constructed, seamless, gapless." His next phrase, too, adroitly combines advertising with a classic African American performative: he "places" himself as a performer by declaring that it's the Mountain Brothers who will "need another one-liter," that is, he inserts a signature into the spot virtually at the outset. Chops provided this exegesis of the phrase *"image is nothin but bluffin"*:

> sprite's catchphrases are "obey your thirst" and "image is nothing"
> so i used the phrases they had, and extended it some.
> to basically just say, around here, image is just a bluff, exterior nonsense, whereas we get to the heart of the matter.

"The city of brotherly love" is of course Philadelphia, but he's specifically referring to "the west side," a predominantly African American part of the city where Chops and Peril both live.

Peril too gets Sprite in at the beginning of his verse and invests it with power, using it to point to his own skill and ability. As he explained to me,

> in the line "this beverage gives leverage" i was saying that drinking sprite gives me an edge over other mc's.
> "i'm the man next to mice" refers to that book "of mice and men" (which i've never actually read). basically, it means i'm a man (or i'm THE MAN) and you're just a tiny little mouse.[12]

Having established his skill, he moves back to the street (the symbolic landscape of hip-hop), where he encounters a *cipher*. As Peril explained,

> a "cipher" is a group of mc's (usually standing in a circle, on the
> street) rhyming. either freestyles or written rhymes. and the
> rhymes may be done a capella, with someone beat-boxing, or over
> an instrumental track. one person starts it off and the next person
> jumps in whenever he/she feels the urge. usually a certain order is
> maintained in the cipher (but not necessarily clockwise or counter-
> clockwise), and if someone rhymes out of turn, he/she is said to be
> "f*ckin' up the cipher." but order of rhyming is not always strictly
> enforced. often times people just jump in and out whenever they
> feel. . . . they usually attract large crowds on the street.

Again, the reflexivity of embedding a description of a performance into the
body of a performed text is classic rap rhetoric. Peril explained that "'ock' is
a slang word referring to any individual; e.g. 'what's up, ock?'" Note his reference to *kids rhymin over beatbox:* hip-hoppers refer constantly to the technologies employed in their compositional process, for example, beatboxes
and mics, but in this case "beatbox" means rhyming out loud over a human
beatbox, or mouth percussion accompaniment—a performative history that
reabsorbs the acoustic percussion/electronic beatbox process back into oral
performance. *Stee* is short for *stee-lo,* a slang word for "style." Peril decides it's
time, in the street narrative he's established, to join the cipher and to show
his stuff. Indeed, *the texture's nice,* but does he mean his poetry or the Sprite?
The two are elided. The ease of his poetry too shifts seamlessly into his own
confidence that *one day* the Mountain Brothers *will be chokin mics for
grands*—that their commercial success is assured. This clever reference to the
industry, to the group's aspirations, and to their unquestioned skill closes his
verse.

In the third and final verse, Styles continues to join references to
Philadelphia, the urban landscape, the Mountain Brothers, and Sprite in slip-
pery metaphorical ways. As Chops noted later,

> unlike chops's and peril's, styles's verse is in narrative story form,
> starting from his place and ending at chops's.[13]

The scene shifts to Chops's apartment, where a *jam,* a music session of some
sort, is taking place; Sprite of course helps out. Sharing Sprites with the
Mountain Brothers shifts to Styles sharing a Sprite with a young woman, a
jawn, on a Philadelphia subway platform. Not only the subway but *jawn*
localizes the scene:

> jawn means woman or girl . . . as a term it doesn't have any impli-
> cations about the type of woman it refers to . . . however, the same
> word is used to mean "thing" (like "could you hand me that jawn
> over there?") in other cities (and philly as well) . . . maybe you could
> read something into the creation of the word from that (i.e. thing
> = woman) but it's not intentional. the word jawn is mostly used in
> the philly area and a little in new york (the use of jawn to mean girl
> however is exclusively a philly thing).[14]

His verse and the spot end with the Mountain Brothers greeting each other
by *giving out pounds*—like shaking hands only striking right fists together—
and, naturally, drinking Sprites.

Textually, this brief moment of hip-hop establishes the Mountain
Brothers as adept in any number of ways—as orators, as street smart, as
objects of admiration by other hip-hoppers. At another level, the Brothers are
proud of their craftsmanship, noting that

> just for your own fun info purposes, notice that unlike many rap-
> pers, we often have polysyllabic rhymes, for instance "rhymin over
> beatbox" and "time to show my stee rocks" in peril's verse makes a
> pair of 6-syllable strings that rhyme with each other. we think this
> is pretty cool too, but . . . anyway it's more cool for listeners to fig-
> ure that out on their own.[15]

Their collaborative composition created another kind of authenticity,
too. When the Mountain Brothers mailed their cassette and press kit to Sprite
for the contest, none of their materials referred to their Asian American identities: no photographs were included, and they referred to themselves only by
their hip-hop names. Unlike some of their other raps, the Sprite spot contains no textual references to their Asian American identities. In short, they
passed as *African* American hip-hoppers, and this careful presentation of self
was a matter of strategy. The Mountain Brothers have learned that they are
most quickly accepted by the hip-hop community if their music precedes any
knowledge of their ethnicity. In other words, they have found that listeners
hear them differently depending on whether they're already known to be
Asian American. Moreover, they have found repeatedly that listeners who
know that they are Asian American beforehand take them much less seriously than when given no racial clues at all, so the Mountain Brothers have
become more and more careful to control listeners' initial reception to their
sound. After reading a draft of this paragraph, the Brothers noted that

> we avoid initially making explicit references to ethnicity so that we
> can be given a fair unbiased listen based on the merits of our music,

lyrics and style, as opposed to avoiding making explicit references
to ethnicity so that we can pass for black.[16]

Over the past few years, they have created two separate sets of promotional
material, one directed toward Asian American audiences that includes explicit references to their ethnicity and another in which their Asianness is
methodically concealed.

Sprite is owned by the Coca-Cola Company. The Sprite contest was
developed and executed by Burrell Communications Group, one of the oldest and largest African American–owned advertising agencies in the United
States, which has overseen the Coca-Cola Company's advertisements for the
African American consumer market since 1973. When the Mountain
Brothers won first place in the contest, Coca-Cola's and Burrell's executives
did not realize that the group was not African American. William Colvard,
the Burrell account executive in charge of the Coca-Cola business, openly
acknowledged that the Brothers' Asian American identity came as a complete
surprise. I asked him if this was a problem or an issue at any point, since, after
all, Burrell Communications Group is in the business of marketing Coca-
Cola products to African Americans. Colvard said,

> Not at all. Coca-Cola's goal was to reach urban teens, and the
> Mountain Brothers are part of that audience. The music was real.
> It was authentic, the best—it was good hip-hop.[17]

Authenticity is a curious measuring rod in American hip-hop, based but not
based in constructions of racial, ethnic, and bodily experience (Wong 1998),
and its merciless standards may as easily condemn as approve. The Mountain
Brothers passed that ultimate test, but they "passed"—in at least two ways—
because they knew the rules of hip-hop authenticity and were savvy enough
to abide by them—on their own terms.

This meeting of the local and the transnational in music production is
no longer unusual. I am not suggesting that the Mountain Brothers have sold
out. Rather, I think that they have adroitly, wisely, and cleverly used all the
means at their disposal to create a space for themselves in the industry. That
particular space may be talked about in a number of different ways. It is a
performative alliance with African American expressive culture—rather than
American popular culture more generally—that hearkens back to other
Asian American musicians participating in African American expressive
forms, and indeed to the birth of the Asian American movement as an
expression of coalition as well as specifically Asian American empowerment.
This is a social space that is racialized in particular ways: as Chris Wang said,
it is Asian American because *they* are. Yet, of course it is—and is not—that
simple. This aural space is defined by Asian American voices making musical

sounds that they are careful to claim as their own, through performance. When the Mountain Brothers urge us to drink Sprite, they become part of the global image factory—that is, they could be seen as coopted—but on the other hand, they are quite openly using it as a step up, as a way to get into the industry, where they will surely rap about far more than Sprite. They are determined both to become part of that bigger system—to reap its rewards— and to remain who they are.

THE RECORDING INDUSTRY, "THE MAINSTREAM," AND LEAKY DIKES

The three companies that I've described, and the Mountain Brothers as an Asian American performance group, have participated in the hegemonies of "the industry" yet, at different junctures, have withdrawn from and resisted it too. What is "the industry"? Or rather, what does it represent for different Asian American performer-producers? How is it imagined, and how is it both used and resisted? "The industry" and "the mainstream" delimit a phantasmatic late capitalist framework that effectively defines and maintains an Elsewhere much as race records did during the first half of this century. It is the marked category against which—through which—Asian American indies and performers define themselves, in much the same way that Asian Americans in general necessarily see themselves as outside the mainstream, even as they aspire to become part of it since success very clearly lies within, not outside, that social geography.

The popular musics created and disseminated by the performers and companies that have been described are at once sites of Asian American empowerment and an interface with cultural technologies located outside Asian American communities. Asian Americans claim rights to particular sounds and technologies through different strategies. I suggest that cultural (re)production, as channeled through music, creates a complex landscape of hearing and speaking—in other words, Asian American musics empower in many ways, not least through the painstaking, mundane creation of explicitly Asian American niches in the late-industrial realities of a transnational music industry. Speaking, listening, consuming, and producing may not be disparate processes; audiences and performers may have overlapping roles in creating new ways of listening and new ways of becoming entitled to hear— not to mention new ways of consuming products that are shaped to varying degrees by identity politics.

How do these cultural workers deal with the slippage between community and mainstream, and commercial success as assimilation? These producer-performers are manipulating the capitalist framework of the mass media in ways that are both mindful and conflicted. Asian Improv has deliberately placed itself outside that framework by becoming a nonprofit organization. AARising aspires to succeed within that framework. Classified Records has perhaps relocated itself as Asian American rather than Filipino American in an attempt to cash in on what they see as an emergent market. The Mountain Brothers try to penetrate the mainstream while maintaining control over their own production from the fiercely local site of their West Philadelphia basement studio.

Every year, the NAACP Image Awards are broadcast on television, honoring positive portrayals of African Americans in television, film, literature, and the recording industry. Lurking behind this annual event is the question of control—the straightforward proposal that more African American producers, directors, writers, and composers are likely to make a difference in the free play of ethnic representation in the media. The Quincy Joneses, Bill Cosbys, Nelson Wongs, and Mark Izus of the world no doubt make a difference, though this is not to say that the problems of reinscription do not lurk under every rock, or perhaps I should say in every inch of celluloid and in every laser track. Cultural theorist John Fiske tells us that a culture of power is a culture of representation (1993, 147). Asian American efforts to reclaim self-representation are necessarily projects of reflexive self-empowerment. Asian Americans in the music biz are thus insurgents of a very special sort, walking a line between capitalist assimilation and the creation of new cultural industries that will allow for different ways of listening.

ACKNOWLEDGMENTS

I am grateful for suggestions from Casey Man Kong Lum, Cynthia Po-Man Wong, and John KuoWei Tchen. Nelson Wong and Kormann Roque were generous with their time and thoughts. All the members of Asian Improv, and especially Francis Wong and Mark Izu, have gone out of their way to answer my questions and to include me in their events. Finally, the Mountain Brothers have been exemplary subjects, patiently sharing their work and their hopes and helping me to incorporate their responses into this essay.

NOTES

1. From a telephone interview, 29 April 1996.
2. From an interview with Scott Jung and Chris Wang in Philadelphia, 29 February 1996.
3. Ibid.
4. The major Third World music recording industries have been based on cassette technology, which carries with it the democratizing possibility of allowing consumers to be producers as well: cassette recording technology can be part of the same equipment that plays sound back, and this simple fact points to the tremendous proletarian potential of cassettes, which essentially took over the Third World in the 1970s (Manuel 1993, 21–35; Wallis and Malm 1984, 5–7). Other recording technologies have also been described as democratizing; Daniel

J. Boorstin, for example, writes that "The phonograph asserted itself in American life largely because it was a democratic instrument. It was a machine which not only repeated experience but democratized it. . . . [W]ithin a decade or two it was one of the primary resources for reaching everybody with music." (American Folklife Center 1982, xii). Thus any technology begs the question of how and why it reaches particular groups, communities, and nations— or does not.

5. The important exception, soon to change, is the communities of Vietnamese, Cambodians, Lao, and Hmong in the United States, who have had to generate their own mass media for over twenty years. The Vietnamese American music and film industry in Southern California has been especially lively (Wong 1994); it will be interesting to see if the lifting of trade sanctions between Vietnam and the United States will be the death knell of the Vietnamese American entertainment industry.

6. From an e-mail conversation, 20 May 1996.

7. From a telephone interview, 29 April 1996.

8. From a telephone interview, 22 May 1996.

9. From a telephone interview, 22 May 1996.

10. All of Chops's textual explanations are from two e-mail notes sent on September 5, 1996.

11. From an e-mail note sent by all three of the Mountain Brothers, 11 September 1996.

12. All of Peril's textual explanations are from an e-mail note sent on September 4, 1996.

13. From an e-mail note sent on 11 September 1996.

14. All of Styles's textual explanations are from an e-mail note sent on September 4, 1996.

15. From an e-mail note sent by all three of the Mountain Brothers on September 11, 1996.

16. From an e-mail note sent by all three of the Mountain Brothers on September 11, 1996.

17. From a telephone conversation with William Colvard on September 2, 1996.

REFERENCES CITED

American Folklife Center. 1982. *Ethnic Recordings in America: A Neglected Heritage.* Washington, D.C.: American Folklife Center, Library of Congress.

Asai, Susan. 1995. Transformations of Tradition: Three Generations of Japanese American Music Making. *Musical Quarterly* 79, no. 3: 429–53.

Baker, Houston. 1993a. *Black Studies, Rap, and the Academy.* Chicago and London: University of Chicago Press.

Baker, Houston. 1993b. Scene . . . Not Heard. In *Reading Rodney King, Reading Urban Uprising,* edited by Robert Gooding-Williams, 38–48. New York and London: Routledge.

Chang, Jeff. 1994. Race, Class, Conflict, and Empowerment: On Ice Cube's "Black Korea." In *Los Angeles—Struggles toward Multiethnic Community: Asian American, African American, and Latino Perspectives,* edited by Edward T. Chang and Russell C. Leong, 87–107. Seattle and London: University of Washington Press.

Cho, Sumi K. 1993. Korean Americans vs. African Americans: Conflict and Construction. In *Reading Rodney King, Reading Urban Uprising,* edited by Robert Gooding-Williams, 196–211. New York and London: Routledge.

Cohen, Norm and Paul Wells. 1982. Recorded Ethnic Music: A Guide to Resources. In *Ethnic Recordings in America: A Neglected Heritage,* 175–250. Washington, D.C.: American Folklife Center, Library of Congress.

Costello, Mark and David Foster Wallace. 1990. *Signifying Rappers: Rap and Race in the Urban Present.* New York: Ecco Press.

Cross, Brian. 1993. *It's Not About a Salary . . . Rap, Race and Resistance in Los Angeles.* London, New York: Verso.

Dyson, Michael Eric. 1993. The Culture of Hip-hop. Rap Music and Black Culture: An Interview. In *Reflecting Black: African American Cultural Criticism.* Minneapolis and London: University of Minnesota Press.

———. 1996a. *Between God and Gangsta Rap: Bearing Witness to Black Culture.* New York: Oxford University Press.

———. 1996b. Tupac: Living the Life He Rapped About in Song. *Los Angeles Times,* 22 September.

Eastman, Ralph. 1989. Central Avenue Blues: The Making of Los Angeles Rhythm and Blues, 1942–1947. *Black Music Research Journal* 9, no. 1: 19–33.

Fiske, John. 1993. *Power Plays, Power Works.* London, New York: Verso.

George, Nelson. 1992. *Buppies, B-Boys, Baps and Bohos: Notes on Post-Soul Black Culture.* New York: HarperCollins Publishers.

Gronow, Pekka. 1981a. The Record Industry Comes to the Orient. *Ethnomusicology* 25, no. 2: 251–84.

———. 1981b. *Statistics in the Field of Sound Recordings.* Paris: Unesco.

Hisama, Ellie. 1993. Postcolonialism on the Make: The Music of John Mellencamp, David Bowie and John Zorn. *Popular Music* 12, no. 2: 91–104.

hooks, bell. 1994. Gangsta Culture—Sexism and Misogyny: Who Will Take the Rap? Ice Cube Culture: A Shared Passion for Telling the Truth. In *Outlaw Culture: Resisting Representations.* New York and London: Routledge.

Jameson, Fredric. 1991. *Postmodernism or the Cultural Logic of Late Capitalism.* Durham, N.C.: Duke University Press.

Jang, Jon, James Newton, Wei Hwa Zhang, Genny Lim, and Francis Wong. 1994. *Up From the Root: Asian American Music and Cultural Synthesis.* A symposium held on 3 March in San Francisco, California. San Francisco: Asian Improv aRts.

Kristof, Nicholas D. 1996. Rappers' Credo: No Sex, Please! We're Japanese. *The New York Times,* 29 January.

Lancefield, Robert. [Forthcoming] Music Making Others: European American Ideas of Asian Alterity and Musical Difference, ca. 1850–1960. Ph.D. diss. in progress, Wesleyan University.

Lum, Casey Man Kong. 1996. *In Search of A Voice: Karaoke and the Construction of Identity in Chinese America.* Mahwah, N.J.: Lawrence Erlbaum Associates.

Manuel, Peter. 1993. *Cassette Culture: Popular Music and Technology in North India.* Chicago: University of Chicago Press.

McLaren, Peter. 1994. White Terror and Oppositional Agency: Towards a Critical Multiculturalism. In *Multiculturalism: A Critical Reader,* edited by David Theo Goldberg. Oxford and Cambridge: Blackwell, 45–74.

Nelson, Havelock, and Michael A. Gonzales. 1991. *Bring the Noise: A Guide to Rap Music and Hip-Hop Culture.* New York: Harmony Books.

Oliver, Paul. 1984. *Songsters and Saints: Vocal Traditions on Race Records.* Cambridge, London, New York: Cambridge University Press.

Park, Dennis, and Dina Shek. 1996. The Chinee Gal from Tokio: Racism and Exoticism in American Popular Songs (1900–1930). Paper presented at the 13th Annual Meeting of the Association for Asian American Studies, Washington, D.C.

Rose, Tricia. 1994. *Black Noise: Rap Music and Black Culture in Contemporary America.* Hanover, N.H. and London: Wesleyan University Press/University Press of New England.

———. 1994a. *Black Noise: Rap Music and Black Culture in Contemporary America.* Hanover, N.H. and London: Weslyan University Press/University Press of New England.

———. 1994b. A Style Nobody Can Deal With: Politics, Style, and the Postindustrial City in Hip-hop. In *Microphone Fiends: Youth Music and Youth Culture.* Edited by Andrew Ross and Tricia Rose. New York and London: Routledge.

Schreiber, Norman. 1992. *The Ultimate Guide to Independent Record Labels and Artists: An A-to-Z Source of Great Music.* New York: Pharos Books.

Slobin, Mark. 1982. *Tenement Songs: The Popular Music of the Jewish Immigrants.* Urbana: University of Illinois Press.

———. 1993. *Subcultural Sounds: Micromusics of the West.* Hanover, N.H.: Wesleyan University Press/University Press of New England.

Spottswood, Richard K. 1990. *Ethnic Music on Records: A Discography of Ethnic Recordings Produced in the United States, 1893 to 1942.* With a foreword by James H. Billington. Urbana: University of Illinois Press.

Stanley, Lawrence A. 1992. *Rap: The Lyrics.* New York: Penguin.

Sykes, Charles. 1996. Local Configurations of "Soul": The Motown Sound and the Detroit African American Community. Presentation at the University of Pennsylvania, 22 April.

Taylor, Timothy D. 1997. *Spread the Music All Over the World.* Forthcoming.

Toop, David. 1991. *Rap Attack 2: African Rap to Global Hip Hop.* 2nd ed. London: Serpent's Tail.

Tsou, Judy. 1996. Images of Chinese in American Popular Sheet Music. Paper presented at the annual meeting of the Sonneck Society, Falls Church, Va.

Vernon, Paul. 1995. *Ethnic and Vernacular Music, 1898–1960: A Resource and Guide to Recordings.* Foreword by Benno Haupl. Westport, Conn.: Greenwood Press.

Wallis, Roger, and Krister Malm. 1984. *Big Sounds from Small Peoples: The Music Industry in Small Countries.* London: Constable.

Walser, Robert. 1995. Rhythm, Rhyme, and Rhetoric in the Music of Public Enemy. *Ethnomusicology* 39, no. 2: 193–217.

Wilson, August. 1981. *Ma Rainey's Black Bottom.* New York: Plume.

Wong, Cynthia Po-Man. 1996a. "Asian for the Man!": Stereotypes, Identity and Self-Empowerment in Asian American Rap. Unpublished paper presented at the annual meeting of the Mid-Atlantic Chapter of the Society for Ethnomusicology, Baltimore, Maryland, 24–26 March.

———. 1996b. "We Define Ourselves!": The Negotiation of Power and Identity for Asian Americans in Hip-hop. Unpublished paper presented at the 13th annual meeting of the Association for Asian American Studies, Washington, D.C., 29 May–2 June.

Wong, Deborah. 1994. I Want the Microphone: Mass Mediation and Agency in Asian American Popular Music. *The Drama Review* [T143] 38, no. 2: 152–67.

———. 1998. The Asian American Body in Performance. Forthcoming in *Music and the Racial Imagination,* edited by Philip V. Bohlman and Ronald Radano. Chicago and London: University of Chicago Press.

Yanow, Scott. 1994. Enthusiasm. *Jazziz* 11, no. 2: 28–33, ff.

Zheng, Su de San. 1993. Immigrant Music and Transnational Discourse: Chinese American Music Culture in New York City. Ph.D. diss., Wesleyan University.

COMPANION CD SELECTION

Track 25. The Mountain Brothers, Sprite commercial.

ADDITIONAL SOURCES

For Further Reading

Chang, Jeff. 1994. Race, Class, Conflict and Empowerment: On Ice Cube's "Black Korea." In *Los Angeles—Struggles toward Multiethnic Community: Asian American, African American, and Latino Perspectives,* edited by Edward T. Chang and Russell C. Leong, 87–107. Seattle and London: University of Washington Press.

Decker, Jeffrey Louis. 1994. The State of Rap: Time and Place in Hip-hop Nationalism. In *Microphone Fiends: Youth Music and Youth Culture,* edited by Andrew Ross and Tricia Rose. New York and London: Routledge.

Flores, Juan. 1994. Puerto Rican and Proud, Boyee!: Rap Roots and Amnesia. In *Microphone Fiends: Youth Music and Youth Culture,* edited by Andrew Ross and Tricia Rose. New York and London: Routledge.

Lipsitz, George. 1994. We Know What Time It Is: Race, Class and Youth Culture in the Nineties. In *Microphone Fiends: Youth Music and Youth Culture,* edited by Andrew Ross and Tricia Rose. New York and London: Routledge.

Rose, Tricia. 1994a. *Black Noise: Rap Music and Black Culture in Contemporary America.* Hanover, N.H. and London: Wesleyan University Press/University Press of New England.

———. 1994b. A Style Nobody Can Deal With: Politics, Style and the Postindustrial City in Hip-hop. In *Microphone Fiends: Youth Music and Youth Culture,* edited by Andrew Ross and Tricia Rose. New York and London: Routledge.

Walser, Robert. 1993. *Running with the Devil: Power, Gender, and Madness in Heavy Metal Music.* Hanover, N.H.: Wesleyan University Press.

Wei, William. 1993. *The Asian American Movement.* Philadelphia: Temple University Press.

CHAPTER 13

Constructing Communities and Identities

Riot Grrrl New York City

Theo Cateforis and Elena Humphreys

*I*n this chapter, Theo Cateforis, a doctoral student in musicology at the State University of New York at Stony Brook, and Elena Humphreys, a master of fine arts graduate from the same institution, examine the musical activist movement Riot Grrrl. A contemporary, largely gender-based, underground community, Riot Grrrl emerged in the early 1990s in various local punk scenes throughout the United States. Cateforis and Humphreys analyze how young women in these punk scenes used Riot Grrrl as a means of solidifying a community around female issues, carving new creative spaces within the domain of the traditionally exclusive male punk musical lifestyle. From the politics of Riot Grrrl fanzine publications to the socially charged musical statements of various Riot Grrrl bands, the movement has profoundly affected the 1990s alternative musical culture. Focusing on the grass-roots impetus behind this sociomusical phenomenon, the coauthors recount the initial formation and activities of one regional chapter in the larger riot grrrl landscape—that of Riot Grrrl New York City. Cateforis, whose scholarly interests revolve around issues of genre, style, and musical analysis in punk, new wave, and alternative rock, and Humphreys, who along with being one of the founding Riot Grrrl New York City members in 1992, has long been a participant in the New York punk scene as a musician and artist, come to this writing project as a team of outside and inside ethnographers. Together they present Riot Grrrl New York City through a mixture of personal depiction, interviews, and theoretical interpretation, giving special attention to the group's *negotiations with private and public identity and the outside media. Given the obstacles women have generally met as participants, and particularly as instrumentalists, in twentieth-century popular music, Riot Grrrl's liberating attitudes and confrontational ideologies act as a positive outlet, one that has opened countless new avenues for women in rock.*

■ ■ ■ ■

> Like she-devils out of Rush Limbaugh's worst nightmare, a battery of young women with guitars, drums and a generous dose of rage stampeded into popular consciousness earlier this year [1993]. They do things like scrawl SLUT and RAPE across their torsos before gigs, produce fanzines with names like *Girl Germs* and hate the media's guts. They're called Riot Grrrls and they've come for your daughters. (France 1993, 23)

Throughout 1992 and 1993, numerous sensationalized accounts, like the above passage from *Rolling Stone* magazine, appeared in such newsstand publications as *Spin* (Nasrallah 1992), *Newsweek* (Chideya 1992), *Seventeen* (Malkin 1993), and *Glamour* (Borchers 1993) describing a new youth subculture that had emerged out of the American underground punk movement. Riot Grrrl, as the confrontational name suggests, consisted of teenage girls and women who had claimed the innocent freedom of girlhood and adolescence and transformed it into a riotous, raging growl. Riot Grrrl's aggressive stance was evident most visibly in the music of punk bands, as, for example, *Bikini Kill* and its lead singer, Kathleen Hanna, whose lyrics in such songs as "Suck My Left One" stood as a defiant blast against the dominance of patriarchy in American society.[1]

On a more private level, Riot Grrrls organized meetings where they could question gender roles and confront their identities while speaking openly about their experiences with rape, sexuality, racism, oppression, and domestic violence. Most observers considered Riot Grrrl to be a new wave of feminism, supposedly drawing inspiration from such feminist bestsellers as Susan Faludi's *Backlash* and Naomi Wolf's *Beauty Myth* and from empowering, autonomous performers like Madonna.[2] The media characterized Riot Grrrl as a national phenomenon dispersed throughout various American cities and towns: "a support network of activist 'girls' who are loosely linked together by a few punk bands, weekly discussion groups, pen-pal friendships and more than fifty homemade fanzines" (Chideya 1992, 84). Descriptions like these, though, fail to distinguish how different regional Riot Grrrl groups reflect the very real cultural separations that mark America's diverse urban and rural landscape.

This ethnographic essay traces the formation of one specific Riot Grrrl group in the geographic region of New York City, detailing their activities in that city's small, independent punk community from the autumn and winter of 1992 through the spring of 1993.[3] As with any ethnographic research, this essay reveals as much about its authors as it does its subjects. Theo Cateforis is a musicologist living just outside of New York City who studies various alternative rock and punk music styles. Elena Humphreys is an artist and musician who has spent many years in the New York City punk scene and was an active member of Riot Grrrl New York City (hereafter referred to as Riot Grrrl NYC). Together, our study, which joins Elena's voice with the voices of other women involved in Riot Grrrl NYC, reveals the combined perspectives of an "outside" ethnographer and an "inside" ethnographer. Above all, in this essay we will focus on Riot Grrrl as an empowering idea central to the women and girls involved in Riot Grrrl NYC's social collective. Our ethnographic narrative is framed by some basic questions: How were girls and women introduced to Riot Grrrl, and what purpose did it serve in their lives? How, through such activities as music making, did Riot Grrrl NYC relate to the city's established Punk community? In what ways did the members of Riot Grrrl NYC build an internal group identity? Lastly, how did Riot Grrrl NYC negotiate its external, or public, identity and reconcile the gaze of the media?

NEW YORK PUNK AND RIOT GRRRL NYC

The New York City punk scene out of which Riot Grrrl NYC evolved has a long history that dates back to the late 1960s and early 1970s.[4] This scene coalesced in 1974 and 1975 when such artists as Patti Smith and bands like Blondie, The Ramones, Talking Heads, and Television began playing and socializing at a lower east side club: CBGBs.[5] Of these groups, The Ramones most typified an angry, edgy, unrefined sound, which would prove influential among the numerous British punk bands who followed in the wake of the Sex Pistols' success in England. The Ramones played short, clipped songs that featured distorted guitars, minimal, repetitive chord progressions, sharp, declamatory vocals, and a propulsive rhythm section. In the mid to late 1970s their simple, direct music stood as an antithesis to the excessive technology and indulgent instrumental virtuosity associated with the majority of large stadium and arena bands dominating the record industry. Punk bands challenged this hierarchy, proving that music making was not an exclusive domain but rather that it could and *should* be open to anyone.

In the late 1970s and early 1980s American punk became known by a new prefix—hardcore—and its sound was characterized by tempos much faster than that of earlier punk bands. Where the early New York punk scene had been unified by a sense of musical experimentation and a fairly ragged, intense sound, the new hardcore punk scene became codified around distinct musical traits. In particular, bands started displaying the increased instrumental technical proficiency necessary for the blistering speeds that the hardcore style dictated. Audiences began more and more to expect and demand that punk bands have a certain level of competency both on their instruments and in their songcraft. Punk rock had become competitive, and within this arena fans were less accepting of bands who sounded relatively amateurish. During this same period, hardcore punk began to take the shape of an especially male-dominated subculture. Women found themselves on the periphery of punk's musical endeavors, excluded from predominantly male bands. At live shows they felt marginalized, often forced to the back of the venue, away from those male audience members who were slamming into one another and participating in a form of hardcore punk dancing known as slamdancing or thrashing. Gavin van Vlack, a member of the 1980s New York hardcore band Absolution, describes how the area reserved for thrashing, referred to as "the pit," encouraged ritualistic male bonding:

> If you don't want to get hurt, you don't step into the pit. It's all a part of it. Also you get your aggressions out and they're letting their aggressions out. You're bound to get hurt. The big macho guys showing how much they can take. Showing their physical prowess. Yeah, it's a rite of passage thing. (Hurley 1989)[6]

Punk scenes in other cities in the United States during the 1980s suffered as well from similar stifling environments. In 1990 three women in Olympia, Washington—Molly Neuman and Alison Wolfe, who together eventually would form the band Bratmobile, and Tobi Vail, one of the members of Bikini Kill—decided to react against that city's stagnant male-dominated punk scene. They wanted to create an environment where other women would feel more encouraged to learn how to play instruments, form bands, participate in shows, and ultimately voice their political awareness. Through a series of meetings, they attracted other interested women, and soon they adopted the name "Riot Grrrl" as a descriptive phrase for the group's feminist-based ideas. During 1991, various people from Riot Grrrl Olympia either visited or relocated to the Washington, D.C., area, and by 1992, Riot Grrrl DC had developed as a large and active contingent. During the spring and summer of that year, two events in Washington, D.C., finally led to Riot Grrrl's explosive dissemination. First, in early April many women interested in Riot Grrrl met in Washington at the pro-choice rally, March for Women's Lives. Then, almost four months later, Riot Grrrl DC was host to the first national Riot Grrrl Convention. The event, which met for three days, drew a wide range of participants who attended workshops on such topics as "Rape," "Unlearning Racism," "Fat Oppression," and "Domestic Violence." The convention also featured presentations by poets and spoken-word artists but was focused primarily around performances by numerous all-female bands. Afterwards, many girls and women who had attended the convention returned to their cities, colleges, or hometowns determined to begin their own Riot Grrrl chapters. In New York City, the women who began recruiting for a Riot Grrrl group received their first responses from women and girls already in fledgling local punk-rock groups, or from those female members of the local punk community interested in joining a band. Elena Humphreys recalls this early social dynamic:

> I was at a house party of a friend of mine, Tina [Lagen], who I worked with. There were ten or twenty people there all hanging out, just women. It was about fifty percent gay, fifty percent straight women who all knew each other from work, or from the punk scene in New York. Tina was starting a band with Jill [Reiter] and this girl Glynis and they needed a bass player. I mentioned I had a bass but I didn't know how to play it. They said I should be in the band anyway and to come to the first practice. At this party Tina was handing out fliers and wanted to start a Riot Grrrl New York City. A couple days after our first band practice, the first Riot Grrrl NYC meeting occurred which I had learned about from the flier. Tina had another band, Delta Dawn, and the two bands and four other girls made up the first meeting. (Humphreys 1995)

Riot Grrrl NYC also brought together a variety of women whose backgrounds were not necessarily in music but rather reflected New York City's specific position as a thriving underground media and arts capital. Situated near such institutions as New York University and the Parsons School of Design, various liberal presses—for example, the *Village Voice*—and numerous art galleries and shops, the Riot Grrrl NYC meetings became a haven for many high school girls and college educated women who were interested in activist politics. Many of the women drawn to the meetings were already familiar with the alternative scene and had received Riot Grrrl fliers at local events, such as "Wigstock," a large annual New York City festival celebrating gay cultural diversity. Others, however, had relatively little experience with music or the New York punk community. Two members of Riot Grrrl NYC, Sarah Valentine and Diana Morrow, describe how, at first, they saw the group as a positive avenue to the New York punk scene and feminist politics:

> Initially my involvement with Riot Grrrl was supposed to be as a journalist. I was an intern at an underground anarchist newspaper, and my editor wanted me to do a story on Riot Grrrl. At the time, I was very interested in discovering more about music and wishing to hang out with people who I could do that with. Going in there, I didn't expect to be involved with it, I expected just to be a journalist . . . [but, eventually] I felt compelled to stay. (Valentine 1995)

The first time I heard about Riot Grrrl was at a Take Back the Night march. Someone gave me a flier, and then later I saw a girl [in one of my classes at the Parsons School of Design] who had a necklace or something that had Riot Grrrl on it, and I asked her about it and she told me to come to the meeting . . . [I got involved] because I was looking for some sort of activist outlet and there wasn't really one that I could relate to. I had gone to a couple of WAC [*Women's Action Coalition*] meetings and they were horrible. (Morrow 1995)

As one of Riot Grrrl NYC's fliers declared, the group "comprises individuals who determine our mood and direction."[7] But the group also set certain borders around their collective ideological identity. In the same flier, Riot Grrrl NYC defined their constituency:

Girls/women 16 to ? primarily involved in alternative music scenes. we are bisexual, gay and straight. multicultural. multifaceted. we are diverse in beliefs but concur on this: sexism, homophobia and racism run rampant in our "scenes." we want to do something about it. now. ("Is She a Riot Grrrl?" flier)

Most noticeably, this statement excludes through its gender-based terms, the presence of boys and men. And it is clear that such definitions often had a ruinous effect on the tenuous relationship that Riot Grrrl as a whole enjoyed with various existent underground scenes. Editorials began to appear within the alternative presses, for example, characterizing Riot Grrrl as a group that believes "males are responsible for all the world's problems" (Goad 1994). Many people accordingly perceived that Riot Grrrl was a group exclusionary, and thus hostile, to men. Yet, in truth, most Riot Grrrl groups did not present themselves as such. Rather, as Riot Grrrl NYC's members explained, the male-dominated punk scene had excluded women's voices for so long that unless a group like Riot Grrrl carved out its own space, women would never have the opportunity to work *within* the punk scene. Thus in promoting a "constructive solidarity between women," Riot Grrrl ultimately sought to break down gender barriers and secure "mutual respect and appreciation between women and men in [their] creative efforts" (Is She a Riot Grrrl? flier).

The community that Riot Grrrl NYC fostered in their first meetings during the waning months of 1992 began in relative isolation. The women normally would gather in one of the members' kitchen or living room areas, nestled away in an apartment in downtown Manhattan. Spaces such as these provided a safe atmosphere conducive to the sense of support the women and girls were seeking. Even more so, these spaces reflected the reality of the members' living circumstances. For in New York City there are virtually no houses; many residents involved in the alternative scene, therefore, live in the most convenient, economical apartment space available. As a result, the alternative community is widely dispersed. Unless the members of Riot Grrrl NYC chose to live as "squatters," holding their meetings illicitly in abandoned buildings, they would not have access to any large personal or communal spaces.[8]

These factors differed considerably from the social dynamics of Riot Grrrl groups in other regions. In Washington, D.C., for example, Riot Grrrl grew out of a punk community that, for many years, had been gravitating around small neighborhoods and housing complexes. Since the early 1980s the Washington hardcore punk scene has revolved around Dischord House, a home out of which Ian MacKaye, of the band Fugazi, operates the local record label Dischord Records. Likewise, many members of the Washington, D.C., punk scene often meet at the Embassy, a sizable house capable of accommodating numerous people. The members of Riot Grrrl NYC debated whether or not they too should try to locate a public meeting space. On the one hand, some of the members were concerned that in its first few months Riot Grrrl NYC had not expanded far beyond a handful of friends and acquaintances. Even though the group had been announcing its meetings via fliers and posters, these were often lost amidst the dozens of other fliers and posters plastered around the city each week advertising a dizzying array of new alternative cultural events. Furthermore, since most women or girls in the city were understandably hesitant to attend an event listed at the private residence of someone they did not know, Riot Grrrl NYC was not attracting many new members. On the other hand, if the group moved to a public space they would risk possible intrusions upon their private meetings. Eventually Riot Grrrl NYC did arrange with a local co-optive punk record store, Reconstruction Records, to hold their publicized meetings in the store's space after it had closed for the night. Located on East Sixth street in the heart of New York's East Village, the store provided a meeting space much less threatening to newcomers and interested outsiders.

On one occasion, some of the male members from the Reconstruction Records collective, who had not been informed of Riot Grrrl NYC's special arrangement, accidentally walked in on a meeting and were asked by the group to leave. The store members contested the group's private claim to the store's public space, however, insisting that Riot Grrrl NYC had unrightfully commandeered a collective punk domain. Uncomfortable incidents such as these typified Riot Grrrl NYC's difficult transitions between private and public meeting spaces. These negotiations of space are especially striking for they seem to reinscribe the underlying gender divisions that govern private and public spaces in many traditional patriarchal societies—divisions where the house is intimate and secretive and the private domain of women, while the outside world is an open meeting place and the public domain of men.[9] That Riot Grrrl NYC favored the sanctity offered by a private space reflects the gendered nature of the sensitive personal experiences that women were recounting and confronting during group meetings. Should the members of the group know in advance that males might be involved in a meeting, they could allow for the men's participation in the discussions. Once, male musicians in the local band Vitapup, who were sympathetic to Riot Grrrl's cause and wanted to participate by playing in a benefit for the group, were allowed to attend a special meeting on the condition that they wore dresses. By complying with these gestures, the men openly compromised their gender roles and, accordingly, neutered their positions of male power. Such occurrences were exceptional, however. Although Riot Grrrl NYC advertised open meetings for the last Wednesday of every month, inviting men to attend, none ever appeared. As one Riot Grrrl observed, "[the men] weren't really interested in coming, they just wanted to assert their power by having the opportunity to come" (Humphreys 1995).

SUBVERSIVE POWER: RIOT GRRRL NYC AND FANZINES

Of all the projects the members of Riot Grrrl NYC discussed at their meetings, the most consistently realized took shape in the group's published fanzines. Fanzines have long enjoyed a tradition in punk scenes as alternatives to the mainstream music press. Their contents range from contentious editorials, music reviews, interviews, and media clippings to poetry, artwork, and politically pointed anecdotes. Fanzines are easy to construct and reproduce. Beyond the material cut and pasted on the fanzine's pages, all one requires to manufacture the final product is access to a xerox machine. Even before Riot Grrrl had been widely adopted as a revolutionary moniker, Olympia-based fanzines, such as *Jigsaw, Girl Germs* (written by members of Bratmobile), and *Bikini Kill,* had served as effective means for communicating immediate and unmitigated feminist viewpoints to other regional areas, in ways that helped spark activism and awareness among women in various local punk scenes.

The majority of Riot Grrrl fanzines represented the efforts of either individuals or perhaps two or three collaborators. When Riot Grrrl NYC planned their chapter's fanzines, however, they wanted to capture the pluralistic composition of their collective. Therefore, they conceived their fanzine as a group project. Diana Morrow describes how Riot Grrrl NYC organized their fanzine production through special meetings:

> There were maybe ten girls squished into this tiny New York apartment living room/bedroom. Everybody brought a little thing that they did, whether it be a poem or a drawing or whatever. And we

sat there and actually cut and pasted and put things together in some kind of order. Everybody brought something, and everybody contributed to the making and the laying out of the pages, and eventually we would go down together to Kinko's [a copy/print center] and xerox it. (Morrow 1995)

Because the fanzines originated in this manner, they normally displayed a fragmentary character. Looking through the collage of material that populates each issue, however, one notices that the contributors address some basic themes:

1. Raising awareness and encouraging critical thought: In the fanzines, one might find a newspaper article reporting or detailing acts of sexual abuse, or homophobic or racist hatred. The third issue of *Riot Grrrl NYC,* for example, carries a newspaper clipping—"Stalked By Neo-Nazi Terrorists, Lesbians Flee Underground"—about seven lesbian women who had been chased out of Oregon and were seeking refuge in San Francisco. Scrawled in at the end of the article are added comments encouraging readers to send relief aid to the women. Dotting the pages of fanzines, as well, one finds short essays or pieces asking readers to consider the issues surrounding such topics as pornography, the dangers of smoking, or the horrific realities of incest. Or a contributor might simply include references to provocative literature, ranging from samples of ecofeminist poetry to the critical writings of bell hooks.[10]

2. Personalizing issues of sexual identity and experience: Within the fanzines' pages some Riot Grrrls share their poetry, fiction or artwork. Authors might depict, from a woman's perspective, the muted horror of sexual abuse or rape. Other submissions describe intimate lesbian encounters and awakenings. Some entries confront the reality of such eating disorders as bulimia and anorexia. Above all, most of the authors draw attention to women's bodies, exposing how they are often violated through the force of male possession, judged and demeaned through societal definitions of femininity, and ultimately imprisoned by the machinations of capitalist culture.

3. Subverting Images of Women: Perhaps the most striking aspects of the fanzines resonate in their visual content. In each issue, Riot Grrrls freely plunder images of women, from photographs to cartoons and drawings, and recast them in a jumbled, decontextualized fashion, around the fanzine's prose and clippings. Judith Butler has commented how such disruptive actions potentially "make gender trouble" (Butler 1990, 34). That is, by mobilizing stereotyped images of women in a subversive manner, one can demonstrate that these images are not "natural" but rather constructed versions of a feminine gender that is molded, shaped, and perpetuated by society and the mass media. The cover of issue number 4, from January 1993, serves as an excellent example (Fig. 13.1). Here, three contrasting images compete for the reader's attention. The image in the lower left-hand corner, a seated woman,

Figure 13.1. Fanzine Images: The cover of *Riot Grrrl NYC* 4. Photo by Elena Humphreys.

legs crossed and surrounded by brick, intently loading a rifle, emphasizes Riot Grrrl's determined feminist, activist stance. In the lower right-hand corner, a drawing shows a girl scout troop and its two leaders. Most likely lifted from a girl scout manual, the image and an accompanying text that describes in detail a girl scout induction ritual, are reclaimed by Riot Grrrl to symbolize their own group's solidarity. The act, however, is brazenly ironic, creating a paradox between the combined girl scouts and riot grrrls imagery. A swirl of conflicting meanings comes to the surface: in one sense, the image of the young girl scouts is positive and empowering; it emphasizes the pre-adolescent freedom that Riot Grrrl, by its very namesake, in some ways hopes to recapture and celebrate. At the same time, though, the girl scout troop members, dressed in uniform and standing at attention before the two women, present a negative image of conformity and subserviance. The drawing foregrounds the power structure and socialization process inherent in becoming a girl scout. Ultimately this is a process that Riot Grrrl, as a leaderless group composed of individual voices, insistently denies. Lastly, in the upper right-hand corner, two cartoon women apparently are modeling the issue's cover-price placard. Their exaggerated features, dominated by glowing smiles, are entrenched stereotypes of American beauty and femininity. Inside the fanzine, though, one finds an article exposing the realities behind these ideals:

An ineluctable part of modeling is the pressure to retain your ethe-
real look against the ravages of time. Low-calorie is your god; zits
are your devil. Most models starve themselves. They smoke heavily
and drink gallons of coffee to throttle their appetites. (*Riot Grrrl
NYC* 4 (1993): 13)

In this light, the cartoon images appear doubly, and sadly, unreal. And it is in
such instances as these that the texts of the fanzines seem most powerful; for,
rather than criticizing the women in the images, the reader is instead led to
question the patriarchal forces in our society that drive women to aspire to
such mentally and physically damaging standards. Early Riot Grrrl fanzines
are overflowing with similar prose and imagery that seek not only to strip
away the veneer suffocating women in society but also to deploy strategies
and advice by which women can reclaim their power as individuals.

RIOT GRRRL AND MUSIC

From Riot Grrrl's earliest stages, the movement enjoyed its greatest exposure
via its musical manifestations and associations. In 1992 and 1993, various
Olympia and D.C. bands, such as Bikini Kill, Heavens To Betsy, and
Bratmobile, and England's Huggy Bear, produced and distributed their music
through small independent record labels like Kill Rock Stars, securing Riot
Grrrl's visibility throughout America and the United Kingdom. On a more
local level, we want to examine *how* and *why* the act of musical performance
was integrated as part of Riot Grrrl NYC's social configuration. Many members of Riot Grrrl NYC had little or no musical experience and joined the
group because they were seeking a safe environment where they could learn
various instruments and create music expressing their uninhibited viewpoints. It was for this reason, among others, that Jill Reiter first decided to
join Riot Grrrl NYC. Jill had been involved with the punk scene in New York
and was struggling to learn guitar. Like other aspiring New York women
musicians, however, she found herself disenfranchised. The New York punk
scene was largely monopolized by all-male bands, and because punk musicians rarely were willing to give women lessons on their instruments, this
network seemed resistant to most women's musical endeavors. In Riot Grrrl
NYC, though, Jill found a supportive forum where musicians could practice,
make mistakes, grow, and experiment. In this environment, she was able to
form the band Double Zero. If Jill's band, in their early developmental stages,
had performed at a club for a predominantly male audience, they would have
faced a group of adversarial spectators, predisposed to dismiss their music.
But playing their initial shows for Riot Grrrl NYC members, they were
assured of an audience they *knew* would offer not only encouragement but
also advice and constructive criticism. In this sense, Riot Grrrl NYC meetings

sometimes functioned as musical workshops. Those women who were accomplished musicians offered to share their experience and to work with women who were beginning on their instruments. The members of Riot Grrrl NYC thus forged in the male-dominated punk scene a new female-gendered oral musical culture. Within Riot Grrrl's safe space, they essentially initiated a closed musical transmission that was capable of surviving across generations of women and girls.

Riot Grrrl was especially important for lesbian women like Jill, because for the first time they had an opportunity within their own musical scene to express their desires and explore their identities. Before Riot Grrrl NYC's formation, the New York hardcore punk scene of the 1980s had been tainted by severe homophobic outbursts, effectively alienating many of the community's gay and lesbian members. Historically, however, punk had never been an avenue frequently traveled by lesbian musicians. Feminist and lesbian music more often was the exclusive province of folk performers involved in independent women's music labels like Olivia records, or was more known through more such prominent artists as Tracy Chapman and Michelle Shocked. In New York City, many gays and lesbians also clustered around the club culture of techno, rave, and house music. As various writers have discussed, within these gay and lesbian communities, the prominence of role playing, "camping" or "masquerading" gendered identities, has long distinguished the interaction between the scene's participants (Case 1989, Butler 1990, Peraino 1992, Currid 1995, Robertson 1996). Male members of the house music communities who dress as drag-queen disco divas, women who assume roles of the masculine "butch" and feminine "femme dykes"—these are both measures of camp. Their deliberate posturing makes conspicuous their adopted gender roles. And, ultimately, their actions expose gender as a mask, part of a costume we all wear throughout our daily interactions. Camp thus acts as "a performative strategy, as well as a mode of reception, [which] commonly foregrounds the artifice of gender and sexual roles." (Robertson 1996, 14). Riot Grrrl NYC attracted many lesbian and bisexual women, and resultantly the ironic, and often humorous, gender manipulations associated with camp's discursive maneuvers began permeating the music of many Riot Grrrl bands.

Double Zero's "Gas, Food, Satan" revels in this practice of masquerade (Track 26). On the surface, the song is couched in typical raucous punk anger, characterized by its distorted guitars, raspy, shouted vocals, and rough, direct production values. But from the moment the lead singer interrupts the introductory stuttering drum cadence with a stream of random phrases, "big wheels walking, 'n I feel shocking, eyeballs whopping," she sets an uproarious satiric tone. She adopts the role of the macho hard-rock male lead singer, creating a composite persona constructed out of stock conventions. The opening section's chugging, syncopated, two-bar riff provides a backdrop for her

Figure 13.2. Cartoon grrrl imagery: poster for a Double Zero performance. Photo by Elena Humphreys.

first litany of loose shouted signifiers: "four-wheel, ten-gauge . . . you are my gas station . . ." In the chorus that follows, she wraps herself more clearly in the guise of the male outlaw, on the run stealing and killing at will:

> Everything I own, I've stolen
> Everyone I know is no one
> Every time I kill in your world,
> An angel gets her wings

This is a more powerful and purposeful section, underscored by repetitive guitar riffing and a driving backbeat in the drums.

The next section of the song is more restrained and effectively serves as a foil, offsetting the momentum built up through the chorus. The singer recedes into a spoken narrative that relates the hardships of outlaw life. Her voice sounds desolate, tinged with a regret mirrored in the accompaniment of the sighing, melodic bass chords. In a normal rock song setting, such direct vocal expression and somber musical shading would invite the listener to join the singer in reflecting upon the harsh realities of his chosen lifestyle. But "Gas, Food, Satan" parodies these sentiments. The barren wasteland that the singer conjures forth is a cartoonish terrain littered with incongruous symbols of masculinity: *"Out here it's all about dope and drugs, and four wheel drive, and meat."* Combined with the band's convincing musical stylistic appropriations, the vocalist's delivery sounds all the more amusing. Near the end of "Gas, Food, Satan," the song's rock groove momentarily dissolves into a menacing, rumbling bass glissando over which the singer slowly builds to a frenzied climax: *"In my dreams, I'm running across that open field, out to the highway."* This neatly outlines the song's overriding trope—the liberating "open road" that is mythologized in countless male rock anthems, stretching from Steppenwolf's "Born To Be Wild" through Van Halen's "Runnin' with the Devil."[11]

When Double Zero engaged such masquerades at their live shows, they were entertaining an audience fully aware of the camp display unfolding before them. As they simultaneously played upon—and claimed for their own—these well-worn tokens of male empowerment, they reinforced a sense of community between performers and spectators. Where women musicians in punk traditionally had found themselves objectified under the gaze of a primarily male audience, Riot Grrrl performances subverted such situations. During Double Zero's performances, band and audience were equal participants in the masquerade. The women in the audience gazed at the band, and the group returned the spectators' gazes, enacting a sexually charged atmosphere between the bodies on stage and the bodies in the pit. Such performances were instrumental in the formation of a strong New York City queercore movement, signalling the insurgence of gay and lesbian voices in the punk community.

Queercore was already in its nascent stages on the West Coast when Selena Wahng, an accomplished bassist and singer, moved from San Francisco to New York in the late summer of 1992. Her punk band, Lucy Stoners, had appeared with three other bands earlier in the year on a groundbreaking underground seven-inch single, "There's a Dyke in the Pit," a record whose jolting title deftly captures the male sexual paranoia and insecurity that dominated the hardcore punk scene of the 1980s. Almost immediately upon her arrival in New York, Selena attended a Riot Grrrl NYC meeting. She was already familiar with the Riot Grrrl movement and hoped the group would provide for her an outlet where she could continue her musical efforts. While Selena had been using her music to politicize her gendered position as a woman, an Other in society's eyes, at the same time she also saw Riot Grrrl as a place where she could explore her ethnic background and her experiences as a different type of Other: a Korean-American woman involved in the punk scene. Traditionally, punk communities throughout the United States have always held limited appeal for groups outside the white middle-class social strata. In the 1980s, white racist, patriotic Skinhead groups, though sometimes not directly related with the punk community, had especially damaged much of the scene's reputation through their rhetoric and violent demonstrations at punk shows.[12] Only with the appearance of groups such as Riot Grrrl were these social and political values contested.

Selena Wahng's "Killing for Pleasure" (Track 27) is a composition that relates experiences from a vantage point firmly outside of punk's normal young, white male constituency. As she describes, the song, on which she sings and plays bass, drum beats, and samples, represents "the sound of rape repeating over and over again" (Wahng 1995).[13] These sounds show the influences of two divergent musical styles. On the one hand, she draws upon the musical tradition of the shaman—in Korean society, a powerful female authority figure who communicates with spirits through ritual practices. Together with the song's constant, pounding percussive attacks, Selena's oscillating background voices, droning and chanting throughout, imitate the shaman's ceremonial incantations and musical accompaniment. On the other hand, the song derives its chaotic energy from punk rock. In particular, the two foreground elements, Selena's distorted, detuned electric-bass melody, and her screaming vocal projections, vibrate with punk's buzzsaw rage. Of these two, it is Selena's wailing voice that most of all enwraps the listener. Her screams are controlled yet unpredictable, sometimes repeatedly mimicking the melodic material of the bass and the background vocals, and other times twisting into irregular garbled, guttural, reverbed shapes. In the context of the song, their meaning seems double-edged. In one respect the screams are stimulating. We identify emotionally with their visceral timbre, their release of rage and frustration, their rousing display of power. But the screams are also horrific. They all too easily resonate with the tortured pain and experience of rape. That "Killing for Pleasure" exudes such intensity is a testimony to the identification and intersubjectivity of the performer's voice with those voices of the listening audience. In Riot Grrrl NYC, such musical performances served to strengthen the group's communal foundation.

PUSSYSTOCK, RIOT GRRRL AND THE MEDIA

The members of Riot Grrrl NYC realized early on that if they were to fund any musical activities or other projects the group was interested in, they would need to raise money. Since music was the most visible component and certain to draw the most interest, they decided to organize and sponsor a benefit concert, an event which they chose to name "Pussystock," an amusing twist on the American pop-culture icon. Riot Grrrl NYC could only hold this benefit, however, if they secured the proper public space. ABC no Rio, a well-known local punk rock collective and club, made their performing area provisionally available for the event, allowing Riot Grrrl control of the concert's arrangement, promotion, and contents. At the initial Pussystock meetings, each Riot Grrrl member volunteered the name of a local or East Coast band that they thought would be appropriate for the benefit. The bands that eventually agreed to play the benefit included the Riot Grrrl NYC band Delta Dawn; two groups from New York City, Wives and Vitapup; The Maul Girls (New Jersey); Bimbo Shrineheads (Connecticut); Slant 6 (Washington, D.C.); and a local performance artist, Penny Arcade, who would act as emcee. In most alternative or punk scenes, small bands and artists such as these release their music through independent labels and neither can afford nor desire any outside management. They generally operate in a fairly autonomous fashion, handling their own correspondence and arranging their own tour schedules. One can find the band's mailing address or phone number on their cassette or seven-inch vinyl releases, or attached to the end of some fanzine review. Riot Grrrl NYC simply sent out invitations to each of the bands, offering not only to pay the expenses for their travel into the city but also to provide for them free lodging and a home-cooked dinner. After enough bands had been contacted and had confirmed that they would participate, members committed to different promotional activities. For the benefit, which was to occur in January 1993, they made fliers, contacted various local underground radio stations, and advertised on bulletin boards throughout the city's village area.

At the show, the predominantly female performers voiced a noise, anger, and celebration that set in motion an exciting set of parameters:

> It was exhilarating and thrilling and really wonderful, because it was a world that we had created and which we were participating in and leading and experiencing our own power that we had as women. And it was alternative, queer, punk women at that, not just upper middle class [activist women] . . . real grass rootsy, strong individuals, experiencing something that they had created. (Valentine 1995)

The members of Riot Grrrl NYC set no age restrictions on the Pussystock show and, as was customary in the punk scene, only charged five dollars admission.[14] Since Riot Grrrl NYC had asked only obscure punk bands to play, they expected a small audience typical for the New York punk community and ABC no Rio. The event, however, drew a larger crowd than anticipated and unfortunately ushered in a more pernicious element as well. ABC no Rio's small performance space was overrun by interested media parties who had no connection with the punk community. Their curiosity added a new dimension to Pussystock, one that trampled the benefit's underlying principles. Another member of Riot Grrrl describes how the media ultimately disrupted the benefit's atmosphere:

> Somebody got hold of the fliers and we had camera crews from Germany, Canada, Australia, Japan coming in and trying to get in free, annoying people with their lights and cameras. People were interviewing girls who weren't even involved with Riot Grrrl, and asking them about Riot Grrrl and making their words some quintessential statement on Riot Grrrl. Media crews were saying [to the members of Riot Grrrl] "We're doing you a favor, so we should get

in free." But this was a benefit and these people were bringing in like thirty people to shoot film . . . and people couldn't dance at the show because the camera crews were right up front documenting stuff. They were interviewing people in the bathroom, it was just a mess. It got to the point where we had to start throwing people out. (Humphreys 1995)

Through Pussystock, Riot Grrrl NYC had witnessed firsthand the havoc that an intrusive media could wreak on their endeavors. While this was the first manifestation of a truly ravenous press corps that they had seen, the other major regional Riot Grrrl groups had held antagonistic relationships with the mainstream media for practically an entire year. Because Riot Grrrl NYC encountered, and was affected by, problems similar to those that other Riot Grrrl groups faced, it is worth examining in depth the terms of Riot Grrrl's relationship with the national media.

On a basic level, the members of Riot Grrrl NYC voiced their dissatisfaction with the press's activities in a manner that echoed the timeworn complaints of *any* person or group subject to the interpretation of the printed word. That is, they felt that the media, by either decontextualizing the words of Riot Grrrl members, fabricating their own Riot Grrrl quotes, or misconstruing the group's purpose, were in some way misrepresenting Riot Grrrl. While even the most distorted accounts of Riot Grrrl generally professed their sensitivity or sympathy towards Riot Grrrl's feminist activist concerns, these same media reports refused to accept that Riot Grrrl was not a stable entity, but rather a diffuse collective of individuals each seeking their own form of empowerment. Ultimately, the press devised tactics by which they could consolidate a packaged image of Riot Grrrl and sell it to the public. Some of these means were blunt, others more insidious.

The article that Riot Grrrls across the country most unanimously decried appeared in the national music magazine *Spin*. In this article, the journalist describes a scenario from the 1992 DC Riot Grrrl Convention: A teenage girl, Erika Reinstein, walks past a group of onlookers "startled by her appearance."

> Reinstein's jeans were slung low, and her midriff exposed . . . a message written in thick black marker on her stomach: RAPE . . . Reinstein wrote RAPE on her belly to break the silence surrounding the crime. (Nasrallah 1992, 78–80)

Any injustices Reinstein had unmasked, however, were silenced by *Spin* in favor of a fashion statement. On the page facing the above text, the reader sees an airbrushed photograph of a pouting lipsticked woman with the words *Riot Grrrls* stenciled across her arm. While the conjunction of text and imagery would lead readers to assume the photograph was of Reinstein, in fact *Spin* had substituted in her stead a photograph of a glamorized—and unidentified—model. An even more troubling, though less cited, article appeared in the major British weekly music newspaper *Melody Maker* (Joy 1992). The newspaper featured as its cover story a report on Riot Grrrls and "the new girl revolution." Adorning the cover was a photograph from the Re/search archives, a picture of two scantly clad women mudwrestling, one standing triumphantly over the other, arms akimbo and smiling confidently at the camera.[15] While these women obviously had no relation to Riot Grrrl, the newspaper completed the travesty by inscribing over the picture an invitation to the reader to join the women frolicking in the mud: "Riot Grrrls! You wanna play . . .?" What were the chances that for most of the paper's readers the cover page provided any effect other than mere titillation? How many of these readers would look beyond such images and read about the issues that were confronted by a Riot Grrrl fanzine?

Not all articles resorted to such extreme measures. Instead, more commonly, the authors would tacitly acknowledge that Riot Grrrls were "diverse" or "atypical," but then proceed to sketch out their own reductive, homogenous description of Riot Grrrl:

> While no Riot Grrrl could be considered typical, Tiffany, a student at a small, Catholic, New England college, displays a few common traits: "People here think I am weird becaue I am political and I go to the dean's dinner in a little black dress with big boots and a shaved head and I study a lot." Smart, literate, and mad as hell, Grrrls began with young women like Tiffany. (Nasrallah 1992, 80)

> Meetings, which now go on in enclaves on the East Coast and in Toronto, draw women as young as fourteen and as "old" as twenty-five, mostly with cropped and/or dyed hair, bright red lips, and body paint. (Bernikow 1993, 165)

> The [fan]zines reflect the style of the Riot Grrrls themselves, who mix baby-doll dresses and bright red lipstick with combat boots and tattoos. (Borchers 1993, 134)

> The Riot Grrrl refusal to conform to fashion dictates, however, has created a "look" of its own . . . So you'll see Riot Grrrls in fishnet stockings and army shorts, cinch-waisted dresses with combat boots, or miniskirts with long underwear. (Malkin 1993, 81)

While such descriptions as these diminished and damaged Riot Grrrl's stance as a collective group of *individuals,* they also provided the movement with wide public exposure. Many of Riot Grrrl NYC's members thus reacted ambivalently towards the media:

> If Riot Grrrl had stayed out of the media, we would have reached other people in other cities through [fan]zines, but we wouldn't have reached people outside of the underground network. It was like hot and cold with those things. Part of me was like "I don't want an article in *Seventeen* magazine because they're gonna say really dumb things." Yet, how do you reach the kid in Oklahoma if the only records they have [available to them] are *Steely Dan.* (Humphreys 1995)

The members of Riot Grrrl NYC had learned from Pussystock that they somehow had to protect themselves from the media's probing gaze. After the benefit, the group met and decided they would follow the example set by the Riot Grrrl chapters in Olympia and Washington, D.C., and institute a media blackout. They no longer welcomed any members of the press to the meetings, and would only grant interviews under the stipulation that the journalist talk with *all* the women and girls involved in the group. Though inquiries from the press would never fully subside, they did begin gradually to abate.

Despite Riot Grrrl NYC's souring experience with the media, Pussystock had been an overwhelming success, and the group agreed they should start planning another benefit immediately, an event reasonably enough entitled "Pussystock II." At the same time that Riot Grrrl NYC was attracting more women from the alternative scene, the group was also encountering some growing pains. Specifically, Riot Grrrl NYC recognized that their group, which was predominantly white, middle-class women and girls, was not significantly diversified. The privileged socioeconomic stature enjoyed by some Riot Grrrls in various regional groups had led many critics to join in a wholesale dismissal of Riot Grrrl's activities. In Riot Grrrl NYC, one of the group's more outspoken members, Claudia von Vacano, had attempted to rectify the situation, soliciting contributions from Latino, African, and Asian women to feature in her fanzine *Lost ID.* And for Pussystock II, Riot Grrrl even placed on the opening-night show a well-known local gospel group, Faith. But such ventures did not dramatically alter the group's predominant cultural composition. From its very origins the Riot Grrrl movement had been embedded in punk communities, and thus Riot Grrrl NYC's limited social makeup continued to reflect the white middle-class complexion of the larger punk subculture itself. At best, with Pussystock II, which took place in early May 1993, the members of Riot Grrrl NYC found themselves a much more known quantity in the public's eye, and thus capable of drawing a more varied crowd than the previous benefit's audience. Sarah Valentine had written a full-page article describing the benefit for a local community newspaper, *Downtown,* and consequently a larger number of men and older women from outside the New York punk community attended the shows.

Pussystock II extended across five nights at five different venues and featured numerous local female and mixed-gender bands who, for one reason or another, had not been able to play for the first benefit. The range of bands was diverse: some bands—for example, Chickenmilk and Sexpod—played a melodic "pop" style of punk. Another band, No Commercial Value, veered more towards ska-influenced punk.[16] God Is My Co-Pilot mixed eclectic styles from funk to polka in a noisy experimental post-punk collage. Riot Grrrl NYC, as a whole, prepared more fully for the event. Two members, Elena Humphreys and Tina Lagen, had contacted each of the bands before the benefit, and received tracks that they included on a cassette compilation entitled *Mudflower*, produced through their own independent label, Flytrap records. Most importantly, Riot Grrrl NYC briefed the audiences at the shows—the press were allowed no pictures or interviews. The group had prepared a press release containing brief quotes from a large number of Riot Grrrl's members. These were the only statements to which they allowed the media access.

Pussystock II was an enormous success and established Riot Grrrl NYC as one of the most active group chapters in the country. For many of the women involved in the group, this proved to be a culminating point in their activities. In the strenuous months throughout the winter of 1992 and spring of 1993, they had gone through various rites of passage. The majority of Riot Grrrl NYC members from this period soon drifted away from the group. Speaking with the members of Riot Grrrl NYC three years after these events, we find the movement's loose revolutionary slogans realized in a manner quite unlike the press's distorted vision of a "female utopia" (Malkin 1993, 81). More realistically, Riot Grrrl NYC served as a supportive workshop that fostered, among its members, practical communicative and artistic skills applicable far beyond the group's small social domain. Sarah Valentine now works as a promoter and specializes in shows featuring female punk-rock bands that highlight women musicians and artists. Diana Morrow, who edited issues of the Riot Grrrl NYC fanzine, published in the spring of 1995 her premiere issue of *Princess* magazine, a glossy fanzine combining theoretical analysis and personal writings on feminist, queer, racial, and class issues. Another member of the group, Abby Moser, realized her creative goal and completed a documentary film project about Riot Grrrl NYC entitled *Riot Grrrl NYC*. As Selena Wahng describes, the time these women spent in Riot Grrrl NYC ultimately proved most important, both as a point of initiation and as a momentary cathartic release:

Riot Grrrl is really good for very young girls, their first contact with feminism and organization. It really can't serve as anything more elaborate . . . I think to get up there on stage and scream and yell and play loud music is a healthy outlet . . . The act of doing that is important. Riot Grrrl is all about speaking out and inhabiting your anger and your pain in that way. But I also feel that after you do that for whatever amount of time, you have to start exploring other things deeper than that. You can't just be stultified in this moment of anger that you felt at some past time. (Wahng 1995)

RIOT GRRRL: A POSTSCRIPT

While most of those members who had been involved with Riot Grrrl NYC during 1992 and 1993 eventually left the group, Riot Grrrl groups still meet in New York City and across the country. Many of the young girls and women in Riot Grrrl NYC today have no tangible connection with the women from the beginning New York chapter. Such a rapid decay and growth rate between generations would indicate that Riot Grrrl's communities are not modeled upon stable lineages. Rather, Riot Grrrl is wrested from history, perpetually reinventing its identity in accordance with the goals and concerns of new Grrrls. Precisely because Riot Grrrl does not adhere to one agenda, the movement has succeeded beyond its formative generations. For the moment, the media no longer considers Riot Grrrl a shocking proposition, and thus it seems unlikely that the generation of girls and women currently involved with Riot Grrrl will soon suffer again the degree of lavish mainstream attention that Riot Grrrls previously attracted. What is more interesting for the cultural analyst, though, is to trace the ways that the word *Grrrl* has loosed itself from the movement and achieved a strong presence elsewhere in popular culture. On the one hand, *Grrrl* has accrued its own significance to the extent that one finds it linked to various popular trends. Articles in *Seventeen* (Solin 1995) and *Wired* (Cross 1995), for example, have contained profiles on a "Biker Grrrl" and a "Modem Grrrl" respectively. A recent anthology collecting interviews with such women rock musicians as Courtney Love, Kim Gordon, and Liz Phair, cobbles together artists under one uniform title: *Grrrls* (Raphael 1996).[17] In each of these cases the author uses *grrrl* as a descriptive means of filling out a gendered character profile—a rebellious, daring sensibility that breaches convention in some fashion. In this sense, Riot Grrrl has remained in the public sphere as a positive and powerful signifying idea. On the other hand, as the word *Grrrl* gains more familiarity through commercialization, Riot Grrrl is trivialized and its potential as a liberating signifier reduced. In its wake, though, Riot Grrrl has affected most powerfully the complexion of the American underground rock scene. As we write this essay, the number of mixed-gender and all-female rock and punk bands in the mid-1990s has escalated beyond a point that any people in the alternative music scene in 1990 or 1991 could have realistically imagined or foreseen. This remains Riot Grrrl's most visible and audible legacy.

NOTES

1. Kathleen Hanna's lyrics from the second verse of "Suck My Left One" (Bikini Kill KRS-204, 1992) are typical in their directed outrage:

> *Daddy comes into her room at night*
> *He's got more than talking on his mind*
> *My sister pulls the covers down*
> *She reaches over, flicks on the light*
> *She says to him: "Suck My Left One, Suck My left One."*

2. During the late 1980s and early 1990s academics were fascinated with Madonna's position as a potentially subversive political force in popular culture. The culminating point was perhaps Cathy Schwichtenberg's 1993 collection of essays, *The Madonna Connection.*

3. Throughout this essay we will differentiate in a general sense between communities and scenes. Communities consist of a stable population, who are united by some sense of common history and tradition. Scenes, on the other hand are more diverse and represent what Will Straw refers to as a "cultural space in which a range of musical practices coexist" (1991, 373). For a detailed discussion of communities and scenes, see Straw's article as well as that of Holly Kruse (1993), who argues the importance of translocal scenes in alternative music.

4. For the most thorough descriptions of the New York Punk scene's formative years, see Roman Kozak (1988) and Clinton Heylin (1993).

5. CBGBs did not begin as a punk club. The club's moniker is shortened from its proper title: CBGB and OMFUG. This stands for Country, Bluegrass, Blues and Other Music For Urban Gourmets.

6. Hurley (1989). This book has no page numbers; the quote is taken from the section entitled "The Clubs."

7. Quoted from a Riot Grrrl NYC flier, the header of which contains a drawing of a winged angel accompanied by two questions: "Is She a Riot Grrrl?" "Are you [a Riot Grrrl]?"

8. Squatting is common in the New York City punk community. Groups of punks will move into vacant public buildings, connect electrical, gas, and water services, and renovate the building for living accomodations. They are always in danger, however, of being evicted by the city.

9. For classic discussions of the dialectical conception of private and public space, see Pierre Bourdieu's extensive anthropological writings on the Kabyle tribal members of Algeria. In recent years, ethnomusicologists have both elaborated on and problematized these gendered divisions of space. Jennifer C. Post (1994) provides a summary of the relation between public/private gendered space as it specifically relates to musical performance.

10. bell hooks has dealt with numerous feminist topics in her writings and in particular has addressed issues concerning African American women in today's society.

11. For a detailed analytical discussion of Van Halen's "Runnin' with the Devil" and the signification of freedom and power in heavy metal, see Walser (1993, 41–54).

12. For a concise discussion of the relationship between Skinhead and Punk subcultures, see O'Hara (1995, 33–43).

13. From notes on the recording provided by the composer/performer.

14. Many clubs in New York City cater only to crowds of ages twenty-one and over or set an

age limit at eighteen. Occasionally bands and management will allow special "all ages" shows, admitting audience members under the age of eighteen. Most punk bands who play the smaller clubs, such as ABC no Rio, refuse to charge over five dollars at their shows. This tradition has its most noticeable roots in the Washington, D.C. punk scene and is still upheld by such successful bands as Fugazi, who consistently sell out large clubs and small theater venues across the country.

15. Re/search is a publication series that includes volumes on various unusual pop-cultural styles and genres, bizarre subcultural phenomenons, and controversial performance artists.

16. Ska is fast-tempo, rhythmically jerky, Jamaican dance music that gained notoriety among punk crowds in England in the late 1970s.

17. Of the artists Raphael interviews, only one group, Huggy Bear, is directly aligned with Riot Grrrl. The others fall more loosely under the amalgam "women in rock."

REFERENCES CITED

Bernikow, Louise. 1993. The New Activists: Fearless, Funny, Fighting Mad. *Cosmoplitan* (April): 162–65, 212.

Borchers, Karen R. 1993. Grrrl Talk. *Glamour* (May): 134.

Bourdieu, Pierre. 1977. The Dialectic of Objectification and Embodiment. In *Outline of a Theory of Practice,* translated by Richard Nice. Cambridge: Cambridge University Press, 87–95.

Bourdieu, Pierre. 1979. The Kabyle House or the World Reversed. In *Algeria 1960,* translated by Richard Nice. Cambridge: Cambridge University Press, 133–53.

Butler, Judith. 1990. *Gender Trouble: Feminism and the Subversion of Identity.* New York: Routledge.

Case, Sue-Ellen. 1989. Toward a Butch-Femme Aesthetic. In *Making a Spectacle: Feminist Essays on Contemporary Women's Theatre,* edited by Lynda Hart. Ann Arbor: University of Michigan Press.

Chideya, Farai. 1992. Revolution, Girl Style. *Newsweek,* 23 November: 84–86.

Cross, Rosie. 1995. Modem Grrrl. *Wired* 3, no. 2: 118–19.

Currid, Brian. 1995. "We Are Family": House Music and Queer Performativity. In *Cruising the Performative: Interventions into the Representation of Ethnicity, Nationality, and Sexuality,* edited by Sue-Ellen Case, Philip Brett, and Susan Leigh Foster. Bloomington and Indianapolis: Indiana University Press, 165–96.

France, Kim. 1993. Grrrls At War. *Rolling Stone* 8–22 July: 23–24.

Goad, Debbie. 1994. Riot Grrrls Rrreally Borrring. *Your Flesh* 29: 22.

Heylin, Clinton. 1993. *From The Velvets to The Voidoids: A Pre-Punk History for a Post-Punk World.* New York: Penguin.

Humphreys, Elena. 1995. Interview.

Hurley, Bri. 1989. *Making a Scene: New York Hardcore in Photos, Lyrics and Commentary.* Boston: Faber and Faber.

Joy, Sally Margaret. 1992. Revolution Grrrl Style Now! *Melody Maker* 10 October: 30–32.

Kozak, Roman. 1988. *This Ain't No Disco.* Winchester, Mass.: Faber & Faber.

Kruse, Holly. 1993. Subcultural Identity in Alternative Music Culture. *Popular Music* 12, no. 1: 33–41.

Malkin, Nina. 1993. It's A Grrrl Thing. *Seventeen* (May): 80-82.

Morrow, Diana. 1995. Interview.

Nasrallah, Dana. 1992. Teenage Riot. *Spin* (November): 78–81.

O'Hara, Craig. 1995. *The Philosophy of Punk.* San Francisco: AK Press.

Peraino, Judith. 1992. "Rip Her to Shreds": Women's Music According to a Butch-Femme Aesthetic. *Repercussions* 1, no. 1: 19–47.

Post, Jennifer C. 1994. Erasing the Boundaries between Public and Private in Women's Performance Traditions. In *Cecilia Reclaimed: Feminist Perspectives on Gender and Music,* edited by Susan C. Cook and Judy S. Tsou. Urbana: University of Illinois Press, 35–51.

Raphael, Amy. 1996. *Grrrls: Viva Rock Divas.* New York: St. Martin's Griffin.

Riot Grrrl NYC. 1992–93. "Is She a Riot Grrrl?" Flier.

———. 1992. *Riot Grrrl NYC 3.* Fanzine.

———. 1993. *Riot Grrrl NYC 4.* Fanzine.

Robertson, Pamela. 1996. *Guilty Pleasures: Feminist Camp from Mae West to Madonna.* Durham, N.C.: Duke University Press.

Schwichtenberg, Cathy. 1993. *The Madonna Connection: Representational Politics, Subcultural Identities, and Cultural Theory.* Boulder, San Francisco, Oxford: Westview Press.

Solin, Sabrina. 1995. Biker Grrrl. *Seventeen* (June): 54–56.

Straw, Will. 1991. Systems of Articulation, Logics of Change: Communities and Scenes in Popular Music. *Cultural Studies* 5, no. 3: 368–88.

Valentine, Sarah. 1995. Interview.

Wahng, Selena. 1995. Interview.

———. 1995. Notes to "Killing for Pleasure."\

Walser, Robert. 1993. *Running With The Devil: Power, Gender, and Madness in Heavy Metal Music.* Hanover, N.H.: Wesleyan University Press.

COMPANION CD SELECTIONS

Track 26. Double Zero, "Gas, Food, Satan."

Track 27. Selena Wahng, "Killing for Pleasure."

ADDITIONAL SOURCES

Selective Bibliography, Audiography, Videography

Studies on alternative music and underground music scenes and communities may lead the researcher down various alleyways. In general, tracking down the music of local bands on small record and cassette labels and locating such primary sources as fanzines can prove a frustrating task. Many records and fanzines are ephemeral, enjoying only limited publication runs. Furthermore, because these usually are produced and distributed directly by individuals, not companies, the address that you find listed on the back of a record or in a fanzine from four or five years ago may no longer be valid. We have included in this bibliography, however, several sources for either the most current or well-known recordings and literature from Riot Grrrl bands and groups. With the recent surge in popular-music studies, especially in England and the United States, there is a wealth of secondary literature on punk music and subcultures available at most university research libraries. Only those books notable for their seminal theoretical studies or concise, informative contents are listed here.

Riot Grrrl NYC

For recordings such as the *Mudflower* compilation (cassette only) and Riot Grrrl NYC fanzines from the period 1992–1993 contact Flytrap Records, P.O. Box 188, Cooper Station, New York, NY 10003.

Riot Grrrl (and related) Fanzines

Factsheet Five: the best guide to current fanzine literature, is a large semimonthly fanzine review that has a section devoted exclusively to Grrrl fanzines. It is available at most alternative or underground bookstores, or by mail: P.O. Box 170099 San Francisco, CA 94117.

Riot Grrrl Press: a mail-order catalog and distributor that focuses specifically on women's and girls' fanzines: 1573 N. Milwaukee Ave. Suite 473, Chicago, IL 60622.

Princess: a post-Riot Grrrl NYC publication concentrating on diverse feminist, queer, racial, and class issues: 151 First Avenue, Suite 129, New York, NY 10003.

Riot Grrrl (and related) Record Labels

Kill Rock Stars: released Bikini Kill's self-titled influential 1992 record (KRS-204), and has a vast selection of compilations, spokenword recordings, and Riot Grrrl–related music. You can contact the label for a full catalog: 120 NE State St. Suite 418, Olympia, WA 98501.

Outpunk: the leading West Coast Queercore label, released the groundbreaking seven-inch compilation single "There's a Dyke in the Pit" (Out 5). You can contact the label for a catalog and copies of the fanzine *Outpunk:* P.O. Box 170501, San Francisco, CA 94117.

Punk Studies

There are literally dozens of full-length books on British Punk Rock. While Jon Savage's *England's Dreaming* (New York: St. Martin's Press, 1992) provides a captivating historical narrative, Dave Laing's *One Chord Wonders* (Philadelphia: Open University Press, 1985) remains the definitive theoretical and stylistic study of the late 1970s British punk movement.

Craig O'Hara's *The Philosophy of Punk: More Than Noise!!* (San Francisco: AK Press, 1995), written from an insider's point of view, is an especially informative account of the American punk subculture.

Videos

Abby Moser's documentary *Riot Grrrl NYC* is a compelling film that expands upon, in visual and aural terms, many of the issues discussed in our essay. Also of interest is Lucy Thane's documentary "She's Real, She's Worse Than Queer; British Riot Grrrl Now." For more information on both these films, you may contact the following address: 138 Ludlow St., New York, NY 10002.

Index